The Supreme Court on Trial

The Supreme Court on Trial
Judicial Activism or Democratic Dialogue

Kent Roach

A Quicklaw Company

Published in 2001 by
Irwin Law
Suite 930, Box 235
One First Canadian Place
Toronto, ON
M5X 1C8

Cover Photo: Philippe Landreville
Design and typesetting: Sonya V. Thursby, Opus House Incorporated

ISBN: 1-55221-054-5

National Library of Canada Cataloguing in Publication Data

Roach, Kent, 1961-
    The Supreme Court on trial : judicial activism or democratic dialogue

Includes bibliographical references.

ISBN 1-55221-054-5

    1. Canada. Supreme Court. 2. Political questions and judicial
    power — Canada. I. Title.

KE8244.R62 2001   347.71'035
C2001-902462-2

Printed and bound in Canada

1 2 3 4 5   04 03 02 01 00

For my teachers

Contents

Preface

The recent personalization of the judicial activism debate in Canada and its focus on the role of the so-called Court Party of law professors, law clerks to the Court, and interest groups that appear as intervenors before the Supreme Court[1] make it necessary for me to respond to those who may attempt to discredit this book on the basis of my previous experience. As a former clerk to Justice Bertha Wilson, I might be thought by some to be an apologist for the work of the Court and for its decisions that are associated with judicial activism. I am indeed sympathetic to many of the Court's interventions on behalf of unpopular minorities and the accused, but not because I believe that the Court has a monopoly on wisdom or should always have the final word. Rather, I believe that democracy is improved when we are forced to consider the effects of our actions on the unpopular and the disadvantaged and that an independent and courageous judiciary is the best institution we have to remind us of those concerns. Any fears that I will be too soft on the Court should be rebutted by the fact that, as a law professor, I earn my livelihood by criticizing the Court both in the classroom and in the law reviews. One of the reasons for writing this book is my concern that the Court may pay too much attention to the critics of judicial activism and may become too deferential in its work. This restraint would deprive Canadians of the checks and balances produced by having both a strong Court and a strong Parliament and a more self-aware and self-critical democracy.

My *pro bono* work as counsel for a number of Aboriginal and civil liberties groups who appear as intervenors before the Court should not disqualify me from contributing to the debate.[2] Those who represent groups before the Court are in a good position to understand why these people go to the Court and the difficulties they face. Such groups often fail to persuade the Court to see matters their way. They also understand that occasional hard-won judicial victories can turn into legislative or administrative defeats. I do not doubt that my prior experiences influence the views expressed in the book, but ask only that they be considered and judged on their own merits and not dismissed out of hand on an *ad hominem* basis.

I write this book not as a former clerk or a person who occasionally represents intervenors before the Court, but as an academic interested in the history, politics, and law of the *Canadian Charter of Rights and Freedoms*. In this book, I continue to take a new legal process approach, one that refuses to focus on judicial decisions as the inevitable end point of legal disputes. My previous work has concluded that the Supreme Court has frequently not had the last word on *Charter* remedies or *Charter* matters affecting the criminal justice system and that Parliament has frequently been able to reply quickly and effectively to the Court's decisions.[3] I approach the judicial activism debate with the assumption that all branches of government have something to offer, though they also have blind spots and limitations. My legal process approach disposes me to examine judicial decisions as only the start of a process that allows for responses by legislatures, the executive, and society. I am attracted to theories that see judicial review as part of an ongoing dialogue with legislatures and societies because such theories do not assume that judicial decisions are self-executing or the final word. The back and forth between courts and legislatures, which has been part of the common law and now is part of the *Charter*, allows people to participate in different ways through different institutions. Democracy can be enriched — made more self-aware, self-critical, and real — when the extremes of judicial and legislative supremacy are avoided and courts and legislatures do what they do best and respond to the inevitable shortcomings of the other.

Part 1
What is Judicial Activism?

Chapter 1
The Supreme Court on Trial

In many high-profile cases the Supreme Court of Canada has found new rights for unpopular individuals and minorities in the 1982 *Canadian Charter of Rights and Freedoms* and has placed new obligations and restraints on governments: it has struck down abortion laws, extended gay rights, recognized Aboriginal rights, given tobacco companies the right to advertise, and required the police to obtain warrants before they conduct searches. These cases make good news because they produce clear winners and losers. On decision day the nine unelected judges on the Supreme Court have the last word.

The Court's new power and prominence has led to new levels of criticism. Governments have found themselves on trial before the Court, but the Court itself has been placed on trial by politicians and the media. Canada's two national newspapers and Her Majesty's Loyal Opposition, first the Reform Party and now the Canadian Alliance, have loudly complained that the Court has engaged in "judicial activism" by inventing rights for minorities and criminals and by imposing them on the majority of Canadians. Recent debates have been driven by neo-conservative or right-of-centre concerns that the Court is too solicitous of the rights of criminals, Aboriginal people, and minorities. Previous debates, however, have featured arguments from the left that the Court has been too generous in protecting the rights of corporations and other powerful interests.

The Supreme Court is on trial. Vic Toews, the former attorney general of Manitoba and the Canadian Alliance's Justice critic, told Parliament in the spring of 2001 that the Court has "engaged in a frenzy of constitutional experimentation that resulted in the judiciary substituting its legal and societal preferences for those made by the elected representatives of the people," producing "legal and constitutional anarchy."[1] John Crosbie, the former Conservative minister of justice, has accused the judges of using the *Charter* "to elevate themselves above the two other branches of government," so that parliamentary supremacy has been replaced by judicial supremacy.[2] Other concerns about the Court have been raised in a less extravagant manner. Allan Blakeney, the former social democratic premier of Saskatchewan, and Peter Lougheed, the former Conservative premier of Alberta, have joined together to express concerns about the growth of judicial power in the two decades since they helped frame the *Charter*. They have called for increased use of the power to enact legislation, notwithstanding *Charter* rights, in order to assert "the supremacy of elected people as distinguished from appointed judges" and to "develop some creative tension between the legislatures and the courts when the courts are moving into areas which have been the traditional preserve of the legislatures."[3] The Supreme Court has been put on trial and found guilty of being undemocratic.

The Supreme Court has also put itself on trial. The Court's early approach to the *Charter* was shaped primarily by three judges: Chief Justices Brian Dickson and Antonio Lamer and Justice Bertha Wilson. Long before the enactment of the *Charter*, Chief Justice Dickson, a former corporate lawyer from Manitoba, had creatively and boldly reshaped the criminal law, family law, and private law to take account of changing social and economic needs, the importance of not punishing the morally innocent, and other principles. Chief Justice Lamer, a former defence lawyer and law reform commissioner, also took a creative approach to law reform, especially of the criminal law. Justice Wilson, the first woman to sit on the Court, was a law reformer; while still on the Ontario Court of Appeal she had invented a new tort of discrimination. Today some members of the Court seem uncomfortable with the legacy left by these judges. In an extraordinary public interview, Justice Michel Bastarache, a former law dean who was appointed by Prime Minister Chrétien in 1997 and who remains the youngest member on the Court, indicated that he has been "more conservative than the majority of the court over the last few years," in particular, the recently retired Chief Justice Lamer. In Justice Bastarache's view, the Court has gone "too far" in inventing an exclusionary rule beyond the level Parliament intended and in protecting "ill-defined" Aboriginal rights. It should be careful not to extend rights beyond the area "Parliament really wanted to protect" or to have its legitimacy questioned by being "consistently seen by a majority of the people as going too far, as extending rights, as having ... an agenda ... that's not something we want."[4]

The Court has not been oblivious to the concerns that many have voiced about judicial activism. In its decisions it has reminded the politicians that they entrenched the *Charter* and that they have plenty of opportunities both to place reasonable limits on *Charter* rights and to override some *Charter* rights. Both former Chief Justice Lamer and present Chief Justice Beverley McLachlin have made headlines by expressing concerns about "court bashing" and by denying claims that the Court has been "hijacked by interest groups."[5] Lamer came out of retirement to complain that members of the Canadian Alliance, the neo-conservative official Opposition that has been most critical of judicial activism, require "a crash course on constitutional law."[6] In any event, the Court is now being praised by some and criticized by others for demonstrating increased deference towards legislatures. The issue of whether the Court is being activist or restrained figures prominently in media accounts of its work.

All this discussion of judicial activism and restraint, of liberal and conservative wings, makes the Canadian Court seem more like the American Court. Seven of ten Canadians now see the Supreme Court as being prone to partisan politics some or most of the time, almost as many as the eight of ten Americans who hold similar views about their highest court.[7] One of the chief powers of the United States president, the most powerful person in the world, is to appoint judges to the United States Supreme Court, "the most extraordinarily powerful court of law the world has ever known."[8] This status was again confirmed in the 2000 presidential election. Many people believed that the most significant issue in the election was the kind of judges the two candidates would appoint to the Supreme Court. As if to underline its importance and power, the Court, bitterly divided between its conservative majority and its more liberal minority, intervened on flimsy constitutional grounds to end vote recounts in Florida — in effect awarding the presidency to George W. Bush. Many Canadians believe we are heading down the American road to judicial supremacy and politics. It is a bumpy, undemocratic, and dangerous trip.

If I were an American, I would be concerned about judicial activism. My politics would not matter. Throughout its long history the United States Supreme Court has thwarted the political wishes of elected governments on the left and on the right. Today the Court manages to annoy both conservatives and liberals. However, as a Canadian, I am not worried that the Supreme Court of Canada will, in the long run, thwart the determined will of elected governments, and I do not believe that Canadians should be concerned either. This book will explain why.

One reason that does not explain my lack of fear of judicial activism is a faith that Canadian judges will always make correct decisions.. The nine justices on our Supreme Court are human and they will make decisions that many people will believe are mistaken and even misguided. It is especially difficult to ask the Canadian public to have complete faith in the judges of the Supreme Court when they are appointed without any published shortlist or public hearings and after only a phone call from the prime minister. In any event, the issues the Court is required to address — from abortion to capital punishment to euthanasia — are intensely controversial, and there is usually no clearly right answer. Most Canadians could name some Supreme Court decision they believe was a grievous mistake. Law professors and philosophers love to construct elaborate theories that, to their own satisfaction at least, establish that judges always reach the right answers and that their decisions are always consistent with democracy. The problem is that very few people ever agree with their theories or how they should be applied in particular cases. I will not offer a new theory to ensure that judges reach the right answers. Rather, I will outline a process by which society can struggle for the right answers in a manner that respects both rights and democracy and includes both the Court and Parliament.

If judges cannot be relied on to discover right answers, how can Canada avoid the travails of judicial activism that have haunted American history and that continue to bedevil that country? The answer in my view lies in understanding the differences between the two constitutions. The American *Bill of Rights* was added to the American Constitution in 1791, a time when it took six days to travel from New York to Boston, when women and African Americans could not vote, and when people were worried about soldiers being quartered in their houses. The *Charter* was added to the Canadian Constitution in 1982, a time of air and space travel, more or less universal suffrage, and concern about nuclear disasters. Not surprisingly, the *Charter* accommodates the democratic and modern state much better than does the American *Bill of Rights*. The more democratic nature of the *Charter* is based on the fact that Canadian legislatures can respond to the Court's decisions with ordinary legislation that limits or override rights, without having to rely on the drastic responses of changing the Constitution or the Court.

The framers of the *Charter* were well aware of the sometimes unfortunate American experience with judicial activism. They took important and innovative steps to balance the potential of judicial activism under a constitutional bill of rights with the ability of the strong legislatures produced by the Canadian parliamentary system to limit and even override rights as interpreted by the Court. The *Charter* broke new ground by avoiding the dangers of both judicial supremacy, which gives unelected judges the last word, and legislative supremacy, which gives elected politicians the last word. Instead, it promotes and structures democratic dialogues among courts, legislatures, and society about the way rights and freedoms will be treated. The key is section 1 of the *Charter*, which allows legislatures to justify reasonable limits on the rights that the Court finds in the *Charter*. This innovative provision not only recognizes the reality that rights are not absolute — even the Americans recognize that one should not be allowed to shout "Fire" in a crowded theatre — but provides legislatures with a vehicle to respond to judicial decisions and to justify contextual departures from the principles that the Court recognizes. The Canadian Court may say that hate speech or flag burning is a protected form of expression, but Parliament still retains the option of justifying ordinary legislation that restricts these dubious forms of speech as a reasonable limit on that right. In contrast, once the American Court decides that burning a cross or a flag is speech, then, following the absolutism of the First Amendment, Congress shall make no law abridging free speech. The *Charter* invites democratic dialogue about how to respond to the Court's decisions; the American *Bill of Rights* often ends it.

On top of section 1 of the *Charter*, Canadian legislatures also retain the power to enact legislation notwithstanding certain *Charter* rights. This override power has rarely been used, but it provides an important safeguard against judicial decisions that the politicians are truly prepared to denounce as unwise and illegitimate. Amid much controversy, Quebec used the override to reinstate a requirement that all commercial signs be in French a few days after the Supreme Court struck down the law as an unreasonable limit on freedom of expression. The elected politicians of Alberta could have exercised this power when the Court read protections for discrimination against gays and lesbians into its human rights code, but they chose not to do so. Alberta has, however, invoked the override to prevent the courts, for five years at least, from even considering whether gays and lesbians should be able to marry. Reports of the death of section 33 have been exaggerated, and governments that have used it have had no trouble in getting re-elected. The Canadian *Charter* does not give fallible and unelected judges the last word over matters that involve rights and freedoms. All that governments need to do is to take responsibility for enacting ordinary legislation that justifiably limits or clearly overrides rights as interpreted by the Court. The answer to objectionable judicial activism under the *Charter* is legislative activism.

The difference between the Canadian *Charter* and the American *Bill of Rights* is widely appreciated abroad. New Zealand, Israel, and South Africa enacted bills of rights in the 1990s that virtually copied section 1 of the *Charter*, and the United Kingdom has recently enacted a bill of rights that allows something like our section 33 override. At home, however, the differences between the *Charter* and the American *Bill of Rights* have too often been ignored or disparaged. First the left and now the right have mimicked American critics of judicial activism without adequate attention to the ability of Canadian legislatures to limit or override rights declared by the Court. The Canadian debate about judicial activism remains mired in the deep tracks and dead ends of the American debate. Canadians are losing sight of the genius of the

Charter, which gives *both* judges and legislatures robust roles in determining the way rights are treated in our free and democratic society. Too much fear of courts may deprive judges of their ability to make us aware of the effects of governmental actions on fundamental values and the rights of minorities. Too much faith in courts may make us unable to respond confidently and democratically to judicial decisions on important questions of social policy. This book is an attempt to assess the debate about judicial activism, but ultimately to move beyond it to a recognition of the unique structure and genius of the *Charter* in promoting democratic dialogue about the treatment of rights and freedoms.

There has so far been more heat than light in public debates about judicial activism. Critics have often trivialized the reasoning of the courts and ignored the many options that legislatures have to respond to most *Charter* decisions. Defenders have often focused on the excesses of the critique, downplayed the reality of reasonable disagreement with the Court's decisions, and relied on the unsatisfying defence that politicians should not complain because they gave judges the power they now exercise. The debate has been plagued by hyperbole on both sides. The *Charter* is neither an invention akin to "the invention of penicillin and the laser"[9] nor one that has destroyed Canadian democracy, so that "a Speech from the Throne cannot be properly interpreted until one has heard the 'Speech from the Bench.'"[10] The judicial activism debate deserves better than the inflated rhetoric that both sides have exchanged.

Both critics and defenders in the current debate over judicial activism are creating some dangerous illusions. The critics of the Court create the illusion that some groups — "Charter Canadians,"[11] or "the Court Party"[12] — are protected by courts and win every time they walk into the imposing building that houses the Supreme Court. As someone who has had the privilege of representing Aboriginal and civil liberties groups that have intervened in the Court, I wish it were so easy. The Supreme Court, which has generally been more receptive to rights claims than other courts, rejects two-thirds of all *Charter* claims it hears.[13] Some minorities may be able to attach themselves to specific rights in the *Charter*, but, in every case, governments and majorities can attach themselves to section 1, which allows reasonable limits on rights to be justified. Even in the third of *Charter* cases that the government loses, the Court's decisions are often not the last word. Judicial wins for minorities and the accused can easily turn into political defeats. There is already plenty of "creative tension" between courts and legislatures, including some "in-your-face" legislative replies that have essentially reversed the Court's *Charter* decisions (and have been subsequently accepted by the Court with surprising equanimity). It is a mistake for those either sympathetic or hostile to particular *Charter* claims to think that courts always recognize and vindicate rights or that, when they do recognize rights, they necessarily have the last word. The rights of minorities and the unpopular are far more fragile than either side of the judicial activism debate suggests. One of the greatest dangers of judicial review may be the idea that we can rely on the courts to protect rights. In a democracy, and especially under the *Charter*, you always need more than the Court on your side.

The Voyage Ahead

Although concerns about judicial activism are sometimes raised in contexts such as civil litigation,[14] I will focus on the role of the Supreme Court of Canada in interpreting the *Charter* and Aboriginal and treaty rights. This book joins the ongoing debate about judicial activism and argues that the extent of judicial activism in Canada has been seriously exaggerated and, in any event, is not to be feared as inconsistent with democracy. Ultimately, however, I hope to move beyond the judicial activism debate by suggesting that the structure of the Canadian Constitution makes even arguably activist judicial decisions a legitimate, but not final, contribution in a self-critical, self-aware, and energetic democratic debate about the way we will treat rights in our free and democratic society.

When not thrown around as an epithet, judicial activism is a complex subject. In order to understand what judicial activism means, we must visit many places and meet many people. The first leg of our journey will take us to foreign lands and back in time. Our first stop will be the United States, because the American experience casts a long shadow over debates about judicial activism in Canada and elsewhere. The next stop will be back in time, to understand that Canadians complained about judicial activism long before anyone heard of the *Charter*. The framers of the *Charter* accommodated concerns about judicial activism when they drafted the *Charter*, and their decisions have had an important influence in other countries that have since adopted their own bill of rights. We will then visit both the serenity of the ivory tower and the hurly burly of newsrooms and political backrooms to understand how judicial activism has come to be defined as a problem in Canada since the enactment of the *Charter*. Finally, we will step back from all this activity and criticism to ask ourselves what people really mean when they say that the Court has engaged in judicial activism. These conclusions often depend on unarticulated but controversial views about judging, rights, and democracy. Before critics assert that a court has engaged in judicial activism, and by doing so suggest that the judges have acted improperly, they should be required to explain what they expect from judges as well as their understanding of rights and democracy.

To facilitate a more transparent debate, I will outline four main components of judicial activism. The first is that judges engage in judicial activism when they make the law in their own image. Although they both stress the law-making powers of judges, the left tends to stress the indeterminacy of text and adjudication, while the right emphasizes the Court's inability to follow the text and the clear intent of the framers. The second component is that judges engage in activism when they are eager to make law and do not avoid or minimize constitutional judgments whenever possible. The third is that judges engage in judicial activism when they give the rights of individuals and groups primacy over the public good. The left tends to focus on individual rights as trumps over collective and group rights, while the right is concerned about group rights and a general inflation of rights. Both critiques are premised on scepticism about the rights claimed in *Charter* litigation and the assumption that courts will apply rights as trumps, without adequately balancing them with competing social interests. The fourth element of judicial activism is the idea that judges, when they displace policies established by legislatures and the executive, have the final word and act in an undemocratic manner. Both left and right critics tend to assume an American-style judicial supremacy that discounts the ability of legislatures to modify or override judicial decisions under sections 1 and 33 of the *Charter*. They also tend to make idealistic and majoritarian assumptions about the way that legislatures and executives represent the democratic will. The four strands of judicial activism — judges making law, judges being eager to make law, judges giving rights primacy, and judges having the final word — will provide the organizing framework for Part Two of the book.

This second leg of our journey will focus on the last two decades of Canada's experience under the *Charter*. We will address the extent to which the Canadian Supreme Court has engaged in judicial activism by the way it interprets the *Charter*. We will look at cases in which the Court has been accused of inventing a right to abortion, an automatic exclusionary rule, equality rights for gays and lesbians, voting rights for prisoners, special and generous rights for Aboriginal people, and processes to determine judicial salaries and an obligation to negotiate the breakup of Canada. We will also examine the claim that the Court has been too eager to make law under the *Charter* and to hear from interest groups. Judicial review in Canada is not simply about the rights that the Court recognizes, but the limits on those rights it accepts as reasonable. To this end, we will see how the reasonable limits section of the *Charter* has evolved as the Court responded to the left critique of judicial activism and recognized that the vindication of rights was not a cost-less exercise. The Court has given the legislature a greater margin of deference not only with respect to social policies such as mandatory retirement but in much of the criminal law. With little support in the text, the Court has also created government powers to place limits on Aboriginal rights, including rights in treaties signed long ago, and then expanded the grounds from legitimate concerns about conservation of natural resources to concerns about the economic interests of the non-Aboriginal majority. The record with both *Charter* and Aboriginal rights suggests that rights are a long way from being the absolute trumps over collective interests that many of the critics of judicial activism imagine. Finally, we will examine governmental responses to the minority of *Charter* cases that governments lose. When legislatures have failed to respond, this reaction has reflected more a lack of governmental will than any judicial supremacy. In many other cases, [15] new legislation has been enacted to advance society's interests in police powers, criminal laws, and restrictions on tobacco advertising. Legislatures often have a range of legitimate responses, as can be seen by the variety of actions already taken by some provincial legislatures in response to the Court's decision about the equal treatment of gay and lesbian couples. *Charter* decisions have often produced a democratic dialogue among the court, legislatures, and society. This dialogue is far from a judicial monologue in which the Court necessarily asserts the final word.

In the last leg of our journey we will try to escape from the bog of the perpetual American debate about judicial activism and find firmer ground to reconcile the role of the Court under the *Charter* with democracy. The path forward requires escaping the extreme positions advanced by both the critics and the defenders of judicial review as well as careful attention to the firm terrain provided by the structure of the Canadian Constitution. On the one hand, the critics of judicial activism overstate their case when they argue that judges have a blank cheque under the *Charter*, that they can avoid tough *Charter* issues, that they vindicate rights at all costs, and that they impose the final word on society in an undemocratic form of judicial supremacy. [16] Take the abortion issue. The Court tried unsuccessfully to duck the issue of whether the fetus had rights under the *Charter*, only to be summoned back in the twenty-second week of Chantal Daigle's pregnancy to decide whether an injunction prohibiting her from obtaining an abortion should be overturned. Unlike the American decision of *Roe* v. *Wade*, which prescribed a trimester-by-trimester abortion policy, the Court's decision striking down the abortion law did not prescribe an abortion policy for Canada. Even if the fetus did not have rights, Parliament could act to protect it. What prevented a new law on abortion was not the Court or the *Charter*, but a tied vote in the Senate and the Mulroney government's lack of courage on this difficult issue. On the other hand, defenders of the *Charter* and the Court overstate their case to the extent they suggest there is any reliable way to ensure that the justices on the Supreme Court always get it right. Again, abortion is a good example, as the justices took a variety of inconsistent approaches in their decisions on abortion. It is an unhelpful myth that there is a reliable formula or theory that produces right answers in the difficult cases the Court hears or that ensures that those decisions are always consistent with democracy. Judges can legitimately reach a number of different results, and citizens can reasonably disagree with many of the Court's decisions.

The way out of the dead end of an American-style judicial activism debate requires us to step back and see the *Charter* not so much as a revolution, but as a continuation and enrichment of the ability of courts and legislatures to engage in dialogue under the common law. In many fields of public law that are now dominated by the *Charter*, judges have traditionally engaged in activism to the extent they have enforced fairness values associated with a common law or judge-made bill of rights. For example, in their hurry to pass criminal laws, legislatures often forgot to ensure that people should be punished only if they were at fault. In their desire to regulate, legislatures often forgot to ensure that people would have an opportunity to participate before a bureaucrat makes a decision affecting their lives. The courts have traditionally used the common law to remind politicians and bureaucrats about fairness values that they were likely to neglect. At the same time, the Court did not necessarily have the final word when it enforced common law presumptions of fairness. Our elected representatives could always limit and even override the rights in the common law bill of rights with clear statements in publicly debated legislation. The values of the common law constitution often prevailed — not because of judicial supremacy, but because elected governments were understandably unwilling to be held accountable for explicitly spelling out their desires to treat people unfairly. Under the *Charter*, judges continue to call attention to values such as fairness and the rights of minorities that are liable to be neglected by government, but they are now guided by a democratically enacted text. As under the common law, the *Charter* decisions of judges are not necessarily the final word. Legislatures can still respond with ordinary legislation. To be sure, the requirement that governments justify violations of the rights found by the courts is more rigorous than before the *Charter*, but it is not an impossible task or one that ignores the role or abilities of elected governments. As a final democratic fail safe, legislatures retain the power they had under the common law to avoid the process of justification by enacting legislation that operates notwithstanding most *Charter* rights. The *Charter*, however, enhances democracy by requiring the legislature to revisit the matter when the override expires after five years.

Talk of dialogue between the Court and the legislature is common, but it seems odd and confusing to many. People think of courts as laying down the law, and not as engaging in dialogue with people or even their governments. Nevertheless, the Supreme Court itself has recognized that the structure of the *Charter* means it may not have the final word. It has lent some support to the idea that the legislature can act on its own interpretation of the *Charter*, even when it is different from the Court's, and that the legislature can hold the Court accountable when it has stepped too far away from the democratic mainstream.[17] Such strong theories of dialogue effectively allow the legislature to shout at the Court. In my view, shouting should only occur in those extraordinary circumstances when the legislature believes it must reverse a completely unacceptable *Charter* decision and is prepared to use the section 33 override. This override governs shouting matches by ensuring that, after a five-year cooling-off period, the legislature has an opportunity for sober second thoughts when it decides whether the override should be renewed.

Dialogue works better when there is no shouting and when people are prepared to learn from each other. The best dialogue is a respectful conversation among those who have different abilities, concerns, and perspectives and who are prepared to expand the debate beyond a particular point of disagreement. Section 1 of the *Charter* contemplates such a conversation. It promotes a constructive and respectful dialogue in which courts and legislature can each do what they do best without competing over who is the best interpreter of the *Charter* or who has the most popular support. It allows courts to bring concerns about respecting rights to the attention of governments who might otherwise be inclined to ignore them or not be candid about limits placed on them. In turn, section 1 allows governments to explain to the courts and the people their regulatory ambitions, the alternatives considered, and the tradeoffs made. This type of conversation allows courts and legislatures to stick to what they both do best and to learn things from the other they would otherwise not appreciate. It permits both courts and legislatures to speak in strong but distinct and complementary voices.

Canadians and those other countries with bills of rights influenced by the *Charter* can enjoy the benefits of both judicial and legislative activism. We can have strong and principled judicial decisions that remind us of the importance of fundamental values, fair procedures, and the rights of minorities and the unpopular, while not, as in the United States, having to live with decisions we find misguided or unacceptable unless we can change the constitution or the Court.

My conclusion that the *Charter* is not fundamentally different from the common law will be disquieting to both sides in the debate on judicial activism. Those concerned about judicial activism will be reluctant to see the *Charter* as a continuation of a common law tradition they believe is consistent with majoritarian democracy, limited rights, and limited judicial law making. Defenders of the Court and the *Charter* will be reluctant to admit that we have not travelled so far from a common law heritage that often inadequately protected the rights of minorities and the unpopular. There is no guarantee that judicial decisions under the *Charter* will either prevail or be rejected. This is the price that must be paid for the responsibility that comes with democracy and self-government. The *Charter* and the courts cannot save us from ourselves. The Supreme Court is on trial and we, as citizens, are on trial. But that is the way it should be in a democracy.

Chapter 2
The Endless American Debate

To understand why people in Canada are concerned about judicial activism, it is essential to understand judicial activism in the United States. The United States Supreme Court has a two-hundred-year history of enforcing the *Bill of Rights,* and this history dramatically demonstrates the dangers of judicial activism. The Court's ruling protecting the property rights of slaveholders was reversed by a constitutional amendment only after the bloody Civil War. The Court's decisions striking down the New Deal during the Great Depression of the 1930s forced the president to threaten to pack the Court with six new judges, before the Court itself backed off in what has come to be known as "the switch in time that saved nine." The Court's finest hour was its 1954 decision that racially segregated public schools were unconstitutional, but that decision itself reversed an earlier one that "separate" could be "equal." It also faced massive resistance, and public schools remained segregated until the courts ordered busing, a very unpopular remedy. The Court's decisions over the last four decades establishing detailed rules regulating abortion and police powers, prohibiting school prayer, and allowing flag burning have also been unpopular, but generally impervious to change.

Even a short history of the United States Supreme Court should shake any complacency about the possible dangers of judicial activism. Those on the left have bitterly complained of judicial activism that struck down government regulation, and those on the right have severely criticized the Court's usurpation of democracy on many social issues. Today, the United States Supreme Court is hounded from both sides and there is very little that Americans can do about the Court's decisions.

The Fragility of American Judicial Review

The framers of the American Constitution did not stipulate clearly whether federal courts such as the Supreme Court should be able to enforce the constitution against the federal and, especially, the state governments. Alexander Hamilton, one of the leading architects of the 1787 constitution, was the most inclined to give the independent judiciary this power. Nevertheless, in response to many who opposed judicial review as an almost monarchical power — something that was taken very seriously in the wake of the American Revolution — Hamilton stressed that the judiciary was the "least dangerous branch" of government. Possessed with "neither Force nor Will but merely judgment," the Court "must ultimately depend upon the aid of the executive arm even for the efficacy of its judgments." Hamilton also argued that the ability of the legislature to impeach judges would help to prevent "deliberate usurpations on the authority of the legislature."[1] The United States Supreme Court was on precarious ground from the start.

A 1793 Supreme Court decision requiring a state to defend its actions in federal court was reversed by a 1798 constitutional amendment that federal courts could not entertain lawsuits brought against states by citizens of other states or countries. Well into the twentieth century, controversy continued about the extent to which the *Bill of Rights* applied to state governments. The First Amendment, for example, provides only that "Congress shall make no laws" abridging freedom of speech, religion, and assembly. The battle cry of the rights of the states to govern themselves free of federal interference continues to be an important feature of arguments against the power of the federal courts to enforce the *Bill of Rights*. Many people oppose judicial activism not only because the judges of the Supreme Court are unelected but because they are part of the federal government. When the Supreme Court intervened in the 2000 presidential election, millions of Americans saw it as both judicial interference with democracy and federal interference with the states.

The American origins of judicial review are found in the curious case of *Marbury* v. *Madison*.[2] The case was brought by Marbury, who had been given a patronage appointment as a justice of the peace in the dying days of an old administration. The new administration under President Thomas Jefferson refused to make the appointment, and Marbury went to court. The Supreme Court indicated that Marbury was entitled to the appointment, but decided that, under the constitution, it did not have jurisdiction to force the president to make the appointment. The case is now famous for the Court's emphatic statements that the constitution was the supreme law and "it is, emphatically, the province and duty of the judicial department, to say what the law is." This argument has been used again and again by the Court to justify the supremacy of its rulings in the face of opposition. In the actual case of *Marbury* v. *Madison*, however, it was used to "reject and assume power in the same breath" and to avoid a confrontation with a new Jefferson administration that would likely not have obeyed the Court's order to make good on the patronage appointment. President Jefferson was no friend of the Supreme Court and he believed that the previous administration, "defeated at the polls, have retired into the Judiciary and from that bar-ricade" they hoped to oppose his more populist regime.[3] Jefferson also believed that the president could act on his own interpretation of the constitution, even if the Court had reached a different interpretation.

Subsequent presidents were no more inclined to accept the Court's power to enforce the constitution than was Jefferson. President Andrew Jackson, who had made his fame as an Indian fighter, refused to enforce a landmark Court opinion holding that the states had no power over Cherokee land. He is reported to have said: "The Chief Justice has made his decision and now let him enforce it."[4] There is a long and often ugly history in the United States of elected officials defying the decisions of courts, often in the name of states' rights or because they disagreed with the way the courts interpreted the *Bill of Rights*.

Slavery and Segregation

Alexis de Tocqueville, the insightful French aristocrat who visited America in the early nineteenth century, was struck by the power of the American judiciary. His 1846 warning that, "if ever the Supreme Court came to be composed of rash or corrupt men, the confederation would be threatened by anarchy or civil war"[5] was prophetic. In 1857 the Court decided that Dred Scott, a former slave, was not a citizen able to bring a suit in the courts to be declared free, on the basis of having lived in free states and territories. Black people were not citizens, but, in the Court's hateful words, "articles of merchandise" and "a subordinate and inferior class of beings." The Court could have thrown out the case merely on the invidious basis that Scott was not a citizen with standing to bring a lawsuit. Nevertheless, it went beyond what was necessary to decide the case and declared that the federal government had acted unconstitu-tionally in prohibiting slavery in the western territories. Such a prohibi-tion, it said, would deprive slave owners of their property without due process of law and just compensation, as required under the Fifth Amendment.[6] The Court effectively constitutionalized slavery and indi-cated that Congress's long-standing Missouri Compromise was uncon-stitutional because it was premised on half of the western territories being free. Attempts were made to respond to *Dred Scott* by amending the constitution to extend the Missouri Compromise through to California, but they failed.

Weak and fearful politicians are often only too happy to leave divi-sive and delicate issues to the Court. Torn between Southern and Northern factions in his Democratic Party, President James Buchanan argued at his inaugural (shortly before the release of the *Dred Scott* decision, but after one of the Southern justices had tipped him off to the result) that the slavery issue "legitimately belongs to the Supreme Court of the United States, before whom it is now pending, and will, it is understood, be speedily and finally settled." Once the Court's decision was handed down, he argued that it made Kansas "as much a slave state as Georgia."[7] In contrast, the next president, Abraham Lincoln, drew a careful distinction between respecting the Court's resolution of the dispute in *Dred Scott* and rejecting its larger policy implications. At his first inaugural after the Southern states had already formed the Confederacy, Lincoln argued that "the candid citizens must confess that if the policy of the government upon vital questions affecting the whole people is to be irrevocably fixed by decision of the Supreme Court, in the instant they are made, in ordinary litigation between parties, in personal actions, the people will have ceased to be their own rulers, knowing, to that extent, practically resigned their government into the hands of that eminent tribunal."[8] Lincoln's elegant arguments against judicial supremacy on the slavery issue did not win the day.

Dred Scott was eventually reversed, but only after the bloody Civil War in which over half a million died and after three postwar constitutional amendments. The Thirteenth Amendment prohibited slavery, the Fourteenth Amendment provided that all persons born or naturalized in the United States would be entitled to the rights of citizens, and the Fifteenth Amendment provided that the rights of citizens to vote would not be denied by either the federal or the state government "on account of race, color, or previous condition of servitude." The Supreme Court did not appear to have learned a lesson from the Civil War. It interpreted the last two amendments restrictively, so that states retained the rights to prohibit women from practising as lawyers and the federal government could not enforce voting rights or prohibit racial discrimination in public accommodation. This restrictive line of cases culminated in the infamous *Plessy* v. *Ferguson*[9] decision, in which the Court held that a law requiring separate railway cars for blacks and whites did not violate the Fourteenth Amendment as long as the segregated facilities were "equal." The Fourteenth Amendment was not "intended to abolish distinction based upon color, or to enforce social, as distinguished from political equality, or a commingling of the two races upon terms unsatisfactory to either." Justice Harlan, a Southerner, correctly predicted in dissent that, by allowing "the seeds of race hate to be planted under the sanction of law," the Court's decision would "prove to be quite as pernicious as the decision made by this tribunal in the *Dred Scott* case." *Plessy* legitimized the apartheid of the Jim Crow era. It would take another sixty years before the Court would attempt, often without success, to dismantle it.

Lochner, the New Deal, and the Switch in Time That Saved Nine

At the same time as it was upholding laws requiring racial segregation, the Court was striking down many attempts by governments to regulate a rapidly industrializing nation. In the 1890s the Court recognized "substantive due process," which meant that the right not to be deprived of life, liberty, or property without due process went beyond the right to a fair trial before being jailed to include freedom to contract without interference by government regulation. This expansive and libertarian mandate for judicial review led to the invalidation of fifty federal and four hundred state laws between 1898 and 1937.[10] This was the *Lochner* era, and it still influences debates about judicial activism.

In *Lochner* v. *New York*[11] a bakery owner successfully challenged a New York law that restricted his workers to a sixty-hour work week. The Court concluded that the law restricted the "right to purchase or sell labor," which was part of the liberty protected under the Fourteenth Amendment. Bakers were not "wards of the State" and they should be free to decide for themselves how many hours they wished to work without "meddlesome interference" from the state. It was "unreasonable and entirely arbitrary" for the legislature to conclude that a baker who worked eleven, as opposed to ten, hours a day would be unhealthy. Two powerful dissents were written. Justice Harlan, the dissenter from the separate but equal case, argued that "whether or not this be wise legislation is not the province of the court to inquire," and that the legislature was entitled to make good-faith efforts to promote health and safety. Justice Oliver Wendall Holmes, the great judge and sceptic, was even more cutting as he argued that the Court was reading laissez-faire economics into a constitution that "is not intended to embody a particular economic theory." Despite these powerful dissents, the *Lochner* Court went on to strike down various attempts to establish minimum wages and maximum hours as infringements of freedom of contract. It also struck down closed-shop agreements as a violation of freedom of contract and used injunctions against unions on the basis that they threatened the property rights of corporations.[12] In the 1910s and 1920s, progressive politicians proposed that Congress be allowed to overrule the Court's constitutional decisions. They could not, however, win widespread support for such radical constitutional reform. The Court was reading its economic preferences into the constitution and having the last word when doing so.

The *Lochner* Court relied not only on "substantive due process" to protect absolute freedom of contract but also on a restrictive approach to the powers of the federal government. The federal government could not prohibit monopolies within states and could not enact a 2 per cent income tax.[13] This last decision involved a successful lawsuit by share-holders to stop a corporation from paying taxes. It meant that, during the Robber Baron era of capitalist expansion, the federal government could not impose income or corporate tax. It took eighteen years to reverse the decision through the enactment of the Sixteenth Amendment in 1913. The Court also struck down federal attempts to regulate child labour. A constitutional amendment to reverse this decision was approved in Congress in 1924, but it gained assent from only twenty-eight of the required thirty-six states.[14] There was no practical way to change judicial decisions short of the extraordinarily difficult process of securing a con-stitutional amendment or having the Court overrule itself.

The confrontation between the laissez-faire *Lochner* Court and more interventionist governments came to a head over President Franklin Delano Roosevelt's attempts to implement a New Deal during the Great Depression. Roosevelt had been elected in 1932 in a landslide and brought many bright young men to Washington, but his election promise of a New Deal was shut down by the unelected old men on the Court. After the Court overruled a major part of the New Deal which imposed minimum wage, maximum hour, and trade practices over var-ious industries, a bitterly disappointed Roosevelt called the Court's deci-sions the most important since *Dred Scott*, causing cheeky reporters to inquire whether he proposed a constitutional amendment or a war to reverse them.[15] The next year the Court also struck down federal attempts to raise the depressed prices of farm commodities. Justice Stone, who would later lay the basis for a new kind of judicial activism, dissented on the basis that "the removal of unwise laws from the statutes books lies not to the courts but to the ballot and to the processes of dem-ocratic government."[16] The majority of the Court remained confident, however, that the constitution restricted the federal government and oblivious to the plight of farmers and the millions of unemployed dur-ing the Depression.

The Court and the Roosevelt administration were on a collision course. The spirit of the debate is captured by the titles of some of the books that were published by the Court's many critics in the 1930s: *Government by Judiciary, Congress or the Supreme Court: Which Shall Govern America?, Nine Old Men,* and *Lawless Judges.* For some, the Court had become a "dictator over the American people" that "deliberately applied [its]economic principles and prejudices rather than the existing laws."[17] A more moderate critique written by Roosevelt's attorney gen-eral (who would later serve on the Court) argued that "the vice of judi-cial supremacy, as exerted for ninety years in the field of policy, has been its progressive closing of the avenues to peaceful and democratic conciliation of our social and economic conflicts," whether it be the Missouri Compromise on slavery invalidated in *Dred Scott* or the New Deal measures struck down by the *Lochner* Court.[18] The Court was imposing absolute rights and preventing democratic compromises and accommodations.

In a 1937 "fireside" radio broadcast, Roosevelt criticized the Court for "acting not as a judicial body, but as a policy-making body" or a "super-legislature ... reading into the Constitution words and implications which are not there, and which were never intended to be there ... In our courts, we want a government of laws and not of men."[19] He appealed to the idea that the Court was departing from the clear intent of the constitution. Other critics, influenced by legal realism, which stressed the discretion that all judges inevitably exercised, argued that what was required was different men on the Court. In any event, there was a wide consensus that something must be done about the Court. Roosevelt proposed legislation that, under the guise of helping the elderly Court with its workload, would allow him to add up to six new justices. The Court-packing plan was resisted in many quarters because it attacked the independence of the judiciary. One of the most passionate defenders of the nine-man Court argued that "if the United States has the good fortune to escape the wave of dictatorial rule now sweeping over many parts of the world, we shall doubtless look back upon this attempt to pack the Supreme Court as one of the darkest hours of our history."[20] Roosevelt never expanded the Court, but his desperate and dangerous plan underlined the paucity of means that governments have to respond to judicial decisions under the American Constitution.

In a series of 1937 judgments — the "switch in time that saved nine" — the Court suddenly abandoned the approach taken by the *Lochner* Court. Roosevelt remarked that "the old minority of 1935 and 1936 had become the majority of 1937 — without a single new appointment of a justice!"[21] The turning point was a case that upheld a minimum wage for women, even though the Court had previously struck down minimum wages for both women and minors. The majority concluded that "the Constitution does not speak of freedom of contract. It speaks of liberty and prohibits the deprivation of liberty without due process of law ... But the liberty safeguarded is liberty in a social organization which requires the protection of law against evils which menace the health, safety and morals of the people." Better late than never, the Court took judicial notice of "the unparalleled demands for relief which arose during the recent period of depression and continue to an alarming extent." The community was entitled to regulate "unconscionable employers" who would act in "selfish disregard of the public interest" by paying less than a living wage. The old guard as represented by a three-judge minority bitterly complained that the Court was amending a constitution that should not "change with the ebb and flow of economic events."[22] The Court had indeed moved from the extremes of judicial activism to judicial restraint in a very short time.

One of cases signalling the end of the *Lochner* era was the 1938 *Carolene Products* decision, which upheld federal legislation regulating the shipment of milk between states. The Court created a presumption that legislation rests "upon some rational basis within the knowledge and experience of the legislator." In a footnote that has since become famous, Justice Stone hinted that this presumption of constitutionality might not apply to "legislation which restricts those political processes which can ordinarily be expected to bring about the repeal of undesirable legislation," such as restrictions on freedom of expression or the right to vote. The Court's new deferential approach might also not apply to "statutes directed at particular religious, or national or racial minorities," on the basis that "prejudice against discrete and insular minorities may be a special condition, which tends seriously to curtail the operation of those political processes ordinarily to be relied upon to protect minorities, and which may call for a correspondingly more searching judicial inquiry."[23] Written at a time when African Americans were forced by law to use separate washrooms and ride at the back of the bus, this footnote laid much of the basis for the second generation of Supreme Court activism.

After the close call of the switch in time, the Supreme Court was not even willing to protect discrete and insular minorities for some time. The Court upheld the wartime internment of Japanese Americans and the conviction of Communists during the McCarthy era.[24] Excessive concern about avoiding judicial activism can result in the independent courts not exercising their power to protect minorities and the unpopular. In 1940 the Court upheld mandatory flag salutes in schools on the basis that judicial intervention would "make us the school board for the country. That authority has not been given to the Court, nor should we assume it." Three years later the Court reversed itself in recognition that the mandatory flag salute discriminated against minorities such as the Jehovah Witnesses. Extreme judicial deference towards other institutions of government was replaced by equally extreme judicial activism, based on the idea that "the very purpose of a bill of rights was to withdraw certain subjects from the vicissitudes of political controversy, to place them beyond the reach of majorities and officials."[25] The *Bill of Rights* was not designed to enhance and enrich democratic debate, but to withdraw rights from democratic debate. The Court lurched from the extremes of a *Lochner* activism that disregarded the role of the legislature to regulate the economy, to a temporary deference that threatened to undercut its anti-majoritarian role, and then back again to extreme activism that sought to withdraw the rights of discrete and insular minorities from democratic debate. There was little attempt to find any middle ground between the dichotomy of judicial activism and judicial restraint, a compromise that would allow both strong courts and strong legislatures to co-exist and thrive.

The Post-Second World War Civil Rights Era

Although the Court at times held that particular segregated facilities were not equal, the separate but equal doctrine of the 1896 *Plessy* v. *Ferguson* case remained law until it was reversed in 1954 by the Court's decision in *Brown* v. *Board of Education*.[26] In that momentous decision, newly appointed Chief Justice Earl Warren, a former prosecutor and Republican governor of California who was destined to become the Court's most famous liberal activist, was able to get all nine judges to agree to a short judgment that separate facilities in public education were inherently unequal. Today *Brown* is regarded as perhaps the greatest victory for justice in the twentieth century, but not at the time it was rendered. The decision was released on what its Southern opponents called "Black Monday." Almost one hundred Congressmen signed the "Southern Manifesto," which criticized the decision as "a clear abuse of judicial power" that "climaxes a trend in the Federal Judiciary to legislate, in derogation of the authority of Congress[,] and to encroach upon the reserved rights of the States and the people." Eight of the eleven former Confederate states passed laws purporting to declare the *Brown* decision null and void on the basis of states' rights. Attempts were also made in Congress to declare that separate but equal was the correct interpretation of the constitution and to limit Supreme Court justices to four-year terms.[27] Fierce Southern resistance meant that only 1.2 per cent of African American children in the South attended school with whites a decade after the Court decided *Brown*.[28] Even in the calmer atmosphere of the law reviews, respected commentators questioned the decision's respect for freedom of association and "neutral principles."[29] The decision that, today, is rightly seen as the Court's greatest triumph was originally denounced in some political and academic quarters as arrogant judicial activism that invented absolute equality rights and imposed them on an unwilling majority in defiance of states' rights.

The Court accommodated some of the resistance to *Brown* by allowing lower courts to engage in "all deliberate speed" in desegregating public schools.[30] It could tolerate delay, but not outright defiance, and stepped in to issue a stern judgment signed by all nine justices that Central High in Little Rock should admit black students even if that meant violence and disorder. Citing *Marbury*, the Court asserted in the strongest terms that it was "supreme in the exposition of the law of the Constitution" and that, whether the South liked it or not, *Brown* was "the supreme law of the land."[31] President Eisenhower, who had so far done nothing to defend *Brown* and who would later remember his appointment of Earl Warren as chief justice as "the biggest damned-fool mistake I ever made," reluctantly sent federal troops to ensure that the Court's order could be implemented. Despite this intervention, the Court did not approve of judicially ordered busing plans to integrate schools until 1971. Even then, it stressed that remedies were only justified to the extent they responded to intentional constitutional violations and that "remedial judicial authority does not put judges automatically in the shoes of school authorities whose powers are plenary. Judicial authority enters only when local authority defaults."[32] A strong remedy that had been used against unions in the *Lochner* era — people could go to jail for violating an injunction — was now used to desegregate schools. Liberals who had once feared injunctions as being anti-union now praised them. Conservatives who had once praised them now condemned them as a sign of an "imperial judiciary" intent on producing "disaster by decree." Both Presidents Nixon and Ford unsuccessfully attempted to have legislation enacted to restrict court-ordered busing.[33] As the progressive critics of the *Lochner* Court had done, conservative commentators criticized the courts for substituting their views for democratically accountable authorities, for enforcing extreme versions of rights, for going beyond the words of the constitution, and for imposing detailed and coercive remedies. The sides had switched, but the debate about judicial activism remained the same.

The activism of the Warren Court was by no means restricted to racial discrimination. On "Red Monday" in 1957 the Court ruled against the investigative powers of the House of Representative's Un-American Activities Committee, provoking attempts in Congress to put matters of national security out of the Court's jurisdiction.[34] In the early 1960s the Court banned prayer and Bible reading in public schools as violating the First Amendment's prohibition on the establishment of religion, causing one Congressman to complain that the Court had "put Negroes in the schools and now they've driven God out."[35] More than 150 resolutions were introduced in Congress to overrule the Court's controversial rulings on the separation of church and state, but "because of delays by House Committees, and filibusters on the Senate side, these efforts proved fruitless."[36] It was difficult to formulate legislative replies to Court decisions in the congressional system of checks and balance and loose to non-existent party discipline. When the Court's decisions were not simply disobeyed, they were the final word.

The Court's activism also affected criminal justice. Chief Justice Warren, the former prosecutor, extended to the states the rule that illegally obtained evidence be excluded at trial. He required police officers, on pain of exclusion of any evidence obtained, to administer *Miranda* warnings about the right to legal counsel before interrogating suspects. The Warren Court effectively extended the right against self-incrimination from the courthouse to the police station. Richard Nixon was elected president in 1968 on a law-and-order platform that argued that the Court, under Warren, had "weakened the peace forces against the criminal forces in this country."[37] In that year Congress enacted legislation that purported to repeal *Miranda*. Given the tradition of judicial supremacy in defining the law, courts ignored this legislative attempt to reverse the Court's constitutional decision, something that had been affirmed recently by a more conservative Court on the basis that "Congress may not legislatively supersede our decisions interpreting and applying the Constitution."[38] In the early 1970s the Court struck down many laws requiring the death penalty, but changed its mind shortly thereafter. It now upholds the death penalty, despite strong evidence of wrongful convictions for murder and systemic discrimination in its use. The Supreme Court has the final word on many controversial issues of criminal justice.

The power of the Court brought greater attention to its workers as well as its work. In 1957 a former law clerk (and the present chief justice), William Rehnquist, wrote a magazine article complaining that the "political cast of the clerks as a group was to the 'left' of either the nation or the Court" and that the clerks demonstrated an "extreme solicitude for the claims of Communists and other criminal defendants, expansion of federal power at the expense of State power, great sympathy towards any government regulation of business — in short, the political philosophy now espoused by the Court under Chief Justice Earl Warren."[39] The Court's many critics bashed not only the clerks but the judges. Unsuccessful attempts were made to impeach Warren for the Court's soft-on-crime and communism decisions. Attempts were also made to impeach Justice William O. Douglas, a famed nonconformist and environmentalist, after his fourth marriage, this time to a twenty-three year old.[40] In a destructive and often futile manner, conservative critics launched personal attacks on those who worked in the Court.

The Court also revived substantive due process, but now based it on the right to privacy, as opposed to the freedom of contract of the *Lochner* era. In 1965 it struck down a Connecticut law making the sale of contraceptives illegal, on the basis that it violated the right to privacy. Douglas argued that the right of privacy was "older than the Bill of Rights" and found that right in the "penumbras" of enumerated rights.

Justice Black, who was famous for his reliance on the literal words of the *Bill of Rights*, complained in dissent that, although he liked his "privacy as well as the next one," he was "nevertheless compelled to admit that government has a right to invade it unless prohibited by some specific constitutional provision." He feared that the Court's open-ended approach would make it "a day-to-day constitutional convention" with "broad, unbounded judicial authority."[41] Although the Court claimed it was not reproducing the substantive due process of the *Lochner* era, because it was not sitting "as a super-legislature to determine the wisdom, need, and propriety of laws that touch economic problems, business affairs or social conditions," many were not convinced. Critics complained that the Warren Court was maximizing its law-making power by making sweeping statements that were not necessary to decide the particular dispute before it and were not sufficiently related to its past precedents.[42] The case for avoiding and minimizing constitutional judgments is strong when the Court has the last word in matters involving the constitution.

Then came *Roe* v. *Wade*. [43] In 1973 the Court decided that a woman's right to privacy included a more or less absolute right to have an abortion in the first trimester. The state's interest in protecting the fetus became compelling only at viability. Dissenting judges criticized the Court for undertaking "judicial legislation" that took a sensitive issue away from the legislatures. The decision invalidated the old Texas law that allowed abortions only when necessary to save a woman's life, as well as many more modern and liberal abortion laws in other states. Some commentators who supported several other parts of the Court's post-Second World War decisions accused the Court of engaging in legislation.[44] Sixty-eight constitutional amendments were proposed in Congress to reverse *Roe* v. *Wade*, but the eventual response was simply to cut off public funds for abortions that were not necessary to save the mother's life or were not the result of reported rape and incest. The Court upheld medicare restrictions on abortion despite objections that the legislature was indirectly prohibiting abortion for poor women when it could not do so directly.[45]

Resistance to *Roe* v. *Wade* was a galvanizing force for the social conservatives of the Reagan revolution. Presidents Reagan and Bush tried to appoint judges opposed to this decision, but the United States Supreme Court has not yet overruled it. A turning point was Reagan's failed 1988 nomination of Robert Bork, an outspoken conservative judge who believes that *Roe* v. *Wade* should be overturned as "the greatest example and symbol of the judicial usurpation of democratic prerogatives." [46] The failure to confirm Bork and the subsequent appointment of a less conservative justice was crucial to the Court's decision not to overturn *Roe*

v. *Wade*. Justice Scalia, like Bork a former conservative academic who believes that judges should enforce only the intent and the clear text of the framers of the constitution, dissented on the basis that *Roe* v. *Wade* was a mistake that the Court should reverse. Scalia noted that "correction through legislative action, save for constitutional amendments, is impossible" and complained that the Court's stubborn decision not to overrule *Roe* v. *Wade* "for as long as the decision faces 'great opposition' and the Court is 'under fire' has a character of almost czarist arrogance."[47] The Court not only has the last word but is reluctant to change its mind.

In many high-profile cases the Court refuses to accept legislative replies that alter its constitutional decisions. In 1989 the Court effectively struck down federal and state laws prohibiting flag burning on the basis that "if there is a bedrock principle underlying the First Amendment, it is that the government may not prohibit the expression of an idea because society finds the idea itself offensive or disagreeable." Congress almost unanimously condemned the Court and quickly enacted a new offence on the flimsy basis that it was concerned only with the physical integrity of the flag, not the message conveyed by burning it. The Court did not blink. In 1990 it stated that "any suggestion that the Government's interest in suppressing speech becomes more weighty as popular opposition to the speech grows is foreign to the First Amendment" and struck the new law down. [48] The only hope of reversing the Court's decision was President Bush's proposed constitutional amendment. The Court also had the last word when Congress, in a rare alliance between the religious right and the secular left, attempted to reverse a Court decision that limited protection of religious freedom. The Court was again not impressed and struck the legislative reply down by concluding that Congress could not exercise its jurisdiction to "enforce a constitutional right by changing what the right is."[49] The Court not only has the last word but is not impressed with defiant back talk by the legislature.

Despite a conscious attempt to use the appointment power to select judges opposed to the legacy of the Warren Court, the contemporary Court continues to be criticized by social conservatives both for its usurpation of democracy and its capture by a liberal Ivy League elite. One controversial decision held that, in the absence of equal facilities, women should be admitted to all-male military academies. In dissent, Justice Scalia alleged that the Court was injecting "the countermajoritarian preferences of society's law-trained elite"[50] into the constitution. Bork similarly argued that the Court used the Fourteenth Amendment "to take basic cultural decisions out of the hands of the people. Culture is made by the fiat of a majority of nine lawyers."[51] In 1996 the Court struck down a Colorado constitutional amendment that prohibited attempts to ban discrimination on the basis of sexual orientation: "[I]f the constitutional conception of 'equal protection of the laws' means anything," it stated, "it must at the very least mean that a bare ... desire to harm a politically unpopular group cannot constitute a legitimate governmental interest." In dissent, Justice Scalia again complained that the Court had taken "sides in the cultural wars ... reflecting the views and values of the lawyer class from which the Court's members are drawn." [52] As in the military schools case, judicial activism was defined as an attempt by the Court to impose elite views on an unwilling majority of the populace. Of course, these arguments could just as easily be made against *Brown* v. *Board of Education.*

Criticisms of judicial activism in the United States today are heard not only from social conservatives but from liberals. The left criticizes the Court for engaging in judicial activism by imposing strict scrutiny on affirmative action programs designed to assist racial minorities and for striking down restrictions on campaign spending.[53] It has also dusted off its criticisms of the *Lochner* Court because the present Court is taking a restrictive approach to the ability of the federal government to regulate social and economic issues. The Court has invalidated twenty-six acts of the federal Congress in the last five years, including gun control and domestic violence laws.[54] The Court's 5 to 4 decision in *Bush* v. *Gore,*[55] which effectively awarded the presidency to the Republican candidate, George W. Bush, by halting vote recounts in Florida, drew strong criticisms from the liberals on the Court. The majority was departing from its usual deference to the states, they claimed, and had engaged in unnecessary activism that was not supported by constitutional principle. The American debate about judicial activism goes round and round and is repeating itself.

The United States Supreme Court today is in the unenviable position of being accused of judicial activism by both the left and the right. The right complains that the Court has not reversed *Roe* v. *Wade*, school prayer, or flag-burning cases and that it remains overly concerned with the rights of minorities and criminals. The left complains that the Court restricts affirmative action and the regulatory powers of the federal government and that it intervened in an unprincipled fashion to give the presidency to a Republican who had promised to appoint conservative judges like Justice Scalia. "And so the debate proceeds, with the two sides talking past one another: democracy versus right versus democracy — point and counterpoint, with all the talk changing few minds."[56] The issue of who gets to appoint justices to the Court was a crucial issue in the presidential election of 2000, for there really is no other way to respond to the constitutional decisions of the Court. Today, the debate about the American judiciary seems more polarized and politicized than in recent memory. From day one, however, a seemingly endless debate about judicial activism has dogged the American project of judicial review.

The Limited Responses That Americans Have to Judicial Activism

Americans are fixated on the Court in part because they have so little power to respond to its decisions. The 1791 American *Bill of Rights* gives the people's representatives very few ways to undo the damage they believe the Court has caused. At different times, conservatives and liberals alike have tried to respond and to reverse the Court's decisions, but with little success. As one conservative commentator has concluded, "the most striking feature of efforts to curb the courts is their marked lack of success."[57] A liberal commentator has similarly observed that attempts to "put the political brakes on judicial power" have been "highly infrequent and largely ineffective" because "the dominant forces of inertia" in the American legislative system "work to safeguard the Court, and indeed are magnified in the case of an attack on the Court's historic independence."[58] In most constitutional cases, the United States Supreme Court has the final word.

CONSTITUTIONAL AMENDMENTS

The most reliably effective response to the Court's constitutional decisions has been the difficult process of amending the constitution, even though an amendment requires two-thirds of Congress and three-quarter of the states. Over the years, six different amendments have been passed to reverse constitutional decisions of the United States. They include the Thirteenth Amendment, which overturned the Court's decision in *Dred Scott* to constitutionalize slavery, and the Sixteenth Amendment, allowing the federal government to collect income tax. As we will see in chapter 3, a constitutional amendment has also been used in Canada to reverse a court decision that deprived the federal government of the jurisdiction to bring in unemployment insurance during the Great Depression. Nevertheless, after the failures of the Meech Lake and Charlottetown accords to amend the constitution, it is extremely unlikely that constitutional amendments could be passed in Canada to reverse an unpopular *Charter* decision. If *Charter* decisions could be changed only by constitutional amendments, there would be a real danger that judicial activism could usurp democracy.

APPOINTMENTS

The second most effective means to respond to unpopular constitutional decisions in the United States is to manipulate the appointment process. President Roosevelt appointed judges opposed to *Lochner* and sympathetic to the New Deal; and Presidents Nixon, Reagan, and Bush (elder and younger) all promised they would appoint judges opposed to *Roe* v. *Wade*. The ability of the president to nominate judges to sit on the Court (who must then be confirmed by the Senate after public hearings) has been said to be an important democratic safeguard that keeps the Court in touch with the political mainstream.[59] Leaving aside for now whether this position is where the Court should be, the appointment process has not proven to be a reliable means to respond to the Court's unpopular decisions. There is no retirement age, and judges have stayed past their prime in the hope of waiting out a president they did not like. Roosevelt was eventually able to appoint supporters of the New Deal to the Court, but he had to threaten to expand the number of seats on the Court when none of the judges retired, even after he won the 1932 and 1936 elections. When a vacancy occurs, presidents have sometimes misread their nominees, with the famous example of a conservative president (Eisenhower) appointing two of the Court's most liberal judges (Warren and Brennan). And, since the failed nomination of Robert Bork, there has been concern that high-profile candidates who have taken controversial positions will be "Borked" and not allowed to sit on the Court. As a result, less well-known and often less-predictable people are appointed to the Court. Once appointed, a justice of the United States Supreme Court can stay for life, unless impeached. The curious decision in *Marbury* v. *Madison* was written in the shadow of a serious attempt to impeach one of the judges who was perceived as hostile to the current administration. Later attempts to impeach members of the Warren Court were not as serious, but were used to express public disapproval of the Court.

One major problem with concentrating on appointments (or impeachments) to respond to unpopular Court decisions is that it requires those opposed to particular decisions to attack or politicize the independent judiciary, rather than the merits of the judgments. In the United States, attempts are often made at the appointment stage to secure commitments from nominees on the way they will decide certain cases. Such efforts are at odds with the idea that a judge, once appointed, will decide cases in an independent manner that is accountable only to the law. There is a strong case for making the appointment process to the Canadian Supreme Court more public and transparent than the present practice of allowing the prime minister to decide, but there is also resistance and little likelihood of significant reform in the near future. The appointment process is, at best, an indirect and haphazard means to respond to Court decisions. If *Charter* decisions could be changed only by the appointment process, there would be a real danger that judicial activism could usurp democracy.

REDUCING THE COURT'S JURISDICTION

Another way to respond to Court decisions is for Congress to redefine the Supreme Court's jurisdiction. This method was taken to deprive the Court of its *habeas corpus* jurisdiction during the Civil War and in subsequent attempts to reconstruct the South. Attempts were also made to take away the Court's jurisdiction to hear matters involving national security or busing.[60] One highly regarded American constitutional commentator concluded in 1982 that he would not know how to defend judicial review "in terms consistent with the principle of electorally accountable policy-making" if Congress did not retain the power to alter the Supreme Court's jurisdiction. He admitted, however, that one problem with his argument was that the power had not been exercised successfully in the last hundred years. The same commentator is now of the view that the Canadian approach of allowing legislatures to override or place limits on rights as interpreted by the Court was a better way to reconcile the Court's power with democracy.[61] Like the appointment process, the response of reducing jurisdiction has the shortcoming of attacking the Court as an institution, not the merits of its particular decisions. If *Charter* decisions could be changed only by Parliament attempting to reduce the Supreme Court's jurisdiction, there would be a real danger that judicial activism could usurp democracy.

DISOBEDIENCE

At various times, Americans have simply refused to obey the Court's more controversial decisions. For over a decade there was little compliance with *Brown* v. *Board of Education*, and most schools and other public facilities in the South remained segregated. This defiance eventually forced courts to order detailed busing orders and to enforce them with the power to hold officials in contempt of court. School prayers continued long after the Court held that they violated the First Amendment's absolute prohibition on the establishment of religion. The police have ignored *Miranda* and other judicial restrictions on their powers. Every year, pro-life forces march on the Court to oppose *Roe* v. *Wade*. Abortion providers in both Canada and the United States have also been subject to criminal attacks. Peaceful civil disobedience is an option in a democracy, but much disobedience to the decisions of the United States Supreme Court has been lawless, violent, and isolated, and, as such, not capable of promoting democracy.

ORDINARY LEGISLATION

The most effective response to the Court's decisions in a democracy should be the enactment of ordinary legislation. Legislatures have always had the option of enacting legislation to revise or even abolish the judge-made common law decisions of the Court. A variety of features of the American system, however, make it difficult to use ordinary legislation to respond to the Court's decisions under the American *Bill of Rights*. One factor is the checks and balances of the American system which set off the power of an elected Senate, House of Representatives, and president, as well as a lack of tight party discipline. This division often makes it difficult to enact ordinary legislation that overrules or modifies decisions of the Supreme Court, especially if the legislation is in a controversial area without a clear consensus or if it is thought to be an attack on the Court. Another factor is the structure of the 1791 American *Bill of Rights,* which does not give legislatures an explicit power either to limit or to override rights as interpreted by the Court. This problem is most dramatic and visible in the context of the First Amendment, which declares that Congress shall make no law abridging free speech. Once the Court has determined that some activity, such as flag burning, is indeed speech, there is little that Congress can do in response.

I do not want to suggest that it is always impossible for legislatures to respond to the Court's decisions. The rights to due process and equal protection should allow for some legislative replies, as they often require only the government to establish a rational basis for the law. Even in the area of speech, a legislature could reply to the invalidation of an overbroad and content neutral restriction with better-tailored legislation.[62] And Congress was able to respond to *Roe* v. *Wade* indirectly by cutting medicare for abortions. At the same time, it is striking that in those cases in which the greatest concern was expressed about judicial activism, legislative replies to the Court's unpopular decisions have played a negligible role. The American legislature was powerless to overturn controversial decisions such as *Dred Scott* on slavery, the *Miranda* rule imposed on police, and the school prayer and flag-burning decisions. The United States Supreme Court is so well entrenched in the traditions of judicial supremacy that it does not seem to be impressed with legislative attempts to revise or reverse its constitutional decisions. As we will see, this is not the case in Canada, where the enactment of ordinary legislation remains the most effective response to the Court's *Charter* decisions. If ordinary legislation was as ineffective in Canada as it is in the United States to respond to the Court's decisions, there would be a real danger that judicial activism could usurp democracy.

Conclusion

The debate about judicial activism in Canada, and elsewhere, is consciously or unconsciously bound up in the American experience. The American franchise on judicial review casts as large and as unhealthy a shadow on judicial review as it does on fast food, music, and the movies. Progressive commentators in Canada have been haunted by the ghost of *Lochner* and by the fear that the Canadian Court would prevent governments from assisting the disadvantaged. Similarly, conservative commentators have been haunted by the ghost of the Warren Court and the fear that the Canadian Court would have the last word on issues such as abortion, police powers, and the rights of minorities. The influence of the American experience is unfortunate because the structures of the American and the Canadian constitutions are fundamentally different. The 1791 American *Bill of Rights* contains no provisions allowing ordinary legislation to limit and even override rights as interpreted by the Court. Combined with the checks and balances of the American congressional system, this limitation promotes judicial supremacy, at least in the absence of the drastic responses of changing the Court or the constitution. The 1982 Canadian *Charter*, like other modern bills of rights, allows legislatures to limit and even override rights, as interpreted by the Court, with ordinary legislation. The parliamentary system ensures that a determined government can quickly enact effective replies to Court decisions. The good news is that a Canadian legislature could override either a *Dred Scott* or a *Lochner*. The bad news is that it could also limit or even override a *Brown* v. *Board of Education*. This capability, however, may be the price that must be paid for a more democratic approach to judicial review.

Before we move on to the *Charter*, however, a brief stop is necessary to understand the Canadian experience with judicial activism in the years before the *Charter*. As we will find in chapter 3, Canadian courts have often failed to come to the defence of minorities and the unpopular, and they have been criticized for engaging in judicial activism the few times they have done so. We will also see that American debates about judicial activism have some resonance in the context of the judicial enforcement of the constitutional division of powers between the federal and the provincial governments.

Chapter 3
Judicial Activism before the *Charter*

Most people think that judicial activism was not a problem in Canada before Prime Minister Pierre Trudeau gave law professors and lawyers the gift of the *Charter*. In fact, complaints that the courts were subverting the intent of the constitution, making bone-headed decisions, and usurping the decisions of elected governments were made long before Canadians ever heard of the *Charter* or Mr. Trudeau. Indeed, judicial invalidation of the Canadian version of the New Deal in the 1930s provoked a greater constitutional crisis than in the United States. In Canada there was no switch in time that saved nine and the judiciary did not back down. The Canadian response was dramatic, as both the constitution and the Court were permanently changed.

The involvement of courts with civil liberties and the rights of minorities is also not a creation of the *Charter*. From Confederation on, minorities appealed to the courts to stop the majority from ignoring or abolishing their constitutional rights to bilingual statutes or denominational schools, to honour Aboriginal land and treaty rights, or to oppose public and private forms of discrimination. The difference under the *Charter* is not that minorities take their claims to court or that litigants are assisted by organized advocacy groups, but that they win the odd case. In the few pre-*Charter* cases in which the Court enforced rights it thought were essential to democracy, the decisions were criticized as undemocratic and overly creative forms of judicial activism. The Canadian commitment since 1867 to federalism and constitutionalism has meant that our courts have always exercised power and tempered majority rule. Those who portray the *Charter* as an entirely novel form of judicial power and restriction on majority rule are ignoring the lessons of our history.

Historical Cases of Minorities Going to Courts

After examining the criminal trials of a variety of Canadians rebels, from the Métis leader Louis Riel to the separatist terrorists of the October crisis of 1970, Canadian historian Kenneth McNaught concluded that Canadian courts had resisted being used as instruments of political change. Critics who see the *Charter* as a revolutionary change in Canadian politics [1] have relied on this opinion, even though Professor

McNaught took pains to exclude the "hundreds of test cases" that fell outside his definition of political trials.[2] Canadian history is full of examples of minorities being forced to take test cases to court because governments were unwilling to respond to their grievances or were eager to hand off difficult issues to the courts.

Riel's Red River Rebellion led to constitutional guarantees through the *Manitoba Act* of 1870 for both the French language and Roman Catholic schools. As the flood of immigrants into the province swamped the original Métis majority, however, the Manitoba legislature in 1890 abolished the use of French in the legislature along with public support for separate schools. There would be no more minority rights. The federal government could have fixed the problem by vetoing the legislation or enacting its own remedial legislation, but it was reluctant to be criticized for intervening in provincial affairs, especially on behalf of a minority. The Franco-Manitoban minority went to court and secured judgments from the County Court of St. Boniface in 1892, 1909, and again in 1976 that legislation making English the only legislative language violated the clear requirements of bilingualism entrenched in the *Manitoba Act*. Unfortunately, the government of Manitoba ignored these rulings. To be fair, it did tell the Franco-Manitoban who won his 1976 challenge to a unilingual parking ticket that he could have a French translation of the relevant legislation — if he was prepared to pay $17,000 in translation costs! In 1985 the Supreme Court had to supervise the translation of all of Manitoba's unilingual laws, a process that took a number of years.

The Catholic minority in Manitoba looked first to the federal government to intervene when public support for Catholic schools was abolished, but it gladly passed the delicate issue of minority rights to the courts. It took five years of constant litigation by the Catholic minority, including two trips to the Supreme Court and two more to Canada's then highest court, the Judicial Committee of the Privy Council in England, for the courts to toss the political hot potato back to the federal government: although no legally enforceable rights had been violated, the courts indicated, the federal government could intervene. The politicians could no longer ignore the issue, and the 1896 federal election was fought on the divisive Manitoba schools question. Wilfrid Laurier became the country's first francophone prime minister in large part by promising the sunny ways of compromise. They ended up not so sunny for the Catholic and francophone minority, which was limited to thirty minutes of religious and language instruction at the end of the school day.[3] The *Charter* does not represent the first time that minorities have gone to court to obtain redress from a legislature dominated by the interests of the majority or that legislatures have tried to off-load controversial issues of minority rights to the courts.

Five well-known suffragettes petitioned the federal government in 1928 that, after almost a decade of women having the vote, it was about time that a woman be appointed to the Senate. Perhaps after one of his regular séances with his late mother, the ever-cautious Prime Minister Mackenzie King decided to pass the issue to the courts. He used a power not available in the United States — the posing of an abstract legal question by way of a reference to the Supreme Court. The reference system was an easy method for politicians to duck issues and, well before the *Charter*, "led to an expanding role for the courts where essentially political problems were seen to be justiciable."[4] Eschewing any concern with the desirability of women being senators or "the political aspect of the question submitted," the Supreme Court unanimously concluded that women were not persons who could sit in the Senate. Noting that all the justices were married to female persons, the Ottawa *Evening Journal* was amazed that they could sit "in their scarlet and ermine and with not a shadow of a smile on their legal faces" conclude "emphatically and unanimously" that women were not persons. "Shame upon you gentleman of the Supreme Court! Where is your gallantry, your chivalry? … It looks as though Bumble ['the law is an Ass'] was right."[5] An appeal was taken to the Privy Council, where the women won their case. They were persons who could pursue the Canadian dream of being appointed to the Senate. In a quote frequently cited by courts in the early days of the *Charter*, the Privy Council concluded that the constitution had "planted a living tree capable of growth" and that it should be given "a large and liberal interpretation," as opposed to a "narrow and technical construction."[6] It is easy to overstate the judicial creativity of this decision, but it did indicate that the courts would be asked to interpret the constitution in a manner that recognized social change, such as the enfranchisement of women and the idea that "the exclusion of women from all public offices is a relic of days more barbarous than ours." Mackenzie King finally relented and appointed a woman to the Senate — not the feminists who had forced the government into Court, but a woman with good connections to the Liberal Party.

Racial minorities also appealed to the courts before the *Charter*, but with much less success. In 1903 the Privy Council rejected the arguments of Tomey Homma that British Columbia could not prohibit him from voting because he was of Japanese origin. Subsequently it rejected challenges to the internment of Japanese Canadians during the Second World War.[7] In 1914 Quong Wing, with the help of the Chinese Benevolent Association, challenged a Saskatchewan law that prohibited him from employing white women. Dissenting judges would have struck the law down as depriving Chinese Canadians "of the ordinary rights of the inhabitants of Saskatchewan," but the majority of the Supreme Court upheld provincial jurisdiction to enact even racist regulations concerning the workplace. The Privy Council refused to hear the case and the law remained on the books in Saskatchewan as late as 1964.[8] Fred Christie went to court in the late 1930s after he was refused service at a tavern in the Montreal Forum because he was black. His defence committee raised money by arguing that "it feels firmly convinced that the Supreme Court of Canada will not uphold this malicious principle of racial discrimination." The Court, however, failed Christie and, in one of its most shameful decisions ever, held that a merchant could refuse to deal with any member of the public for any reason.[9]

The Canadian Jewish Congress, assisted by Bora Laskin, a University of Toronto law professor and future chief justice of Canada, financed and participated in challenges to covenants that prevented land from being sold to Jews. In 1945 a trial judge in Ontario stuck down such racist restrictions as contrary to public policy, relying on the *Charter* to the United Nations and arguing that "the common law courts have, by their actions over the years, obviated the need for rigid constitutional guarantees in our policy by their wise use of the doctrine of public policy as an active agent in the promotion of the public weal."[10] The Ontario Court of Appeal, however, rejected this approach as too bold and inconsistent with freedom of contract. The Canadian Jewish Congress financed an appeal to the Supreme Court. Although the appeal was successful on the technical grounds that the covenant was too uncertain to be enforced, the congress wanted more from the Court. It issued a press statement indicating that it "would have preferred to see the decision made on the broader base of public policy which per se would have struck a forceful blow against all discrimination."[11] Well before the *Charter*, organized minorities appealed, often unsuccessfully, to the Supreme Court for support.

Aboriginal people also tried to go to court to resist the attempts of governments to abrogate their treaty rights and take their land. In 1911 Prime Minister Laurier observed that "the Government of British Columbia may be right or wrong in [its] assertion that the Indians have no claim whatever. Courts of law are just for that purpose — where a man asserts a claim and is denied by another." Two years later the Nishga formed a land committee to litigate its claims, but in 1927 the *Indian Act* was amended to make it an offence to raise funds for the purpose of pursuing land claims. In 1959 one Indian leader argued, "so long as that title question is not dealt with, every Indian in British Columbia feels that he has been tricked and he will never be satisfied ... Let us say that it be dealt with by the Supreme Court of Canada ... If the case is lost, that would be settled once and for all: if we win, then you will have to deal with us."[12] The Nishga persisted and obtained a ruling from the Supreme Court in 1973 that recognized the concept of Aboriginal title to land. The case helped to force the federal government to recognize Aboriginal rights and to begin to negotiate land claims, including the treaty signed in 1999 with the Nishga. The Nishga, however, lost the 1973 case, with three of the seven judges holding that Aboriginal title had been extinguished by general legislation and a fourth judge dismissing the case on the technicality that the Nishga had not obtained the Crown's consent to be sued.[13] Despite efforts to suppress such litigation, Aboriginal people went to court before the 1982 constitutional recognition and affirmation of Aboriginal and treaty rights.

Throughout our history, minorities have been compelled to go to Court in an often futile quest to have their rights respected. The difference under the *Charter* is not that there is litigation or that it is supported or financed by advocacy groups, but that they have won the occasional case.

Judicial Activism and the Division of Powers

The division of powers is found in the "old" 1867 constitution, formerly known as the *British North America Act*. It divides all governmental powers between the federal government and the provinces. For example, the federal government has the general power "to make laws for the Peace, Order and Good Government of Canada," including the criminal law and laws regulating trade and commerce. The provinces have powers to legislate "matters of a merely local or private nature," including property and civil rights. Many think of judicial enforcement of this division of powers as more democratic and less conducive to judicial activism than the *Charter* because a judicial decision invalidating a particular piece of legislation means only that the other level of government could enact similar legislation. In reality, however, it is not so simple.

A decision under the division of powers can shut down important policy initiatives of elected governments. Restrictions placed by the courts on federal regulation of the economy have generated severe criticism of the constitution and the Court from the left, while judicial restrictions on provincial regulation of free speech have generated similar criticisms from the right. A government frustrated by a judicial decision cannot place limits on or override the division of powers, as is possible with respect to *Charter* rights. Frustration about judicial activism under the division of power has even forced governments to take the drastic step of changing both the Court and the constitution. This reaction follows the pattern of the American debate about judicial activism.

When Confederation was formed in the wake of the American Civil War, it was not certain that the courts would play an important role in enforcing the division of powers. Sir John A. Macdonald, Canada's first prime minister, argued that the centralized federalism he intended would avoid "that great source of weakness which has been the cause of the disruption of the United States. We have avoided all conflict of jurisdiction and authority" and combined "all the advantages of a legislative union under one administration, with, at the same time, the guarantees for local institutions and for local laws."[14] If the provinces exceeded their local powers, the federal government could and did disallow such legislation without judicial involvement. The provinces bitterly resented such political interference by the federal government, and the courts eventually played the dominant role in enforcing the constitutional division of powers. There was a political need for judicial umpiring of the division of powers, and the federal government gradually relinquished enforcement to the judiciary. The courts did not simply grab power.

The courts were, however, subject to intense criticism for the way they exercised their power to interpret the division of powers. The Supreme Court of Canada was perceived as biased towards the federal government, with which it originally shared offices in Ottawa. The Court's first constitutional decision struck down an Ontario liquor licensing law as infringing federal powers over trade and commerce. The decision was strongly opposed by the provinces and was a factor two years later when a bill was introduced to abolish the Court. Later attempts were made by provincial rights advocates to remove scrutiny of provincial laws from the Court's jurisdiction.[15] These early attempts to abolish the Court or to restrict its jurisdiction suggest that constructive dialogue between the Court and the legislatures over the division of powers may be difficult to achieve. The legislature whose law is struck down by the Court has a fairly limited range of reply options. Amending the law to bring it within that government's jurisdiction generally requires drastic changes that will distort the policy that the law is intended to promote. Allowing the other level of government to occupy the field may not result in laws that advance the same policies or any law at all. Federal legislation may not be possible where the provincial law represents only a local majority, and a patchwork of provincial laws may not really replace federal legislation. What is left is often the drastic options of changing the constitution or the Court.

Until 1949 the Judicial Council of the Privy Council was the final court of appeal for Canada, a role it still plays for some other former British colonies. If the Supreme Court in Ottawa had a reputation for favouring the federal government, the Privy Council in London gained one for favouring the provinces. It upheld provincial power to prohibit alcohol and restricted the ambit of federal powers to regulate trade and commerce. Its judgments were applauded by those in the provincial rights movement, who argued that the democratically elected provincial governments should control their own affairs. One of the Privy Council's judges was praised in 1899 by another of the imperial law lords, Lord Haldane, for having "completely altered the tendency of the decisions of the Supreme Court" by recognizing the provinces as sovereign in their spheres, thereby establishing "the real constitution of Canada." Lord Haldane was no less modest about his own contributions to Canadian constitutional law and later boasted that he was the only judge learned enough to write constitutional judgments and that the Canadians in the colonies "now call me the 'father of the Privy Council' and want my portrait hung up there." Haldane was, in fact, praised by the premier of Ontario for giving the constitution a "sane and sound interpretation" that restricted the federal power to make laws for peace, order, and good government to one of responding to emergencies such as war or famine. Everyone seemed happy that the Privy Council in England could shape the Canadian Constitution in the direction of increased provincial rights.

This cozy colonial club of self-congratulation was, however, disrupted when, starting in the 1920s, the Privy Council began to be frequently and fiercely criticized for having "mutilated the constitution" by changing "it from a centralized federalism ... to a decentralized federalism ... contrary to the ideas that were in the minds of the fathers of confederation, contrary to the spirit of confederation itself, and contrary to the early decisions of the courts. We have Lord Haldane to blame for the damage that has been done to our constitution."[16] The imperial law lord was now more likely to be castigated in the colonies than honoured with portraits. Judge bashing is not a new sport in Canada! Complaints that the English judges had illegitimately and unwisely changed the Canadian Constitution reached a crescendo after the Privy Council invalidated the Canadian version of the New Deal. The attack on the Privy Council was shaped both by growing nationalism in Canada and by a concern that the Privy Council, like the American Supreme Court in the *Lochner* era, was blocking much-needed governmental regulation of the economy.

The New Deal Cases

The Canadian New Deal was announced in a radio broadcast by Prime Minister R.B. Bennett shortly before his Conservatives, who had been in power since 1930 and had done little to alleviate the Depression, went to the polls in 1935. A desperate Bennett declared, "I am for reform" and "reform means Government control and regulation. It means the end of laissez- faire." His New Deal was patterned after President Roosevelt's New Deal and included unemployment insurance to deal with unemployment rates as high as 33 per cent, as well as federally imposed minimum wages, maximum hours of work, and marketing legislation to raise depressed farm prices. Like its American namesake, the Canadian New Deal would run into trouble with the courts. Unlike the United States, the judiciary in Canada would not back down.

Mackenzie King and the Liberals were returned to power in the 1935 election. It was far from clear whether King supported the New Deal, but the ever-cautious yet consummate politician was once again only too happy to hand another political hot potato to the courts via the reference procedure. King shipped off the entire New Deal to the Supreme Court, which, in a series of reference cases, struck down federal marketing[17] and unemployment insurance schemes[18] as infringing provincial jurisdiction, but divided 3 to 3 on whether the federal government could legislate maximum hours and minimum wages under its power to implement treaties. Appeals were taken to London, and the Privy Council declared that the marketing and unemployment insurance schemes, as well as the minimum wage and maximum hours schemes that were based on international standards, were an unconstitutional invasion of provincial jurisdiction over property and civil rights. The division of powers remained "watertight compartments," even though "the ship of state now sails on larger ventures and into foreign waters."[19] In theory, the decisions striking down federal legislation should have meant that the provinces were free to enact the measures, but the Privy Council warned that even if the provinces and the federal government could cooperate, "the legislation will have to be carefully crafted, and will not be achieved by either party leaving its own sphere and encroaching upon that of the other."[20] F.R. Scott, the McGill law professor and co-founder of the socialist Canadian Co-operative Federation, warned that "the courts have created a no man's land in the Constitution and are able to invalidate any marketing legislation they do not like."[21]

The Privy Council also refused to hold that the Depression was an emergency that would authorize exceptional federal powers. F.R. Scott, who won the Governor General's Award for poetry, later wrote:

'Emergency, emergency,' I cried, 'give us emergency,
This shall be the doctrine of our salvation.
Are we not surrounded by emergencies?
The rent of a house, the cost of food, pensions and health,
the unemployed,

These are lasting emergencies, tragic for me.'
Yet ever the answer was property and civil rights,
And my peace-time troubles counted as nothing.[22]

In the chaos and desperation of the Dirty Thirties, Scott was less poetic in expressing his anger at the Privy Council. He denounced the decisions as "a national set-back of grievous proportions" that left Canada "even more helpless than she was in 29 to deal with the problem created by a changing economic system." He criticized the court for importing an American version of states' rights contrary to the clear intent of Sir John A. Macdonald and the other Fathers of Confederation. Echoing American criticisms of the *Lochner* Court, he also argued that the Privy Council was reading in "doctrines of laissez-faire" into the constitution. He threw in more than a little Court-bashing by suggesting that only "foreign judges ignorant of the Canadian environment and none too well versed in Canadian constitutional law could have caused this constitutional revolution." Scott's conclusion was unequivocal: the "Privy Council is and always will be a thoroughly unsatisfactory court of appeal for Canada in constitutional matters." [23]

Scott's views were shared by many in the 1930s. Professor W.P.M. Kennedy of the University of Toronto criticized the Privy Council for holding that "the social lines must not obliterate the legal lines of jurisdiction"[24] and called for both an abolition of appeals to the Privy Council and a complete redesign of the 1867 constitution. A 1939 Senate report criticized the Privy Council for having "repealed by judicial legislation" the centralized federalism intended by the Fathers of Confederation and concluded that the Privy Council had made the "most serious and persistent deviation ... from the actual text of the Act."[25] Some criticized the Privy Council for departing from what they believed to be the clear words and intent of the constitution; others criticized it for not interpreting the constitution to evolve with the times and particularly the Depression; and some did both. [26] Canadian scholars also attacked the Privy Council on much the same basis that the Americans attacked the *Lochner* court: for "its lamentable technique of interpretation and because it frustrated regulatory and social welfare legislation, which could be effected only by a strong federal government."[27] The Privy Council, composed of unelected judges in the mother country, was an easy target for criticism in the Depression.

All this court bashing had an effect. In 1939 a bill terminating all appeals to the Privy Council passed second reading in Parliament. The parliamentarians interrupted their debates about the difficulties the federal government faced responding to unemployment in the cities and poverty on the farms to discuss abolishing appeals to the court that had made their response to the Depression considerably more difficult. The mover of the bill noted that, with the exception of some with "legal learning" and "business expertise ... public opinion in Canada is favourable to this bill." Other parliamentarians complained that the Privy Council's "narrow interpretation" of the constitution had deprived the federal government of much-needed powers.[28] Giving vent to its anger at the Privy Council's decisions striking down the New Deal, Parliament was prepared to abolish it as a court for Canadians during the Depression. Appeals to the Privy Council were not actually abolished for a decade, but only because the ever-cautious King referred the constitutionality of the bill to the courts and the Second World War delayed the Privy Council from signing "its own death warrant."[29] The decade of delay does not diminish the fact that the abolition of appeals to the Privy Council was a response to the way that it had restricted federal powers.

The cases striking down the New Deal precipitated not only a change in the final court but also a change in the constitution. With one in five Canadians "on the dole" at some time during the Depression, a number of provinces were willing to give the federal government power to implement unemployment insurance right after the Privy Council held, in 1937, that it had no such power. Unanimous provincial consent could not be obtained until 1940, when the federal government was given the explicit constitutional power to bring in unemployment insurance. Unfortunately, this date was too late for the millions of unemployed during the Depression. The New Deal cases underline the fact that the constitutional division of powers affects the ability of governments to regulate the economy much more than does the *Charter*, which contains no property rights. They also suggest that a government whose law is invalidated under the division of power may have few avenues of response short of the drastic and desperate ones of trying to change either the constitution or the Court. Without anything similar to the limitation power under section 1 of the *Charter* or the override power of section 33, the division of powers comes much closer to the American model of judicial supremacy than does the *Charter*.

The Alberta Social Credit Cases of the 1930s

The Depression was a desperate time, and it was most desperate on the Prairies, which turned into a dust bowl of crop failure, despair, and hunger. In 1935 the people of Alberta put their faith in "Bible Bill" Aberhart, a radio evangelist who ran the Calgary Prophetic Bible Institute. Aberhart became premier of the first Social Credit government in the world. Social Credit was based on the idea that there was poverty in the midst of plenty because people did not have enough money to buy up the available goods. Aberhart promised to give Albertans a $25 dividend each month, so they could purchase more and limit the debts they owed to the banks out east. It was no wonder that he was swept into power with fifty-six of sixty-three seats. His election promises, like the New Deal, would be blocked by the courts.

Aberhart's populist government distrusted lawyers and legal arguments, a mistrust that only increased when its own attorney general resigned after he concluded that bills introducing the Social Credit platform were unconstitutional.[30] The government would not allow threats of interference by the courts or the federal government to get in the way, and it went ahead with the legislation. The federal government disallowed much of it, but again quickly passed the hot Alberta file to the Supreme Court in a series of references. The Court held that Alberta's attempts to control banking, finance, and credit infringed federal powers over banking and currency. Aberhart and his lieutenant, Ernest Manning, were furious with the Court, which they associated with eastern "money power," and argued that "there is no British constitution that would prevent any province taking wise steps to feed and clothe the people within its own bounds."[31] The rejection by the courts of the Social Credit measures had a profound effect on the movement. There was no further serious attempt to achieve Social Credit by legislation, although the government would continue in power by blaming eastern interests, including the Court, for its failure to fix the Depression. In theory, a federal government could introduce Social Credit, but such a government could not be elected nationally. Even more clearly than in the New Deal cases, the courts interpreted the division of powers to thwart the introduction of radical, albeit somewhat whacky, economic reform. The Alberta Social Credit continued in name only when Ernest Manning became premier after Aberhart died. A generation later, Manning's son, Preston, would feature concerns about judicial activism in the western-based Reform Party's platform. A sense of history is very helpful in understanding contemporary concerns in western Canada about judicial activism being imposed from Ottawa.

The war between the Supreme Court and the Alberta Social Credit government had cultural as well as economic dimensions. Aberhart, an authoritarian drillmaster who brooked no dissent, attempted in the *Alberta Press Bill* to regulate the bad press his programs received by requiring newspapers to run corrections and reveal sources. The Supreme Court characterized the bill as "retrograde," based on the premise that "Social Credit doctrine must become, for the people of Alberta, a sort of religious dogma of which a free and uncontrolled discussion is not permissible." This not-so-subtle dig reflected the fact that Aberhart's

Prophetic Bible Institute had spread the word about evangelical Christianity and Social Credit throughout the province. In its *Alberta Press* case, the Court went beyond its holding that the bill was an invasion of the federal power to enact criminal law to suggest that it was inconsistent with the preamble of the constitution, which contemplated a constitution similar in principle to that of the United Kingdom. The very idea of a parliament required freedom of expression, because elected legislatures "derive their efficacy from the free public discussion of affairs, from criticism and answer and counter-criticism, from attack upon policy and administration and defence and counter-attack; from the freest and fullest analysis and examination from every point of view of political proposals." This decision was a democratic defence of judicial invalidation of a law enacted by the elected government. It was based on the idea that some rights enforced by the courts facilitated democracy. The Court also appealed to a sense of national citizenship by arguing that Alberta could not interfere with the rights of its citizens "as citizens of Canada ... to express freely ... untrammelled opinion about government policies and discuss matters of public concern."[32] In some ways, the Court's stern rejection of Alberta's attempts to control the press and its insistence on national rights of citizenship foreshadowed the Court's subsequent showdown with Alberta over gay rights under the *Charter*. Under the division of powers, however, the Alberta government was powerless and did not even have the option of invoking the override.

The Quebec Cases of the 1950s

The Court's decision to strike down the *Alberta Press Bill* on the basis of an implied bill of rights in the constitution indicated its growing concern about civil liberties. This trend culminated in a series of cases from Quebec in the 1950s. In one decade the Court overturned the sedition conviction of a Jehovah's Witness; struck down closing laws for Roman Catholic holidays, a Quebec city bylaw used to restrict the activities of the Jehovah's Witnesses, and Quebec's padlock law making it illegal to use premises to propagate communism; and awarded damages against Maurice Duplessis, Quebec's autocratic premier, for arbitrarily revoking the liquor licence of a Jehovah's Witness. Like the *Alberta Press Bill* case, these cases are widely praised today for their recognition of civil liberties,[33] but they were criticized at the time as unwarranted and creative incursions by an unelected and unrepresentative Supreme Court in Ottawa on majority preferences in Quebec. They lent "creditability to [Duplessis's] claim that Ottawa was meddling ignorantly and recklessly in Quebec's affairs."[34] A sense of history is again helpful in explaining concerns in Quebec about judicial activism being imposed from Ottawa.

In 1951 the Court overturned the seditious libel conviction of a Jehovah's Witness for distributing a tract called *Quebec's Burning Hate for God and Christ and Freedom Is the Shame of All Canada*. Justice Ivan Rand, a Harvard-trained lawyer who would become the first Supreme Court judge famous for his activism on civil liberties issues, concluded "with the greatest of respect" that the courts in Quebec (one of which had referred to the Witnesses as a "bunch of crazy nuts") "have lost sight of the fact" that the tract was "an earnest petition to the public opinion of the province to extend to the Witnesses of Jehovah, as a minority, the protection of impartial laws."[35] Rand saw the issue in this civil libertarian light, but most in Quebec saw the Witnesses' appeal as a blasphemous attack on the Roman Catholic faith of the majority in the province. The Court also rejected Quebec's arguments that its padlock law prohibiting the use of houses for the "propagation of communism or bolshevism" was a legitimate attempt to safeguard its local "intellectual and spiritual life against subversive doctrines."[36] The influential newspaper *Le Devoir* questioned whether "the Supreme Court would be as careful in an opposite case when it would be a question of protecting provincial jurisdiction from a federal intrusion." It also concluded that "one of the most profound differences that exist between us and English Canadians ... is a question of knowing whether the defence of freedom must go so far as to defend and to respect an alleged right to propagate error."[37] Many in Quebec, including the judges from Quebec on the Supreme Court, saw these cases as "not involving civil liberties at all or else involving a civil liberty of Quebec citizens not to be subjected to aggressive or insulting religious proselytising activities."[38]

As with the Alberta cases in the 1930s, there were cultural dimensions to the Quebec cases of the 1950s. The Supreme Court seemed not to be sensitive to the majority faith in Quebec when it accepted the argument of Henry Birks and Sons, a favourite of Montreal's anglophone and Protestant establishment, that bylaws requiring it to close on Catholic holidays should be struck down because only the federal government could regulate religion under its criminal law powers.[39] The famous *Roncarelli* v. *Duplessis* case pitted anglophone McGill law professor Frank Scott against University of Montreal law dean Lucien Beaulieu as counsel. Scott won, as the autocratic but popular Duplessis was held liable for over $46,000 in damages for arbitrarily revoking "forever" the liquor licence of a Jehovah's Witness. All these cases are today rightly remembered as civil liberties classics, but it is often forgotten just how unpopular Jehovah's Witnesses and communists were in Quebec because they attacked the Catholicism that, at the time, was the root of Quebec's identity. The Supreme Court's decisions were praised by radi-

cals in Quebec such as Scott and his friend Pierre Trudeau, both impa-
tiently waiting for the Quiet Revolution of the 1960s, but they were significantly ahead of popular opinion in Quebec during the 1950s.

In most of these cases the Supreme Court had the final word
because it based its ruling on the constitutional division of powers. In
theory, the federal government could enact its own padlock act or a law
closing shops on Catholic holidays, but in theory only. The recognition
of Catholic holidays and the fight against communism were not pressing issues on the national stage. Judicial enforcement of the constitutional division of powers can be quite intrusive when it frustrates a local
majority that cannot command a national majority. Under the *Charter*,
the legislature whose law is struck down has the option of re-enacting
similar legislation and defending its right of reply as a reasonable limit
on the right as interpreted by the Court. If push comes to shove, the legislature can even enact legislation notwithstanding most rights in the
Charter. When that part of Bill 101 which required that commercial signs
be only in French was struck down by the Supreme Court, Quebec,
within a matter of days, re-enacted the requirement, notwithstanding
the right to freedom of expression in the *Charter*. In the division of powers cases of the 1950s, Quebec generally did not have this option.

In one of the 1950s cases, Quebec did have the option and it quickly and vigorously exercised its right of reply. In 1953 the Court struck
down a Quebec City bylaw prohibiting the distribution of pamphlets
without the permission of the chief of police. The plaintiff, Laurier
Saumur, who was a Jehovah's Witness, alleged that the bylaw was "discriminatory, vindicative, oppressive, constitutes an abuse of power and
is therefore unconstitutional, illegal, null and void."[40] Both the trial
judge and the Quebec Court of Appeal upheld the bylaw as a valid
"police regulation" governing the streets. In a 5 to 4 decision, the
Supreme Court reversed, with four judges holding that the bylaw
exceeded provincial powers in its attempt to regulate free speech and
free religion. Justice Rand echoed the *Alberta Press* case and argued that
the Jehovah's Witnesses were entitled to their freedom as "citizens ...
not of this or that province but of Canada." Four other judges, including
the three from Quebec, concluded that the bylaw was a valid provincial
attempt to regulate either religion or the streets. Citing testimony from
a Witness at trial who had argued that the Catholic Church was "pictured
in the Bible as a whore," Chief Justice Rinfret concluded that Quebec
City, which he noted had a 90 per cent Catholic population, had "non
seulement le droit, mais le devoir, d'empecher la dissemination de
pareilles infamies." The fifth and swing judge based his decision to
strike the Quebec bylaw down not on the basis of the constitution, but

a pre-Confederation statute that protected freedom of religion.[41]

Quebec quickly responded to the unpopular decision by amending the pre-Confederation statute to provide that it did not constitute the free exercise of religion to distribute pamphlets door to door or to make speeches that contained "abusive or insulting attacks against the practice of a religious profession or the religious beliefs of any portion of the population of the Province." The new legislation did not name the Jehovah's Witnesses, but clearly targeted their practices. For good measure, it declared that insulting other religions endangered "the public peace and good order in this Province" and was prohibited.[42] This "popular" legislation "served Duplessis well electorally" [43] and constituted an "in-your-face" reply that effectively reversed the Supreme Court's decision. The day after this law was passed, Saumur again went to court to challenge it on the basis that it was "expressly designed to override the decision of the Supreme Court and is contrary to law and an effort to undermine the constitution of the country and to destroy civil liberties."[44] He unsuccessfully tried to have the court consider testimony to the effect that Duplessis had threatened the Jehovah's Witnesses with prosecutions under the new law. Duplessis died in 1959, but the litigation went on. The Supreme Court avoided the issue of the constitutionality of Quebec's reply legislation by dismissing Saumur's second challenge in 1964 on a technical basis: his fear that he might be charged under the new law, it said, did not give him a sufficient interest or standing to challenge the law.[45] Quebec's quick and effective reply to *Saumur* underlines its opposition to the Supreme Court's decision.

The *Saumur* case and Quebec's hostile and in-your-face reply to it is the exception, not the rule, because the Court's decision was ultimately based on an interpretation of a statute, not the constitutional division of powers. Judicial decisions interpreting statutes, unlike the constitutional division of power, can be limited or overridden by the enactment of ordinary legislation. If the *Saumur* case had occurred under the *Charter*, Quebec would also have had reply options, including the possibility of an in-your-face reply that rejected the Court's ruling as simply wrong or unacceptable. Quebec could have defended the legislation it enacted as a reasonable limitation on freedom of expression designed to provide protection against religious insults. It would have had an opportunity to justify its objectives in regulating the Witnesses' activities to the courts. It could have avoided this process by enacting the reply legislation, notwithstanding the *Charter* right of freedom of expression. The people would have been alerted to what was being done, and the courts would have been prevented for a time from invalidating the reply legislation. The override would also have ensured sober second thoughts about this heated dialogue by expiring after five years, on the eve of the Quiet Revolution. If renewed, it would expire and be debated every five years. As matters stood, the legislation remained on the books until it was repealed in 1986 in order to bring Quebec's laws in compliance with the *Charter*.[46] For better or for worse, the determined will of the majority in Quebec would not have been thwarted under the *Charter*. The division of powers is more absolute than the *Charter* because, under it, the provinces are absolutely prohibited from enacting legislation designed to address matters that the Court classifies as criminal law. Contrary to those who argue that the division of powers is more democratic because the Court simply decides what level of government can enact legislation, the greater danger of judicial activism and supremacy that imposes the Court's final word on the legislature may be under the division of powers rather than under the *Charter*.[47]

Conclusion

Canadians expressed concerns about judicial activism long before anyone heard of the *Charter*. The Privy Council was accused in the 1930s of subverting the intent of the Fathers of Confederation to create a centralized federalism and of preventing the federal government from enacting a New Deal to deal with the Great Depression. Unlike the situation in the United States, the judges first in Canada and then in England did not back down. They effectively prevented the introduction of the New Deal by the federal government, and Social Credit by the government of Alberta. Governments had little choice but to accept these judicial decisions, even though they thwarted the popular will and frustrated attempts to alleviate the Depression. The eventual response to the New Deal cases was dramatic and drastic and will be familiar from the discussion of the American experience with judicial review. Canada changed both the Court and the constitution. Legislation was proposed in 1939 to abolish appeals to the Privy Council, and the constitution was amended in 1940 to give the federal government a new constitutional power to bring in unemployment insurance. Unfortunately, these drastic responses to the New Deal cases came too late for the millions of unemployed and poverty-stricken Canadians who suffered through the Depression. The danger of the Court having the final word under the division of powers does not, however, mean that judicial activism is equally to be feared under the *Charter*. As we will discuss in chapter 4, the *Charter* is more flexible than the division of powers because legislatures have the power to justify limits on *Charter* rights as interpreted by the courts, and they can even enact legislation notwithstanding *Charter* rights. Unpopular *Charter* decisions, unlike the New Deal or the Alberta Social Credit cases, but like the judge-made common law, can be altered by ordinary legislation without changing the Court and the constitution.

Since Confederation, unpopular minorities have gone to court when they have suffered discrimination from the majority. The courts have often turned their back on such claims and, when they have not, their decisions have frequently been criticized as judicial activism. The *Alberta Press* case of the 1930s and the Quebec cases of the 1950s indicate how the Supreme Court, long before the *Charter*, was prepared to pit itself against majority sentiment and strike down laws because they infringed civil liberties that the Court believed were essential to democracy. These cases raise the question of whether today's Supreme Court decisions on gay or Aboriginal rights, which are criticized as judicial activism, will be praised in half a century as high-water marks in ensuring that minorities are treated justly and that Canada is free and democratic.

Chapter 4
The *Charter's* Influential Response to Judicial Activism

Those who created the *Charter* in 1982 were well aware of the benefits and the dangers of judicial activism. Prime Minister Pierre Trudeau, who, because of his radical reputation, had been unable to get a job as a law professor in Quebec during the Duplessis regime, saw a lack of respect for the rights of individuals and minorities as an obstacle to democracy and a sense of Canadian citizenship. For him, a Supreme Court interpreting a *Charter* could be an instrument of national unity as well as the expression of a liberal concern for the rights of individuals and minorities. Although Trudeau leaned towards judicial supremacy, he knew, as a constitutional scholar, that the courts were unpredictable. They had interpreted the division of powers in a manner never imagined by the framers of the 1867 constitution and, south of the border, they continued to surprise many people.

Provincial opposition to the *Charter* came from both the left (the social democratic government of Saskatchewan) and the right (the conservative governments of Manitoba and Alberta). The western premiers were suspicious of giving a federally appointed Supreme Court in Ottawa the final word on matters of social or economic policy. They remembered the New Deal and the Social Credit cases of the 1930s, in which the courts had thwarted attempts by both the federal and the provincial governments to alleviate the suffering of the Depression. Their suspicions about the Supreme Court in Ottawa were not alleviated when it failed to protect provincial jurisdiction over resources from the federal National Energy Program in 1980. The provinces were also familiar with the American experience with judicial activism and feared that a bill of rights would give the Court in Ottawa the final word on many social and regulatory matters within their jurisdiction. They would be especially affected by the recognition of property and Aboriginal rights, which would affect their jurisdiction over property and natural resources, as well as due process rights, which would bind their police and prosecutors. Most of the provinces favoured the retention of legislative supremacy.

As individuals, those who framed the *Charter* might not have been able to agree on a document that combined the benefits of strong judicial review and strong legislative review of judicial review. Left to its own devices, the federal government might have produced a bill of rights without a limitation clause and certainly without an override. The provinces might have retained legislative supremacy or a bill of rights that preserved as much legislative supremacy as possible. Together, however, the two levels of government devised a creative compromise that combined the virtues of both judicial and legislative activism. Non-governmental groups also played an important role. The federal government was prepared to water down many of the rights of the *Charter* to get the provinces on side. It was most committed to minority language rights, not due process rights for those accused of crime, or equality rights for women or minorities, or land or treaty rights for Aboriginal people. When the provinces did not agree to a weak *Charter*, the federal government allowed social groups — defence lawyers and civil libertarians, women's and other equality-seeking groups, and Aboriginal groups — to participate in the drafting. It often followed their recommendations, and the result was a much stronger *Charter* than one that would have emerged from backroom intergovernmental wheeling and dealing.

The *Charter* that all governments except the separatist government of Quebec eventually agreed upon was innovative. It was certainly different from the American *Bill of Rights*. Property rights were omitted, and affirmative action was specifically allowed for both disadvantaged groups and residents of provinces with higher than average unemployment. The ability of courts to strike down unconstitutional legislation and award remedies for constitutional violations was specifically recognized. Every one of the broad and robust rights in the *Charter* — the fundamental freedoms, democratic rights, mobility rights, legal rights, equality rights, and minority language rights — was subject to a general limitation provision that allowed governments to enact laws that imposed reasonable limits that were demonstrably justified in a free and democratic society. As a final failsafe, legislatures could enact legislation notwithstanding the fundamental freedoms and the legal and equality rights. This override of rights would expire after five years, but could be renewed. The *Charter* was a unique and innovative Canadian invention: it allowed strong courts interested in protecting rights to co-exist with strong legislatures, which could take democratic responsibility for limiting and even temporally overriding rights as interpreted by the courts. The *Charter* was the product of people who understood the dangers of unfettered legislative and judicial supremacy.

The *Charter*'s combination of strong courts that could enforce rights and strong legislatures that could limit or deny rights has been influential in the development of subsequent bills of rights. Trudeau, a self-proclaimed citizen of the world, must have been proud to see how widely the innovations in the *Charter* have been embraced abroad. New Zealand, Israel, and South Africa have all copied the general reasonable-limits provision of the *Charter* in bills of rights enacted in the 1990s. New Zealand, Israel, and the United Kingdom have all followed the override in providing that their legislatures can enact legislation that expressly derogates from rights in their bills of rights. As is so often the case when Canadians travel in foreign lands, the main asset of the *Charter* has been that it is not American. It combines the civil law tradition of codifying abstract rights and principles with the common law tradition of allowing the elected legislature to take responsibility for limiting and even overriding in particular contexts the rights that the court has recognized. It also builds on other post-Second World War bills of rights, which generally recognize that the state can enact some necessary and proportional limits on rights. The *Charter* has been attractive in countries that want to give the independent judiciary a stronger role in protecting rights and freedoms, but have been unwilling to follow the American example of giving the Court the final word. In a typically inclusive, understated, and compromising Canadian manner, it quietly works out a new approach to the dilemma of judicial activism that has plagued the Americans for over two hundred years.

Negotiating the *Charter*

As a young reforming justice minister on the verge of becoming prime minister, Pierre Trudeau signalled in 1968 the Liberal government's interest in entrenching a bill of rights. This proposal set off a sophisticated debate about its merits. Many spoke about the danger of giving judges the final word on matters of rights.[1] Although the opponents of a bill of rights ultimately lost that battle, they had an important impact on how the *Charter* was structured and in making Canadians aware of the dangers of American-style judicial activism. The result was a compromise that did not particularly please purists of either judicial or legislative supremacy: it gives courts strong powers to enforce individual and group rights by striking down legislation, but also gives legislatures strong powers to justify limits on such rights and even override them for a temporary period of time. It has been argued that the *Charter's* "innovative and useful structure for avoiding political/judicial stalemates" was produced more "by political circumstances rather than genius."[2] Politics did indeed play an important role. Nevertheless, the *Charter's* creative and innovative combination of judicially enforced rights for individuals and minorities and legislative powers to limit and even temporally override those rights was a stroke of collective genius. In many respects it resembles the Confederation compromise between the individualistic principle of representation by population and the communitarian principle of federalism. In their collective wisdom, the framers of the *Charter* worked out a new and important response to the dilemma of judicial activism — one that has since been followed in other parts of the world.

During the final push in 1980 and 1981 towards the *Charter*, two premiers — Allan Blakeney, the socialist premier of Saskatchewan, and Sterling Lyon, the Tory premier of Manitoba — took strong and principled stands against adopting an American-style bill of rights. Lyon, a staunch monarchist, opposed the *Charter* on the basis that it could lead the country down "the slippery slope of republicanism." Canada should avoid "the experience of our neighbours to the south, where judges create rights — on occasion in direct defiance of the people's elected and accountable representatives." His government stood for "the Federal, parliamentary and monarchical system in Canada which needs the support of all good Canadians at this time considering the kind of attack under which these three items of our traditions are presently facing."[3] Lyon's opposition to the *Charter* was based on a traditional defence of parliamentary sovereignty and the idea that unelected judges had no business interfering with legislation. The night the federal government and all the provinces except Quebec finally came to a deal that would allow the *Charter* to be entrenched, but subject to the notwithstanding clause, Lyon was campaigning in Manitoba for an election he would lose. He could live with the override because it preserved parliamentary supremacy by allowing legislatures to have the last word under the *Charter*.

Lyon was joined in his concerns about the *Charter* by Allan Blakeney. These Prairie premiers were at opposite ends of the political spectrum, but they were both concerned about giving the courts powers to trump the legislatures. Like Lyon, Blakeney argued that the entrenchment of the *Charter* was a "matter foreign to Canadian constitutional practice and tradition." He did not, however, base his opposition solely on tradition, but was concerned that the *Charter* made false promises and gave the courts excessive power. For him, the *Charter* ran the danger of being "just chest thumping and ... not dealing with the essential problems of operating a society and of drawing these lines." Whatever a bill of rights guaranteed, rights were not and could not be absolute. Thus the rights rhetoric of the *Charter* was misleading: "I tend not to be in favour of a ringing declaration of what we say we are going to do when we know we are not going to do it and to allow the judges to put in the qualifications."[4] In an effort to win support from Blakeney and other provincial premiers, the *Charter*, when introduced in September 1980, had a broad limitation clause that allowed legislatures to place "reasonable limits as are generally accepted in a free and democratic society with a parliamentary system of government." It also departed from the American *Bill of Rights* by not including property rights, which were subject to day-to-day limitation by all sorts of regulation by provincial governments. The watered-down version of the *Charter* also contemplated that many restraints on the police would ultimately be defined by Parliament, not the courts.

Blakeney's concerns about the *Charter* were not completely met by a broad limitation clause that would allow judges to uphold generally acceptable limitations on rights. He argued that courts were at a disadvantage compared with governments in assessing difficult choices and tradeoffs. "The essence of government is making a fair number of these qualifications and I say that judges are not well qualified to do this. They do not have the expertise or the staff. They cannot set up task forces and they cannot find out what the problems are. They may not be terribly sensitive to what the people want." Testifying before the Joint Committee on the Constitution in November 1980, he indicated that he could go along with entrenchment of the *Charter*, but "with a non obstante clause because basically the courts are good places to decide individual cases of human rights issues, but bad places to decide broad social policies in the guise of deciding issues of human rights."[5] There was precedent for the override in statutory bills of rights at the federal level and in Alberta, Saskatchewan, and Quebec.

The override was brought into the patriation debates in a 1979 speech by Paul Weiler, a Canadian who held a professorship at the Harvard Law School. Weiler confessed that he had always "been ambivalent about the idea of a constitutional Bill of Rights in Canada," in large part because he had been highly critical of the Supreme Court's performance in the past. He had even made a controversial proposal that the enforcement of the division of powers be taken away from the Court entirely. Nevertheless, he saw an important distinction between judicial enforcement of the division of powers and the *Charter*. In most cases the *Charter* would be applied, not against the actions of elected legislatures, but to officials, most notably the police. Even when legislation was challenged, "a majority vote in the legislature is not a democratic talisman," especially in the Canadian parliamentary system of strict party discipline and tight control by the prime minister. Weiler proposed that legislatures have the ability to enact laws, notwithstanding the *Charter*, as "a creative compromise between the British version of full-fledged parliamentary sovereignty and the American version of full-fledged judicial authority over constitutional matters." Unlike the situation in the United Kingdom, aggrieved citizens could use litigation to engage their governments "in a dialogue of principle" and not "be fobbed off as a troublemaker who is raising issues too touchy to be handled by politicians, and who does not represent enough votes to carry political clout anyway." Unlike the system in the United States, however, governments would not have to accept judicial solutions to complex issues of social policy if they were prepared to enact legislation notwithstanding the *Charter* and "take the flak for such a measure."[6] It was acceptable to give Parliament the final say, "so long as it does so in accordance with a procedure which clearly focuses political responsibility for such action."[7] Weiler's understanding of the democratic nature of the *Charter* built more on his understanding of the common law, in which courts required legislatures to make clear statements when they wished to infringe civil liberties, than on the constitutional division of powers, in which the courts enforced absolute limits on legislatures.[8] Like the common law, the *Charter* could enhance democracy by requiring the legislature to take responsibility for the way it and its officials treated rights and freedoms.

Most attention by far has been focused on section 33 as the Canadian answer to the dilemma of judicial activism, but other features of the *Charter* were designed with this issue in mind. The debate about the constitutionality of affirmative action that was raging in American courts was settled with section 15(2), which provided that equality rights did not preclude affirmative action programs for disadvantaged groups and individuals. Mobility rights were similarly qualified to allow affirmative action for residents of provinces with above-average unemployment. Property rights were excluded from the *Charter* because of a concern about repeating the *Lochner* experience of judicial interference with government regulation and redistribution. The fear of substantive due process was so great that the framers avoided even the use of the phrase "due process" in defining the procedural guarantees of the *Charter* and used, instead, what non-lawyers might think was the broader concept of "fundamental justice." The *Charter* recognized that courts could strike down unconstitutional laws and award "appropriate and just remedies." Unconstitutionally obtained evidence could be excluded, but, unlike in the United States, only if, in all the circumstances, its admission would bring the administration of justice into disrepute.

The most important feature in the *Charter* to respond to the danger of judicial activism has turned out not to be the section 33 override, but the ability of governments under section 1 to enact laws that contain reasonable limits on *Charter* rights. In response to concerns expressed by women's and civil liberties groups, section 1 was changed in 1981 to require limits that were "prescribed by law" and "demonstrably justified in a free and democratic society." This restriction placed a stricter standard of justification on governments than a previous version drafted to win provincial support, but it still contemplated that limits on rights as interpreted by the courts could be imposed by ordinary legislation. Section 1 was modelled after limitation clauses found in post-

Second World War rights documents, but went beyond these documents in its generality. Section 1 applied to every *Charter* right and at all times, not only in emergencies. It did not attempt to enumerate or limit the valid reasons legislatures might have for limiting rights for objectives such as public safety, health, or the rights of others. Section 1 recognized that it was only "chest thumbing" to think that rights were absolute; rather, governments should take democratic responsibility and be able to justify the limits they placed on rights to both the people and the courts. By following and expanding on the ability of the modern state to justify reasonable, necessary, and proportionate limits on rights in post-Second World War bills of rights, section 1 distinguishes the *Charter* from the 1791 American *Bill of Rights,* which in its First Amendment emphatically proclaims that "Congress shall make no law respecting an establishment of religion; or prohibiting the free exercise thereof; or abridging the freedom of speech or of the press; or the right of the people peaceably to assemble."

The requirement in section 1 of the *Charter* that limits on rights be prescribed by law followed common law traditions of demanding clear statements for the infringement of rights. It enhances democracy by requiring legislatures to articulate, and presumably to debate, the limits they place on rights. Section 33 similarly requires legislatures expressly to declare that legislation will operate notwithstanding certain *Charter* rights. It also requires the legislature to revisit the matter in calmer times when the override expires after five years. Section 1 and section 33 remain distinctive features of the *Charter* that would be unthinkable to most Americans, who believe that rights are absolute and that courts should have the last say on rights. Lyon and Blakeney lost the battle not to entrench the *Charter*, but their concerns about judicial activism and their faith in legislatures helped ensure that the Court under the *Charter* would not necessarily have the last word.

As Premier Blakeney explained in November 1981, the *Charter* as enacted "guarantees the protection of individual rights and freedoms while recognizing that in some cases that protection remains the ultimate responsibility of parliament and the legislatures and not the courts."[9] The "constitutional escape valve" of section 33 allows "parliaments and legislatures to make ultimate social decisions."[10] It could be used if the courts invalidated union shop agreements as infringing freedom of association, minimum ages for drinking or driving, mandatory retirement as age discrimination, or capital punishment as cruel and unusual punishment. "Appointed courts ... who were ill-equipped to make decisions on these broad social questions" should not have "unfettered power" on such issues.[11] At least at that time, Blakeney had satisfied himself that courts would not have the last word on vital matters of social policy. In subsequent years, he has expressed concerns that governments have not used section 33 enough. This may be true, but if blame must be assigned, it should be directed at those governments and not the *Charter* he helped design.

As a protest against the enactment of the *Charter*, the separatist government of Quebec attached the override to all its laws. The Supreme Court deferred to the legislative will and declined to second-guess the way the override was used. It was up to the people at election time, not the court, to decide whether a government should be disciplined for using the override.[12] The Saskatchewan government under Conservative Grant Devine became the second government to employ the override to ensure that the courts would not prevent strikers from being ordered back to work. The Devine government was re-elected shortly after the override had been used, as was the Conservative Klein government in Alberta when it used the override to outlaw gay marriage. Section 33 "ensures that no one has the final word" because of the requirement that the override expires (but can be renewed) five years after its use. By these means it achieves "a subtle and effective check on both legislative and judicial power."[13] At the same time, the focus on the rarely used override discounts the more important role that section 1 of the *Charter* plays in restraining judicial power and disciplining legislative power. Section 1 has proven to be the vehicle that has allowed legislatures to have the last word on social policies such as mandatory retirement and labour relations. Courts have also recognized under section 1 that legislatures have certain advantages in deciding what trade-offs and limitations should be made on rights. As we will see, many countries that have enacted bills of rights since the *Charter* have been attracted to the idea that ordinary legislation can be used to justify reasonable limits on rights and even to override or derogate from rights as interpreted by the Court.

The *Charter* Is Exported Abroad

The differences between the Canadian *Charter* and the American *Bill of Rights* have been better appreciated abroad than at home. Given the heavy export trade in the *Charter*, Canadians may soon add copies of the *Charter* to the maple leafs we sew on our backpacks to distinguish ourselves from Americans.

The most influential innovation of the Canadian *Charter* has been section 1, which allows legislatures to enact and justify reasonable limits on all *Charter* rights. Unlike the 1950 *European Convention on Human Rights* (now incorporated in English law) or the 1966 *International Convention on Civil and Political Rights*, section 1 does not attempt to prescribe or restrict the reasons that elected governments may have to place limits on rights, and it does not provide that some rights are not subject to legislative limitation.[14] Rather, it provides that the *Charter* "guarantees the rights and freedoms set out in it subject only to such reasonable limits prescribed by law as can be demonstrably justified in a free and democratic society." An almost identical provision is contained in the 1990 New Zealand *Bill of Rights*,[15] and a similar provision is found in Israel's 1992 *Basic Law on Human Dignity and Liberty*.[16] A key provision in the 1996 South African *Bill of Rights* is not only patterned after section 1 of the *Charter* but also contains an elaboration of the process that Canadian courts have used in determining whether legislated limits on rights are reasonable.[17] A general limitation provision transforms the nature of judicial review by avoiding many of the dangers of American-style judicial supremacy. It contemplates a dialogue between courts and legislatures about rights and justifications for limiting rights. This dialogue has its origins in the ability of legislatures to clearly displace judge-made common law. Section 1 also embraces ideas of justification and proportionality that are often implicit in the development of the common law and found in the law of many countries. At the most basic level, section 1 requires the court to demand that the legislature be clear about when and why it has limited rights.

The ability of the legislature to justify limits on rights also opens the possibility that social and economic rights might be entrenched without giving unelected courts a final say on the complex budgetary priorities of governments. In South Africa, rights to housing, health care, and social assistance are all protected, but subject to the qualification that the state "must take reasonable legislative measures within its available resources, to achieve the progressive realization of these rights." Following a similarly deferential approach that the Supreme Court of Canada applies to rights that involve the allocation of scarce resources, the South African court has deferred to reasonable and good-faith decisions taken by the government in the distribution of scarce and limited resources.[18] As in Canada, however, this deference is not absolute. In a recent case dealing with the right to housing, the South African court has warned that "to be reasonable, measures cannot leave out of account the degree and extent of the denial of the right they endeavour to realize ... If the measures, though statistically successful, fail to respond to the needs of those most desperate, they may not pass the test."[19] The issue is not one of judicial enforcement of absolute rights, but of requiring the state to justify its often inarticulate silence when rights are denied. The more drastic the violation of the right, the greater the obligation on the state to justify its conduct. Seen in this light, a bill of rights is not about judges withdrawing rights from political dispute, but more about requiring politicians to justify their infringement or neglect of rights.

Section 1 is not the only provision of the *Charter* which has been copied in subsequent bills of rights. Section 15(2) recognizes the regulatory ambitions of the modern state by deeming that affirmative action programs to assist disadvantaged groups and individuals do not violate equality rights. The 1996 South African Constitution follows section 15(2) by deeming that affirmative action measures do not violate equality rights. The recognition of property rights in that *Bill of Rights* is similarly qualified so that property rights should not impede "the state from taking legislative and other measures to achieve land, water and related reform, in order to redress the result of past racial discrimination."

Some recent bill of rights also provide equivalents to the ability of Canadian legislatures to enact legislation that overrides rights under section 33 of the *Charter*. One of Israel's *Basic Laws* has a provision like section 33 of the *Charter*, and the override has been used to prevent the importation of non-kosher meat to that country.[20] The 1990 New Zealand *Bill of Rights* contemplates that legislation can be introduced and enacted, even though the attorney general has declared it to be inconsistent with the bill's rights and freedoms. The courts cannot strike down such legislation because that power is specifically denied to courts under the *Bill of Rights*. Moreover, a clear statement of a legislative intent to violate rights means that the legislation should not be read down by the court to conform with the rights. The United Kingdom's *Human Rights Act of 1998* also follows the Canadian override by providing that Parliament can enact legislation that is declared by the responsible minister to be incompatible with rights in the *European Convention* and by providing that derogations from the *Convention* must be reviewed and approved by Parliament every five years. Like the New Zealand *Bill of Rights*, the *Human Rights Act of 1998* instructs courts to interpret legislation as consistent with the rights in that document only "so far as it is possible to do so."[21] Thus, a clear statement of parliamentary intent to enact laws, notwithstanding the rights of the *European Convention*, should be free from judicial interference. New Zealand and the United Kingdom have followed Canada in allowing strong legislatures to counter the power of strong courts.

New Zealand and the United Kingdom have not followed Canada in giving courts the power to strike down legislation that is inconsistent with their bills of rights. The most courts in these two countries can do is to declare that legislation is incompatible with a right, but without striking the legislation down.[22] The United Kingdom and New Zealand have taken this weaker approach to rights protection in part because of concerns that the Canadian practice of allowing courts to strike down legislation is too American and may too easily thwart the wishes of democratically elected governments.[23] But the differences between the seemingly milder-mannered "Clark Kent" English and New Zealand approaches and the bolder "Superman" Canadian *Charter* can be overstated.[24] The main difference between British and New Zealand declarations of incompatibility and Canadian declarations of invalidity is where the burden of legislative inertia is assigned. In Canada, those who have their rights unreasonably violated by legislation enjoy the burden of legislative inertia. The legislature must respond under sections 1 or 33 if it wishes to re-enact a similar law, which will be applied prospectively. In the United Kingdom and New Zealand, the legislature enjoys the burden of inertia. The legislature must enact corrective legislation if the rights declared by the courts are to be respected either prospectively or retroactively. The burden of legislative inertia can often be important and even decisive. In my view, the Canadian approach is preferable because it gives the aggrieved and successful litigant a tangible remedy and gives minorities and the unpopular the benefit of legislative inertia, all without necessarily giving the courts the final word. Arguments about where the burden of legislative inertia should be assigned should not obscure the fact that both the Canadian and the New Zealand/United Kingdom approaches are rooted in the common law, to the extent that they all allow ordinary legislation to limit or override a court decision declaring rights. Under both systems, the ultimate result will depend on how the courts and the legislature interact over matters affecting rights and freedoms. Both the Canadian and the New Zealand/United Kingdom approaches are miles away from the American *Bill of Rights*, in which the Court is truly a supreme Superman and the legislature is powerless to limit or override the Court's decisions with ordinary legislation.[25]

There is even a chance that Parliament in the United Kingdom, for all its concern about preserving parliamentary sovereignty by not allowing the courts to strike down laws, may find it more difficult than Canadian legislatures to displace judicial decisions. The reason is that two key rights in the *European Convention* — the fair trial and equality rights — have no internal limitation clauses or mini-section 1 clauses, which are found in most of the other rights in the *Convention*. The failure to have an explicit limitation clause does not mean that courts do not balance conflicting interests when deciding whether the right in question is violated. The balancing that occurs is internal balancing of the kind that American courts engage in when determining whether expression — fighting words, shouting "Fire" in a crowded theatre, and so on — constitutes speech that is protected under the First Amendment. Once the courts have conducted their internal balancing and decided that something does indeed violate the right to a fair trial of Article 6 or the prohibition of discrimination in Article 14 of the *European Convention*, they must declare the right, however defined and balanced, as more or less absolute. Without being able to rely on an explicit limitation clause like section 1 of the *Charter*, Parliament in the United Kingdom may find itself in a box. It may have to accept judicial decisions about the meaning of these rights unless it is prepared to enact reply legislation that, as under section 33 of the *Charter*, has an express declaration of Parliament's intent to contravene the fair trial or equality rights in the *Convention*. Anything less than an express declaration of incompatibility would present a danger of the courts reverting back to their previous interpretation of what compliance with the particular right requires. This process would be *Charter* review with no section 1 and only section 33. The Canadian experience suggests that explicit derogation from rights will be rare and controversial, as opposed to the more common practice of responding to court decisions with legislation that can be defended as a reasonable and proportionate limit on the right. Without something like section 1 of the *Charter* to rely upon, Parliament in the United Kingdom may have difficulty replying to and revising some judicial decisions without pulling out the big and controversial gun of explicitly overriding the right through a derogation or express declaration that the legislation is incompatible with the *Convention*.

The Canadian experience also suggests that the most democratic form of dialogue between the courts and Parliament may occur when the courts use their power to declare legislation to be incompatible with *Convention* rights. Parliament will, if it so desires, then have an opportunity to fashion corrective legislation in the way it pleases. A dialogue may emerge, with the courts primarily being concerned with rights and Parliament primarily concerned with the reasons for limiting rights in specific contexts. There is some reason to believe, however, that the most common judicial response in the United Kingdom will not be to trigger this highly visible dialogue with a declaration of incompatibility, but simply to interpret legislation so that it is consistent with rights in the *Convention*. The courts will essentially fix the legislation so that it is compatible with their interpretation of the relevant rights. The Supreme Court of Canada has been cautious not to use creative forms of interpretation to render all legislation consistent with the *Charter*. It has been concerned that judicial reliance on such an interpretative approach could deprive the government of an opportunity to argue that, although legislation violates a right, it is justified as a reasonable limit on that right.[26] Courts in the United Kingdom may frustrate dialogue with Parliament if they distort Parliament's intent in order to interpret legislation so that it complies with the *Convention*.[27] Parliament can always reply to creative interpretations of the Court, but at least with fair trial and equality rights it may feel compelled to accept the interpretation of those rights or to make an express declaration of incompatibility and even derogation from those rights. The absence of a general limitation clause and judicial reliance on strained interpretations to make legislation consistent with the *Convention* may unwittingly conspire to give the courts the last word. This would be quite ironic, given the government's desire to preserve parliamentary sovereignty and avoid Canadian-style entrenchment.

The structural differences between the Canadian *Charter* and these other modern bills of rights should not be ignored, but there is a danger of losing the forest for the trees. All these modern bills of rights, whether entrenched or not, whether granting courts the power to strike down legislation or not, are united in the ability that determined legislatures retain to enact ordinary legislation that clearly limits or derogates from rights as interpreted by the courts. This ability makes all these modern bills of rights more congruent with the common law and more democratic than the American *Bill of Rights,* under which constitutional decisions are generally final, absent changes to the constitution or the Court. Modern bills of rights are united in allowing both courts and legislatures to play important roles in determining how rights and freedoms will be treated and in not withdrawing issues affecting rights from genuine political debate that culminates in the enactment of legislation. The *Charter* is a prototype of a democratic form of common law constitutionalism that gives both courts and legislatures strong voices in determining the treatment of rights and freedoms and that promotes continuing dialogue among courts, legislatures, and society about these matters. Under the *Charter*, the dangers of judicial activism can be met by legislative activism in which a parliament takes responsibility for limiting or derogating from rights as interpreted by the courts.

Common Law and Democratic Constitutionalism

There are important continuities between the new constitutionalism, as represented by modern bills of rights, and the best of the common law in protecting rights. By the best of the common law, I do not mean that judges can invalidate laws because they determine them to be "against common right and reason, or repugnant, or impossible to be performed,"[28] or that the common law protects rights as "trumps" and "vetoes on the politics of the nation."[29] Giving the courts the final power to strike down laws in that way would raise the problem of judicial supremacy, and of judges having the last word, that has bedeviled the Americans under their *Bill of Rights*. [30]

By the best of the common law, I mean a process in which the courts apply presumptions that Parliament will respect rights unless Parliament has, in the clearest of possible terms, spelled out for the people and the court its intent to violate the rights defended by the Court. [31] Much administrative and criminal law, two areas of public law that dominate litigation under bills of rights, is made by courts in such a presumptive fashion. Courts have long read in concerns about fairness that are often not apparent to the naked eye reading the statute. For example, most criminal laws simply prohibit some dastardly deed and do not say anything about whether the prosecutor has the burden of proof or whether fault must be proven. It is the courts, not the legislature, which presumes that prosecutors are required to prove guilt, including the accused's subjective fault, beyond a reasonable doubt. A similar story can be told about administrative law, as legislatures rarely provide for hearings, reasons, or access to courts. Courts use common law presumptions that the legislature intends to respect rights to enforce concerns about fairness that are liable to be neglected or ignored by legislatures. How can this robust form of judicial law-making — judicial activism if you will — be consistent with democracy?

One approach would be to argue that such rights are essential to a meaningful democracy. This may well be so, but such a conclusion would require agreement about what constitutes democracy. I will take a simpler and less contentious approach. The common law is democratic because the legislature can always come back at judge-made norms by clearly stating its desire to treat people in a manner that the court has found to be unfair. Parliament can tell the courts and the people that it really wanted to send people to jail who were not at fault; to make important decisions without giving them an opportunity to participate or litigate; or to expropriate their property without compensation. The common law approach to protecting rights enhances democracy both by making legislatures address concerns about fairness they would rather ignore or finesse and by allowing the legislature to reverse or revise the court's decision provided it takes democratic responsibility for doing so. As I will suggest at greater length in chapter 14, the *Charter* can be seen as enrichment of the common law method of protecting rights because legislatures can generally limit or override rights if they are prepared to enact ordinary legislation to that end. Unlike the liberal approach of the American *Bill of Rights*, which is designed to "withdraw certain subjects from the vicissitudes of political controversy, to place them beyond the reach of majorities,"[32] the *Charter* stimulates democracy by reminding legislatures about rights and by putting them into political play. Under the *Charter*, courts require legislature to address questions of rights, but judicial decisions are not necessarily the final word about rights if the elected government is prepared to take responsibility for limiting or overriding rights.

In a society that respects its courts and is concerned about compliance with domestic and international standards of rights protection, the common law approach of courts enforcing presumptions of respect for rights may often produce a similar result to that under the American *Bill of Rights*, in which the Court enjoys judicial supremacy when it enforces rights. The key difference, however, is that respect for rights under the common law approach is produced by the decision of the elected government of the day not to make clear legislative statements (with the consequent debate at home and abroad) necessary to override rights. In Canada, this respect is produced by the explicit or implicit decisions of governments not to enact new legislation that limits or overrides the rights declared by the Court. When the Alberta government did nothing in response to the *Vriend* decision extending gay rights, it was because the people's elected representatives were not sufficiently concerned about the Court's decision to enact reply legislation limiting or overriding the rights articulated by the Court, and not because of American-style judicial supremacy, where the Court's word is final in the absence of the drastic responses of changing the constitution or the Court. Dialogue between the court and the legislature under both the common law and modern (but not American) bills of rights is based on "active citizenship,"[33] because it is about whether elected governments will use their powers to limit or override rights as declared by the Court.

The difference between modern bills of rights, such as the Canadian *Charter*, and the common law is more one of degree than of kind. They both draw on the idea implicit in the common law that "the more substantial the interference with human rights, the more the court will require by way of justification before it is satisfied that the decision is reasonable."[34] Most legislation in response to judicial decisions will be justified as reasonable limitations on the right as contemplated under section 1 of the *Charter*. The legislature will clarify its objectives and its alternatives to the court. Legislation that simply rejects or reverses the court's decision may require the more drastic response of enacting legislation in formal derogation of rights, as contemplated under section 33 of the *Charter*. The option of enacting ordinary legislation intended to limit or override rights as defined by the Court is not open under the American *Bill of Rights*. In the United States, governments are generally left with the even more drastic and difficult responses of changing the Court or the constitution if they are not prepared to accept the Court's decisions.

Conclusion

One of the goals of this book is to suggest that modern bills of rights allow citizens — the ultimate reference point in a democracy — to enjoy the benefits of both judicial activism and legislative activism. The courts should fearlessly use their independence to make clear the importance of values — fair process, respect for fundamental values, and the rights of unpopular minorities — that are liable to be neglected by parliamentarians and administrators. At the same time, members of parliament can use their powers to depart from and even reverse the Court's decisions, provided they are prepared to justify their decisions to their constituents and, increasingly in this globalized age, to the world. As the United Kingdom's highest judicial official has noted, modern bills of rights seem designed to ensure that human rights should "not be a matter of fudge," that departures from rights "should be conscious and reasoned departures, and not the product of rashness, muddle or ignorance," and that they should be justified "openly and in the full glare of parliamentary and public opinion."[35] Such an approach ensures a democratic process that neither ignores nor guarantees rights. At times, this is a scary thought, but it is the best we can and should hope for in a democracy.

Canada produced an innovative and modern bill of rights in 1982 that is fundamentally different from the 1791 American *Bill of Rights*. It has subsequently influenced the development of bills of rights in many other countries, but its democratic ability to allow judicial activism to be countered by legislative activism has been better appreciated abroad than at home. In the early years of the *Charter*, the Supreme Court warned of the danger of importing "into the Canadian context American concepts, terminology and jurisprudence," which were not appropriate because the American *Bill of Rights* did not have "the internal checks and balances of ss.1 and 33." Canadians can have the advantages of a strong Court that robustly protects rights and freedoms, while not necessarily giving the nine unelected judges on the Supreme Court the final word. The Court wisely warned that Canadians would do themselves a "disservice to simply allow the American debate to define the issue for us, all the while ignoring the truly fundamental structural differences between the two Constitutions."[36] Despite these fundamental structural differences, the judicial activism debate in Canada has tracked the American one, as we will see in chapter 5. This replication of the American debate on judicial activism has done Canadians a disservice by "ignoring the truly fundamental structural differences between the two Constitutions."

Chapter 5
An American Debate Comes to Canada

Since the enactment of the *Charter*, Canadians have played out the American debate about judicial activism at an accelerated pace. Throughout the 1980s a number of commentators on the left expressed concerns that the Court was *Lochnerizing* the *Charter* in a manner that would thwart legislative attempts to assist the disadvantaged and strike down progressive social legislation. In the 1990s Canadian commentators on the right duplicated American criticisms of the Warren Court by arguing that the *Charter* had given the courts too much power to enforce the rights of minorities and criminals and that courts had invented rights not found in the constitution. Despite their different politics, these critics of judicial activism share much in common. They all believe that judges can read their personal preferences into the *Charter*; they are all sceptical about the rights asserted in *Charter* litigation; and they all have faith in majoritarian forms of democracy and legislative supremacy. The American flavour of Canadian debates about judicial activism is regrettable to the extent that it ignores crucial differences in the structures of the Canadian and American constitutions, most notably the increased ability of governments under the Canadian parliamentary system to use the room provided by sections 1 and 33 of the *Charter* to respond to *Charter* decisions. It is understandable, however, given that most of what has been written about the role of courts under bills of rights has been shaped by the overpowering American experience.

Judicial activism is not a disease that doctors can diagnose with some degree of certainty. At best, it is an elaborate concept and, at worst, a label used to reach provocative conclusions without explaining them. Because judicial activism exists primarily in people's mind, it is necessary to understand the minds of a variety of thinkers who are not household names. By the end of this chapter we will see that this exercise is not entirely academic. The professors and others who have defined judicial activism as a problem that Canadians should be concerned about now see their ideas reflected in newspapers, party platforms, and even the judgments of the Supreme Court.

The Left Critique of Judicial Activism under the *Charter*

Allan Blakeney was the leading left critic of giving judges the last word under the *Charter*, and, as premier of Saskatchewan at the time the *Charter* was drafted, he played an important role in obtaining the inclusion of the section 33 override and the omission of property rights. Despite these significant achievements, others on the left continued to issue warnings throughout the 1980s about the dangers of judicial activism under the *Charter*. The focus of these critics' concerns were several early *Charter* decisions which held that large corporations enjoyed rights against unreasonable searches and seizures, mobility rights to pursue a livelihood, and rights not to be required to close on Sundays for religious reasons. These critics feared a Canadian version of the *Lochner* era in which corporations and the advantaged would use the *Charter* to repeal legislation enacted to assist the disadvantaged.

Andrew Petter, who had worked as a lawyer for the government of Saskatchewan before becoming a law professor and who later became a key Cabinet minister in British Columbia's socialist government, was one of the most influential critics of the *Charter* and the dangers of judicial activism. He argued that the *Charter* would protect the advantaged, such as corporations, who had the money to litigate and an incentive to resist state intervention, but would do little for the disadvantaged, who would not have the resources to litigate and who required "greater intervention by the government as a means of achieving social justice." [1] Writing in 1987, he observed that the Supreme Court had taken "an overtly activist posture" by recognizing *Charter* claims in eleven of its first twenty-two cases. This record "does not mean that the Court is about to displace Parliament as the primary law-making body in Canada," but it was wrong to assume that the Court's activism was costless. Returning to a theme that Blakeney had often expressed, Petter argued that "the Court does not have the luxury of expanding rights in the abstract. Rather, it must trade off the interests of some in favour of the interests of others." Rights were really just interests that competed with other interests. The Court's "hidden ideology of the state as inhibiting rather than promoting human rights" and of "negative freedom" ignored "the possibility that government action might facilitate individual freedom ... of the less powerful in society who depend upon government to provide and protect their rights and freedoms." [2] For example, Petter feared that the court's "overt activism" in defining due process rights and excluding unconstitutionally obtained evidence would "weaken the ability of the state to protect those in society who are most vulnerable to criminal activity," including women and the poor. [3]

Similarly, workers might be harmed if the court required warrants for safety inspections or struck down mandatory retirement as a form of age discrimination.

Petter argued that the *Charter* was, "at root, a 19th century liberal document set loose on a 20th century welfare state."[4] This criticism downplayed several important features of the *Charter* that Blakeney and others had secured. The *Charter* recognized the role of the positive state in promoting rights and freedoms through the ability of governments to justify limits on rights under section 1. Section 15(2) allowed governments to adopt affirmative action measures to assist disadvantaged groups, and section 6(4) allowed governmental programs to assist socially and economically disadvantaged people in provinces with rates of unemployment higher than the national average. The *Charter* also contemplated group rights in the form of minority language rights and the rights of Aboriginal peoples, while not entrenching what nineteenth-century liberals would have believed was a key human right: the right to property. It also provided that the individual rights in the *Charter* should be interpreted in a manner consistent with other rights and values, including Aboriginal and treaty rights, multiculturalism, the equality of women and men, and denominational school rights. Finally, section 33 provided the ultimate safeguard against the danger that the Court would *Lochner*ize the *Charter* in a way that prevented elected governments from implementing a fundamental aspect of their platforms.

Michael Mandel of Osgoode Hall Law School is another left critic of the *Charter* who was concerned that the courts and the *Charter* conceived government as the enemy, at a time when the most disadvantaged groups in society were in need of public power. *Charter* victories were not without cost, and the price could well be paid by workers, the unemployed, and crime victims who might be even more disadvantaged than the successful *Charter* applicants. *Charter* litigation was an expensive, elitist, and dishonest form of politics that could capture the energies of progressive forces. Even the odd *Charter* victory in court would be illusory. If the courts had recognized a constitutional right for unions to strike (which they did not), this would "not at all have meant guaranteeing it. It would have meant only the judicial regulation of its restrictions, with wide deference to the economic judgment of governments." In the end, Mandel rejected "the utter uselessness of legalized politics in the face of massive social inequality," but was vague about what should be done other than to abandon "legal politics" in favour of "a strong, responsive, democratic politics."[5]

Another left critic of judicial activism was Allan Hutchinson, again from Osgoode Hall Law School. He argued that the *Charter* was, "at root, a liberal document" that embraced "the American tradition of liberal law and politics" and "withdrew large areas of social regulation from the legal reach of elected bodies." He heaped scorn on those who saw *Charter* review as a form of dialogue that could enhance democracy. "Ordinary people do not take part in constitutional litigation," he argued, "and, therefore, never have the democratic opportunity to speak for themselves. It is almost perverse to liken judicial review to a dialogue between citizens and the state about the reasonableness of government action ... Democracy demands that citizens be more than eavesdroppers at the doors of power." Hutchinson was also vague about what should be done, except for the idea that "direct citizen involvement is always to be preferred to constitutional litigation."[6] At this point he did not see majoritarian and populist democracy as a threat to unpopular minorities.

The left also criticized the indeterminacy of both the rights and the limitations contained in the *Charter* and the power it gave unelected and elite judges to impose their views. They described Court decisions not to apply the *Charter* to the common law, to find that unions did not have a constitutional right to strike, and to allow corporations to benefit from the protection of fundamental freedoms and legal rights as evidence of judges' lack of concern about the exercise of private and corporate power, their hostility to labour, and their sympathy for corporations. These views echoed the critics of the *Lochner* Court and their Canadian counterparts, such as F.R. Scott, who were suspicious of the motivations behind the judicial dismantling of the New Deal. The new left critics were also inspired by the critical legal studies movement, which questioned whether it was possible to separate law from politics. Petter and Hutchinson combined to argue that "rights are like tools. The purposes they serve depend upon the hands that are placed upon them and the minds that direct those hands." Section 1 was even less determinate than rights, because "balancing is little more than a convenient device enabling the judiciary to place its political thumb upon the illusory constitutional scales of justice."[7] Although the left's understanding of adjudication was more sophisticated, it created the impression that judges had a more or less blank cheque and that they usually made their cheques out to the interests of the powerful. As we will see, the ideas of both judicial freedom and judicial bias were picked up and given a different spin by a new generation of conservative critics of judicial activism.

In the 1990s the left began to realize that the major threat to progressive causes was not so much the *Charter* and the courts, but democratically elected neo-conservative governments. Some began to realize that it was a mistake to exaggerate the democratic potential of legislatures and to deny the ability of courts to advance democratic values.[8] As the 1990s drew to a close, even Professor Hutchinson reconsidered his previous antipathy to the *Charter* and the courts. Although disclaiming "a root-and-branch rejection" of his earlier views, he now gave them "a more pragmatic and less dogmatic spin" that focused more on the substantive contributions of courts and legislatures than on ideal and formal understandings of adjudication and democracy. Hutchinson no longer assumes that all legislative policies are inherently democratic and all judicial policies are anti-democratic. Rather, he said, courts "have a vital and complementary role to play in the 'continuous process of discussion and reflection' about what democracy means and demands." This discussion sounded a lot like the dialogue he had previously scorned. A key factor in Hutchinson's conversion was his recognition that the critical account of the *Charter* "has played into the hands of right-wing populist groups." The socially conservative Reform Party "has deployed the sweeping rhetoric of critical jurisprudence to challenge the activism of the Supreme Court in dealing with, among other matters, gay rights and aboriginal land claims. In a very smart move, the Reform Party has been able to hide its particular homophobic and racist agenda in a more general and less offensive critique of court activism." [9] Hutchinson now resists giving conservative critics of the Court the high ground of democracy and urges a more contextual debate that allows for the possibility that courts may contribute to genuine democracy.

The early left critique of the *Charter* was united by its suspicions that appointed judges would favour corporate and other powerful interests and, like the *Lochner* Court, thwart the ability of legislatures to implement progressive reforms to assist the disadvantaged. The left academic critics paid scant attention to the ability of legislatures to respond to judicial decisions under sections 1 and 33 of the *Charter* and often assumed that the *Charter* was simply a Canadian version of the American *Bill of Rights*. With respect to the Court's performance, the left critics often took an unbalanced approach that, ironically, ignored the effects that their own warnings about judicial activism were having on the Court's increasing deference to the difficult distributional decisions made by the legislatures. They made much of the fact that the first successful search and seizure challenge was made by a large corporation against anti-combines investigators, but they largely ignored the Court's subsequent decisions that allowed governmental officials ample powers to conduct searches on those individuals and corporations that entered a regulated field.[10] Similarly, they focused on the Court's 1985 decision to strike down Sunday closing laws enacted for religious reasons, but not its decision a year later to accept Sunday closing laws as a reasonable attempt to provide workers and the community with a common day of rest. Sunday closing laws were eventually repealed by elected governments, including left-wing governments. The economic forces that were leading to Sunday shopping and depriving workers of power and security could not so easily be blamed on the Court and the *Charter*.

The early critics laid some of the corrosive groundwork for a later generation of conservative critics of judicial activism. The left critics expressed romantic but underdeveloped views of democracy. They seemed to favour some type of direct democracy, without coming to grips with the failures of pure majoritarianism or the danger that unpopular minorities could be scape-goated in the name of democracy. To his credit, Hutchinson changed his tune when he realized that conservative and populist forces that rallied under the banner of democracy were often hostile to the rights of gays and Aboriginal people. The early critics were also sceptical about many *Charter* rights as negative and individualistic protections from the state. They sometimes discounted the value of *Charter* litigation to some disadvantaged individuals and minorities, especially in the criminal process. They also sometimes ignored the fluidity of *Charter* discourse about rights and their reasonable limitation. In their efforts to illustrate how much freedom judges had under the *Charter*, they also created an impression that judges had something of a blank cheque under the *Charter*. Whereas the left critics feared that judges would use this freedom to assist the advantaged in society, conservative critics would soon argue that judges had used the very same freedom to assist minorities who had not properly advanced their objectives through the legislature.

The Right Critique of Judicial Activism under the *Charter*

The left criticism of judicial activism that dominated scholarly debate in the 1980s was gradually replaced in the 1990s by a critique that came from the right of centre. Whereas the left had taken its cues from Premier Blakeney, the new critics on the right followed in the footsteps of the Tory premier of Manitoba, Sterling Lyon, who opposed the *Charter* as an unnecessary departure from parliamentary supremacy. Like the left critics, the conservative critics were also drawn to American analogies based on a concern about judicial supremacy. The fear was not so much that the Canadian court would repeat the mistakes of the *Lochner* Court, but that it was following the Warren Court by inventing rights for minorities and criminals and imposing them against the wishes of majorities and their democratically elected governments. Although its politics were quite different, the new right critique of judicial activism followed the older left critique in stressing the freedom of judges under the *Charter*, being sceptical of the rights claimed in *Charter* litigation, and in endorsing majoritarian theories of democracy.

The most prominent and controversial critique of the *Charter* and judicial activism from the right of centre has been made in a series of books and articles by University of Calgary political scientists Ted Morton and Rainer Knopff. These two authors have had a long interest in judicial politics, but their criticisms of the Court, the *Charter*, and the problem of judicial activism became sharper and louder throughout the 1990s. During this time they also became more active in the media and in politics. They were associated with conservative political parties, and Morton was elected as one of Alberta's senators-in-waiting under the Reform Party's platform of establishing a "triple E" Senate — elected, equal, and effective.

Morton and Knopff were concerned that activist judges had used their "judicial discretion" to "create new rights," such as the right to abortions, Aboriginal rights, and gay rights — all in defiance of the intent of the framers of the *Charter*.[11] Anything beyond the discovery of clear answers in the text created a danger of turning the *Charter* into "a 'blank cheque' to posterity, on which each generation of judges can scrawl what he likes."[12] They discounted the possibility that the freedom of judges could be constrained and guided by constitutional text, precedents, and traditions and by the need to "provide a compelling account of what the Charter requires."[13] They also argued that the Court, eager to interpret the *Charter* in its own image, had cast aside traditional adjudicative restraints and become "more a de facto third chamber of the legislature than a court."[14] Their criticism of the "oracular court" was influenced by the American example, in which the courts are constitutionally restricted to deciding live controversies. In contrast, Canadian governments have always been able to refer abstract legal questions to courts and have often been eager to hand the Supreme Court political hot potatoes (see chapter 3).

Although they were once sympathetic, Morton and Knopff now dismiss the idea that the *Charter* can promote a dialogue between the Court and the legislatures. Writing in 1992, they were willing to concede that "the judicial perspective may ... round out the process of deliberating about public policy" and that a decision invalidating a law under the *Charter* could be likened to a presidential veto in the American system that "can often be circumvented or even overridden."[15] Relying on the inability to enact new abortion amendments to the *Criminal Code* after *Morgentaler* and on Alberta's decision not to invoke section 33 to override the *Vriend* decision extending protection against discrimination to gays and lesbians, they now conclude that what is described "as a dialogue is usually a monologue, with judges doing most of the talking and legislatures most of the listening ... legislative non-response in the face of judicial activism is the normal response in certain circumstances."[16]

As we will see in chapter 10, even the failure of legislatures to reply to Court decisions in this skewed data set cannot be blamed entirely on the courts or the *Charter*.

Morton and Knopff's criticism of judicial activism depends on a minimization, if not outright rejection, of the rights of minorities and an acceptance of a majoritarian understanding of democracy. Most *Charter* cases do not involve the denial of core rights, but, they argue, reasonable disagreements about the periphery of rights in which temporary minorities should graciously accept defeat by temporary majorities. Morton and Knopff's majoritarian premises even seem hostile to federalism, as they unapologetically invoke Lord Durham — the British aristocrat who advocated legislative union between Quebec and Ontario as a means to end the "vain endeavour to preserve a French-Canadian nationality" — as the proponent of a parliamentary sovereignty that would protect rights through a system of checks and balances. The *Charter* Revolution is "deeply and fundamental undemocratic," they say, because it is "anti-majoritarian" and because it "leads to a moral inflation of policy claims and substitutes the coercion of court orders for the persuasion of parliamentary (and public) debate."[17]

According to Morton and Knopff, a "Court Party" of state-supported "post materialist elites" has given minorities a disproportionate and unwarranted ability to use litigation to reverse the policies of democratically accountable arms of government. The Court Party is part of a "revolt of the elites" in which a left-leaning state-supported knowledge class in the law schools and beyond imposes its agenda for "life-style issues" on an unwilling majority.[18] The Court Party is defined broadly to include official language minorities, civil libertarians, equality seekers, social engineers, and post-materialists and their supporters in the law schools, the judiciary, and governments. This broad definition strains the idea of a party. Moreover, these constituencies do not rely on the Court for their power. For example, the feminist Legal Education and Action Fund (LEAF) has frequently lost battles in court over sexual assault law (against civil libertarians who are also part of the Court Party), only to obtain some spectacular victories by taking a short walk over to Parliament. The state support that Morton and Knopff stress some members of the Court Party receive also suggests that democratically accountable institutions have found that such groups can play a role in governance in a multicultural and pluralist society. It is simplistic to blame interest groups and a focus on single issues on the Court and the *Charter*. With or without the *Charter*, governments would have considered at least some of the demands made by the diverse groups associated with the Court Party.

Morton and Knopff must also struggle to reconcile their Court Party thesis with the fact that its members — for example, the Canadian Civil Liberties Association and LEAF — frequently oppose each other on a broad range of issues. In their desire to identify the Court Party as left wing, they ignore right-wing uses of the constitution such as the National Citizens Coalition's successful and repeated challenges to election spending limits, interventions by conservative groups such as REAL women, pro-life religious groups, non-Aboriginal fishing interests, and anti-gun control groups. They also ignore the fact that once a constitutional question has been set in the Supreme Court, the attorneys generals of all the provinces can intervene, usually to oppose *Charter* claims, and outnumber the nongovernmental groups that appear before the Court.[19] Finally, they ignore the historical record that some of the minorities they identify as part of the Court Party have, since Confederation, gone to Court. The only difference is that they win a few cases under the *Charter*.

Another conservative critic of judicial activism is McGill political scientist Christopher Manfredi. He can visualize only one clear choice: judges restricted by the intent of the framers of the constitution, or judges with a discretionary power to make law without any constraints other than judicial will. Following the American dichotomy between procedural and substantive due process, he argues that the emergence of "substantive review" under the *Charter* risks constitutionalizing the personal policy preferences of judges on a broad range of issues. The Court's decision that a no-fault offence violated the principles of fundamental justice "had no source other than judicial will," and its decision not to restrict equality rights to the nine listed groups may "eventually come to mean any failure by an identifiable group to achieve its policy objectives through the political process" will violate the *Charter*.[20] Once the Court does not find clear answers in the framers' intent and the text of the *Charter*, then judges have an essentially blank cheque to write their policy preferences into law.

The *Charter*, unlike the American *Bill of Rights*, provides structural outlets in both sections 1 and 33 for legislative replies to judicial decisions, but Manfredi finds they do not respond adequately to the dangers of American-style judicial supremacy. Section 1 is not adequate because judges still retain the right to determine whether legislation enacted in response to Court decisions is reasonable, and they may not have access to the legislative and social facts necessary to establish that legislated limitations on rights are reasonable. Manfredi recognizes that section 33 offers a possible antidote to the dangers of judicial supremacy. In 1993 he wrote that section 33 "can have a positive impact by encouraging a

more politically vital discourse on the meaning of rights and their relationship to competing constitutional visions than what emanates from
the judicial monologue that results from a regime of judicial supremacy."[21] More recently, however, he has declared that that "the decline, if
not the actual death, of section 33 has had a profound impact on the leg-
islative-judicial relationship," effectively making the judiciary supreme.
The adverse reaction that Quebec received for its use of the override to
require commercial signs to be only in French has so delegitimized section 33 that he believes it is "disingenuous"[22] for the Court to rely on the
availability of the override as a response to judicial supremacy. Reports
of the death of the override may, however, be exaggerated. Manfredi
relies on Alberta's failure to invoke the override after the Supreme Court
read in sexual orientation to its human rights code, but he does not deal
with Alberta's subsequent use of it to outlaw gay marriage. A theory of
dialogue between courts and legislatures cannot be built exclusively
around the rarely used override, but section 33 still provides the ultimate weapon should legislatures be unwilling to accept court decisions
and be prepared to justify their actions to an alerted public. If section 33
is not used to correct judicial decisions that the public finds fundamentally unacceptable, the fault seems to lie more in the public's acceptance
of the infallibility of judicial declarations of rights or the government's
lack of will than in the structure of the *Charter* or the Court.

Manfredi is concerned that "judicial supremacy ... is overtaking
constitutional supremacy" as legislatures are forced to accept the Court's
interpretation of the *Charter* as the only legitimate interpretation, even
though judges are no more infallible than legislators.[23] Constitutionalism
is offended as much by unlimited judicial power as by unlimited legislative power. As we will discuss in chapter 13, his solution is to return
to the radical American idea that the legislature can act on its own interpretation of the constitution, even when the courts have interpreted the
constitution differently. "Genuine dialogue only exists when legislatures
are recognized as legitimate interpreters of the constitution and have an
effective means to assert that interpretation." On this basis, he classifies
most legislative replies to court decisions as "negative" forms of dialogue, because any legislative compliance with judicial decisions suggests a "hierarchical" rather than an "equal" relationship between the
court and the legislature.[24] He is also concerned that legislative acceptance of judicial decisions will result in policy distortion. Even when the
Supreme Court has given legislative interpretations of the *Charter* a
wide margin of deference, Manfredi remains unimpressed because the
legislature had itself based its interpretation of the *Charter* on dissenting
judgments in the Court. He remains concerned that *Charter* review will
distort the policies of the legislatures and convinced that genuine dia-

logue will occur only if legislatures are not forced to accept the Court's interpretation of the constitution.[25]

In 1995 the prestigious *McGill Law Journal* published a lead article by Professors Robert Hawkins and Robert Martin of the University of Western Ontario entitled "Democracy, Judging and Bertha Wilson." Martin's previous work had demonstrated the close relation between the left and the right critique of the *Charter* and judicial activism, and he had foreshadowed the work of Petter and Mandel by warning that the Court could *Lochnerize* the *Charter*.[26] A decade later, however, Martin concluded that the Court had not read in laissez-faire values to the *Charter*, but had capitulated to feminists and other interest groups of the Court Party. Hawkins and Martin base their criticisms of judicial activism on both a formalistic and positivistic understanding of adjudication and a majoritarian understanding of democracy. Constitutional interpretation must be based on the "ordinary and plain meaning of words" or else amount to "judicial amendment" of the constitution based on the "subjective preferences" and "will" of the judges. Democracy is based on legislative supremacy, and judicial review is undemocratic because it "gives judges the last word on what is or is not constitutional." They ignored the ability of Canadian legislatures to respond to court decisions under sections 1 and 33 and believed the only alternatives were the dichotomies of legislative supremacy or judicial supremacy. When push came to shove, Hawkins and Martin were more committed to their majoritarian view of democracy than to fidelty to constitutional text. They criticized affirmative action as offensive to "the basic principles of liberal-democratic constitutionalism," even though it was clearly contemplated and authorized by section 15(2) of the *Charter*.[27] They also criticized as "undemocratic and unjudicial" attempts by judges such as Justice Wilson to understand the perspectives of those, such as women and minorities, who claimed that their rights had been violated by the majority. Not only should excluded groups not complain but the judiciary should not attempt to appreciate their perspectives.

In the end, the criticisms made by these conservative commentators about judicial activism depend on particular and controversial views of judging, rights, and democracy. They all see adjudication in positivistic terms that suggest that if there is no clear answer in the text, judges must exercise an unfettered discretion informed by their own subjective value preferences. They are also all sceptical about whether real rights are at stake in *Charter* litigation or only policy choices, or "the ordinary vicissitudes of democratic politics."[28] In their urge to pronounce dialogues between courts and legislatures under the *Charter* to be monologues based on American-style judicial supremacy, they all discount the ability of the strong governments produced by the

Canadians parliamentary system to limit and even override rights as declared by the Court. The conservative critics of judicial activism all embrace majoritarian understandings of democracy that suggest that individuals and minorities that bring *Charter* litigation should accept the treatment they receive from the legislature on a win-some lose-some basis. It is easy to be concerned about judicial activism if you believe that judges exercise an open-ended discretion, that majorities as expressed in legislatures do not violate real rights, and that those aggrieved by the decisions of the majority should not really complain.

Similarities between the Left and Right Critiques of Judicial Activism

Despite occupying opposite poles of the ideological spectrum, there are remarkable similarities between the left and the right critiques of judicial activism. Although they start from very different premises when it comes to judging, they end up in much the same place. The left critics begin with the proposition that legal norms, particularly the abstract ones that are entrenched in the *Charter*, are inherently indeterminate. Judges are often left with a strong discretion in interpreting these provisions. The left fears that judges will exercise this discretion to benefit corporations and other advantaged sectors of society, in large part because judges are wealthy lawyers. In contrast, the right critique begins from the proposition that judges should follow the clear intent or words of the framers of the constitution. They quickly conclude that this is not being done and that judges have a strong discretion to do what they want. Critics on the right also believe that judges will exercise this discretion according to their own preferences and experiences, but conclude that it will benefit the minority interests of the Court Party that influence judges through law schools, judicial education, and interest groups. Critics of judicial activism on both the left and the right share the view that judges are generally free to legislate their preferences into the constitution, but differ widely in the prediction of what the preferences of the judges will be.

The left and the right critics of judicial activism also share similar understandings of democracy. Both are enthusiasts for direct and majoritarian democracy, although they again have very different predictions about what it will produce. In the absence of direct democracy, they are willing to defer to the legislative process they both see as the best approximation of the democratic will. It is interesting to speculate why commentators with different politics would both celebrate legislative supremacy. It may have something to do with the "tory touch"[29] in Canada's political culture which has produced both conservative and

socialist governments. This dynamic was certainly present at the creation of the *Charter*, as both the Tory premier of Manitoba and the
socialist premier of Saskatchewan objected to the entrenchment of the
Charter on the grounds that a Supreme Court in Ottawa would limit the
sovereignty of their democratically elected governments.

Another similarity between the left and the right critics is their
common unease with the rights claimed in *Charter* litigation. The left
criticizes the vision of rights expressed in the *Charter* as impoverished
in its individualism and its conception of the state as the enemy. The
right is concerned with group rights, inflation of rights, and the divi-
siveness of rights discourse, which allows no compromise and makes little room for the public interest and a common identity. The *Charter* has
given a number of groups — women, Aboriginal and disabled people,
linguistic, ethnic, and racial minorities — a stake in the constitution.
These groups, who form the core of the Court Party, "see their fate as
affected by the evolving meaning attached to particular constitutional
clauses."[30] The investment of these minorities in their rights makes legislative and constitutional compromises difficult, as witnessed by the
demise of both the Meech Lake and Charlottetown accords, and may
erode a sense of national citizenship.

There may be something to this critique of rights consciousness,
but all the blame cannot be placed on the *Charter* and the Court.
Linguistic minorities, feminists, and Aboriginal people all had a certain
amount of political power before their rights were entrenched in the
Charter. The fact that they successfully lobbied for special rights is a tes-
tament to their political influence. The *Charter* recognizes groups' rights,
but not as absolutes. It does not ignore the public interest as articulated
by our representative institutions. Legislatures and the public have their
own section in the *Charter* every bit as much as the minorities of the
Court Party. They can justify reasonable limits on rights in the public
interest under section 1 of the *Charter* and they can even override rights
under section 33 of the *Charter*. The Court itself is receptive to strong
arguments by elected governments that rights must be limited in the
public interest. The rights that are recognized in the *Charter* make governance more complex and difficult, but the *Charter* offers no support
for the idea that rights, however robustly asserted, are absolute.

Reality Check: Other Perspectives on Judicial Activism and the *Charter*

The excesses of both the left and the right critiques of judicial activism
are revealed by comparing them to the more balanced assessment of the
Court's power offered by University of Toronto political scientist Peter

Russell.[31] Russell, Canada's pioneer political scientist in studying the courts, opposed the introduction of the *Charter* and is no cheerleader for courts or lawyers.[32] Given this view, one might expect he would reach the same conclusion as other critics about the dangers of judicial activism under the *Charter*. Professor Russell, however, is too good a social scientist to let ideology get in the way of the facts.

Russell acknowledged that the *Charter* would give the Supreme Court more power, but warned about overestimating the change or ignoring the power that courts already had when developing the common law, interpreting statutes, and enforcing the constitutional division of powers. Most *Charter* review, he argued, would be directed at the actions of bureaucrats, not legislatures. When laws were struck down, they would often be old laws that were not central to the government's agenda. When important laws were struck down, there was still "the possibility of an interesting interchange between the judicial and the legislative process. Perhaps only Canada, still teetering uncertainly between British and American models of government, could come up with the legislative review of judicial review" contemplated in sections 1 and 33 of the *Charter*.[33]

Russell recognized that the Court was quite active in recognizing claims in the early years of the *Charter*, but he also concluded that "it would be difficult to contend that the courts' audit of this part of our criminal law constitutes a serious challenge to parliamentary sovereignty" because "few of the laws overturned by the courts have represented major policy interests of contemporary governments."[34] In 1988 he noted that the Court had applied "the brakes to the Charter express," partly in response to the left critique of judicial activism. At the same time, he also concluded that the left critique was overstated, because the Court was more interested in criminal justice reform than in "promoting privatization or rolling back the welfare state."[35] "There is not much empirical evidence to support" the concerns of either the left or the right about judicial activism, he claimed, given that "none of the key economic and social policy interests of government — monetary and fiscal policy, international trade, resource development, social welfare, education, labour relations, environmental protection — have been significantly encroached by judicial enforcement of the Charter." The Court's performance in recognizing about a third of the *Charter* claims it hears "has probably kept the Court in line with the mainstream of political opinion in the country," even though it was "far too restrained for proponents of judicial activism and not nearly deferential enough for advocates of judicial self-restraint."[36] Russell's important work suggests that someone who is no fan of the *Charter* can conclude, after a balanced examination of the evidence, that judicial activism is not a pressing problem in Canada.

The Popular Criticism of Judicial Activism

Russell's moderate conclusion does not mean that judicial activism cannot be manufactured by opinion makers to be a problem. The left critique of the *Charter* in the 1980s, confined as it was to the law journals and the academic lecture circuit, had relatively little popular appeal. The critics made some appearances on the op-ed pages of newspapers, but no national newspaper or national political party adopted their critique of judicial activism as its own. In contrast, the more recent right critique of judicial activism has been embraced in the editorial pages of two national newspapers and in the platform of Her Majesty's loyal Opposition. In the late 1990s judicial activism was presented as a new and important problem in Canadian politics. How did this happen?

THE REFORM PARTY

An important factor in raising concerns about judicial activism was its inclusion in the platform of the Reform Party, a western-based populist and neo-conservative party founded by Preston Manning, which became the official Opposition in Canada. The role of the Reform Party in making judicial activism an issue underlines the continued importance of parties and Parliament in Canadian politics. In 1998 the Reform Party devoted a day in Parliament to debating the resolution that "federal legislation should not be altered by judicial rulings." Reflecting a "framers'-intent" approach embraced by conservative critics of judicial activism in both the United States and Canada, Reformers defined judicial activism as "rulings by judges which go well beyond the intent of the law and in fact substantially change the law to the point where judges have taken on the role of legislators or law makers as opposed to simply interpreting and applying the law."[37] The focus of concern that day was a ruling by the Ontario Court of Appeal that a legislative definition of "spouse" should be read as referring to same-sex couples. In reply to the specific motion, members of the Liberal Party, the New Democratic Party, the Bloc Québécois, and the Progressive Conservatives all accused the Reform Party of homophobia. The Reform Party was not deterred. For it, the issue was whether Parliament or the courts was supreme, and parliamentary supremacy was the only democratic approach.

Gerry Ritz of Reform argued "that the practice of allowing judges to rewrite statutes, order public money spent and change the very meaning of our language to suit special interest agendas can only mean that parliament will become unnecessary."[38] Liberal Shaughnessy Cohen replied that "unconstitutional legislation is usually replaced by legislation which is designed to accomplish similar objectives in a more constitutionally tailored form. This dialogue enhances the democratic process." Cohen, who was a lawyer, accurately noted that courts only rarely rewrote statutes to make them constitutional, but when they did, "legislatures are free to respond by correcting legislation with limitations that may be justified under section 1 of the charter."[39] Cohen's argument about the reality of dialogue between courts and legislatures was more accurate, but the Reform Party's simpler contrast between undemocratic judicial law-making and democratic legislative law-making was easier to understand and captured the imagination of at least the media, if not the public.

In his reply to the 1999 Throne Speech, Preston Manning, then leader of the Opposition, argued for greater attention to a "simple principle: that Parliament makes the law, the executive administers it, and the courts interpret it ... in recent years we have seen these lines increasingly blurred ... [as] the courts increasingly encroach on the prerogatives of Parliament to the point that one might argue that one cannot fully interpret the speech from the Throne until after hearing the speech from the bench."[40] For Manning, once courts go beyond interpreting a law to ascertain Parliament's will, they illegitimately make the law. The *Charter* had replaced the supremacy of Parliament with the supremacy of the Supreme Court, by giving that court "the ultimate right of interpretation." He assumed judicial supremacy and attacked the *Charter* as an American import "without any of the checks and balances on the three branches of government found in the American Constitution." He ignored the fact that the centralized Canadian parliamentary system (one he wanted to change with an elected Senate and looser party discipline) actually made it easier for Canadian governments to reply to the Court's decisions.

Manning's reply to the Throne Speech was also remarkable because it criticized fourteen different judicial decisions as examples of "political and social activism by the courts." Manning echoed Richard Nixon's attack on the Warren Court by criticizing the Canadian Court under the leadership of Chief Justice Lamer for being soft on crime.[41] He also criticized cases involving minorities, including those involving the francophone minority in Alberta (*Mahe*), the hearing impaired (*Eldridge*), and gay and lesbian couples (*M. v. H.*). He gave special prominence to two cases that he portrayed as involving both crime and minorities. The Court's 1985 *Singh* decision to give refugee applicants the right to an oral hearing had handed "to those engaged in people smuggling and to illegal entrants, regardless of their status, all the legal tools required to fight deportation hearings ... This is an issue of law and order. It is an issue of criminal justice." Similarly, a British Columbia case that ordered a new trial because the accused was not provided with a French-language interpreter (*Beaulac*) was criticized. Manning also challenged the Court's decisions recognizing Aboriginal title (*Delgamuukw*) and fishing rights (*Marshall*). In a 1998 op-ed piece in the *Globe and Mail*, he appealed to a majoritarian understanding of democracy by arguing that, unlike the Supreme Court, "no Parliament, regardless of its partisan composition, would ever propose a conception of aboriginal title that would lead to a legal claim by 3.5 percent of the population of B.C. over virtually all the land and resources of that province." He then proposed that the "federal government itself legislate a definition of aboriginal title that is in the interests of all British Columbians, rather than leave this task by default to the Supreme Court."[42] Manning's critique of judicial activism was based on both form and substance. The Court's interventions were opposed on the basis that rulings by unelected judges were undemocratic and that they advanced the rights of minorities.

The new Canada Act proposed by the Reform Party also made concerns about judicial activism a central part of its platform. A Judicial Review Committee of the House of Commons would "ensure the supremacy of the elected representatives of the people of Canada and the accountability of the judiciary." As in the United States, it would hold hearings "on the qualifications and judicial philosophy" of Supreme Court nominees. As we saw in chapter 2, the appointment process is one of the few ways that American governments can respond to the Court's constitutional decisions. The same parliamentary committee would also review all Supreme Court decisions to determine whether they "violate the basis upon which Parliament passed legislation or the original intent of the Charter and Rights and Freedoms and whether any legislative action is necessary to restore the legislation or the application of the Charter to its original intent."[43] The judicial philosophy of the Reform Party was very American. It was based on coordinate construction that suggested that Parliament should act on its own understanding of how the *Charter* should be interpreted, even if the Court has interpreted the *Charter* in a very different way, and on a framers'-intent approach to judicial review embraced by conservative American judges such as Robert Bork. The Reform proposal would give Parliament a large role in curbing the Court when it strayed from what the legislators believed to be the original intent of the constitution.

In an attempt to widen its western base, the Reform Party renamed itself the Canadian Alliance. The platform of the Alliance is not as developed, but its members continue to express many of the same concerns about judicial activism as the Reform Party. The Alliance tried to make the reluctance of the Liberal government to use the override to reinstate an offence of possession of child pornography, which had been struck down by courts in British Columbia, an issue in the 2000 federal election. Vic Toews, the Alliance's justice critic and a former Conservative attorney general of Manitoba, argued that the Court, under former Chief

Justice Lamer, had engaged "in a frenzy of constitutional experimentation that resulted in the judiciary substituting its legal and societal preferences for those made by the elected representatives of the people ...
Our democratic principles and institutions are too important to be
hijacked by a non-elected political judiciary."[44] Lamer, now retired from
the bench, responded with the comment that "the Alliance members
should take a crash course on constitutional law" because of "half-
cocked" criticisms of the judiciary and their failure to understand that
the politicians had given the Court new powers under the *Charter*. The
public brawl continued as Lamer's comments then drew rebuttals from
members of the Alliance, who explained that the official Opposition was
not "attacking them personally. We attack the types of decisions when
we think they are judge-made and not Parliament-made." Ted Morton,
described not only as a constitutional law expert but as an Alliance supporter, argued that "it's Lamer that misunderstands the role of the judiciary ... They are not immune to criticism. They are not infallible. They
do not have a monopoly on Charter interpretation."[45] The concerns of
conservative critics of judicial activism are not just academic — they
continue to be reflected in the platform of the official Opposition.

THE MEDIA'S EMBRACE OF THE JUDICIAL ACTIVISM CRITIQUE

Another factor in the popularity of the conservative critique of judicial
activism was its embrace by the media. Originally limited to conservative periodicals, this support quickly spread to Canada's two national
newspapers. The new "anti-institutional"[46] approach to reporting on the
Court that emerged in the late 1990s is captured by the titles of two long
articles that appeared in the small conservative periodicals *Next City* and
Western Report in 1998: "Robed Dictators" and "Benevolent Monarch."
The imagery of the Court as a monarch is a powerful one that often
appears in popular criticisms of judicial activism.[47] The *Next City* article
relied heavily on the American experience and suggested that, "while
many pro-choice activists applaud the 1988 Morgentaler ruling, they
ought to reflect on the prospects of conservatives one day regaining
ascendancy on the Supreme Court and defying Parliament by banning
all abortions." It complained that, "thanks to the arbitrary will of
Supreme Court judges, the law in Canada is no longer permanent, fixed
and knowable." The best way to end "a courtroom coup" by the "robed
dictators" was to abolish the *Charter*, which the writer, like Sterling
Lyon, characterized as "an alien and unnecessary United States-style
innovation that is incompatible with our traditions of parliamentary
democracy."[48]

The *Western Report* article was more intemperate. It left the impression that the Court's concern for the rights of the accused was related to Chief Justice Lamer's previous career "defending murderers, drunk drivers and white collar criminals, which earned the nickname 'Tony the Fixer.'" The author, like Canadian Alliance leader Stockwell Day (who settled a libel action after he accused a defence lawyer of supporting child-molesting), did not seem to understand that defence counsel play a vital role in the adversary system and should not to be tarred by their professional association with their clients. The article also featured arguments that decisions such as *Vriend* were undemocratic and that "no one cares what you think or how you vote. Whether you agree or not with the prevailing charter interpretation is inconsequential — you are bound by the judge's decision." This opinion ignored the point that the Alberta legislature could have reversed the Court's decision to read sexual orientation into the Alberta human rights code with the override. The article even featured a bizarre allegation that the professional exchanges between Canadian and Israeli judges were "suspect and highly prejudicial to an impartial hearing of any issues involving Jews or Judaism." [49] It would be tempting to dismiss these articles as the work of a right-wing fringe, except that many of their themes reappeared within a year in the mainstream media.

Shortly after these articles appeared, the phrase "judicial activism" began to be used with greater frequency in the mainstream media. "Suddenly, it seemed, someone had declared open season on judges' power and the media were beginning to give prominence to people who question whether the Supreme Court had seized too much authority over lawmaking in Canada."[50] There were a few dissenting voices, including *National Post* columnist Andrew Coyne, who pointed out that courts struck down laws in controversial decisions well before the *Charter*,[51] and *Edmonton Post* editorial writer Susan Rutton, who argued that the judicial activism debate was an American import fuelled by "right-wingers" who were angry with court decisions on "gay and aboriginal rights."[52] Nevertheless, even with a few voices expressing dissenting views, judicial activism was packaged by the media as a new, contentious, and exciting issue.

In their own distinctive styles, the *Globe and Mail* and the *National Post* expressed concerns about judicial activism. In October 1999 the *Globe and Mail* ran an editorial entitled "Judicial activism is not a figment of the imagination," which argued that the *Charter* "had substantially increased judges' power to strike down legislation *and* to effectively amend it for the same reason." On the basis that the legislature, not the Court, ought to rewrite the law, the Court was criticized for read-

ing in protection against discrimination on the grounds of sexual orientation into Alberta's human rights code. Citing the *Marshall* case, which
found an Aboriginal fishing right in a reference in a treaty to the provision of truckhouses, the paper also suggested that "appointing judges
who resist aggressive extensions of judicial interpretations is one route
to righting the balance" between courts and legislatures.[53] The *Globe* has
drawn a distinction between debates about the Court's role, which are
"perfectly proper in a democratic society," and "attacks about the quality of individual judgments and the reputations of certain judges."[54]

Compared with the *National Post,* the *Globe* was restrained in its
criticism of judicial activism. As *Post* columnist Andrew Coyne accurately observed: "For the *National Post* and for the ultraconservative legal
theorists it has adopted and promoted, the day the Charter of Rights and
Freedoms became law, in the words of one, Canada 'surrendered any
claim to democratic self-government' ... The *Post* is against any attempt
on the part of unelected judges to impose their will on a democratically
elected legislature."[55] In its editorials, the *National Post* argued that judicial activism — "the process by which judges subvert the will of
Parliament by striking down laws or 'reading in' new elements to old
laws ... is very real ... Canadians have been outraged as the courts have
used the Charter to tweak or abolish dozens of laws, including the abortion law, the Lord's Day Act, restrictions on pornography and voluntary
school prayer, and laws that kept incompetents from fighting fires."[56]
The *Post* has not restricted its criticism of judicial activism to its editorial pages. A 1999 article featured various conservative critics who argued
that the Court has a "left-wing, feminist and intolerant bias" that reflected the "values of one very small but incredibly powerful segment of
Canadian society — the liberal educated elite." Mirroring conservative
critics of the Warren Court who also argued that the law clerks were ide-
ologically biased, the article went on to contend that "central to the
court's shroud of secrecy are the law clerks ... The average age of a clerk
is 27. They are mostly women."[57] Although this article reflects many of
the themes of the earlier articles in *Next City* and *Western Report,* it
received much more attention and creditability because of its placement
on the front page of a national newspaper. Chief Justice Lamer even
responded to this extraordinary article with a letter to the editor to point
out that he had been misquoted.[58]

THE JUDGES RESPOND

Chief Justice Lamer did more than just write a letter to the editor. At the
1998 Canadian Bar Association meetings he complained about the tenor
of media criticisms of court decisions and speculated about "whether
judges, or maybe through their chief justices, should be rolling up the

sleeves of their judicial robes and involving themselves in these public discussions more directly."[59] The judges found themselves in a difficult position as they responded to accusations that they had engaged in improper judicial activism. The fact that they did respond probably reflects the reluctance of others, notably attorneys generals and lawyers' groups, to come to their defence. It might also reflect a reluctance in Canada's concentrated media to publish defences of the Court submitted by law professors and others. In any event, by 1999 Chief Justice Lamer seemed less feisty towards the critics of judicial activism and expressed concerns that, "as a result of virulent or harsh comments by the press or public, the most popular thing to do might become the outcome ... Judges are human beings. I would be remiss if I were to say that we are superhuman or that we are not influenced sometimes."[60] After Chief Justice Lamer's early retirement, Chief Justice McLachlin continued the trend to public defence of the Court's work by telling the *National Post,* shortly after the publication of Morton and Knopff's book *The Charter Revolution and the Court Party,* that "any suggestion that the court has been hijacked by interest groups is totally false." Two of her colleagues also denied the claim that the Court had been captured by either intervenors or law clerks, but also indicated there was less of a need for intervenors.[61] In their extrajudicial activities, at least, the Court was clearly listening to those who criticized it for judicial activism.[62] What about in their judgments?

EFFECTS OF THE CRITIQUE OF JUDICIAL ACTIVISM ON THE COURT

Justices on the Supreme Court regularly receive more detailed assessment and criticism of their work than most of us will receive or hope to receive in our lifetime. They hear about their decisions not only in the newspapers but also in law reviews, including one that is devoted entirely to assessing and criticizing their work. I remember reading these reviews the year after I had clerked at the Court and finding many of them to be unduly critical. Nevertheless, I soon got over my sensitivity and joined my fellow law professors in criticizing the Court both in the law reviews and the Monday morning quarterbacking of instant media responses to the Court's work. Although judges cannot be pressured and lobbied, they are, like the rest of us, not immune from the criticism they receive. There is some evidence that the Court has not ignored the critique of judicial activism that has swirled around it for the last twenty years. Listening to one's critics in itself is not bad, but the ultimate question is whether it improves the Court's work.

The left critique seems to have influenced the Court: it pulled back from its initial enthusiasm for striking down laws and created a greater margin of deference for legislatures when they attempted to assist the disadvantaged and allocate scarce resources among competing groups. Contrary to the fears expressed by Petter and others, the Supreme Court upheld both Sunday closing laws and mandatory retirement as reasonable limits placed by the legislature on rights. The Court was alive to the danger that the *Charter* could "become an instrument to roll back legislation that has as its object the improvement of the conditions of less advantaged persons."[63] In a 1989 decision that upheld Quebec's ban on advertising aimed at children, the Court indicated that it would not force the representative and elected legislature "to choose the least ambitious means to protect vulnerable groups."[64] The next year the Court upheld mandatory retirement as a reasonable, albeit discriminatory, employment policy. It stressed the point that both Blakeney and Petter had made about legislatures being in a better position than courts to make tradeoffs between competing demands and rights. The fear that the *Charter* would be used to assist corporations and the advantaged also influenced the Court as it restricted its interpretation of equality rights to laws that discriminated against the nine enumerated groups and other similar discrete and insular minorities and as it reduced the restrictions that the *Charter* imposed on the regulatory state. Even in the criminal law field, the Court recognized that broad and unlimited *Charter* rights might harm victims as it upheld laws targeting hate speech and pornography that harmed women and children and as it accepted limitations on the rights of the accused in other cases. The left critique may not have won popular or partisan support, but it provided a progressive justification for the courts to slow down and back off from their initial enthusiasm for using the *Charter* to strike down state activity.

There are some signs that the conservative critique of judicial activism may also be affecting the Court. The Supreme Court's decision acquitting Donald Marshall of fishing eels without a licence recognized a limited treaty right for the Mi'kmaq to fish and trade for a moderate livelihood.[65] The recognition of even this limited right unfortunately provoked violence as non-Aboriginal fishers vandalized lobster traps set by Aboriginal fishers out of season. Although the government seemed less than prepared for the decision, the Court took much of the criticism. *Globe* columnist Jeffrey Simpson argued that the Court was acting "as a battering ram" and seemed "to be ahead of political bodies and courts in finding and broadening aboriginal rights." He noted that while "supporters of robust judicial activism" praised the United States Supreme Court's decision in *Brown* v. *Board of Education*, which held that racially segregated public schools were unconstitutional, they often forgot that the Court revisited the case the next year to allow "all deliberate speed" in desegregation.[66] Simpson might have mentioned that, three years later, the United States Supreme Court stood up to the open defiance of a court order to desegregate Central High in Little Rock, Arkansas. In any event, the Court eventually did respond to the uproar over the *Marshall* decision, but in a manner quite different from the "all deliberate speed" sanctioned in *Brown II* or the "this is the law, obey it" spirit of the Little Rock case.

As the violence in Burnt Church flared a month after the Court's decision, an intervenor representing non-Aboriginal fishers took the extraordinary step of applying for a rehearing to allow the Crown to justify restrictions on the treaty right. The Crown had an opportunity at trial to make the case for such external limitations on the treaty right, but chose not to do so. After receiving written submissions only from the parties and intervenors, a unanimous judgment signed by the Court denied the motion. (Justices McLachlin and Gonthier had dissented in the first judgment and found that the treaty right had expired, but joined in the second judgment.) The Court, however, wrote forty-eight paragraphs in this second judgment limiting the ambit of its original ruling by pointing out that the treaty right did not involve trade in logging, minerals, or off-shore natural resources. It also indicated that a wide range of objectives, including "the interest of the non-natives," could be pursued by the government in placing further external limits on the treaty right and that it was possible to justify the same licensing and closed season rules for Aboriginal fishers as for non-Aboriginal ones. [67] Although the Court dismissed as a political argument the idea that Aboriginal rights should not inconvenience non-Aboriginal people, the effect of the second judgment was to underline the limited nature of the treaty right and the broad range of options — including imposing the same rules on Aboriginal and non-Aboriginal fishers — that the government could pursue. Picking up it cues from the Court's second judgment, the federal government would now charge Donald Marshall for fishing without a licence, even though he had been acquitted in the first judgment on the basis that this activity was part of his treaty rights. Although much of what the Court discussed in *Marshall II* was based on prior law expanding the basis for limiting Aboriginal and treaty rights, its extraordinary form left many with the impression that the Court was not oblivious to the adverse public reaction to the case. Chief Lawrence Paul of the Mi'kmaq complained that the Court had "backtracked" and "given in to mob rule and vigilantism ... it has hurt its credibility today."[68]

Justice Bastarache, the Court's only judge from the Maritimes, did not sit on the case, but subsequently provided a revealing glimpse of how the *Marshall* controversy looked to one justice on the Court. He said in a controversial media interview that "the first reaction of the public, especially in the Maritimes, is that the court was very result-oriented and was inventing rights that weren't even in the treaties that were brought before the court in that case ... The second problem, I think, was also that the court was maybe seen as being unduly favourable to the native position in all cases, and that it sort of has an agenda for extending these rights, and that it has no concern for the rights of others." [69] His point may have been to rebut such inaccurate perceptions of the Court's jurisprudence,[70] but his comments also offer some support for those who believe that the Court in *Marshall II* had gone out of its way to limit the ambit of an unpopular decision and to recognize the legitimacy of the interests of the non-Aboriginal majority.

In 1999 the Court also appeared to back away from another unpopular decision, one that gave trial judges and defence counsel access to the private records of complainants in sexual assault cases. Parliament had responded to the 1995 decision with an "in-your-face" parliamentary reply that has been described by a number of commentators as "a direct, almost point by point repudiation of the majority judgment ... vindicating the approach taken by the minority."[71] Of all the frequent legislative replies to the Court's decisions, this one was the most difficult to accept without the use of the override because it was so directly at odds with the Court's previous decision and so closely based on the position of the minority in the Court. The near unanimous Court upheld the new legislation (in one of his last judgments before he retired, Chief Justice Lamer dissented on the basis that the Court was allowing Parliament to dilute the prosecutor's disclosure obligations under the *Charter*). There was a tone of deference to the legislature in the judgment. The Court stated that its 1995 judgment "was not the last word on the subject"; that it was prepared to assume "a posture of respect towards Parliament"; that it was "somewhat accountable" to Parliament; and that courts "do not hold a monopoly on the protection and promotion of rights and freedoms." [72] The Court's understanding of its relationship with Parliament is in a state of flux, but this case provides some support for the idea that Parliament can act on its own interpretation of the *Charter*, even when the majority of the Court has reached an opposite conclusion, and that Parliament can hold the Court accountable by reversing one of its *Charter* decisions without using the section 33 override. Giving Parliament such a strong role in its dialogue with the Court may discount the unique role of the independent judiciary in standing up for the rights of those unpopular people who are accused, sometimes falsely, of committing crimes.

The Court has also become much more deferential to Parliament's decisions to enact mandatory minimum sentences. In a judgment writ-

ten by Justice Lamer in 1987, the Court struck down, as grossly disproportionate to what was required to punish, rehabilitate, and deter small
time offenders, a mandatory minimum sentence of seven years for
importing drugs. This was a bold decision in many ways, but one that
still left Parliament with options if it wished to impose mandatory sentences on big-time offenders. By 2000, however, the Court was prepared
to uphold a mandatory minimum sentence of four years' imprisonment
for a thirty-five-year-old man with no prior convictions who lived with
his mother and who had drunkenly and negligently, but unintentionally, shot and killed a friend who was helping him deal with the breakup
of a relationship.[73] The next year the Court also upheld life imprisonment with no parole eligibility for ten years as applied to Robert
Latimer, the Saskatchewan farmer who murdered his twelve-year-old
daughter Tracy because of his concern that she would suffer severe pain
from surgery. Although the Court agreed that the mandatory penalty
was not necessary to deter or rehabilitate Mr. Latimer, it stressed that
Parliament was entitled to use the penalty to try to deter others and to
denounce the serious crime of murder. The unanimous Court noted that
it was up to the Cabinet to decide whether to grant Mr. Latimer mercy
and that "the choice is Parliament's on the use of minimum sentences."[74]

A week after its decision in *Latimer*, the Court won praise from the
police and governments for upholding the offence of possession of child
pornography that had been struck down by two levels of British
Columbia courts as an overbroad restriction on freedom of expression
verging on thought control. The law defines child pornography as pictures of those under eighteen years of age engaged in explicit sexual
activity, or depicting their sexual organs for a sexual purpose, or written
material advocating sexual activity with those under eighteen years of
age. The Supreme Court reversed the British Columbia courts and
upheld this law by interpreting it so that it did not apply to innocent
baby-in-the-bath pictures and works of art, and by reading in two limited exceptions for private writings and private representations of the
accused engaged in lawful sexual activity. Three judges would not have
read in even these limited exceptions. This decision, along with a decision not to strike down customs legislation or to supervise custom officials after they had discriminated against a gay bookstore by detaining
books and sex-education material at the border, and the unanimous
decision to uphold the mandatory sentence in the *Latimer* case, all won
praise from the *National Post*. The Court was now using "a fine scalpel
to excise only those parts of the laws deemed unlawful or overbroad …
instead of imposing broad, sweeping measures" that would have struck
down democratically enacted laws. Another *Post* story suggested that

"criticisms of judicial activism were muted in 2000" as a "revamped bench" under the leadership of Chief Justice McLachlin had not struck down a single law in that year.[75]

A few weeks later, however, criticisms of judicial activism were heard once again when the Court abandoned its previous position that Canada could extradite fugitives to face the death penalty. In 1991 a divided Court had allowed escaped murderer Robert Kindler and mass murderer Charles Ng to be sent to the United States to face the death penalty. A decade later, in a case involving Glen Burns and Atif Rafay, eighteen-year-old Canadians accused of murdering Rafay's mother, father, and sister with a baseball bat in the United States, a unanimous Court indicated that in all but the most exceptional cases, the *Charter* required the Canadian government to obtain assurances that the death penalty would not be imposed before fugitives were extradited. Unlike in the *Latimer* case, the Court would not defer to the minister's discretionary decision to grant mercy when the issue was death. The Court relied on a growing awareness of wrongful convictions as a reason for its courageous change of heart and disclaimed primary concern with the morality and effectiveness of the death penalty. Citing the South Africa Constitutional Court, which had, to much public criticism, struck the death penalty down in 1996, it argued that the special and unique duty of the independent judiciary was to protect "the worst and weakest among us."[76] The Canadian Alliance expressed fears that Canada would become a safe haven for murderers, even though the Americans soon provided the assurances that the death penalty would not be applied. Burns and Rafay were sent back to the United States, where, if convicted of the brutal murders, they face life imprisonment without parole. Op-eds appeared in both the *National Post* and the *Globe and Mail* criticizing the Supreme Court justices for the "imperial arrogance" of imposing their "personal beliefs" on capital punishment on elected governments in Canada and the United States.[77] The Court was back — and so too were the critics of judicial activism.

It may be too soon to make firm conclusions about the precise influence of the conservative critique of judicial activism on the Court, but there likely will be some impact. In itself, the impact is not objectionable and shows that the Court is prepared to listen and learn from its many critics. As discussed above, the left critique was influential in making the Court realize some of the distributional implications of its *Charter* decisions and the danger that recognizing all *Charter* claims may harm legislative attempts to advance the interests of the disadvantaged. These developments, however, seem to be consistent with the Court's role under the *Charter* in protecting disadvantaged minorities and the unpopular. Some of the more recent developments, however, may undercut the Court's anti-majoritarian role because the justices seem to be sensitive to the concerns of conservative critics who champion majoritarian views of democracy and are sceptical about whether the unpopular individuals and minorities who seek relief from the courts have real rights.

Conclusion

The judicial activism debate that has emerged in Canada since the *Charter* is an unfortunate example of a branch-plant mentality that ignores the differences between the *Charter* and the American *Bill of Rights*. The left critique of the *Charter* and judicial activism in the 1980s direly warned of the dangers of the *Charter* being *Lochner*ized by judges hostile to state intervention. The right critique of the late 1990s made equally dire warnings that the Court was following the Warren Court and inventing rights for criminals, minorities, and others who could not advance their agenda through the legislature. Both set of critics largely ignored sections 1 and 33 of the *Charter* and the strengths of governments produced by the Canadian parliamentary system, assuming that judges would, as under the American *Bill of Rights*, have the last word.

Critics of judicial activism on both the left and the right stress the freedom that judges have to impose their own values when interpreting the constitution. They pay little attention to the need for judges to justify their decisions in terms of the text of the *Charter*, precedents, and traditions. Although the left is most concerned about individual rights, and the right is most concerned about group rights, critics of judicial activism share a scepticism about the rights enforced in *Charter* litigation and have a common concern that the courts will take an absolutist approach to rights and ignore competing rights and interests. Critics of judicial activism also assume that democracy is eroded whenever state action is struck down by judges. They pay little attention to differences between invalidating the actions of bureaucrats and the legislatures and between invalidating old legislation that may not be supported by the current government and legislation that is central to the government's agenda. They also discount Canadian traditions of federalism, minority rights, and common law constitutionalism, which restrain and even frustrate the will of current majorities. After examining both the American and the Canadian debates about judicial activism, it is now possible to move on to the difficult and often neglected task of defining exactly what people mean when they complain about judicial activism.

Chapter 6
Four Dimensions of Judicial Activism

The next time people complain about judicial activism, ask them to tell you what they mean by this phrase. If the answer is not simply silence, it may be interesting and surprising. Judicial activism can be a code word for unarticulated yet strongly felt social anxieties. Judicial activism in the United States may be a shorthand way for conservatives to express concerns about a liberal culture that allows abortion, flag burning, and the interconnected issues of crime and race. Judicial activism debates in Australia are frequently concerned with Aboriginal issues, those in Israel often revolve around the role of religion in public life, and those in the United Kingdom may reflect debates about that nation's relation to Europe. In Canada the judicial activism debate in the 1930s was tied up in a nationalist and centralist hostility towards the Judicial Committee of the Privy Council in England. Western alienation from the governing elites in Ottawa, including the Supreme Court, played an important role in the way that the Alberta Social Credit Party in the 1930s and the Reform Party in the 1990s defined judicial activism as a problem. There is more to many discussions of judicial activism than meets the eye.

Most commentators never bother to define precisely what they mean by judicial activism. The accusation of judicial activism is thrown around to bolster disagreements about particular judicial decisions and to imply judicial overreaching, if not actual impropriety. Debates about judicial activism can be frustrating in part because of the absence of definitions. Reliance on the shorthand code word of judicial activism means that the implicit assumptions that are made about judging, rights, and democracy are not identified, even though they may be controversial. It is too much to expect agreement about what judging, rights, and democracy should entail — these are eternal questions of jurisprudence and politics. However, it is not too much to expect that those who engage in debates about judicial activism should define what they mean by this loaded and slippery term.

The contrast between judicial activism and restraint has been used as a focus for complex debates about the nature of constitutional interpretation and the degree of freedom judges have when interpreting the text of the constitution and their own precedents. Those who see adjudication as a matter of following the clear intent of enacted law often criticize what they believe to be the exercise of unfettered and presumptively illegitimate judicial discretion as judicial activism. The term judicial activism has also been used to describe bold and broad techniques of judicial decision making, with judicial restraint being associating with avoiding or minimizing constitutional judgments that are not absolutely necessary to settle live disputes. Judicial activism is also used to describe an absolutist approach to rights, as embodied in the First Amendment tradition of allowing no laws to restrict free speech. Finally, judicial activism is often associated with the idea of judicial supremacy that occurs when a legislature has little choice but to accept the Court's constitutional judgment as the final word. The idea that judges should follow the intent of the framers of the constitution, avoid or minimize constitutional judgment, enforce rights in an absolute manner, and have the last word are all deeply rooted in debates about American constitutional law. The judicial activism debate is embedded in the American experience of judicial review, but, with the practice of judicial review, it has spread throughout the globe.[1] As the judicial activism debate goes global, it is important that it not proceed on assumptions that, however accurate in the context of the American *Bill of Rights*, may not be applicable in countries that have modern bills of rights and parliamentary systems of government.

Popular Understandings of Judicial Activism

Much popular discussion of judicial activism is based on a simple and stark distinction between judges *finding* the law in the clear words and intent of the legislators or *making* the law by acting in a legislative fashion. One conservative critic of judicial activism has complained that "policy-making judge-politicians have no regard for rules fixed and announced beforehand; instead they lurch from one inconsistent ruling to another ... Thanks to the arbitrary will of Supreme Court judges, the law in Canada is no longer permanent, fixed and knowable. The law is no longer changeable exclusively by Parliament or a provincial legislature."[2] The author's assumption that the law could be "fixed and knowable" subject only to legislative change would be amusing to most who have studied the common law. The common law is constantly evolving as it balances competing values in a changing society. With Justice Dickson taking the lead, the Supreme Court in the 1970s significantly altered its understandings of fairness in family law, criminal law, and administrative law — all without reliance on the *Charter*. As Justice Wilson has suggested, if the critics of judicial activism wish "to label judges politicians because they have the power 'to determine which rights prevail when rights are in conflict' or 'to sort out the priorities of society,'" they "should blame the common law."[3]

Another element of popular discussions of judicial activism is the assumption that, because the judiciary is not elected, it must be undemocratic. This idea is conveyed by the emotive imagery of "robed dictators," "benevolent monarchs," and an aristocratic "jurocracy." The relation of both judicial and legislative law making to democracy is, however, more complex than labels and name calling. In debates about judicial activism, democracy often means rule by the majority of the people and by their elected governments. At the same time, however, many would define as undemocratic any actions by legislatures that denied fundamental rights such as freedom of expression. In any event, governments are often not elected with a majority of the votes and, between elections, those with a majority in the legislature have significant freedom to enact legislation that may not accord with what the majority wants. Although judges cannot be removed because the public does not like their decisions, they read the papers and live in the world, and it would be unrealistic to conclude that they do not consider how their decisions will be received by governments and by the public. Elected governments are not perfectly accountable to the people, and unelected judges are not completely unaccountable to governments and the people. The dichotomy between the undemocratic judiciary and the democratic legislature is as simplistic and inaccurate as the dichotomy between making and applying the law.

Another feature of the popular debate about judicial activism is the assumption that a court's judgment constitutes the final word about rights. People tend to think of courts as institutions that lay down the law and settle matters once and for all. The strong pull of the American model of absolute rights and judicial review also means that most people assume that the constitutional rulings of courts are final. This assumption may explain negative reaction to Quebec's use of the override in response to the Court's ruling that the requirement in Bill 101 — that commercial signs be only in French — was an unreasonable limit on freedom of expression. The public debate outside Quebec did not reflect a widespread recognition that freedom of expression was not absolute and that Quebec had legitimate powers both to limit rights under section 1 of the *Charter* and to override them under section 33. One survey suggests that over two-thirds of the public support the idea that when the Court says a law is unconstitutional, the Court, as opposed to the legislature, should have the final say.[4] Public support for judicial supremacy can be used, as in the Bill 101 case, to mobilize public support for a popular judicial decision, but it may also be turned against the Court when it makes an unpopular decision on matters such as criminal justice. Better public understanding of the complex structure of the *Charter* and the ability of governments to respond to judicial decisions under sections 1 and 33 might change the popular debate about judicial activism and make the public more accepting of the ability of legislatures to limit or override rights as interpreted by the Court. However popular, the dichotomy between judicial and legislative supremacy is as simplistic and as inaccurate as the dichotomy between applying and making the law.

In summary, three themes emerge from popular discussions of judicial activism. The first is that judicial activism is seen as judicial law making involving the exercise of open-ended judicial discretion contrasted with judicial application or discovery of a fixed and pre-existing law. The second is that judicial activism is characterized as undemocratic, on the basis that judges, in contrast to legislatures, are not elected. The final theme is that judicial activism occurs when judges lay down the law and declare absolute rights in a way that many assume must be accepted by citizens and their governments as the final word.

Three American Approaches to Judicial Activism

Although no one definition has achieved common currency, various commentators have attempted to define judicial activism. Some definitions focus on one issue, such as the ability of judges to make law or the ability of judges to impose their policies on governments. More helpful definitions recognize that the term is used in a complex fashion and attempt to identify multiple dimensions of judicial activism. Most of the writing about judicial activism has been American and has focused on either criticizing or defending the activism of the Warren Court. The assumptions made by those on both sides of this debate should not unthinkingly be transferred to the different context of the *Charter* or other modern bills of rights.

Richard Posner, a prolific academic and conservative judge appointed by President Reagan, has defined judicial activism in a one-dimensional manner as revolving around the "court's power over other government institutions."[5] A judge who believes in judicial restraint will worry about the acceptability of his or her decisions to governments and society and the danger of being swamped by litigation directed at the other branches of government. Posner's lack of concern about how the restrained judge reaches a decision with respect to other branches of government leads him to the absurd position of arguing that a decision overruling *Marbury* v. *Madison*, the Supreme Court's oldest and most important precedent establishing the right of the Court to strike down an unconstitutional law, would be an act of judicial restraint because it would decrease the power of the federal judiciary over the other branches of government. Posner's definition seems designed to shelter conservative advocates of judicial restraint from criticism that they employ activist and perhaps unnecessary means to achieve their goal of deferring to elected governments.

Posner views activism as a zero-sum game in which every extension of judicial power must be at the expense of legislative and/or executive power. He makes no distinction between judges restraining elected legislatures and unelected officials, such as the police, and assumes that judicial interference with the decisions of either are undemocratic. His definition of judicial activism is tailored to the particular structure of the American *Bill of Rights*, which has no provision that allows legislatures to reply to Court decisions by limiting or overriding the rights proclaimed by courts. The absolutist structure of the American *Bill of Rights* helps promote a zero-sum approach that ignores the possibility that some forms of judicial activism could be matched by legislative activism.

The conservative scholar and judge Robert Bork concludes that judicial activism allows judges to implement "an elite moral or political view [that] may never be able to win an election or command the votes of a majority." He captures the historical evolution of concerns about judicial activism from the laissez-faire *Lochner* court to the egalitarian Warren Court by arguing that "the opinions of the elites to which judges respond change as society changes and one elite replaces another in the ability to impress judges."[6] This approach has influenced Morton and Knopff, who criticize the Canadian Supreme Court for making decisions that benefit a Court Party of "post-materialist elites" who, they also argue, could not find support for their policies in the legislative arena.[7] The problem is that the criteria of an elite's minority sentiment is radically indeterminate, to the point of being a code word. To brand minority sentiment "elite" is, at best, a highly subjective process and, at worse, an attempt to whip up populist opposition. It also falls prey to the impoverished moral vision of public choice theories[8] by suggesting that all minorities are special-interest pleaders opposed to the public interest. Bork would place the robber baron capitalists who benefited from the *Lochner* era in the same company as African Americans and the accused who benefited from the decisions of the Warren Court. A more helpful question is to ask whether the particular minority that may be supported by a particular Court decision requires support from an independent judiciary. Minorities that are vulnerable to discrimination and chronic neglect of their interests may require Court support, whereas large corporations and otherwise advantaged individuals that are disadvantaged by one law may not. Finally, the idea that any judicial decision that does not reflect "majority sentiment" is an objectionable form of judicial activism undercuts any anti-majoritarian role for the Court. If majorities should rule unhampered by decisions that never reflect "minority sentiment," it is difficult to understand why unelected and independent courts should be given the power of judicial review.

Ronald Dworkin, who teaches jurisprudence at Oxford and at New York University, is famous for his theory that judges should attempt to find the right answers in hard cases by interpreting the abstract principles of the constitution, and that judicially enforced rights should trump legislatively crafted policy. Dworkin once cheerfully associated his position with judicial activism and argued that judicial restraint had to be based on a scepticism about whether individuals had rights that could be enforced against the majority or a belief that deference to the legislature would produce fairer and sounder decisions about rights. Allowing the legislature to decide the ambit of rights violated the principle that "no man should be judge in his own cause," because "decisions about rights against the majority are not issues that in fairness ought to be left to the majority."[9] Judicial activism was, in Dworkin's view, preferable to judicial restraint because it allowed judges to do their job of interpreting and applying the moral principles of the constitution. Dworkin's work is helpful in demonstrating that one's position on judicial activism and restraint is inescapably tied with one's position on the existence of rights. Dworkin has subsequently refined his defence of judicial activism by disassociating himself from a "crude activism" that would allow a judge to substitute his own sense of good policy or even justice for that of the legislature. Instead, legitimately activist judges must "enforce the Constitution through interpretation, not fiat, meaning that their decisions must fit constitutional practice, not ignore it."[10] Dworkin's evolving sense of the limits of activism reflects the general jurisprudential turn in debates about judicial activism by suggesting that activism that does not make sense of the integrity of the existing legal materials is illegitimate and should be rejected.

Dworkin's political defence of judicial activism is troubling because it is based on assumptions of judicial supremacy and the idiosyncratic structure of the American *Bill of Rights*. In 1977 he recognized that "judicial activism involves risks of tyranny," but concluded: "We must not exaggerate the danger. Truly unpopular decisions will be eroded because public compliance will be grudging, as it has been in the case of school prayers, and because old judges will die and retire and be replaced by new judges appointed because they agree with a President who has been elected by the people."[11] This argument constitutes a rather unconvincing defence of judicial activism by its foremost theorist. It suggests that if judges cannot be relied upon to get the right answers (those suggested by Dworkin's theory), the only control on judicial activism is defiance of the rule of law through grudging public compliance and political manipulation of judicial appointments. Dworkin has subsequently argued that the moral victories of the right kind of judicial activism outweigh the losses caused by wrong-headed activism and the costs of judicial restraint.[12] His utilitarian calculus is debatable. It is not clear that the moral victory of the Court holding that racial segregation was unconstitutional — a decision that was successfully resisted for some time — makes up for the wrong-headed activism of defending slavery in *Dred Scott* or laissez-faire economics in *Lochner*. If this is the best that Dworkin, as the foremost theorist of judicial activism, can do, it is no wonder that Americans have been so concerned with judicial activism. It is perhaps unfair to criticize Dworkin for this lame defence of judicial activism: it may be the best he has, given his decision to build a theory of judicial review around the American *Bill of Rights*, and not a modern bill of rights that allows ordinary legislation to place limits or even override rights as interpreted by the Court.[13]

Non-American Approaches to Judicial Activism

Conservative Americans, such as Bork and Posner, and liberal Americans, such as Dworkin, who discuss judicial activism have more in common than they might realize. They all assume that judicial activism is a zero-sum proposition. Whatever the courts decide, the legislature cannot decide. American approaches are often based on a false choice between the extremes of judicial and legislative supremacy, with little attention to the prospect of dialogue between courts and legislatures.[14] The dichotomous American approach to judicial activism reflects the endless cycle of debate about activism and restraint in that country. Conservatives denounce liberal decisions restraining governments as creative judicial activism. The Court eventually changes and conservative judges make decisions that liberals criticize as crude activism. Much energy is spent on trying to define a role for the Court that is consistent with democracy, with little attention paid to how legislatures should respond, once the Court has made its decision, because, in the absence of changes to the Court or the constitution, there is often little that the legislature can do. The debate about rights, activism, and restraint in the United States goes on and on, with little progress being made.

Those who are less rooted in the American tradition of judicial supremacy have, however, taken a more helpful approach to judicial activism. The key is their recognition of the ability of legislatures under modern bills of rights to limit and override rights as interpreted by the court. They reject the dichotomy between judicial supremacy under the American *Bill of Rights* and the legislative supremacy formerly enjoyed by the English Parliament as having "no sense of the post-war model of constitutionalism,"[15] as represented by modern bills of rights that allow legislatures to limit and derogate from rights. After examining the decisions interpreting the 1950 *European Convention of Human Rights*, Paul Mahoney, a European lawyer and scholar, rejected the dichotomy between judicial activism and restraint that pervades much American writing on the subject. The European Court of Human Rights had been activist in interpreting rights, to hold, perhaps contrary to the intent of the framers of the 1950 *European Convention*, that whipping was inhuman and degrading punishment and that consensual gay sex was protected under the right to privacy. At the same time, however, the European Court was restrained in invalidating state action only if it went beyond the range of reasonable options open to democratic governments. The ability of elected governments to justify contextual and proportional limits on even broad rights made judicial activism and judicial restraint "two sides of the same coin."[16] The Court's margin of appreciation allowed the judicial creativity inherent in judicial interpretation of vague and open-ended rights to be balanced with judicial deference to justifiable policy choices made by legislatures. It is possible for the Court to be activist when interpreting rights, but restrained when determining whether limits on those rights had been justified.

This analysis can be taken beyond the decisions of the courts. A judicial willingness to accept justifiable limits on rights enables the legislature to craft replies to most court decisions. Even judicial decisions that would normally be defined as activist because they invalidate legislation and are based on creative interpretations of the bill of rights, may not be the final word if the state is prepared to take democratic responsibility for enacting new legislation to limit or derogate from the rights proclaimed by the Court. The dangers of judicial activism are mitigated not only by the Court's willingness to find some limits on rights to be justified but the ability of legislatures to enact new laws in response to the Court's decision. For example, the United Kingdom in 1988 proclaimed a formal derogation after the European Court held that the detention of suspected terrorists constituted an unjustified violation of the *Convention*. This derogation is preserved under the *Human Rights, 1998*, but, like overrides under section 33 of the *Charter*, is subject to review every five years. Once the American model of judicial supremacy is left behind, it becomes possible to decouple judicial activism from judicial supremacy and to make judicial activism more conducive to democracy. Modern bills of rights that allow legislatures to limit and even derogate from rights open the possibility that judicial activism can be matched by legislative activism, especially in those countries in which a parliamentary system produces strong governments to balance off strong courts. In contrast, most American debates about judicial activism have been based on the false choice between the extremes of judicial and legislative supremacy and between strong courts and weak legislatures.

Defining the Dimensions of Judicial Activism

One of the dangers revealed by previous attempts to define judicial activism is a tendency to ignore questions of degree and context. The empirical record of the Supreme Court, which finds an unjustified violation in about a third of *Charter* cases, suggests that any analysis should make room for the existence at any one time of contradictory tendencies to be both active and restrained.[17] A related danger of dichotomy is that the vast majority of definitions of judicial activism leave no space for middle ground between the extremes of judicial and legislative supremacy. Judicial activism and judicial restraint can be complementary, especially when the structure of the constitution invites courts, first, to define rights and, second, to determine the reasonableness of the legislature's limitations on those rights. Courts can be active in interpreting rights, but restrained in judging limits on rights or imposing remedies for their violation.

Another weakness of many approaches to judicial activism is their static and legalistic focus on the judgment of the Court as opposed to the options they leave to other branches of government. Knopff and Morton come closest to overcoming this difficulty when they draw a distinction between negative and positive activism, on the basis that the later involves the judges telling the legislature what it must do.[18] Implicit in the idea of negative activism is the notion that the legislature has a range of options after the Court has invalidated legislation or some executive act. To be sure, simple judicial nullification of legislative action can be judicial activism, but the range of reply options is an important component of the degree of judicial activism. The Court's word on judgment day is not necessarily the final word, and legislatures have a wide range of possible responses to activist decisions. We should be careful to avoid assuming the American model of judges having the last word, short of changes to the constitution or the Court. Under modern bills of rights, judicial activism that invalidates state action on the basis of creative and broad interpretations of the constitution and absolutist definitions of rights can be countered and even nullified by legislative activism in the form of reply legislation that justifies limitations on rights or even overrides the Court's decision.

Building on these attempts to define judicial activism and incorporating questions of degree, the structure of the Canadian Constitution, and the possibility of legislative replies to Court decisions, I will now offer my own definition of judicial activism that will provide the structure for Part Two of this book. Following the breadth of the judicial activism debate, my definition requires four components. The first concerns the degree to which judges are free to read their own preferences into law when interpreting the constitution. The second is the degree to which judges are eager to make constitutional judgments not necessary to decide a live dispute. The third concerns the extent to which courts recognize rights as trumps over other social interests, and the extent to which they defer to other social interests. The fourth concerns the extent to which Court decisions displace those of the legislature and the executive and the extent to which courts have the final word in their interactions with those institutions. This institutional and political dimension of judicial activism requires consideration of the options that legislatures have to respond to the Court's judgment.

My four dimensions of judicial activism should be viewed in a cumulative manner. Even if a judge engages in judicial activism by creatively interpreting a right or deciding a constitutional issue that is not necessary to resolve a live dispute, he or she may still recognize that society has placed a legitimate limit on such a right. If the judge does not accept the legislative limitation on the right, the dangers of judicial activism can still be mitigated by the legislature formulating an effective reply to that judicial decision. Judicial activism can occur at each stage, but the strongest form of judicial activism would occur when the Court not only eagerly declares broad rights and rejects limitations on them but also rejects the legislature's attempt to reply to the decision and justify new limitations placed on the rights proclaimed by the Court. It is only at this final stage that the legislature has to consider using the override, let alone the drastic options of changing the Court or the constitution.

JUDICIAL ACTIVISM 1: JUDGES MAKING LAW

The first component of my definition of judicial activism concerns the process of judging and refers to the extent to which judges are free to read their preferences into the constitution. Critics of judicial activism on both the left and the right have made much of the ability of judges to make law and impose their own views and preferences on the vague words of the constitution. Conservatives are especially fond of positing a dichotomy in which judges either follow the clear intent and language of the framers or are left with a freewheeling discretion to legislate on the basis of their own subjective preferences. The idea of judicial activism — as judges making, as opposed to applying, law — figures to an even greater extent in most popular discussions of judicial activism. Both popular and academic debates about judicial activism have taken a jurisprudential turn, which focuses on the way judges make their decisions. The danger, however, is that this focus will privilege those who argue that judges can, and should, find determinate answers in the text and intent of the constitution and see any exercise of judicial creativity as an illegitimate imposition of the will of judges. This controversial and positivistic view of adjudication has been embraced by conservative critics of judicial activism, but framing the debate in this way virtually ensures a conclusion that judges are engaged in an illegitimate form of judicial activism when they exercise any creativity in their interpretation of the constitution. It also ignores the creativity that courts already exercise in formulating the common law and in interpreting statutes

Critics of judicial activism often subscribe to the idea that if judges do not find the law in pre-existing standards set by the legislature, they must exercise a strong discretion that is virtually indistinguishable from legislating their subjective views or preferences into the law.[19] In essence, this argument is the more sophisticated academic version of the popular dichotomy between applying pre-existing law and making new law. The critics believe that once the law runs out, a judge can turn nowhere except to his or her own personal values or politics. As we discussed in chapter 5, critics on the left fear that judges will use this strong discretion to favour corporations and other advantaged members of society, while critics on the right fear that judges will use it to benefit the intellectual elites with whom they identify. In chapter 7 I will explore a number of decisions to see if there is indeed evidence that judges have such a strong discretion. The alternative hypothesis to the stark dichotomy between making and finding law is that, while judges must exercise some creativity in interpreting the broad guarantees of the *Charter*, it is a creativity that is constrained and guided by the text of the constitution, legal traditions, and precedents. Dworkin's later work is helpful in distinguishing between a crude and unjustifiable form of activism, in which judges ignore text, precedent, and traditions, and a justifiable form of activism, in which the judges engage in a good-faith effort to make sense of such materials when reaching their conclusion. This distinction also helps explain why judges generally do not assert their personal preferences in their judgments, but attempt, often in painful detail, to explain and justify their decisions in light of the relevant text and precedents and the arguments of the parties.

JUDICIAL ACTIVISM 2: JUDGES BEING EAGER TO MAKE AND IMPOSE THE LAW

Judicial restraint is often associated with a judicial unwillingness to decide constitutional issues unless absolutely necessary to settle live disputes. A restrained judge would deny standing to litigate to anyone not entitled to a remedy to resolve a concrete and live dispute. A restrained judge would also cautiously decide one case at a time, not make any broader pronouncement than necessary to resolve the dispute, and avoid remaining entangled in a dispute after pronouncing judgment.

In the debate about judicial activism, it is important not to import unwarranted assumptions from the American Constitution, which, unlike the Canadian Constitution, restricts judges to deciding live controversies and will not allow governments to refer abstract questions to the courts. Much of the American interest in avoiding or minimizing constitutional judgment is related to the fact that when the Court speaks in a constitutional voice, it often has the last word. Avoiding or minimizing constitutional judgment can be seen as a means to reduce the likelihood and consequences of judicial error and to increase the space for legislatures, given judicial supremacy, once the Court has actually made a constitutional judgment.[20] As we saw in chapter 3, Canadian governments have long dumped abstract and politicized references on the Court which are not connected with live disputes. This tradition continues under the *Charter* and, arguably, should make the Court somewhat more willing to hear cases brought by citizens who also represent a vision of the public interest. The structure of the *Charter* is relevant to whether courts should minimize and avoid constitutional judgments. Even broad judicial rulings under the *Charter* can be subject to contextual exceptions that can be justified by the government under section 1 of the *Charter*. Nevertheless, the idea that a restrained Court should avoid and minimize constitutional judgments whenever possible has become a live issue in Canada and elsewhere.[21] Canadian conservative critics of judicial activism have taken the Court to task for being eager to be an "oracular" court, one that decides constitutional issues that are not necessary to resolve a live dispute and to hear from not only governments but non-governmental groups who claim to represent the public interest or some segment of society affected by the Court's decision. Moreover, there are some signs that an increased willingness to avoid or minimize constitutional judgments may be one of the responses of the Canadian Court to criticisms that it has engaged in judicial activism. A judicial eagerness to decide constitutional issues, as well as a judicial willingness to make law, will therefore be examined as forms of judicial activism.

JUDICIAL ACTIVISM 3: JUDGES USING RIGHTS TO TRUMP OTHER VALUES

The third dimension of judicial activism focuses on the extent to which judges recognize constitutional rights as trumps over other social interests and competing rights. An activist judge insists, in Ronald Dworkin's memorable phrase, on rights as trumps over social interests, while a restrained judge would be open to the possibility that limitations on rights can nevertheless be justified. Most judges will define rights with some attention to competing social interests. Even under the American *Bill of Rights*, which has no formal limitation clause, not every form of expression will be protected as free speech, not every claim of privacy will be protected, and the Court will factor in social interests in determining whether the state has acted without due process or denied equal protection of the law. My concern is not only with the extent to which competing social interests are considered in defining the ambit of the right, but with the willingness, once the right has been defined, for the Court to consider the government's case for limiting that right because of competing social interests and rights. Here the *Charter* and other bills of rights with explicit limitation clauses ensure that the government has the fullest opportunity to justify limitations on rights. The *Charter* embraces a decidedly non-absolutist approach to rights. "Like most post-war constitutions, it ... has avoided hard-edged, American-style proclamations of individual rights ... The drafters recognized that 'most controversies about rights involve subtle choices or balances between individual and community interests.'"[22] The reasonable-limits provision in section 1 of the *Charter* can be contrasted with the absolutist language of the First Amendment, which influences the entire American experience of rights. Conservatives like Bork and liberals like Dworkin differ dramatically in what they think constitutes a constitutional right, but they agree that whatever the Court decides is a constitutional right is generally the final word on the matter, no matter what the legislature says in reply.

Judicial activism would occur under modern bills of rights if courts were dismissive of the reasons given by the state to justify restrictions on rights. An activist judge would be inclined to think there is only one right answer to the difficult issues posed in constitutional cases, while a restrained judge would be willing to be educated by the government about the reasons why limits must be placed on rights and why other alternatives will not be as effective in advancing the legislature's options. This does not mean that judges should mechanically defer to the state, but, rather, that they should ask whether the state has justified the limits it has placed on rights and listen carefully to the state's answers.

JUDICIAL ACTIVISM 4: JUDGES HAVING THE LAST WORD

The fourth and final dimension of judicial activism focuses on the extent to which judicial decisions permanently displace policies established by other arms of government. The issue of displacement involves not only the immediate question of whether a particular court decision conflicts with policies established by other arms of government, but the way that conflict is ultimately resolved. Many approaches to judicial activism are overly narrow and legalistic because they examine but one issue: whether there is conflict on judgment day. This focus ignores the options legislatures have to respond to court decisions. These options range from the extremes of amending the constitution, changing the Court, or disobeying the Court's decision to the somewhat less drastic option of a formal derogation from the right as interpreted by the court or simply reformulating the policy in a manner that may well be found acceptable by the Court. Too much writing about judicial activism focuses only on whether there is conflict between the Court and the government on judgment day, and does not explore the issue of how that conflict is ultimately resolved. A related failing is that most accounts of judicial activism ignore the important question of whether the Court has invalidated an important policy initiative of the current government or an older law or the exercise of bureaucratic discretion that may not represent the policy of the current government. To say that judicial invalidation of a key part of a recently elected government's platform and of a police officer's illegal use of discretion are both judicial activism is like saying that a bottle of home-made plonk and a Châteux Latour are both wine.

This institutional dimension of judicial activism should make room for the dialogue between courts and legislatures that can occur when legislatures under modern bills of rights place limits on or override rights as declared by the Court. It also introduces further qualitative questions of degree into the judicial activism debate. The extent to which a judicial decision that invalidates legislation is activist will depend on the range of options open to the legislature in fashioning a reply. A decision that leaves the legislature only with the option of derogating or overriding the rights will be more activist than one that allows the legislature a range of options that can be defended as reasonable limits on the right as interpreted by the Court. Decisions that force legislatures to distort their preferred policy when formulating a reply will be more activist than those that allow the legislature to respond with only minor adjustments to their policy. Assessing the options that legislatures have to respond to judicial decisions should be an important component of debates about judicial activism under modern bills of rights.

Conclusion

Judicial activism involves complex questions of how judges decide cases as well as their relations with the legislature. Whether there has been judicial activism is not susceptible to simple yes/no answers and requires attention to questions of degree and context. Judicial activism should be examined in a multi-tiered fashion. The next four chapters will address each tier in turn to provide a sense of the extent to which the Canadian Court has made law in its own image, been eager to make and impose such laws, imposed its own view of rights as an absolute trump and had the final word. It should be recalled, however, that judicial activism, in creatively and boldly interpreting rights, can be countered by judicial deference in accepting limits on rights and by legislative activism that produces new and ordinary legislation that justifies limits on or derogates from the rights as interpreted by the Court.

Debates about judicial activism have been aggravated by an assumption made by the many American commentators who have dominated the debate that the only choices are between legislative supremacy, with its dangers of the tyranny of the majority, and judicial supremacy, with its danger of the tyranny of unelected judges. This zero-sum approach explains the endless cycles of heated debate in the United States between those who, at different times, fear legislative supremacy and those who fear judicial supremacy. The choice between strong courts and weak legislatures that is presented in many debates about judicial activism is, however, unnecessary and unhelpful. It is possible, indeed desirable, and conducive to a self-critical and robust democracy to have both judicial activism and legislative activism. Modern bills of rights provide a way to back away from the endless American debate about judicial activism. We can have the benefits of judicial activism, in which courts protect fundamental values and the rights of minorities, and legislative activism, which allows legislatures to justify in an open and democratic fashion legislation designed to limit or even derogate from the rights that the fallible Court has declared.

Part 2
The Extent of
Judicial Activism

Chapter 7
The Constrained Creativity
of Judicial Law Making

The *Charter* is littered with vague phrases that give judges considerable room to make law. Already, judges have interpreted the *Charter* in ways that the framers did not expect. Parliamentarians assured both pro-choice and pro-life groups that the *Charter*'s guarantee of fundamental justice was neutral on abortion because it protected fair process alone and not substantive values such as privacy. Yet only three years after the *Charter* was drafted, the Supreme Court rejected the dichotomy between substantive and procedural fairness. Three additional years later, it invalidated the abortion law. The framers also believed that the Canadian rule for the exclusion of unconstitutionally obtained evidence would be much more moderate than the American rule because it only required exclusion when, in all the circumstances, the admission of the evidence would bring the administration of justice into disrepute. The Court, however, has created an absolutist exclusionary rule. In 1982 the framers decided not to include sexual orientation as a prohibited ground of discrimination, but in 1995 the Supreme Court unanimously held that it was a prohibited ground. In the *Marshall* case that led to violence in Burnt Church, New Brunswick, the Court found an Aboriginal right to commercial fishing in a reference to the maintenance of "truckhouses" in a 1760 treaty. It has mandated a complex process for determining judicial salaries over an impassioned dissent that it was exceeding its role by inventing a procedure nowhere spelled out in the constitution. It also relied on unwritten constitutional principles to suggest that, in some circumstances, the rest of Canada should negotiate separation with Quebec. The language of the constitution and the intent of the framers do not seem to have constrained the judges.

The critics of judicial activism look to these cases as proof that judges are free to inject their own subjective preferences into the law. Those on the right criticize judges for departing from the clear intent or words of the framers. Those on the left stress the indeterminacy of the vague phrases of the *Charter* and of adjudication in general. Both argue that judges will read their biases and preferences into the *Charter* and that this gloss is illegitimate because no one elected the judges. The right fears judicial preferences for unrepresentative minorities, while the left fears judicial favouritism towards corporations and other advantaged members of society. The idea of unconstrained and undemocratic judicial law making is central to critiques of judicial activism.

In this chapter, I will examine the claims of judicial law making made by the critics of judicial activism. I will make no attempt to deny that judges exercise creativity as they interpret the vague provisions of the *Charter*. Reasonable people disagree about what is involved in fundamental justice or what brings the administration of justice into disrepute. Moreover, individual judges do make a difference. Justice Michel Bastarache has indicated that, on criminal matters, he is more conservative than the majority of the Court, and particularly former Chief Justice Antonio Lamer.[1] Not many would disagree. Nevertheless, I will deal the critics of judicial activism a significant blow if I can establish that judicial creativity is not open-ended, but rather constrained and guided by the need for judges to provide a good-faith interpretation of the text of the *Charter*, precedents, and traditions. The essence of the judicial activism critique is not that judges must make judgment calls — surely that is why we have judges and appeal courts — but rather that they are free to read their own view of the world and the good life into the *Charter*.

The Court's Interpretative Methodology

Chief Justice Brian Dickson was an innovative judge who, even before the enactment of the *Charter*, was prepared to reshape important areas of criminal law, family law, and private law. In one of the first *Charter* cases he set out an approach to interpreting the *Charter* that has influenced all those who have subsequently interpreted that document. He conceded that the meaning of the *Charter* "cannot be determined by recourse to a dictionary, nor for that matter, by reference to the rules of statutory construction." Invoking the famous living-tree metaphor employed by the Privy Council to hold that women were persons who could be appointed to the Senate, he argued that "the task of expounding a Constitution is crucially different from that of construing a statute."[2] These statements have led some to accuse the Court of going beyond the bounds of legitimate interpretation — of changing elms to willows.[3] Justice Bertha Wilson, who was even more inclined than Chief Justice Dickson to strike down laws under the *Charter*, warned that while the living-tree metaphor was "harmless ... so long as it is used merely to suggest that a constitution must adapt and grow to meet modern realities," it could "become dangerous and anti-democratic if it were used to justify the shaping of the constitution according to the personal values of individual judges."[4]

Viewed in the abstract, Chief Justice Dickson's statements about the differences between statutory and constitutional interpretation are misleading: they underestimate the creativity required when judges interpret statutes, and they overestimate the freedom judges have when they interpret the *Charter*. Well before the *Charter*, judges would presume that legislation respected an "ideal constitution" or a "common law Bill of Rights"[5] unless there was a clear legislative intent to displace such judge-made values. Large areas of public law such as criminal law and administrative law are based on judicially created presumptions that the legislature intended only to punish those at fault and to treat people fairly. This judicial law making is not even prompted and guided by an authoritative text of a democratically enacted law like the *Charter*. As Justice Wilson argued in a 1989 lecture, in response to an early conservative criticism that "the breadth and vagueness of the Charter gives the courts almost unlimited power," the critics of judicial law making should blame the common law, not the *Charter*.[6] Too many criticisms of judicial activism under the *Charter* do not acknowledge the law-making power that judges have when they formulate the common law or interpret statutes.

The freedom that judges have when interpreting the *Charter* is not unlimited. In the very case in which he endorsed a living-tree approach to *Charter* interpretation, Chief Justice Dickson also concluded that "the proper approach to the interpretation of the Canadian Charter of Rights and Freedoms is a purposive one" in which the Court interprets the language of the *Charter* in light of the purposes and interests it was meant to protect. The purposive approach to *Charter* interpretation is not based on the judge's own sense of morals or postmodern literary deconstruction.[7] It was first recognized in 1584 by an English judge who, quite sensibly, concluded that statutes should be interpreted in light of the "mischief" they were intended to remedy.[8] Although sometimes challenged by the more formalistic "plain meaning" rule, the mischief rule was included in Canada's original *Interpretation Act* enacted in 1849. To this day, that Act instructs judges that every statute is remedial and shall be given "such fair, large and liberal construction and interpretation as best ensure the attainment of its objects."[9] The purpose of the *Charter*'s guarantee against unreasonable searches and seizures was to protect reasonable expectations of privacy. It was this purpose, not the dictionary meaning of "unreasonable," "search," or "seizure," that determined the ambit of the guarantee. This interpretation allowed the Court in subsequent cases to hold that the provision was infringed by electronic and video surveillance, even though such technologies might not fit dictionary meanings of searches and seizures. The purposive approach to protecting privacy was not, however, a blank cheque for judges. It applied only to reasonable expectations of privacy, and the Court has not applied it to give criminals an absolute right of privacy or corporations freedom from state regulation.

The Court's purposive approach to *Charter* interpretation is also tempered by other factors. A year after he urged judges to give the *Charter* a generous and liberal interpretation designed to achieve its purposes, Chief Justice Dickson warned that they should also be careful "not to overshoot the actual purpose of the right or freedom in question" and to pay attention to the "linguistic, philosophic and historical contexts" of *Charter* rights.[10] This contextual approach to *Charter* interpretation has influenced the Court to restrict equality claims to those that result in broader forms of discrimination and affronts to human dignity; to resist *Charter* challenges to separate schools;[11] to reject the one-person/one-vote standard imposed by the Warren Court in the United States as inconsistent with Canadian history and geography;[12] and to be extremely cautious about recognizing economic rights under the *Charter*, given the absence of property and other forms of economic rights in the *Charter*.[13] The Court has not embraced a revolutionary approach to interpreting the *Charter* that is insensitive to text or tradition, or the traditional ways that judges interpret statutes. This does not mean that some cases do not push the envelope and that reasonable people will not disagree with the Court's judgments. Nevertheless, when interpreting the *Charter*, judges are obliged to make sense of the democratically enacted text and are not free to read their own preferences about how the world should work into the law. This is a fairly minimal claim about the constraints that text imposes on judges when interpreting the *Charter*, but it is all that is necessary to counter the robust claims of judicial creativity made by many critics of judicial activism.

The Judicial Creation of Substantive Due Process?

Section 7 is perhaps the most open-ended right in the *Charter*. It provides that "[e]veryone has the right to life, liberty and security of the person and the right not to be deprived thereof except in accordance with the principles of fundamental justice." The governments who participated in the drafting of the *Charter* were very concerned about the restraints that it might place on their regulatory activities, which routinely deny people the freedom to do what they want. For this reason, they departed from the comparable Fifth Amendment of the American *Bill of Rights* in two important respects. First, there is no reference in the *Charter* to property rights. Some have regretted this omission, but it significantly reduces the ambit of judicial scrutiny of government regulation. The second change was that Canadian governments were required to act in accordance with the principles of fundamental justice, as opposed to the American phrase "due process of law." Barry Strayer, a senior civil servant who helped draft the *Charter*, explained that he believed the reference to fundamental justice would protect only "procedural due process" or "fair procedure" in the administration of the law, as opposed to substantive due process, which was used by the United States Supreme Court in the *Lochner* era to invalidate laws that regulated the economy and in *Roe* v. *Wade* to provide women with a right to early abortions.[14] At the same time, the drafters did not use the term "natural justice," which had already been defined by judges as relating to procedural fairness. They also did not follow the 1960 Canadian *Bill of Rights* by restricting the principles of fundamental justice to "a fair hearing," as opposed to the more expansive concepts of the rights to life, liberty, and security of the person.

In one of its first *Charter* cases, the Supreme Court unanimously rejected the idea that courts were restricted to protecting procedural due process under section 7 of the *Charter*. The issue was whether British Columbia could send drivers who drove with a suspended licence to jail for at least a week without proving that they knew or ought to have known that their licence had been suspended. In a landmark pre-*Charter* judgment by Justice Dickson, the Court had already concluded that such no-fault offences offended fundamental principles of criminal law because they could punish the morally innocent.[15] Justice Lamer relied heavily on this pre-*Charter* precedent and warned that the principles of fundamental justice were not found in "the realm of general public policy" associated with substantive due process, but rather with the "basic tenets of our legal system" as found in the common law and in other legal rights in the *Charter*. The relative caution of the ruling is underlined by the fact that Justice William McIntyre, the most conservative judge on the Court and the one least inclined to accept innovative *Charter* claims, agreed with the ruling that fundamental justice meant more than a fair hearing and that the state should not be able to imprison someone who had broken the law without fault.

Despite this caution, the Court's decision was denounced as judicial activism by both the left and the right. The left smelled *Lochner* and argued that the Court was imposing "a narrow and anachronistic view" of the state as the enemy of freedom.[16] Critics ignored the Court's hints that corporations might not be protected under section 7 of the *Charter* because they did not have rights to life, liberty, or security of the person as opposed to property rights. The right smelled *Roe* v. *Wade* and argued that the Court's decision demonstrated "the extent to which judges are potentially free to create whatever principles are necessary to reach the intended result. The Court's power to declare absolute liability offences contrary to substantive fundamental justice ... has no source other than judicial will."[17] This accusation followed the "all or nothing" terms of the

American debate as a false choice between limited procedural review and open-ended and unconstrained judicial policy making. It discounted the way the Court had found a middle way between these extremes and had supported its ruling with the text of the *Charter* and common law precedents. The picture that emerges from this landmark case is not one of free-wheeling judicial activism associated with the American experience of substantive due process, but of substantial continuity with the common law.

The all-or-nothing and American dichotomies of procedural due process, which is concerned only with the fairness of hearings, and substantive due process that allows judges to implement whatever values they favour, do not do justice to the more nuanced and contextual way that the Supreme Court has interpreted section 7 of the *Charter*. This complexity will be seen by the fact that the Court could intervene in the abortion issue in the interest of fundamental justice, but without imposing a final *Roe* v. *Wade*-type solution.

Morgentaler: The Judicial Creation of a Right to Abortion?

For many, the most (in)famous example of judicial activism is the Court's 1988 decision to invalidate Canadian's abortion law. Both pro-life and pro-choice groups campaigned to have their positions entrenched in the *Charter*, but parliamentarians were assured that the *Charter* was neutral on the divisive issue of abortion. This exclusion did not matter to Dr. Henry Morgentaler. He had defied the 1969 abortion law throughout the 1970s by performing abortions in his Montreal clinic. Relying on *Roe* v. *Wade* and arguing that many women did not have access to abortions in a hospital, Morgentaler had challenged the abortion law under the Canadian *Bill of Rights*. These arguments were quickly and unanimously rejected by the Court, which, despite the fact that a jury refused to convict him, convicted and sentenced Morgentaler to eighteen months in jail. Morgentaler was eager to use the *Charter* to resume his battle against the abortion law, and he was soon charged with conspiracy to violate the abortion law by operating a clinic in Toronto. Although a jury again refused to convict Morgentaler, the Ontario courts fairly easily rejected his arguments that the 1969 abortion law violated section 7 of the *Charter*. Many people were therefore surprised when the Supreme Court decided in 1988 that the abortion law was an unjustified violation of section 7 of the *Charter*. It would, however, be a mistake to see the Court's decision as one based on the importation of the substantive due process that the framers of the *Charter* had tried to avoid.

Chief Justice Dickson, with Justice Lamer, stressed that the law interfered with a woman's security of the person by making it a crime to have an abortion outside a hospital and without the approval of a committee of at least three doctors. It was not necessary to decide whether section 7 extended further "to protect either interests central to personal autonomy, such as a right to privacy, or interests unrelated to criminal justice," as the American courts did in *Roe* v. *Wade*. The requirement of committee approval offended the principles of fundamental justice not on the basis of some abstract view of perfect justice, but because it made it impossible for women to secure the legal abortions that Parliament, not the courts, had promised them. Because of the requirement of at least four doctors to run the "cumbersome" committee structure, most hospitals in Canada did not have committees. Women in Newfoundland and Prince Edward Island had to leave their province to obtain a legal abortion. The travel and delay required by the committee system threatened rather than advanced the health of women, even though Parliament had recognized that abortions were justified when a pregnancy would endanger a woman's health. The committees acted in a Kaflkaesque fashion by applying differing definitions of health. Some considered threats to psychological health to be a valid reason for an abortion; others did not. Some applied different standards to married women; others did not. The state could not justify the committee system as a reasonable limit on the rights of women because the "cumbersome" committee structure, with its "arbitrary and unfair" procedures, failed to achieve the balance between the interests of woman and those of the fetus that Parliament had itself set. Chief Justice Dickson's judgment was not judicial activism of the kind associated with substantive due process or *Roe* v. *Wade*. Rather, it was based on a down-to-earth and practical appreciation of the effects of the abortion law on Canadian women, and the failure of the law to live up to the balance between women and the fetus that Parliament, not a judge, had established.

The second main judgment written by Justice Beetz was even more deferential to Parliament. It also stressed that the lack of committees in many parts of the country and delays in obtaining committee approval could endanger the life and health of women who medically required abortions. The committees applied varying and even illegal standards, with some refusing to authorize second abortions or abortions without the consent of the husband. Justice Beetz, however, went out of his way to indicate that Parliament could require some independent medical opinion that the continuation of the pregnancy would likely endanger the woman's health. His decision clearly contemplated that Parliament could enact a new law that stopped well short of abortion on demand and, unlike *Roe* v. *Wade*, could require third party approval of even early abortions.

Justice Wilson was concerned that Parliament might waste "its time and energy" fixing the procedural defects of the legislation without paying attention to the substantive rights at stake. In a manner similar to *Roe* v. *Wade*, she recognized a woman's right to an early abortion. Despite some caricatures of her position as feminist[18] and liberal[19] "gospel,"[20] Justice Wilson stopped well short of constitutionalizing pro-choice as the final solution to the abortion question. She indicated that the protection of the fetus was a "perfectly valid legislative objective ... s.1 of the Charter authorizes reasonable limits to be put upon the woman's right having regard to the fact of the developing fetus within her body ... The precise point in the development of the foetus at which the state's interest in its protection becomes 'compelling' I leave to the informed judgment of the legislature which is in a position to receive guidance on the subject from all the relevant disciplines. It seems to me, however, that it might fall somewhere in the second trimester." Although suggestive of the *Roe* v. *Wade* approach, Justice Wilson's position left room for legislative policy making and did not tie constitutional standards to the changing notion of viability.

Critics of judicial activism look to Justice McIntyre's dissent in this case as "a model of judicial self-restraint."[21] His opinion was an attempt to follow the framers'-intent school of *Charter* interpretation that many conservative critics of judicial activism favour. He argued that the other judgments were premised on a right to abortion that "is devoid of support in the language of s.7 of the Charter or any other section." The problem with this literal approach, which insists that judges can execute only the clear intent and words of the legislature, is that it denies the duty of courts to engage in interpretation of the general phrases found in the *Charter*. For example, Justice McIntyre himself had found that the British Columbia law that sent drivers who drove with a suspended licence to jail, even if they did so "unknowingly and with no wrongful intent,"[22] offended the principles of fundamental justice. Yet there is no statement in the text of section 7 of the *Charter* that no-fault offences that impose imprisonment are prohibited. Justice McIntyre accused the Court in *Morgentaler* of second guessing Parliament's policy choice to allow abortions only when pregnancy could endanger the woman's life or health when, in fact, the majority took pains to use Parliament's own balance of interests as the standard by which to judge the operation of the law. His warning about decisions being based on "how many judges may favour 'pro-choice' or 'pro-life'" ignored the careful limits of the majority's opinion, its acceptance that Parliament could act to protect the fetus, and the middle path that the Court had forged between the all-

or-nothing dichotomy of procedural and substantive due process. A fair-minded reading of *Morgentaler* does not support the claims that unelected judges wrote their views on abortion into the law.[23]

Is judicial invalidation of Parliament's abortion law inherently undemocratic? Those who romanticize the 1969 abortion law as supported by public opinion and "giving something to both sides and taking local opinion into account"[24] ignore that Parliament never authorized or defended the *de facto* local option that emerged under its auspices. The critics of the Court's decision might have a point if our elected politicians had had the guts to defend a law that allowed the abortion committees to make up different standards for different women asking for an abortion and permitted women in Toronto access to abortions, but not women in St. John's or Charlottetown. They did not, and the law that Parliament enacted promised all Canadian women that they could receive an abortion when necessary to protect their life or health. The Court's decision disrupted the *status quo*, but it was a fraudulent *status quo* that promised women equal access, but actually made them subject to regional, substantive, and procedural inequities and unfairness that Parliament had never authorized and could not defend.

The Judicial Creation of an Absolute Exclusionary Rule?

The idea that relevant evidence should be kept out of a criminal trial because the police have violated the accused's rights is inherently controversial. To constant criticisms that it is allowing criminals to go free because constables have blundered, the United States Supreme Court has imposed a more or less absolute rule that unconstitutionally obtained evidence should be excluded from the criminal trial. The American *Bill of Rights* does not provide such a rule, but the Court has deduced it at various times as necessary to respect rights, protect judicial integrity, and deter police unlawfulness. In contrast, section 24(2) of the *Charter* mandates that unconstitutionally obtained evidence shall be excluded "if it is established that having regard to all the circumstances, the admission of it in the proceedings would bring the administration of justice into disrepute."

Section 24(2) was almost left out of the *Charter*. Before the *Charter*, Canadian courts would generally admit relevant and reliable evidence in a criminal trial even if it was illegally or improperly obtained. In an attempt to win support from the provinces, which prosecute most crimes in Canada, the federal government in an early draft of the *Charter* preserved this law and Parliament's ability to legislate with respect to the admissibility of evidence. When the provinces did not agree to the *Charter*, the federal government heard from civil libertarians and defence lawyers who argued that courts should at least be able to exclude evidence obtained through blatant illegalities. The result was section 24(2), which was presented as a compromise between the American rule of excluding all unconstitutionally obtained evidence and the Anglo-Canadian rule of admitting all relevant evidence. One civil servant who helped draft the provision even explained that it would result in exclusion only when "the admission of this evidence would make me vomit, it was obtained in such a reprehensible manner."[25]

Judges soon began hearing many applications that confessions, breathalyser samples, and drugs should be excluded under section 24(2) because the police had violated the accused's rights. The judges did not apply the vomit test, but they stuck close to the text of the provision, often simply concluding that, in their view, the admission of the evidence in the circumstances would or would not bring the administration of justice into disrepute. The problem was that judges had different views about the repute of the administration of justice, and these differences were not usually explained in their rulings. Some judges believed that the justice system should protect rights at all costs, while others believed it should control crime and discover the truth at all costs. The text of section 24(2) was used as a conclusion rather than a reason to explain why the admission of unconstitutionally obtained evidence would, or would not, bring the administration of justice into disrepute.[26] Lawyers and accused could rest assured that they would hear reference to the text of section 24(2), but unless they knew the judges' own views about what the repute of the administration of justice depended on, they would not have a clue whether unconstitutionally obtained evidence would be excluded. Arguments based on the alleged plain or "natural meaning of the term 'disrepute'"[27] disregard the indeterminacy of this concept.

In 1987 the Supreme Court put some flesh on the bare bones of section 24(2) of the *Charter* and gave some reasons why judges should or should not exclude evidence. The case involved Ruby Collins, who, while sitting in a pub in Gibsons, British Columbia, was tackled and choked by a man yelling "Police officer." He found a green balloon containing heroin in Ms. Collin's hand. Would the admission of the heroin bring the administration of justice into disrepute? Some people would be concerned that they could be tackled and placed in a chokehold by the police while sitting in their pub. Many others would be unable to get over the fact that Collins had heroin. The Supreme Court ruled that unless the police officer could show that he had strong grounds to believe that Collins would swallow the heroin unless she was placed in the chokehold, the heroin had to be kept out of the trial in order to protect the repute of the administration of justice.

Writing for the Court, Justice Lamer refused to base the Court's decision on whether the majority of Canadians would be shocked by what the police had done. The public's views were relevant only to the extent that they were reasonable and concerned with the long-term influence of admitting unconstitutionally obtained evidence on the repute of the administration of justice. Besides, he cautioned, "the Charter is designed to protect the accused from the majority, so the enforcement of the Charter must not be left to that majority." In order to give some guidance for judges, Justice Lamer then set out a three-part test to determine when the admission of evidence would bring the administration of justice into disrepute. In the first part of the test, the Court reasoned that an unfair trial would bring the administration of justice into disrepute. It then suggested that there would be an unfair trial if Ms. Collins had been unconstitutionally conscripted to produce incriminating evidence such as a confession, breath sample, or other evidence emanating from her. This conclusion was based on a generous interpretation that extended the right against self-incrimination from the courthouse to the police station. It has been contested by those who take a traditional approach to this right that limits it to the right to refuse to answer questions in court. Nevertheless, the Court's conclusion was not pulled out of the air. It was based on an interpretation of the text of section 24(2) and related constitutional principles, as well as precedents under section 24(2) excluding unconstitutionally obtained breath samples and confessions.

The Court's subsequent interpretation of section 24(2) was logically rigorous. The seriousness of the offence did not justify admitting evidence that would affect trial fairness because "the more serious the offence, the more damaging to the system's repute would be an unfair trial."[28] The seriousness of the violation did not justify admitting evidence because a trial was just as unfair when the police breached the *Charter* in good faith as when they did so in a deliberate and flagrant fashion. The Court also recognized that even the admission of guns and drugs could affect the fairness of the trial if the only way the police could have discovered them was by unconstitutionally compelling the accused to help them build their case. The result has been criticized by many, including Chief Justice McLachlin, for creating an "automatic" exclusionary rule that departed from the text of that section, the expectations of the framers, and what the public would consider behaviour that would bring the administration of justice into disrepute.[29] In a recent public interview, Justice Bastarache has gone further, indicating that he thinks the fair trial test was without "legal support ... an invention of the court, a principle that was created by the court, and I think it's inconsistent with the very wording of [the *Charter*], with the intention of Parliament ... and I also think it's totally unrealistic."[30] Strong words indeed.

The fair trial has not, in fact, resulted in automatic exclusion. The Court has made some pragmatic exceptions, such as when an accused was too drunk to understand his right-to-counsel warning before a breathalyser demand or when he confessed before the police could read him his rights. The Court has also held that the admission of conscriptive evidence that would have been obtained without a *Charter* violation does not require exclusion in order to protect the accused's right to a fair trial.[31] In other words, the heroin would not necessarily have been excluded if Collins had told them where it was hidden, provided the police could establish that they eventually would have found her stash.

Concerns about the judicial creation of an automatic exclusionary rule are even more off-target when we consider the reluctance of courts to exclude evidence obtained without the accused's participation. Under this part of the Court's test, evidence will only be excluded after balancing the seriousness of the violation with the harmful effects to the administration of justice of excluding the evidence. It is here that the evidence is often crucial to a conviction, and the Court has been very cautious, too cautious in my view, in excluding evidence. Perhaps reflecting the Canadian veneration for the Mounties, the Court has been reluctant to find that the police have committed serious violations. Reliance on unconstitutional laws, warrants, and procedures all constitute good-faith excuses to let in unconstitutionally obtained evidence. The Court has also characterized almost all offences, including marijuana ones, as serious and has been reluctant to exclude evidence that is crucial to the prosecutor's case. It has generally characterized *Charter* violations as so serious as to merit exclusion only in cases, such as Collins's, when the police have both flagrantly and violently breached *Charter* rights.

A balanced approach to section 24(2) would conclude that, on the whole, the Court has not created an automatic exclusionary rule. To be sure, the fair trial test has deprived police of confessions and bodily samples that would have provided unconstitutional shortcuts to convictions, and it has prevented the conviction of drunk drivers when the police have not provided them with an opportunity to contact lawyers before providing a breath sample. In cases involving the rape and murder of a fourteen-year-old girl and the murder of an eighty-six-year-old man in his home, the Court's decision to exclude evidence has made headlines,[32] while the accused's subsequent conviction on the remaining admissible evidence barely made the news. Parliament has limited the ambit of the fair-trial test by creating warrant procedures that allow the police constitutionally, and with a warrant, to obtain bodily samples and body impressions from the accused. Criticisms of the fair-trial test as "a collective act of self-immolation"[33] are overblown. Conviction rates remain high and, as Chief Justice McLachlin has recognized, it is a "myth that criminals 'walk' under the Charter."[34] In the near future, the Court may very well respond to the criticism its fair-trial test has received by abolishing or significantly modifying it. This reaction could leave us with a weak exclusionary rule in which the courts are reluctant to criticize police conduct or exclude important evidence in all but the most trivial of cases. Whether one agrees with the fair-trial test or not, it should be recognized that the Court has based this test on a good-faith interpretation of constitutional principles and its precedents. However unpopular they may be, the Court has tried to provide reasons, not simply conclusions, for excluding evidence. Simply reciting the text of section 24(2) might please those who insist on fidelity to the text, but it would not explain why unconstitutionally obtained evidence has been excluded from or allowed into criminal trials.

De-*Lochnerizing* Equality Rights

The guarantee in section 15 of the *Charter* of the equal protection and benefit of the law without discrimination is a provision that could affect every law in the statute book. The business of government is drawing distinctions. An open-ended approach to the broadly worded equality rights could require governments to justify under section 1 most, if not all, of their laws. During the *Lochner* era in the United States, the Supreme Court constitutionalized laissez-faire economics, and advantaged interests such as corporations could easily go to court to oppose the regulatory and redistributive activities of the state. In the early days of section 15, the makers of margarine went to court to complain that they were treated differently from the makers of butter, the owners of movie theatres sued because they were treated differently from video retailers, and the vendors of adult entertainment had the nerve to go to court to complain that they were treated differently from the vendors of other products.[35] Most of these complaints were thrown out of court, but a few courts did strike down laws because they treated similarly situated people differently — by, for example, limiting the size of scallops caught by fishers on different-size boats and by preventing workers covered by workers' compensation from suing their employers for injuries.[36] The large number of cases brought by corporations and other advantaged people demonstrated that equality rights could have *Lochner*ized the *Charter* and provided a vehicle for the courts to strike down much legitimate government regulation.[37]

In its first equality rights case, the Supreme Court made it clear that section 15 of the *Charter* would catch only unequal treatment before the law that resulted in discrimination on the basis of the nine enumerated grounds or similar grounds. In his decision for the Court, Justice McIntyre stressed that the text of section 15 did not provide "a general guarantee of equality ... between individuals or groups within society in a general or abstract sense," but only when laws resulted in discrimination. He warned that, to govern effectively, legislatures must treat individuals and groups in different ways and that mere differences of treatment, even on the enumerated and analogous grounds, did not necessarily violate section 15. Justice La Forest added that he was "not prepared to accept that all legislative classifications must be rationally supportable before the courts. Much economic and social policy making is simply beyond the institutional competence of the courts: their role is to protect against incursions on fundamental values, not to second guess policy decisions." The Court recognized that some of the broader equality tests would take them into *Lochner* territory, and it retreated to a more restrictive approach that required not only inequality but discrimination.

The case was nevertheless a victory for many groups concerned about equality. The Court ruled that the Law Society of British Columbia had discriminated against Mark Andrews, a British subject permanently resident in Canada, by holding that, although otherwise qualified, he could not be admitted to the bar because he was not a Canadian citizen. At first glance the decision to give Andrews some relief seems like a feat of judicial activism, because section 15 of the *Charter* does not specifically prohibit discrimination on the basis of citizenship, only on the basis or race, national or ethnic origin, colour, religion, sex, age, or mental and physical disability. Nevertheless, Justice McIntyre, one of the Court's more conservative judges, held that these listed or enumerated grounds of discrimination were only examples of the more general statement in section 15 that "every individual is equal before and under the law and has the right to the equal protection and equal benefit of the law without discrimination." Non-citizens were "a good example of a 'discrete and insular minority' who come within the protection of s.15" by being analogous to the nine grounds listed in section 15. Justice Wilson also used the phrase "discrete and insular minority," which, although it was taken from the American jurisprudence that backed away from *Lochner*-type activism, had laid the basis for the activism of the Warren Court in protecting African Americans, criminal suspects, and other unpopular minorities from discrimination and abuse. Even Justice Wilson, often thought to be the most activist member of the Dickson Court, warned that courts should look not only to disadvantages imposed by the law being challenged, but to "the place of the group in the entire social, political and legal fabric of our society. While legislatures must inevitably draw distinctions among the governed, such distinctions should not bring about or reinforce the disadvantage of certain groups and individuals by denying them the rights freely accorded to others."[38] The Court's unanimous decision to include, or read in, non-citizens as a group protected from discrimination did not attract any of the criticism that its later decision to include gays and lesbians from discrimination received. In any event, the Court proved that the concept of analogous grounds was not elastic by holding, in short order, that it did not include workers who were denied the legal right to sue their employers for injuries sustained on the job; accused who were denied a procedural benefit because they were tried in a particular province; and those who were required to sue the federal Crown in the Federal Court, as opposed to the provincial superior courts.[39] These decisions made clear that those seeking relief from the Court would have to demonstrate some broader form of discrimination, in addition to a legal inequality. Although its decision to restrict the ambit of equality rights was criticized by most law professors, who urged a broader approach,[40] the Court had decided to focus its powers on protecting the rights of minorities vulnerable to broader forms of discrimination.

The Court's subsequent interpretation of section 15 of the *Charter* was hardly revolutionary, and it rejected most claims of discrimination it heard.[41] It rejected claims by men that their equality rights were violated by the offence of statutory rape or searches by female guards, and it rejected claims by women that not allowing unlimited child-care expenses to be deducted as business expenses or including child support payments in their taxable income violated their equality rights. It also rejected claims that laws prohibiting assisted suicide, requiring severely disabled children to be in special classes, or allowing the Crown to introduce evidence of mental disorder in criminal cases discriminated against the disabled, while holding that the failure to provide sign-language interpreters in hospitals denied deaf people their equality rights. It also rejected a section 15 challenge by religious minorities to state funding of Catholic schools in Ontario. Despite the Court's caution about striking down state action under section 15 of the *Charter*, differences emerged between the judges. Some judges wanted an even more restrictive approach that would allow discrimination even on enumerated and analogous grounds if it were relevant to the functional values of the legislation. The judges who supported this position would have upheld the denial of benefits to common law spouses on the tautologous basis that the legislation in question was designed only to assist couples in traditional marriages. They also would have upheld the denial of benefits to same-sex spouses on the offensive basis that only heterosexual couples could produce children. This approach threatened to return to restrictive pre-*Charter* precedents that ignored discrimination against women on the basis that the denial of unemployment insurance to pregnant women was justified because pregnant women could not work.

In 1999 the Court settled its differences in a unanimous judgment in a case called *Law*.[42] The case involved the claim of Nancy Law, a thirty-year-old widow with no children, who would have received a survivor pension from her husband's Canada Pension Plan contributions if she had been over forty-five years of age, disabled, or had children. Ms. Law was in dire straits, having lost the business she had operated with her deceased husband. Under the existing law, she would have to wait thirty-five years, until she was sixty-five years of age, to receive any survivor's pension. She needed the money now and argued that the legislation discriminated against her on the basis of her age. In the words of the minister who introduced the legislation in 1964, the law assumed that "young widows in their twenties and early thirties usually have little difficulty in finding employment, and of course many of them remarry."[43] Given this type of outdated stereotype, it was not unrealistic for Ms. Law to look to the Supreme Court for relief.

Nancy Law was disappointed. A unanimous Court found that, although the law clearly denied a benefit on the prohibited grounds of age, it was not discriminatory. Adults under forty-five "have not been consistently and routinely subjected to the sorts of discrimination faced by some of Canada's discrete and insular minorities." The search for wider disadvantage that was used when extending the grounds of discrimination beyond those listed was applied to age — one of the specifically listed grounds of discrimination. The Court was "at a loss to locate any violation of human dignity," because the "legislation does not stereotype, exclude or devalue adults under 45." If Ms. Law felt she was excluded from a pension for discriminatory reasons and perhaps even stereotyped as a gold digger or at least as a widow who should get a job, the Court concluded she was not being reasonable. The government had used an "informed generalization," not a stereotype, that young, able-bodied, and childless widows did not need a survivor's pension.[44] Parliament's informed generalization could, however, be another person's stereotype. It is clear from *Law* that not every loss in the political process, or every legal disadvantage even on specifically listed grounds of discrimination such as age, will violate equality rights. Applicants have to demonstrate not only legal inequality and discrimination but an

affront to human dignity and all before the government has an opportunity to justify the violation under section 1 of the *Charter*.

The fact that people are members of a disadvantaged group, even
a severely disadvantaged group, does not mean that they automatically
win their equality rights cases. One case involved the lucrative Casino
Rama run north of Toronto. The Ontario government had reached an
agreement with the Chiefs of Indian Bands in Ontario that millions of
dollars in revenues from the casino would be distributed to the bands
and the bands only. Not surprisingly, some of those who were left out
complained. The groups that went to court were not, however, just anyone looking for a piece of the action, but other Aboriginal people, in this
case a number of Indian and Métis communities and associations that
were not recognized as bands under the *Indian Act*. I volunteered my
time to help represent one of these groups and, without in any way suggesting that the bands are not disadvantaged, believe me when I say that
these groups are also disadvantaged. Aboriginal communities not recognized as bands generally do not receive the benefits that bands receive
from the federal government and, as in this case, they are often ignored
by the provincial government. They must also face the indignity of
being seen by some as "less Aboriginal" than those who have a band card
issued by the Department of Indian Affairs. The litigation was also difficult, as the applicants were opposed by the provincial government, the
federal government, and the bands. A common need for funds among
both the bands and the non-band communities was not enough to establish a violation of equality rights. In one breath, the Court recognized
that Aboriginal people not organized in bands under the *Indian Act* suffered from stereotypes that saw them as less Aboriginal and less
accountable than bands, but in the next breath concluded that the
Ontario government could exclude them from the Casino Rama revenues in order to "develop a partnership or a 'government to government' relationship with Ontario's First Nation band communities."[45] The
Ontario government was allowed to define the purpose of the Casino
Rama project in a manner that excluded other Aboriginal people. The
Court deferred to the government's decision to deal only with the Bands,
even though it excluded other Aboriginal people who very much needed access to the funds produced by the casino.

In *Andrews* and again in *Law*, the Court has restricted the ambit of
equality rights to require, first, discrimination on enumerated and analogous grounds and, second, affronts to human dignity. The Court has
used these tests to reject the vast majority of equality claims it has
heard, even when the unsuccessful applicants are discriminated against
on the basis of specifically listed grounds of discrimination or when they
are clearly and chronically disadvantaged. The Court has stayed well

away from the risk of *Lochnerizing* the equality rights of the *Charter*, and has not given a victory to every discrete and insular minority that has gone to Court.

Judicial Creation of Gay Rights?

Despite the generally restrictive approach taken to equality rights, the Court's decisions involving equality claims by gays and lesbians have attracted some criticism. The Court unanimously decided to "read in" sexual orientation as an analogous ground of discrimination in a 1995 case in which James Egan and John Nesbit, who had been partners since 1948, challenged restrictions that denied them a spousal pension allowance that was available to married and common law heterosexual couples. Egan and Nesbit lost the case. Four judges held that the purpose of the allowance was related to the ability of heterosexual couples to have children. Another judge held that, even though the legislation discriminated against gays and lesbians on the basis of an unwarranted stereotype that they could not have the same form of lasting and supportive relationships as heterosexual couples, the government's policy was a reasonable limit on the right. He stressed that governments could take an incremental approach to addressing discrimination. This decision had to be a bitter blow to the elderly couple who had suffered discrimination together for half a century. Nevertheless, they acted with great dignity throughout the litigation.

Egan and Nesbit's only victory, and it was an important one, was that all nine judges agreed that sexual orientation was an analogous ground of discrimination and that gays and lesbians should be protected from discrimination under the *Charter*'s equality rights. Even the judges who held that the violation was justified, for conservative reasons relating to the traditional family, agreed that sexual orientation was "a deeply personal characteristic that is either unchangeable or changeable only at unacceptable personal costs, and so falls within the ambit of s. 15 protection as being analogous to the enumerated groups."[46] Justice Cory reviewed the history of legal and social discrimination faced by gays and lesbians, including the criminalization of gay sex, the designation of homosexuality as a psychiatric disorder, and hatred and stigma that "has forced many homosexuals to conceal their orientation" with corresponding "costs in the work place, the community and in private life." He also noted that many lower courts had reached similar conclusions and that most human rights codes prohibited discrimination on the basis of sexual orientation.[47] The Court did not justify the need for protection against discrimination on the basis of sexual orientation on the basis of the judges own political or cultural preferences. Instead, a unanimous Court, which included judges attracted to traditional views of the family, justified this decision on the basis of the text and purposes of section 15 and the history of discrimination against gays and lesbians.

Some conservative commentators have criticized the addition of sexual orientation on the basis that it does not accord with the intent of the framers of the *Charter*, who, when they were asked to list sexual orientation as a prohibited form of discrimination, chose not to do so.[48] Similar arguments have been made that the Court defied the framers' intent on the issues of substantive due process and abortion, yet these arguments discount the ambiguity of the text and the fact that judges who made the decisions engaged in a good-faith interpretation of the text of the *Charter*. The framers could have stated explicitly that the nine enumerated grounds were the only grounds of discrimination. The fact that this restriction was not made suggests that, even in 1982, there would have been political opposition to a permanent exclusion of sexual orientation as a prohibited ground of discrimination. Gays and lesbians lost a political battle in 1982 to have sexual orientation listed as an example of prohibited discrimination, but not the constitutional war to have sexual orientation recognized at some point as a ground of discrimination. If they are to be more than speculations, arguments based on framers' intent must make sense of what the framers chose to include and not include in the text of the constitution. They must also make sense of the fact that the nine judges of the Court, including those not prepared to intervene because of their conservative views about the family and their deference to the legislature, all agreed that sexual orientation was a prohibited ground of discrimination analogous to the nine enumerated but non-exclusive grounds of discrimination. The judges who reached this conclusion were not exercising a "policy discretion" that "can just as plausibly defer to the other branches of government as oppose them,"[49] but rather were engaged in a good-faith effort to interpret the constitution in accord with its text and purpose.

Judicial Creation of Prisoner Voting Rights?

Section 3 of the *Charter* guarantees every Canadian citizen the right to vote in federal and provincial elections. It does not say every citizen who is not in prison. The Canadian Constitution differs from the American, which qualifies the right of citizens to vote as not including those who participated in "rebellion or other crime" and has allowed massive and permanent disenfranchisement of felons.[50] Given the clear text, one would expect that conservative critics of judicial activism would applaud judicial decisions holding that legislation that denies prisoners the vote infringes this fundamental democratic right. Yet supporters of framers' intent are inconsistent on this point. Rainer Knopff and Ted Morton have argued that such decisions are examples of an

activist "noninterpretivist" and "living tree" approach to *Charter* interpretation. They defend Justice Sterling Lyon, the former Manitoba premier who opposed the enactment of the *Charter*, in his interpretation of
the right to vote as including the statutory restrictions on prisoner voting at the time of the *Charter*'s enactment; it is, they state, an example
of "a very traditional or interpretivist view of constitutional interpretation."[51] This defence of Justice Lyon's perverse interpretation of the
plain words of section 3 suggests that their preferred approach to
Charter adjudication is less about ensuring fidelity to the text and more
about minimizing the impact of the *Charter*. If anyone does violence to
the text of the *Charter* or engages in judicial discretion that reads his
own personal values into the *Charter*, it is surely Justice Lyon, who
denies that prisoners have been denied the right that they, like every
citizen of Canada, plainly have under the *Charter*. Reasonable people
can disagree about whether particular restrictions on prisoners' clear
right to vote are reasonable. Substantive opposition to prisoner voting
rights should not, however, be dressed up in arguments that judges are
illegitimately reading their personal values into the *Charter* when they
hold that prison disenfranchisement violates the clear right of prisoners,
as citizens, to vote.

Judicial Creation of Aboriginal and Treaty Rights?

There is a perception that the courts have been generous to the point of
excess in defining Aboriginal rights. This impression has been recognized by no less than Justice Michel Bastarache, the judge and former
law dean from New Brunswick who was appointed to the highest Court
in 1997. In controversial comments on the Court's decision finding that
the Mi'kmaq had commercial fishing rights, he commented that there
was a perception, "especially in the Maritimes," that "the court was very
result-oriented and was inventing rights that weren't even in the treaties
that were brought before the court in the case ... the court was maybe
seen as being unduly favourable to the native position in all cases, and
that it sort of has an agenda for extending these rights."[52] I do not know
where people get this perception. It is certainly not from the cases,
which suggest that it is not easy to establish Aboriginal rights. When
Aboriginal people claim rights, they must go to considerable expense to
produce historical evidence about treaties or specific practices and sites
integral to their distinctive societies from the time of European contact
to the present. Even then, courts are very reluctant to define Aboriginal
rights in a broad or unlimited manner.

Aboriginal rights were perhaps the most controversial rights included in the 1982 constitutional package. They were excluded from original drafts of the *Charter*, but included in January 1981 after public hearings. In November 1981, however, they were again dropped at the insistence of British Columbia and other provinces concerned with the effects of such rights on provincial lands and jurisdiction.[53] They were restored after a public outcry, but were qualified by the addition of the phrase "existing," so that section 35(1) of the *Constitution Act, 1982* recognizes and affirms "existing Aboriginal and treaty rights." In its first case, the Court gave meaning to the word "existing" by holding that section 35(1) did not protect rights that were extinguished before 1982. Before 1982, Parliament asserted the power to be able, by legislation, to extinguish Aboriginal rights unilaterally and without the consent of Aboriginal people. The Court held that extinguishment, before 1982, required Parliament to make "clear and plain" its intention to extinguish, and not simply to regulate Aboriginal rights. This requirement was not an "unprecedented ... new invention"[54] by the Court, but part of the courts' traditional stance that the legislature was presumed to respect a wide variety of common law rights unless its intention to violate them was clear.[55] The Court also refused to read the reference to "existing rights" as limiting or freezing the rights "so as to incorporate the specific manner in which it was regulated before 1982." Chief Justice Dickson and Justice La Forest reasoned that "the notion of freezing existing rights would incorporate into the Constitution a crazy patchwork of regulations."[56] This frozen-rights approach would fail to give meaning to the entrenchment of Aboriginal rights and would also mean that governments could not enact any stricter regulation than that imposed in 1982, even if conditions changed. The Court made sense of the qualification of Aboriginal rights as only existing rights while also making sense of the idea that such rights were now recognized and affirmed in the constitution.

In subsequent cases, the Court articulated a restrictive test that required an activity to be part of a practice, custom, or tradition that was integral to the distinctive culture of the Aboriginal group claiming the right at the time of contact in order for the activity to be protected as a section 35 Aboriginal right. Aboriginal rights were limited to those activities that made the culture of the Aboriginal society distinctive or truly what it was; they could not include a practice that was only incidental to a distinctive activity or only a response to European influences. Moreover, there must be continuity between the modern form of the right and its practice before contact with Europeans. As Justice L'Heureux-Dubé argued in dissent, this "harsh burden of proof" required

Aboriginal claimants "to embark upon a search for a pristine Aboriginal society and to prove the continuous existence of the activity."[57] This rigorously historical approach can make Aboriginal rights litigation an expensive form of trial by anthropologist.

The Court's fixation with the point of European contact also created the risk of freezing Aboriginal rights at a point of time that may have had no particular significance to dynamic Aboriginal societies. "Given the generally poor state in which Aboriginal people found the first European explorers to Canada, it is certainly questionable as to what degree of significance they attached to contact with a rag tag group of men in danger of dying of starvation or freezing to death through the winter."[58] A similar approach raises the difficult question: "What would it be like for Canadians to have their fundamental rights defined by what *was* integral to European peoples' distinctive cultures prior to their arrival in North America?"[59] Would there still be slavery? Would women still not have the vote? The Court's application of the term "integral" to the distinctive society test has not been promising for Aboriginal people. Dorothy Van Der Peet was convicted of selling ten salmon on the basis of the Court's conclusion that selling salmon was not an integral activity of the Sto:lo First Nation at the time of contact.[60] Members of the Shawanaga and Eagle Lake First Nations were convicted of illegal bingos on their reserve on the basis that high-stakes gambling was not integral to their distinctive culture at the time of contact. The Court rejected the argument that the band's regulation of gaming was part of their rights of self-government and management of their reserve lands.[61] The gaming rights and exemptions from taxation that some Aboriginal people enjoy, and that are so controversial in some quarters, are largely the product of legislation, not judicial interpretation of Aboriginal rights.

What about the *Marshall* fishing rights case that led to violence in Burnt Church and perceptions that the Court was overly generous to the Mi'kmaq? As often happens, the case was brought on the back of a prosecution of an Aboriginal person. The accused, Donald Marshall, was no stranger to the justice system, having been wrongfully convicted and having served eleven years in prison for a murder he did not commit. When he caught and sold $787 worth of eels, Marshall found himself once again the accused and once again convicted by the Nova Scotia courts, this time of fishing without a licence and in closed season. The Supreme Court's decision to acquit Marshall and to find in a 1760 Treaty of Friendship between the Crown and the Mi'kmaq a right to engage in commercial fishing was greeted with a tidal wave of criticism. The *Globe and Mail* suggested that the case raised "the spectre of the Supreme Court functioning illegitimately to create an unintended right on vague and quasi-historical interpretations."[62] Just how creative was the Court's interpretation?

The written terms of the treaty provided that the Mi'kmaq would "not traffick, barter or Exchange any commodities in any manner but with such persons or the managers of such Truck houses as shall be appointed or Established by His Majesty's Governor."[63] Unlike an earlier treaty, which promised the free liberty of hunting and fishing as usual, a literal reading of this treaty provided the Mi'kmaq no rights at all. In her dissent, Chief Justice McLachlin argued that the peace and friendship treaty had effectively expired. The majority of the Court, however, held that the written terms of the treaty should be interpreted in light of oral understandings that the Mi'kmaq should have access to a harvest of wildlife, so they would have something to trade at the truckhouses and would obtain some benefit from their promises to trade only with the Crown. Justice Ian Binnie, a former Bay Street lawyer, argued that such oral understandings would be incorporated into the interpretation of commercial contracts, let alone solemn treaties, which should be interpreted to include the Mi'kmaq perspective and to uphold the honour of the Crown.

Reasonable people can disagree, but Justice Binnie's approach is arguably more consistent with the continuing constitutional status of the treaty and the parties' understandings when it was negotiated. If the Court erred in finding fishing rights in the treaty, the error was limited because the right was defined in a modest manner. Relying on British notes of the negotiations, Justice Binnie concluded that the purposes of the truckhouse was only the provision of "necessaries," which he interpreted as providing a "moderate livelihood" that "addresses day-to-day needs," but does not allow "the accumulation of wealth"[64] — something like the $787 that Mr. Marshall received for selling 463 pound of eels. Some critics have deplored this internal restriction on the commercial fishing right as not even ensuring that the Mi'kmaq can have the same standard of living as their non-Aboriginal neighbours.[65] In any event, the Court took the extraordinary step of issuing a subsequent judgment, on a motion for rehearing by an intervenor representing non-Aboriginal fishing interests, in which it stressed that the limited treaty right did not apply to logging, minerals, or offshore natural gas deposits and that the government could justify limitations on what was already quite a limited right.

These cases lend little support to the argument that the Court has been overly generous in interpreting Aboriginal and treaty rights. In all cases, the claimant has had to establish with historical evidence the existence of an Aboriginal right, or one that was supported in the text or understandings when treaties were negotiated. Judges have not made up Aboriginal rights and they have been reluctant to recognize rights that go beyond sustenance or the provision of a moderate livelihood. Even if the courts are thought to have unduly expanded the ambit of Aboriginal rights, as we will discuss in chapter 9, the rights are considered by the courts as far from absolute. Governments have robust power to justify external limits on already limited rights for a broad range of reasons, including concerns about non-Aboriginal interests in the resources.

The Judicial Creation of Judicial Compensation Commissions and Obligations to Negotiate Separation

The Supreme Court decided two important cases in the late 1990s not so much on the basis of its interpretation of the abstract rights found in the *Charter*, but on the basis of the underlying principles found in the constitution, including its preamble. The Court's reliance on preambles and general principles here makes the judicial reasoning more abstract and open-ended than in other *Charter* cases. (It should be noted, however, that Preston Manning, among others, has criticized the courts for not paying more attention to the recognition of the supremacy of God in the preamble to the *Charter*.[66]) Both cases emerged from references by governments, suggesting that elected governments may have invited, if not welcomed, the judicial activism that emerged from them.

The first case concerned whether provinces could reduce the salaries of judges as part of a general deficit-reduction strategy. The Court had already established in a number of cases that judicial independence required judges to have financial security from the governments that regularly appear before them as litigants. Relying in part on the reference in the preamble of the 1867 constitution to Canada having a constitution similar in principle to that of the United Kingdom, the Court concluded that judicial salaries must be determined by a process requiring the legislature to consider the salary recommendations of independent commissions. In a biting dissent, Justice La Forest argued that the English Constitution was based on parliamentary supremacy and the Court was unnecessarily creating a commission process that went well beyond the text of the constitution.[67] The imposition of an independent commission process as a constitutional requirement and the reliance on the preamble do indeed push the interpretative envelope. Moreover, the decision was rendered in one of the very few areas where the independent judiciary may be perceived to have an interest in the outcome. Nevertheless, the activism of the *Judges Reference* can be defended on the basis that the Court was ultimately concerned with establishing a fair process, respectful of judicial independence, for establishing judicial salaries. The Court did not attempt to set judicial salaries or to give this power to the independent commissions. Governments can reject the recommendations of commissions so long as they can justify their decision to a court in a manner that is similar to, but less stringent than, the section 1 test under the *Charter*. The Court crafted a fair process respectful of constitutional values — something within its particular competence — as opposed to imposing a final solution.

The Court's second bold foray into the world of unwritten constitutional principles came in the reference directed to it by the federal government on the secession of Quebec. As has happened so often throughout Canadian history, the government used the reference procedure to put the Court in the hotseat, this time after a referendum on sovereignty had been defeated by the narrowest of margins in Quebec. The Court responded to the difficult reference by articulating and relying on the first principles of the Canadian Constitution — democracy, federalism, the rule of law, and the rights of minorities. Although nowhere spelled out as the first principles, all these principles are supported by some aspects of the constitutional text. When faced with the extraordinary prospect of the breakup of the country, the Court decided to rely on basic and abstract principles that were not explicitly written out in the constitution, but were "major elements of the architecture of the Constitution itself and are as such its lifeblood."[68] The Court went on to suggest that, while unilateral secession would be illegal and unconstitutional, there would be an obligation on the rest of Canada to negotiate with Quebec should a sufficiently clear majority vote for separation on the basis of a sufficiently clear question. The decision provided something for federalists who argued that a unilateral declaration of independence would be illegal, and something for separatists who argued that Canada must negotiate separation should the people of Quebec clearly want to leave. The decision has been criticized for contemplating that the constitution might be amended by means that do not follow the formal amending formulae spelled out in the text of the constitution, which could give three and perhaps even one provincial government a veto over the separation of Quebec.[69]

Like the *Judges Reference*, the *Quebec Secession Reference* pushes the interpretative envelope, but can be defended as a decision designed to structure a fair and workable process in an extraordinary situation, without attempting to impose a final solution. The Court disclaimed any power to determine if the majority or the question was clear enough or if the governments were fulfilling their duties to negotiate. It accepted that the elected governments themselves had a role in interpreting whether they were fulfilling their constitutional obligations.[70] The decision left room for Parliament to implement legislation to provide its own procedure for determining the clarity of the question and the majority. As in the *Judges Reference*, the Court was careful to leave the political actors room to move. The unique contribution of the Court's judicial activism in these two extraordinary cases was to structure a process that would allow governments and branches of government to resolve their own disputes in a manner consistent with the complex and multiple values of the Canadian Constitution.

Conclusion

The purposive approach to interpreting the *Charter* is not radically different from the approach that courts have long taken to the interpretation of statutes. Judges cannot depend on dictionary meanings of the text to decide difficult cases and must be guided by both the text and the purposes of the *Charter*. The Court exercises creative powers when interpreting the often vague phrases in the *Charter*, but this power is limited by the need to make good-faith interpretations of the text. Although the Court has been criticized by those who oppose robust interpretations of the right against self-incrimination and its relation to a fair trial, the Court's interpretation of section 24(2) of the *Charter* was a good-faith attempt to elaborate constitutional principles, as opposed to reliance on question-begging conclusions that the admission of evidence will or will not bring the administration of justice into disrepute. Similarly, the Court's conclusion that gays and lesbians are protected under section 15 of the *Charter* is based on its interpretation of the purpose and the text of equality rights. The Court was engaged in a process of interpretation, not the expression of political or cultural preferences or arbitrary will.

Judges cannot simply read their worldviews or political preferences into the *Charter*. As the great American judge Benjamin Cardozo observed: "A judge, even when he is free, is still not wholly free. He is not to innovate at pleasure. He is not a knight-errant, roaming at will in pursuant of his own ideal of beauty or of goodness. He is to draw his inspiration from consecrated principles."[72] Although it rejected a dichotomy between procedural and substantive review when interpreting the guarantee of fundamental justice in section 7 of the *Charter*, the Court has not read the economic agenda of either the right or the left into the *Charter*, nor has it decided on a specific and detailed abortion policy that displaced a role for Parliament. Similarly, the Court has been very cautious when interpreting equality rights not to require governments to justify all the distinctions they draw in legislation under section 1 of the *Charter*. The Court has not interpreted Aboriginal rights at large or attempted to craft a national policy on Aboriginal matters. Instead, it has proceeded in a case-by-case fashion and has relied on historical evidence about the existence of Aboriginal rights in particular locations and treaties. My claim in this chapter is not that judges are infallible interpreters of the constitution or that they do not exercise creativity, but that they are not free to read their own personal preferences into the constitution without justifying them as a good-faith interpretation of the text and the precedents.

Chapter 8
The Limits of Public Law Adjudication

Although the Depression cases of the 1930s and the Quebec cases of the 1950s demonstrate that political controversy is not entirely new to the Supreme Court, the Court's role in Canadian politics has changed significantly in the last quarter of the century. Until 1974 the Court was required by law to hear any appeal in which the litigants — often insurance companies and corporations — had claimed more than $10,000, even if the case raised no legal issues of public importance. Since 1974 the Court has focused more on resolving legal issues of national importance, primarily in the area of public law involving the state. In order to deal with these public law issues, the Court has allowed litigants who are not directly affected by laws to challenge their constitutionality, permitted public interest groups as well as governments to intervene in constitutional cases, and decided moot cases and issues that it could have ducked. Do these changes to the Court's role and practice mean that it has ceased to be a court and now exercises power like a third legislative chamber? Worse still, a legislative chamber that has been captured by certain interest groups? Conservative critics of judicial activism say yes and argue that the Court has become too eager to make law under the *Charter*, to hear from intervenors, and to impose final remedies on government.[1]

Although the Court has changed its procedure to adjust to its new responsibilities under the *Charter* and its new role in Canadian society, it is a mistake to ignore the limits of even public law adjudication. Not just anyone can walk into the Court and start talking about the *Charter*. The image of the Court as an overeager oracle or as a third legislative chamber open for business discounts the continued need for litigants to engage in the formal and costly process of litigation. When the interest group Operation Dismantle wanted to challenge the constitutionality of the testing of cruise missiles in Canada, it did not simply go to the Supreme Court talking about the dangers of nuclear war. It had first to find a trial court with jurisdiction to hear the case, establish standing, introduce into evidence enough facts to decide the case, pay lawyers, and, when it lost because it failed to establish a nexus between the tests and threats to life, be responsible for paying the government's litigation costs.[2] The whole process was far more elaborate than filing a brief with a Senate committee.

The argument that the Court has been captured by certain interest groups is also not compelling. The Court hears from public interest groups on all sides of the issues - pro-choice but also pro-life, Aboriginal groups but also non-Aboriginal groups. The litigants who have benefited from public interest standing have been both liberal advocates of free speech and welfare rights, but also conservative opponents of bilingualism and abortion. The argument that the Court has been eager to make law under the *Charter* is a bit stronger. In the early years of the *Charter* especially, the Court decided more than was strictly necessary to resolve a dispute. This result is hardly surprising, given that the Court can hear only about one hundred cases a year and that governments, litigants, and other judges look to it for guidance. There are some signs that the Court is becoming less eager to decide *Charter* issues and more cautious in defining the breadth of its rulings. At the same time, however, it is not clear that procedural conservatism can be separated from substantive conservatism. A Court that takes a minimalist approach to constitutional adjudication — for example, one that decides Aboriginal claims on an acre-by-acre, species-by-species basis — may, under the guise of procedural purity and neutrality, actually be taking a minimalist approach to rights. Procedural conservatism will only aggravate the considerable difficulties that disadvantaged individuals and groups already have getting their claims heard.

Public Interest Standing

Since the mid-1970s the Supreme Court has been prepared to recognize public interest standing. The Court's first case allowed a politician to argue that official bilingualism was unconstitutional, and its third case allowed anti-abortion crusader Joe Borowski to argue that the abortion law violated the rights of the fetus. Other cases allowed people to argue that they should be able to see the film *Last Tango in Paris* and to challenge welfare cutbacks. These cases, however, show that public interest standing, like intervenor status, is open to all comers and not restricted to the politically correct or left-leaning elites. Should the Court cut back on public interest standing? It already hears very few cases brought on that basis. To deny standing in such cases would amount to an implicit and adverse ruling on the merits. To tell a politician that he could not challenge the constitutionality of official bilingualism would really mean that no one could challenge that policy.

In any event, the Court's receptiveness to public interest standing should not be overestimated. The Court will generally allow public interest standing only if there is no one else more directly affected by the law who can bring the claim. In 1992 the Court had little trouble kicking the Canadian Council of Churches out of court when it attempted to challenge new procedures for determining refugee status under the *Charter*.[3] The Court stressed that individual refugee claimants were more directly affected by the law and, if and when these people challenged the law, the Council might be granted intervenor status. This denial of public interest standing prevented the Court from making a quick and comprehensive decision on the many *Charter* issues arising from the new legislation. It also forced individual refugee applicants, who often did not have funds and found themselves in urgent and dire circumstances, to litigate complex *Charter* issues through confusing and complicated levels of administrative and judicial review. Many of the issues raised by the Council of Churches are still trickling through the system and refugee applicants have had some difficulty raising all the issues that the Council was prepared to argue. Procedural rulings such as the denial of public interest standing affect the substance of the law. Those who urge the Court to return to a procedurally conservative approach should own up to the substantive implications of their recommendations.

The Conservative and Governmental Wings of the Court Party

The idea that some people have disproportionate access to decision makers has always inspired populist resentment. University of Calgary political scientists Ted Morton and Rainer Knopff have made headlines and drawn a rebuttal from Chief Justice McLachlin with their arguments that there is a "Court Party" of postmaterialist elites on the left that have disproportionate access to and influence on the court. There are problems with this thesis, given that the so-called Court Party is not a party, but is bitterly divided on some issues, and that many of the groups classified as members of the Court Party do not rely on the Court for their power. In addition, the Court Party, if it exists, has some conservative members, including the pro-life groups that intervene in abortion cases, the non-Aboriginal fishers that intervene in Aboriginal rights cases, and the attorneys general who can all intervene as of right in constitutional cases. Morton and Knopff's neglect of the governmental and conservative wings of the so-called Court Party suggest that they are most concerned about progressive, as opposed to conservative, groups participating in *Charter* litigation.

The real repeat players who have an advantage in *Charter* litigation are the governments. They have many expert and talented lawyers on salary to defend themselves in *Charter* litigation and they can hire experts and outside counsel if necessary. Public interest groups in

Canada rely on lawyers volunteering their time or the success of applications for legal aid. They intervene in cases often because they do not have the resources to finance a case through all the stages from trial to appeal. Governments retain the ability to quick-start *Charter* litigation by directing a reference to an appeal court or even the Supreme Court. They need not establish standing or even facts to support their case. Public interest groups must do both. Governments must also receive notice and a right to participate whenever anyone challenges a law under the *Charter*. Once a constitutional question is set in the Supreme Court, all the attorneys general have an automatic right of intervention. Governments represent the first eight of the top ten list of intervenors in *Charter* cases before the Supreme Court. The top two intervenors are the attorneys general of Canada and of Quebec, with 126 and 106 interventions apiece from 1984 to 1999. The feminist Legal Education and Action Fund (LEAF) and the Canadian Civil Liberties Association (CCLA), the mighty titans of the Court Party, come in ninth and tenth, with a comparatively modest nineteen and eighteen interventions each. And, in a number of those cases, they cancelled each other out because they were on opposite sides![4] Without public interest intervention, there would be a serious risk of governments dominating constitutional arguments before the Court.

It is a mistake to think that non-governmental groups are always on the side of the person claiming that *Charter* rights have been violated; in almost a third of cases they oppose the rights claims. Wherever possible, the Court has heard from intervenors on both sides of the issue. Both pro-choice and pro-life groups were well represented in the fetal and abortion rights cases of *Borowski* and *Daigle* cases. Anti-feminist groups, religious groups, the police, and non-Aboriginal fishing interests have all been intervenors in *Charter* cases, in addition to the civil libertarians, feminists, and minorities that are associated with the Court Party. Morton and Knopff note with dismay that there were twenty-two intervenors in the Court's first Aboriginal fishing rights case under the 1982 Constitution. In a startling omission that does little credit to their Court Party thesis, they fail to note that interventions by the Assembly of First Nations in support of the Aboriginal accused were more than balanced by interventions by fourteen intervenors representing non-Aboriginal fishing interests (represented by three lawyers with their fifteen minutes each), as well as interventions by the attorneys generals of Ontario, Quebec, British Columbia, Saskatchewan, Alberta, and Newfoundland.[5] In this case, the non-materialist elite - if that is what you must call our First Peoples — was more than countered by those representing the economic interests of other resource users, as well as the public interest represented by seven governments.

As a person who sometimes volunteers my time to represent intervenors before the Court, I would like to think they have some impact. Nevertheless, the evidence does not support extravagant claims about intervenor influence. During the formative early years of the *Charter*, when the Court was the most receptive to *Charter* cases, it actually took a restrictive approach to granting intervenor status to public interest groups.[6] As the Court has heard more intervenors, it has become more stingy in handing out *Charter* victories. Intervenor status generally means being able to submit twenty pages of written argument and fifteen minutes of oral argument before the Court, while the parties generally have forty pages and an hour to make their case. Intervenors can refer to academic articles and other studies, but are bound by the evidence put in by the parties and the constitutional questions set by the Court. Intervenors represent interests that one way or the other will be affected by the Court's decision, and their participation can often increase the quality and legitimacy of the Court's decisions. They allow the Court to be informed, within the discipline of the adversarial system, of the social implications of their judgments. Governments represent one perspective on the public interest, but in a pluralist democracy devoted to self-criticism, this view needs to be balanced by those of non-governmental groups. It is better for the Court to hear from affected interests in an even-handed manner that is subject to adversarial challenge than simply to rely on the Court's own impressions or research or pretend that the cases affect only the immediate parties to the dispute. Conservative groups have as much opportunity to intervene in Court cases as the groups associated with the Court Party. Moreover, governments have an automatic right to intervene in constitutional cases. Governments are the real repeat players who have an advantage in *Charter* litigation.

Process and Substance: Passive Virtues and Constitutional Minimalism

One of the concerns expressed about intervenors is that they will force the Court to deal with issues that are not strictly necessary to decide the case. Intervenors face a dilemma. To get intervenor status, you must establish that you will represent a perspective that would not be represented by the parties, but you will be criticized and perhaps even penalized with costs if you broaden the issues beyond the legitimate purview of the case, as defined by the parties. Intervenors can expose the Court to perspectives beyond those of the immediate parties, but there are limits to how far they can broaden the actual case before the Court.

The idea that the Court should avoid or minimize constitutional judgment has its origins in attempts to limit the dangers of judicial supremacy under the American *Bill of Rights*.[7] It was precisely because the constitutional judgments of the United States Supreme Court were so final and could not be subject to legislative reply that commentators urged that Court to practise the passive virtues of avoiding constitutional judgments and the constitutional minimalism of deciding one case at a time, based on the narrowest grounds possible. Given the ability of Canadian governments to reply to *Charter* judgments under sections 1 and 33, there may be less of a case for such a restrictive approach to constitutional decision making under the *Charter*. The Court can enhance democracy not by avoiding or minimizing constitutional judgment, but by defining broad principles, which can then be subject to limitation by ordinary legislation when required in particular contexts. In any event, it is not clear that the Court can minimize constitutional judgment without minimizing constitutional rights.

In the early years of the *Charter*, the Supreme Court made some decisions it could have ducked. Take the case of Edward Dewey Smith. Mr. Smith was a twenty-seven year old with prior convictions who returned from Bolivia with over $100,000 in cocaine. Applying the seven-year mandatory minimum sentence for importing narcotics to Mr. Smith would not have raised *Charter* concerns about grossly disproportionate punishment. Nevertheless, the Supreme Court used Mr. Smith's 1987 case to strike down the seven-year mandatory minimum sentence for importing narcotics as cruel and unusual punishment on the basis that the mandatory minimum sentence would be grossly unfair if applied to small-time offenders, such as a teenager bringing a joint of marijuana back from spring break.[8] The American courts would never have decided the case on a hypothetical example and would have seen seven years as a light sentence for importing drugs. Can the Court's bold, broad, and even brassy decision be defended? In my view, it can. Prosecutors might never have charged the teenager with importing, but they might have threatened to do so. Moreover, it was a virtual certainty that the mandatory minimum sentence would do injustice to some small-time importer, and such offenders might not have the will or the resources to take their case all the way to the Supreme Court. Finally, the Court's bold decision did not necessarily constitute the final word. As Justice Lamer indicated, Parliament could have replied to the Court's decision with a new mandatory sentence that would apply only to big-time or second offenders. Even bold judgments that could have been avoided need not be the last word under the *Charter*.

The Court has recently grown much more cautious about striking down mandatory minimum sentences on the basis of their effects on hypothetical offenders. It has upheld a mandatory minimum of four years imprisonment for negligent manslaughter with a firearm and has refused to look at actual cases in which the penalty would have been applied to battered women, Aboriginal offenders, and police offenders who negligently killed people with guns.[9] Similarly, in the Robert Latimer case, the Court examined whether life imprisonment without eligibility for parole for ten years was cruel and unusual when applied to Mr. Latimer, and did not examine even more sympathetic cases where the penalty could be applied when the victim asked for assistance in ending his or her life. Although these decisions can be defended on the basis that the Court should decide only one case at a time, it is a mistake to believe that the Court's more cautious approach has not affected the substance of the law. Constitutional minimalism has gone hand in hand with a minimal approach to the right against cruel and unusual punishment. It culminated in the Court's suggestion in *Latimer* that it was up to the Cabinet to grant Mr. Latimer mercy and "the choice is Parliament's on the use of minimum sentences."[10]

A few weeks after the *Latimer* decision, the Court reverted to the bolder and broader approach that characterized the *Smith* case when it held that the *Charter* was violated when any fugitive was extradited to face the death penalty. The Court could have decided the case more narrowly because the applicants, Glen Burns and Atif Rafay, were Canadian citizens who had mobility rights to stay in and enter Canada. It could have decided the case even more narrowly on the basis that the applicants were not only Canadian but eighteen years at the time of the bloody murder of Rafay's mother, father, and sister. The one-case-at-a-time approach would, however, have begged many questions. No execution of most teenagers, but what about nineteen year olds? No execution of pregnant women, but what about after birth? No execution of those with severe mental disabilities, but what about the less severely disabled? This type of gruesome case-by-case approach is used by American courts in death penalty cases, but was eschewed by the Court on the more principled basis that extradition to face the death penalty was fundamentally unjust, given the dangers of executing the innocent. Even then the Court left itself some wiggle room by noting that this principle might not apply in undefined exceptional circumstances.[11] In the death penalty context, a case-by-case approach would have diluted the rights of fugitives and made the law less clear and less principled.

Constitutional minimalism also provides a particular danger of producing a minimal approach to Aboriginal rights. In its first Aboriginal fishing rights case, the Supreme Court articulated a broad test for what constitutes an Aboriginal right, even though the case had to be sent back for a new trial. Chief Justice Dickson and Justice La Forest recognized that Aboriginal rights should be interpreted to provide "a solid constitutional base upon which subsequent negotiations can take place."[12] A similarly broad approach was taken in the *Delgamuukw* land claims case, with the Court again deciding more than was strictly necessary given that the case had to be sent back for a new trial. The Court again expressed a hope that its judgment would provide a solid constitutional base for negotiations to proceed. Some have argued that "the abstract and generalized nature of the advice that was offered takes the Court into dangerous waters" that makes it difficult to predict future cases and that may require the Court "to revise or reformulate the principles."[13] This may be true, but a broad decision at least gave governments and Aboriginal peoples a framework in which to discuss their claims. After years of expensive litigation, it would have been shocking if the Court had said nothing or little about Aboriginal rights in these cases.

The Court's decision in *Marshall II* may suggest a new attraction to a minimalist approach that not only decides one case at a time but minimizes the ambit of Aboriginal rights. After the Court's decision to hold that Marshall had a treaty right to fish for a moderate livelihood, both Aboriginal and governmental leaders, including the minister of Indian affairs, speculated that the decision might have repercussions on other resources and in other parts of Canada. This type of speculation often follows the Court's decisions, particularly in the area of Aboriginal rights, where the objective of much litigation is to establish rules to influence subsequent negotiations. Land claims and other agreements are about negotiating in the shadow of the law, and uncertainty about the breadth of the Court's decisions is often one of the biggest bargaining chips that Aboriginal people bring to the table. In its second judgment, or postscript to the *Marshall* case, the Court wiped some chips off the table by indicating that its decision did not apply to logging, minerals, or offshore natural resources. The Court did not go so far as to say it applied only to eels and not the lucrative lobster fishery, but it might have. The Court's decision in *Marshall* has been praised as an example of a minimalist approach that is "fact-sensitive and context specific" and leaves "more room for dialogue with the legislature than would a court decision announcing a broad or sweeping new rule of law that went far beyond the facts of the case."[14] In my view, however, it is not necessary under the *Charter* to decide cases narrowly in order to facilitate dialogue between the Court and the legislature. Given the ability to justify limits on Aboriginal rights, dialogue can occur whether the Court makes sweeping or narrow decisions. Governments could justify limits on even broadly defined Aboriginal rights that applied to all natural resources. In many Aboriginal rights cases, the dialogue will be negotiation, and not legislation, and all that *Marshall II* accomplished as a minimalist decision was to diminish the bargaining power of the Mi'kmaq by eliminating any doubt that *Marshall I* did not apply to logging and other resources. The logical extreme of a minimalist approach would be to require Aboriginal people to establish their rights on a species-by-species, acre-by-acre basis. This approach would not facilitate the negotiation of treaties, nor would it be neutral on the merits. A minimalist approach that resolves Aboriginal harvesting rights only one prosecution at a time runs the real danger of rendering such rights so difficult and costly to establish in court that they will be illusory.

A Court committed to minimalism would also be eager to avoid constitutional judgment in its entirety whenever possible. The Court has been criticized for deciding the *M. v. H.* case, even though it was moot because this same-sex couple, one of who had contested the exclusion of lesbian couples from support provisions, had reached a financial settlement before the Supreme Court heard the case.[15] It is quite typical for cases heard by the Supreme Court to be effectively resolved, given the years it can take for a case to get there. The Court often hears criminal cases after the accused has served the sentence and the case is technically moot. One of the famous cases it heard from Quebec in the 1950s was also moot because, by the time the Court heard from the person whose premises were padlocked because she was a suspected communist, her lease had expired. It is difficult to believe that, with the *M. v. H.* case fully prepared for argument in an adversarial fashion and the underlying issues having been litigated for much of the 1990s, the Court should have ducked the issue. Such a course of action would only have delayed the inevitable and would have required another gay couple to go through years of litigation to present the issue to the Court. The fact that the Ontario legislature had decided not to include same-sex partners in 1994 could not stop those partners from bringing *Charter* litigation. A couple-by-couple, statute-by-statute approach also would have risked producing a contest about who, between the disadvantaged group and the government, had the deepest pockets to engage in litigation. Even the conservative Ontario government had the good grace to reply to the Court's decision with an amendment not only to the particular law found by the Court to be unconstitutional but to over sixty other laws involving spousal benefits as well. Governments as well as litigants recognize that the Court and the *Charter* must of necessity deal with issues of broad public importance and application.

There may be a case for avoiding or minimizing judgment when the Court genuinely needs more information and argument than has been presented in the case, but there is also often a need for broad principles that can be refined in further cases. Such principles will help governments and affected parties think through questions of rights that might otherwise be ignored.[16] In these still early days of the *Charter*, judges often need to define broad rules rather than duck issues and decide one case at a time. Litigants, lower courts, and governments legitimately look to the Court for guidance. The consequences of broad and even bold constitutional judgments are not as great in Canada or in other countries with a modern bill of rights as in the United States. The *Charter*, unlike the American *Bill of Rights*, allows the legislature to respond by enacting legislation to be defended in a particular context as a reasonable limit on the right as articulated by the Court.

Gentle, Patient, and Flexible Remedies

Conservative critics of judicial activism are concerned that Canadian judges will engage in remedial activism by ordering detailed decrees, such as those used by American judges, to desegregate public schools and to reform conditions in overcrowded and violent prisons. They argue that courts "no longer just tell policymakers what they may not do but also what they must do."[17] The American experience with remedies is frequently misunderstood, as governments frequently helped negotiate the remedial decree and the Court's seemingly extraordinary powers of supervision were derived from the traditions of courts of equity. In any event, the extent of remedial activism under the *Charter* has been greatly overstated and Canadian judges have been careful to craft gentle, patient, and flexible remedies that do not dictate to governments the exact steps to be taken to remedy a constitutional violation. Even in those cases where we most expect courts to lay down the law and issue final remedies, the courts have often deferred to governments with gentle, patient, and flexible remedies.

The Court's most activist remedial decision remains its decision in the 1985 *Manitoba Language Reference* to require Manitoba to translate its unilingual laws. For almost one hundred years, and despite decisions of the County Court of St. Boniface in 1892, 1909, and 1976 pointing out the constitutional promise of bilingualism won by Louis Riel in 1870, the government of Manitoba enacted and published its laws only in English. The Supreme Court in 1979 even struck down the Manitoba law that required statutes to be enacted only in English. Despite these rulings, the government did not translate its old unilingual statutes. It should be no surprise that, after a government has ignored its constitutional obligation for almost a century, judicial patience will be tested. When the issue of Manitoba's unconstitutional and unilingual statute book finally reached the Supreme Court in 1985, the Court nevertheless proceeded with caution. It resisted simply striking down all the English-only statutes, even though such a drastic remedy could have been justified and would probably have produced a constitutional amendment forgiving the obligation to translate the old laws in exchange for a guarantee of French-language services. The Court was concerned that such a drastic remedy would result in a legislative vacuum and threaten the rule of law. Instead, the Court decided to give the unilingual and unconstitutional laws temporary force. Manitoba was given a generous period of time to translate the laws and, in 1992, the Court was still extending this grace period for a date to be decided by the parties.[18] The end result of the Court's supervision in this case was not very creative; it was simply the bilingual statutes that had been clearly required in the constitution since 1870. Although the case indicates that the Court can take active steps to ensure compliance with the constitution, it also demonstrates a judicial willingness to accept considerable delays by governments in implementing constitutional rights.

The Manitoba case set a precedent for affirmative remedies, but there was no flood of cases. A few lower courts in the 1980s experimented with stronger forms of relief to enforce rights to minority language schools,[19] but the Supreme Court has subsequently demonstrated a strong preference for relying on general declarations, as opposed to detailed injunctions, for enforcing even positive rights. Unlike injunctions, a declaration does not allow a court to retain jurisdiction over the case or to use contempt powers should government officials fail to comply with the law. Chief Justices Dickson, Lamer, and McLachlin have all stressed the virtue of declarations in giving governments flexibility to fashion precise remedies that best respond to local circumstances. They have also expressed faith that governments will respond promptly and in good faith to the Court's general and non-coercive declarations.[20]

The Court has been reluctant to order injunctive relief in *Charter* cases. In the *Eldridge*[21] case, involving the equality right of deaf patients to translation services in hospitals, the Court concluded that the appropriate remedy was a "declaration as opposed to some kind of injunctive relief ... because there are myriad options available to the government that may rectify the unconstitutionality of the current system. It is not this Court's role to dictate how this is to be accomplished." The Court even suspended this general declaration for a six-month period in order to allow the government to explore its options and formulate its reply. Despite evidence of systemic targeting of imports from a gay and lesbian bookstore that had resulted in the seizure and often lengthy detention of books and sexual education material at the border (including material that other bookstores had no trouble importing), the Court, in the *Little Sisters* case,[22] declined to do more than simply declare that the customs legislation had been applied unconstitutionally in the past and that new litigation could be commenced if the customs censors did it again. Three judges in dissent found that, given the systemic problems in the past, declaratory relief was not sufficient. Even the dissenters did not propose judicial supervision of custom officials who had such trouble applying legal standards of obscenity, but rather giving Parliament the opportunity to devise a better procedure for determining whether material being imported was obscene. The dissenters recognized that Parliament had a range of response options, including the creation of a new specialized administrative tribunal or relying on criminal prosecutions once the obscene material was received in Canada. Canadian courts have not been eager to duplicate the American experience with "remedial decrees"[23] and have relied on the gentler and less coercive remedy of declarations.

The charge that Canadian courts have engaged in American-style remedial activism is singularly unpersuasive. The judges' remedy of choice in Canada is the declaration of constitutional entitlement that defers to governments to fashion the precise remedy that is required in the particular situation. Even in extraordinary cases such as the *Manitoba Language Reference*, the Court often sanctions delay and defers to the legislature on the details and timing of the precise remedy.

Conclusion

Although the Supreme Court has made changes to account for its new role under the *Charter*, it still remains a court of law - and often a costly one at that. Affected interests must attach themselves to an actual case that has been litigated at great expense to the parties. Public interest standing is generally only available when there is no one more directly affected to make the constitutional argument and when a denial of standing would amount to an implicit denial of the merits of the claim sought to be made. The Court has been willing to hear from intervenors, but they include governments and conservative groups, as well as the left-leaning groups associated with the Court Party. In the early years of the *Charter* especially, the Court articulated broad rules that were not strictly necessary to decide the case. The Court is expected by governments, as well as litigants and other judges, to provide guidance beyond the particular case. There are some signs that the Court may be retrenching and taking a more minimalist approach that decides one case at a time. This more conservative approach, however, cannot be defended on grounds of procedural purity and neutrality. A minimalist approach to deciding cruel and unusual punishment and Aboriginal rights cases may actually go hand in hand with a minimalist definition of those important rights. This trend is unfortunate, because legislatures can respond to even bold and broad judicial rulings by justifying limitations on rights. In chapters 9 and 10 we will examine, first, the limitations that legislatures can place on rights and, second, the way that legislatures have replied to Court decisions.

Chapter 9
Judicial Acceptance of Limits on Rights

Many people probably nodded with agreement when they read Justice Bastarache's comments that the Court "was maybe seen as being unduly favourable to the native position in all cases, and that it sort of has an agenda for extending these rights, and that it has no concern for the rights of others ... you have fishermen who are not very wealthy and whose rights might have been [perceived to have been] overridden by the rights of natives too easily by the court."[1] People tend to think of courts as a place where rights trump over all other interests. If judges decide what constitutes a right and if rights are absolute, then the Court will override competing rights and interests. And there are examples of cases in which the Supreme Court has appeared to be oblivious to competing rights. How else can you explain its decisions to strike down restrictions on Sunday shopping, tobacco advertising, and some of its more controversial decisions recognizing the rights of the accused and of Aboriginal people?

Critics of judicial activism fear that judges will impose absolute rights on society without regard to competing rights and social interests. Conservative critics tend to worry about the inflation of rights, group rights and the rights of the accused. They fear that legalistic and absolute rights talk will make it difficult, if not impossible, to accept the compromises that are often necessary in a functioning and civil democracy. Progressive critics worry that judges will impose a liberal and individualistic view of rights that conceives of the state as the enemy, a view that leaves little room for the promotion of a sense of social responsibility and duty. Much of the anxiety about judicially enforced rights comes from the common opinion that rights are absolute "trumps." The First Amendment of the American *Bill of Rights* supports this absolutist view of rights when it declares that Congress shall make *no* law abridging freedom of speech.

As I suggest throughout this book, however, the *Canadian Charter of Rights and Freedoms* is fundamentally different from the American *Bill of Rights*. Instead of the First Amendment, we have a more modest section 1, which provides that the *Charter* "guarantees the rights and freedoms set out in it," but subject "to such reasonable limits prescribed by law as can be demonstrably justified in a free and democratic society." This approach draws on the modern experience of allowing necessary and proportional limits on many rights, but generalizes it by allowing courts to accept limits on every right for a broad range of reasons. If a good idea gets copied, section 1 is a good idea. It has been duplicated in recent bill of rights in New Zealand, Israel, and South Africa, and the Supreme Court of Canada has invented a process of justifying limitations on Aboriginal and treaty rights even though section 1 does not apply to those rights. Critics of judicial activism in Canada must come to grips with the brooding omnipresence that the limitation provision casts on constitutional rights. It will not do to pretend that this is America, where once a court has defined a right it is often absolute and final. Cries that my rights have been violated play better on the nightly news than in Canadian courts. In court, judges will ask whether the government had a good reason for violating rights.

Section 1 of the *Charter* does not mean that the Court accepts all limits on rights. The legislature must articulate its desire to limit rights, so unelected officials such as police officers, for example, cannot take it on themselves to limit rights without statutory authorization. The requirement that the legislature make clear statements when it intends to limit rights follows common law traditions and enhances democracy. It requires candour and, ideally, legislative and public debate about the limits placed on rights. In addition, governments also must justify limitations on rights by showing that they were aimed at an important objective, that the limitation advances that objective, that there were not other less drastic but reasonable alternatives to advance the objective, and that the overall benefit of the limitation in advancing the objective outweighs the costs of infringing the right. The ability of governments to justify laws that violate rights under section 1 of the *Charter* promotes a dialogue between courts and legislatures, with the courts asking why rights need to be violated, and the legislature explaining why. Section 1, not section 33, is the true engine of dialogue under the *Charter*.

Sunday Shopping

Much about the role and evolution of section 1 of the *Charter* can be understood by recalling a time, one that seems increasing distant and quaint, in which there was controversy over whether people could shop on Sunday. Today, most of us are happy to find any time in our hectic lives to buy groceries and other necessities, let alone worry about the religious significance of Sunday or whether Sunday shopping will disrupt a common rest day to be shared with families and friends.

The first challenge to Sunday closing laws was brought by a Calgary drug store, Big M Drug Mart, which was charged under the federal *Lord's Day Act* for selling groceries on Sunday. As its name implied, this Act was old legislation enacted by Parliament in 1906 after the courts had ruled that the provinces could not require Sunday closing because only the federal government had the power to enforce morality under the criminal law. The Supreme Court struck down the federal *Lord's Day Act* as a violation of freedom of religion that could not be justified under section 1 of the *Charter*. This case was the high-water mark of the Court's early activism; one which minimized the ability of governments to justify limitations on rights under section 1 of the *Charter*.[2] Yet even this case left plenty of room for legislatures to place limitations on rights, provided that those limitations were not designed to abolish or cast aside the right in question.

In holding that the *Lord's Day Act* was not a reasonable limit on religious freedom, Chief Justice Dickson warned that "not every government interest or policy objective is entitled to s. 1 consideration." He dismissed the argument that Sunday closing laws were justified because "the choice of the day of rest adhered to by the Christian majority is the most practical." This reasoning was "really no more than an argument of convenience and expediency and is fundamentally repugnant because it would justify the law upon the very basis upon which it is attacked for violating" the *Charter*. Because the *Lord's Day Act* had been enacted for religious purposes, it was akin to the imposition of a state religion. "The theological content of the legislation remains as a subtle and constant reminder to religious minorities within the country of their differences with, and alienation from, the dominant religious culture ... The Charter safeguards religious minorities from the threat of the 'tyranny of the majority.'" The Chief Justice, who was active in the Anglican Church, tried to walk in the shoes of religious minorities by stating: "If I am a Jew or a Sabbatarian or a Muslim, the practice of my religion at least implies my right to work on a Sunday if I wish. It seems to me that any law purely religious in purpose, must surely infringe my religious freedoms."[3] The Court could not accept limitations on rights that were premised on the rejection of the very values of the right.

Big M Drug Mart indicates that courts will not allow legislatures to use section 1 of the *Charter* to enact legislation that simply disagrees with the purpose of the right. If Parliament really wanted to demand observance of a state religion, it would have to invoke the notwithstanding clause. In the vast majority of cases, however — one study pegs the governmental success rate at 97 per cent[4] — the Court accepts without serious question the legitimacy of the government objective in limiting rights and goes on to focus on the means used to advance its objectives. Even with respect to Sunday closing laws, Chief Justice Dickson made it clear that they could be justified as a reasonable limit of freedom of religion if they were enacted for a secular purpose, such as providing a common family day of rest, that did not reject the freedom and equality of all religions.

Twelve years later in the *Vriend* case, the Supreme Court returned to the idea that the negation of rights was an improper purpose to justify a limitation under section 1. When Delwin Vriend was asked about his sexual orientation, he told. After informing his employer, a private school, that he was gay, Mr. Vriend was fired. Because Alberta was one of the few provinces that did not provide protection in its human rights code against employment discrimination on the basis of sexual orientation, Vriend was out of luck unless he could convince the courts that the Alberta human rights code was unconstitutional. The Court held that Alberta could not justify its refusal to include sexual orientation in its human rights code for any reason that was consistent with equality. The Court rejected arguments that the exclusion of sexual orientation was necessary for reasons of morality, to respond to objections from the majority, or to take an incremental approach to recognizing the rights of unpopular groups. Although these factors may explain why sexual orientation was omitted, they were not pressing and substantial objectives that could possibly justify the violation of the minority's equality rights under section 1 of the *Charter*. Because the exclusion of protection against discrimination on the basis of sexual orientation was "the very antithesis of the principles embodied in the legislation as a whole" (which, like the equality rights in the *Charter*, was concerned with the equal dignity of all persons), there was no pressing objective to justify limiting the equality rights of gays and lesbians. The Court's decision in *Vriend* left Alberta with the drastic options of using the override or repealing its entire human right code. As we will discuss in chapter 10, legislatures typically have a much broader range of less drastic options in formulating replies to the Court's decisions because of their ability to clarify and refine the terms of the debate over justification under section 1 of the *Charter*. Already legislatures have employed a variety of means to respond to the Court's *M. v. H.* decision that gay couples should have the same benefits as heterosexual couples. Cases such as *Big M* and *Vriend* are the exception rather than the rule in holding that a narrow range of government purposes are illegitimate reasons for limiting rights. Nevertheless, they are necessary if legislatures are not to be allowed to abolish the rights of unpopular minorities simply because these lawmakers are opposed to such rights.

The fact that the 1985 *Big M Drug Mart* decision did not prevent provincial legislatures from justifying Sunday as a common day of rest was affirmed when, a year later, the Court upheld an Ontario law requiring stores to close on Sundays. The law had been challenged by both Edwards Books and Nortown Foods. Edwards Books simply wanted to be open on another day of the week in order to sell more books and newspapers, but Nortown Foods closed on Saturday and served a predominantly Jewish clientele. The Ontario legislature had made some allowance for stores that closed on Saturday, but only for small operations with seven or fewer employees. Nortown Foods was too large an operation to qualify for the statutory exemption. The Court recognized that Sunday closing laws still imposed disadvantages on retailers and consumers who observed Saturday as their Sabbath. Nevertheless, a conclusion that the rights of the minority were violated did not end the matter. Chief Justice Dickson recognized that the objective of providing a common rest and family day was important enough to justify limiting *Charter* rights. The crucial question was whether the Ontario legislation violated the rights of Saturday observers as little as possible. A mechanical approach that invalidated the law on the basis of any other less restrictive alternative would have led to the invalidation of the Ontario law, since some other provinces had devised a more liberal exemption policy that allowed all stores closed on Saturday, even bigger stores like Nortown Foods, to open on Sunday. Chief Justice Dickson for the Court found, however, that the Ontario exemption policy was reasonable. The requirement that large stores close on Sunday was designed to give mainly un-unionized and female retail workers the benefit of a rest day. In an oft-quoted phrase, he stressed that the "the courts must be cautious to ensure that the Charter does not simply become an instrument of better situated individuals to roll back legislation which has as its object the improvement of the condition of less advantaged persons. When the interests of more than seven vulnerable employees in securing a Sunday holiday are weighed against the interests of their employer in transacting business on a Sunday, I cannot fault the Legislature for determining that the protection of the employees ought to prevail."[5] This decision was a response to those on the left who had criticized the Court for assuming that the recognition of rights was a costless enterprise.[6] The Court now recognized that maximizing rights in some contexts could invalidate legislation that assisted the disadvantaged and run the risk of duplicating the American experience of the *Lochner* era in which the United States Supreme Court had struck down much economic regulation designed to assist workers.

Justice La Forest was prepared to take an even more deferential approach that would not require the legislature even to attempt to accommodate stores that, because of religious beliefs, closed on Saturday. He argued that what was reasonable depended on the context, and the legislature "must be given reasonable room to manoeuvre to meet these conflicting pressures." Like the left critics of the *Charter*, he recognized that "attempts to protect the rights of one group will also inevitably impose burdens on the rights of other groups. There is no perfect scenario in which the rights of all can be equally protected."

Only Justice Wilson would have struck the Ontario law down. Relying on Ronald Dworkin's theory of rights as trumps, she argued that the Ontario exemption was an unprincipled "checkerboard" compromise that "did not go far enough," because it protected only the religious freedom of small retailers.[7]

Given how critics of judicial activism on both the left and the right would have attacked the Court for following Justice Wilson's approach and invalidating Sunday closing laws, it is ironic that it was the Ontario legislature that opened the door to wide-open Sunday shopping. Soon after *Edwards Books*, the legislature broadened the exemption that the Court had upheld under section 1 so that large stores such as Nortown Foods could open on Sundays and downloaded the issue of wide-open Sunday shopping to the municipalities. This move resulted in "the spectacle in Ontario of a court decision upholding the law, followed by the government acting to repeal it, handing the question over to the municipalities and, via them, to the marketplace." Eventually, the market won. In 1992 a social democrat government in Ontario opted for province-wide Sunday shopping, claiming the need to "respect the choice of consumers" and its inability to "put up a wall up around Ontario."[8] As with many things under the *Charter*, the Court did not have the last word. Now we can shop (and the less advantaged of us be required to work) on Sunday. The reason, however, has more to do with the market than the *Charter* and the Court.

Increasing Deference towards Legislative Limitations on Rights

Edwards Books indicated as early as 1986 that the Court was reluctant to "substitute judicial opinions for legislative ones at which to draw a precise line," at least on social policy issues such as Sunday shopping. The issue was no longer defined as whether the legislature had impaired the right as little as possible, but whether it had impaired the right "as little as *reasonably* possible."[9] Three years later the Court elaborated on the rationale for this increased margin of deference accorded to legislatures in rejecting an attempt by Irwin Toy to strike down a Quebec law that prohibited all advertising directed at children under the age of thirteen. Relying on *Edwards Books*, the Court drew a distinction between, on the one hand, deferring to legislatures when they acted to protect vulnerable groups and allocated "scarce government resources" and, on the other, insisting on the least drastic means when the state acted as "the singular antagonist of the individual whose right was infringed." In the former case, the Court would require the government to have only "a reasonable basis, on the evidence tendered, for concluding that the ban on all advertising directed at children impaired freedom of expression as little as possible given the government's pressing and substantial objective." The Courts would not demand "absolute certainty" in the social science evidence or "require legislatures to choose the least ambitious means to protect vulnerable groups."[10] The Court allowed Quebec to prohibit advertising aimed at all children, even though there was some evidence that the greatest danger of manipulation was with children seven years of age and under. In other words, it deferred not only to the legislature's choice of ends but also to its choice of means.

The *Irwin Toy* distinction between stricter and more deferential forms of section 1 scrutiny was widely perceived as allowing governments increased latitude in resolving controversial and contentious matters of social policy, as opposed to matters of criminal law and procedural protections that were within the traditional domain of the judiciary.[11] For example, it figured prominently the next year when the majority of the Court rejected the claims of university professors that the requirement that they retire at the age of sixty-five constituted unjustified age discrimination. Justice La Forest, who had long campaigned, often alone and in dissent,[12] for a more deferential and flexible approach to section 1 of the *Charter*, now wrote for the majority of the Court. He warned against a "mechanistic" approach to section 1 and suggested that "where government seeks to mediate between competing groups," in this case the professors forced to retire and the young people who could fill their positions, "it is by no means easy to determine with precision where the balance is to be struck." Unlike in criminal cases, where the Court could know with some certainty what the least drastic means was to achieve the objective, mandatory retirement involved the "polycentric" task of allocating scarce resources, in this case positions at universities. Courts should not second-guess how legislatures made these difficult choices.[13] It is clear from these cases that the Court recognized that maximizing rights was not a costless or precise exercise and was prepared to defer to the legislatures' reasonable allocation of resources and choice of means.

A more recent and oft-criticized case may at first glance suggest that the Court has abandoned its increased deference. In *RJR-MacDonald* the Court, in a 5 to 4 decision, held that the government had not justified an absolute restriction on tobacco advertising or the requirement that unattributed health warnings be placed on cigarette packs. In his dissent, Justice La Forest relied heavily on the *Irwin Toy* idea that the Court should defer to the legislature because the judiciary was not a specialist in policy making, as opposed to protecting liberty and fairness in the criminal law. Citing insider documents from the tobacco companies, he was appalled by the millions of dollars that tobacco companies spend on advertising in their attempts to reassure existing smokers and attract new smokers, primarily among the young, by associating smoking with "glamour, affluence, youthfulness and vitality." His condemnation of the tobacco industry, advertising, and the enormous health costs of smoking is powerful. At the same time, his decision optimistically presumes that the government's measures will decrease smoking. It does not really require the government to demonstrate that less drastic means of restricting expression will not advance these important and laudable objectives of discouraging smoking.

Justice La Forest may be right on this particular issue, but the majority's decision striking down the tobacco advertising restrictions did not mark the abandonment of the more deferential approach.[14] Justice McLachlin for the majority of the Court agreed with Justice La Forest that "the context, deference and a flexible and realistic standard of proof are essential aspects of the s. 1 analysis," but stressed that these factors did not relieve the state of "the burden the Charter imposes of demonstrating that the limits imposed on our constitutional rights and freedoms are reasonable and justifiable in a free and democratic society."[15] In other words, whatever the temptation, the justices could not throw the tobacco companies out of court because smoking is bad and they are evil. Consistent with *Edwards Books* and *Irwin Toy*, the majority of the Court was prepared to accept that "the tailoring process seldom admits of perfection and the courts must accord some leeway to the legislator. If the law falls within a range of reasonable alternatives, the courts will not find it overbroad merely because they can conceive of an alternative which might better tailor objective to infringement." In rejecting the trial judge's finding that there was no rational connection between advertising bans and decreased smoking, the Court was also prepared to accept that restrictions on tobacco advertising could serve the end of decreasing consumption, even though there was no scientific evidence of a causal connection.

What the Court could not accept, however, was the complete failure of the government "to explain why a significantly less intrusive and equally effective measure was not chosen."[16] Both Justices McLachlin and Iacobucci were appalled by their belief that the government had refused to disclose to the Court its own studies on the effectiveness of less than total bans on advertising. Justice Iacobucci, a former deputy attorney general of Canada, expressed concern that "the Attorney General of Canada chose to withhold from the factual record evidence related to the options it has considered as alternatives of the total ban it chose to put in place ... Perhaps proof exists for such a ban, but in my view the record does not establish it." In other words, the Court thought that the government, which "should remain non-adversarial and make full disclosure," was hiding evidence in a manner usually associated with the tobacco companies! If the government had been more forthcoming, it is quite possible that the Court would have upheld the advertising ban. The government has the onus of proof under section 1 and, if it has a bad day in court, the Court may strike down legislation that could have been saved by a better defence.

Given the majority's negative reaction to the government's conduct in this case, it is not surprising that the Court concluded that the government had not established that less intrusive restrictions, such as banning only lifestyle as opposed to brand preference advertising or having attributed as opposed to unattributed health warnings, would not advance its important objectives. These less restrictive provisions were quickly adopted by Parliament. They may represent judicial distortion of Parliament's policy, but, as we will see in chapter 10, Parliament could have replied to the Court's perhaps erroneous decision in a stronger fashion. It can only be hoped that this legislation, as well as new requirements for pictures of diseased lungs, hearts, and gums to be placed on cigarette packages, will stem the epidemic of smoking in youth and the resulting cancer in our aging population. At the same time, if we are honest with ourselves, we must admit that the legislation that was struck down was not the magic bullet that would rid us of the tragic blight of tobacco on our society.

Limiting the Rights of the Accused

The increased deference to the legislature on issues such as advertising and mandatory retirement would not have meant as much had the Court continued to insist on a strict section 1 test in criminal law cases, which make up the bulk of all *Charter* litigation. In its most famous section 1 case, the Court had taken a rigorous approach to deciding whether the government could justify restrictions on the presumption of innocence — a traditional fixture that, well before the *Charter*, was celebrated as "the golden thread" of criminal law. The Court held that a law that required anyone found with drugs to prove that they did not intend to traffic in the drugs was an unreasonable limit on the presumption of innocence. The government's objective in attempting to curb drug trafficking was important, but it was irrational to presume that someone with a small amount of drugs was a drug trafficker. Whenever the accused was required to prove something to escape a conviction, there was the less restrictive alternative of giving the accused the benefit of any reasonable doubt.[17] In subsequent cases, however, the presumption of innocence was honoured in its breach as the Court repeatedly held that the government had justified the need to violate the much celebrated golden thread of criminal law in order to control guns and the harms of drunk driving, hate speech, and pimping. Parliament was entitled to presume that anyone habitually in the company of a prostitute was a pimp living off the earnings of prostitution, even though, as noted in dissent, "spouses, lovers, children, parents, room-mates, business associates, providers of goods and services" may all be caught by a presumption that was as wide and irrational as presuming that everyone who had any amount of drugs was a drug trafficker.[18] The distinction between criminal law, which required a strict standard of justification, and social policy, which required more judicial deference, quickly became blurred.

Relying on the social policy cases of *Edwards Books* and *Irwin Toy*, the Court in 1990 upheld a violation of the presumption of innocence that required two young offenders accused of murder to prove that they had the insanity defence, rather than give them the benefit of a reasonable doubt about their sanity. Chief Justice Lamer concluded that Parliament was not required "to roll the dice" and select "the absolutely least intrusive means of meeting its objective," but only to select "from a range of means which impair the presumption of innocence as little as reasonably possible."[19] Only Justice Wilson in dissent focused on the fact that the state was the singular antagonist of the accused, that there was no evidence of a problem with faked insanity pleas, and that many other jurisdictions had the less restrictive alternative of giving the accused the benefit of a reasonable doubt about the insanity defence. Even in the traditional criminal law context, the Court was prepared to defer to Parliament's decisions that the life of prosecutors would be easier if the presumption of innocence was violated.

In the same year the Court again applied the more deferential social policy approach to uphold a restrictive 1985 law that prohibited any public solicitation for the purpose of prostitution. The law itself was a direct response to pre-*Charter* decisions of the Court that had gutted the old law by holding that only "pressing and persistent solicitation" constituted a nuisance that warranted the criminal sanction.[20] Both civil liberties and feminist groups opposed the law, as did a group of prostitutes given intervenor status and represented by Professor Joe Magnet, a former clerk at the Court. The Court Party thesis would thus suggest that the Court should quickly strike down the new soliciting offence. Nevertheless the Court upheld the law and was more deferential to Parliament's efforts to criminalize street prostitution under the *Charter* than before the *Charter*. Chief Justice Dickson stressed that the legislation did not have to be perfect or the least restrictive scheme that could be imagined by the Court to be justified under section 1. Justice Lamer held that the legislation was also justified as a response to the social problems of prostitution, including the victimization and subordination of women and children. He would not "second-guess the wisdom of policy choices made by our legislators" on "contentious" and "morally laden" issues such as prostitution. He also indicated that the courts should avoid the dangers of *Lochner* and not constitutionalize the right of prostitutes to work, even though prostitution itself was perfectly legal. In their dissent, Justices Wilson and L'Heureux-Dubé were concerned, as the entire Court had been before the *Charter*, about the dangers of an overbroad law that would criminalize solicitation — including the "proverbial nod or wink" [21] — which would not result in a public nuisance. Nevertheless, deference was spreading like wild fire to the criminal law, and the majority of the Court in this criminal case was more deferential to Parliament than it had been before the *Charter*.

The Court was prepared not only to defer to Parliament in criminal law cases but also to recognize that some criminal laws involved the claims of competing groups. The players in these new political cases were not only the state and the accused but crime victims and potential crime victims, including women and children. Feminist groups such as the Legal Education and Action Fund (LEAF) most often intervened on the side of the state in criminal cases. In some cases the Court recognized the need for "multifaceted considerations such as the rights of witnesses, in this case children, the rights of the accused and the court's duties to ascertain the truth,"[22] while in other sexual assault cases, such as its decision to strike down the "rape shield" law and to invent a defence of extreme intoxication to sexual assault, it still applied the less deferential standard of seeing criminal cases as a matter in which the state was the singular antagonist of the accused. As we will see in chapter 14, Parliament quickly intervened in the latter cases to reaffirm the importance of the rights of sexual assault victims, women, and children as potential victims of sexual assault. Legislative activism in proclaiming victims' rights has had an impact on the Court, which is now prepared to recognize competing *Charter* rights in criminal cases. It no longer gives an automatic preference to the accused's right to a fair trial, but instead attempts to reconcile that right with the rights of victims to the greatest extent possible.[23] It will "adopt a posture of respect"[24] towards Parliament's attempt to reconcile the competing rights of the accused to a fair trial with the equality and privacy rights of complainants. This relational definition of rights must in difficult cases impose some limitations on the accused's rights. Nevertheless, all this balancing of competing rights takes place outside section 1, under which the government is assigned the burden of establishing that limitations on the accused's rights are prescribed in democratically enacted laws and are justified as reasonable and proportionate limits on rights.

The fiction that a stricter level of scrutiny would be applied in criminal cases was lifted when Justice McLachlin, who had initially resisted the more deferential turn in criminal law, hinted that distinctions between cases that were a "contest between the individual and the state" and cases where greater deference was required to the legislature's reconciliation of "competing rights between different sections of society ... may not always be easy to apply." She went on to suggest that although "the criminal law is generally seen as involving a contest between the state and the accused ... it also involves the allocation of priorities between the accused and the victim, actual or potential."[25] Given that most *Charter* cases arise in the criminal law context and that Parliament has been active in enacting various victims' rights measures, this statement is a significant extension of the Court's increased deference to legislative limitation of rights.

Limiting Freedom of Expression

The Court's increased deference to Parliament's attempts to use the criminal law to protect victims, as well as the differences between the *Charter* and the American *Bill of Rights*, are well illustrated in a series of cases in which the Court upheld crimes based on the content of expression. The First Amendment provides an absolute prohibition on the abridgement of speech, whereas the *Charter* allows reasonable limits as are demonstrably justified in a free and democratic society. The American approach is not completely absolute — obscenity, including child pornography, and fighting words are deemed, however irrationally, not to be speech. At the same time, the United States Supreme Court takes a very hard line against any attempts to regulate the content of speech. Under the *Charter*, the Canadian Court has defined expression more broadly but been much more willing to accept content regulation of speech.

James Keegstra, a former mayor and high school teacher in Eckville, Alberta, was prosecuted under the *Criminal Code* for wilfully promoting hatred against Jews for his theories of a Jewish conspiracy behind depressions, wars, and revolutions. The Alberta Court of Appeal took an American-style approach to freedom of speech and held that speech could not be prohibited because there was no clear and present danger that anyone would act on Keegstra's hateful teachings. In a case in which white youths had burned a cross on the lawn of an African American family, the United States Supreme Court had gone so far as to strike down a law that punished acts designed to insult on the basis of race, colour, creed, religion, or gender as an unconstitutional regulation of the content of speech.[26] The Canadian Supreme Court took a very different approach and stressed that it was precisely because of the hateful content of the speech that Parliament was entitled to prohibit it. Chief Justice Dickson stressed the psychological harm, humiliation, degradation, and risk of violence that hate speech could cause to target groups. Even Justice McLachlin, who would have struck the law down, rejected the "clear and present danger" approach because "to view hate propaganda as 'victimless' in the absence of any proof that it moved its listeners to hatred is to discount the wrenching impact that it may have on members of the target group themselves. For Jews ... statements such as Keegstra's raise very real fears of history repeating itself."[27]

The Court Party was split on this issue, with the majority of the Court following arguments by LEAF and Jewish groups in favour of the law, and the minority following arguments made by civil liberties groups that the law was an overbroad and unnecessary restriction on freedom of expression. The majority adopted LEAF's argument that the offence was supported by equality rights, even though Justice McLachlin argued in dissent that the equality rights in the *Charter* could not apply to the discriminatory teachings of a private citizen, Jim Keegstra. The division on the Court in *Keegstra* disappeared two years later, when the Court unanimously upheld a law against the distribution of obscene material on the basis that the law was a justified response to violent and degrading pornography and child pornography. The law had not been amended since 1959 and it prohibited not only material that combined sex with crime, horror, cruelty, and violence but also the undue exploitation of sex. Nuisance was not an issue, because the video store owner who was prosecuted had posted a sign: "If sex oriented material offends you - please do not enter." Even though the relation between pornography and violence was not clear, the Court deferentially held that Parliament was entitled to its "reasoned apprehension of harm" and could address the "degradation that many women feel as 'victims' of the message of obscenity."[28] The decision has been controversial, but it also indicated the Court's reluctance to strike down criminal laws. Once again, the contrast with the more absolutist American approach to free speech is striking, as the American courts had quickly struck down a law targeting violent, degrading, and dehumanizing pornography as an unconstitutional attempt to regulate the content of speech.[29]

In the recent and controversial case of Robin Sharpe, a British Columbia man charged with the possession and distribution of child pornography, the Court upheld a 1993 law prohibiting the possession of child pornography. The courts in British Columbia had found the offence — prohibiting the possession of any visual representation showing or depicting a person under eighteen years of age engaged in explicit sexual activity or any writings advocating or counseling such sexual activity — was much too broad and invasive of privacy to be upheld in a free society. The Supreme Court disagreed and upheld the broad offence of possession of child pornoraphy. It did create two narrow exceptions in the law for self-created and privately held writings, drawings, and depictions of lawful sexual activity. Nevertheless, it emphatically rejected the idea, accepted by lower courts in British Columbia, that prohibiting the private possession of materials was a "hallmark of tyranny" that could never be justified, or, in American terms, that, "if the First Amendment means anything, it means that a State has no business telling a man, sitting alone in his own house, what books he may read or what films he may watch."[30] Chief Justice McLachlin explicitly rejected the argument "that any Charter right is so absolute that limits on it can never be justified."[31] The existence of section 1 of the *Charter* gives Canadian legislatures much more room to justify limitations on speech than their American counterparts. As we will see, even when section 1 does not apply, the Court has been eager to invent a similar justification process.

Limiting Aboriginal Rights

Aboriginal rights in section 35(1) of the *Constitution Act, 1982* were not granted and guaranteed like *Charter* rights, but were "recognized and affirmed." This terminology acknowledged that they flowed from the fact that Aboriginal people lived as organized societies before Europeans ever came to this country and that many First Nations had signed treaties with the Crown centuries before the *Charter*. When these treaties were signed, no one asserted a clause that the government could justify limits on the often meagre rights in them. The strongest textual basis for an absolute approach to rights is found with respect to Aboriginal and treaty rights, which were not subject to the reasonable limits clause of section 1 of the *Charter*.

In its first case dealing with Aboriginal rights, a prosecution of a member of the Musquem Band for fishing contrary to the terms of a licence, the Supreme Court recognized an ability for governments to limit Aboriginal rights. Chief Justice Dickson and Justice La Forest rejected the argument "that s. 35(1) rights are more securely protected than the rights guaranteed by the Charter." Although recognizing that Aboriginal rights were not subject to section 1 of the *Charter*, they concluded: "[R]ights that are recognized and affirmed are not absolute. Federal legislative powers continue, including, of course, the right to legislate with respect to Indians ... federal power must be reconciled with federal duty and the best way to achieve that reconciliation is to demand the justification of any government regulation that infringes upon or denies aboriginal rights." The Court saw this position as a compromise between two extremes: on the one hand, recognizing absolute rights that would give Aboriginal people "immunity from government regulation in a society that, in the twentieth century, is increasingly more complex, interdependent and sophisticated, and where exhaustible resources need protection and management"[32] and, on the other, a restrictive interpretation of Aboriginal rights which, by incorporating the unfettered power that governments asserted before 1982 to regulate and even extinguish Aboriginal and treaty rights, would make the constitutional recognition of those rights meaningless.

Whatever the merits of allowing governments to place limitations on existing Aboriginal rights that were recognized and affirmed in the 1982 constitutional amendments, the Court's subsequent decision was even more problematic: that the rights in treaties signed hundreds of years before were subject to the same limitation process. The Court recognized that treaties were "analogous to contracts of a very solemn, and special, public nature," but then asserted that, because governments could violate treaties by legislation before 1982, they could justify limits on treaty rights after 1982.[33] The ability of the government to justify limitations on already limited treaty rights, including limitations designed to recognize the interests of non-Aboriginal groups, was again recognized by the Court in its postscript to the *Marshall* case.[34] The judicial invention of a general governmental power to limit all treaty rights has no textual foundation in the text of the treaties or in the *Constitution Act, 1982*. This situation suggests that "activist" decisions that depart from the text of the treaties work not only to the advantage of Aboriginal peoples but also to the Crown. This is not, however, mentioned by conservatives, who criticize the Court for "transforming the treaties" by going beyond their text to include Aboriginal understandings and oral history.[35]

Although the Court in its first section 35 case created an ability for government to limit Aboriginal rights, it also indicated that the government would bear "a heavy burden" in justifying infringements as necessary. First, the limitation would have to be adopted for a "valid legislative objective" that was "compelling and substantial," and not simply "reasonable." The Court rejected the idea that the "public interest" could justify limitations on Aboriginal rights. The vague term "public interest" was simply too broad and too likely to erode Aboriginal rights. Conservation and management of natural resources were valid objectives for limiting Aboriginal rights, in part because these goals were "consistent with aboriginal beliefs and practices, and, indeed with the enhancement of aboriginal rights."[36] Consistent with *Big M Drug Mart*, governments could not limit Aboriginal rights for reasons that were inconsistent with the very existence of such rights.

Following developments under section 1 of the *Charter*, the Court has subsequently retreated from the rigour of its original test for justifying limitations on Aboriginal rights. In a 1996 commercial fishing rights case, the Court held that "objectives such as the pursuit of economic and regional fairness, and the recognition of the historical reliance upon, and participation in, the fishery by non-aboriginal groups"[37] were valid reasons for limiting Aboriginal rights. Long before the violence that followed the *Marshall* fishing rights case, the Court expressed concerns about the effects of recognizing Aboriginal fishing rights on non-Aboriginal fishing interests, which, it should be added, were routinely granted intervenor status in Aboriginal fishing cases. In dissent, Justice McLachlin argued that the recognition of fairness towards non-Aboriginal interests as a legitimate reason for limiting Aboriginal rights "would negate the very Aboriginal right to fish itself ... This is not limitation required for the responsible exercise of the right, but rather limitation on the basis of the economic demands of non-Aboriginals ... To reallocate the benefit of the right from Aboriginals to non-Aboriginals would be to diminish the substance of the right that s. 35(1) of the *Constitution Act, 1982* guarantees to the Aboriginal people" in a manner that should occur only by treaty or by constitutional amendment.[38] Her argument was essentially that the Court was allowing Aboriginal rights to be limited for the reasons it had rejected in the *Big M Drug Mart* case — that the wishes and interests of the majority were opposed to the very idea of rights that would inconvenience them.

The Court's expansion of the range of legitimate reasons for limiting Aboriginal rights became even broader the next year in its controversial *Delgamuukw* decision. The judgment is best known for its discussion of Aboriginal title to land that has been claimed in most of British Columbia. What is less well known is that the Court sanctioned a staggeringly broad array of reasons for limiting and infringing Aboriginal title to land. Chief Justice Lamer indicated that "the range of legislative objections that can justify the infringement is fairly broad ... In my opinion, the development of agriculture, forestry, mining, and hydroelectric power, the general economic development of the interior of British Columbia, protection of the environment or endangered species, the building of infrastructure and the settlement of foreign populations ... are the kinds of objectives that ... in principle, can justify the infringement of aboriginal title."[39] In other words, the public interest can now justify the infringement of Aboriginal title to land. In its efforts to recognize the impact of Aboriginal rights on the non-Aboriginal majority of British Columbia, the Court has run the risk of making Aboriginal rights hostage to the interests of the majority, including "the economic interests of large corporations."[40]

The lynchpin of the justification process was originally the idea that Aboriginal people should have priority in the exercise of their rights over the claims of non-Aboriginal people, who do not have special rights to fish or hunt. Limitations on Aboriginal rights could be justified if necessary for conservation, but the Aboriginal people had the first claim on what could be caught consistent with conservation. As under section 1, however, the Court became more deferential as it realized that maximizing rights for one group would have adverse effects on another group. The group that would suffer in this context was not a minority, but the non-Aboriginal majority, who, particularly in the West, expressed concerns about the adverse effects of special rights for Aboriginal people. In a 1996 Aboriginal commercial fishing case, Chief Justice Lamer indicated that, as under the minimal impairment test in section 1, "where the government is balancing the interests of competing groups," courts should "not scrutinize the government's actions so as to determine whether the government took the least rights-impairing action possible." Rather, courts should be concerned only with the general "reasonableness of the government's actions, taking into account the need to assess 'conflicting scientific evidence and differing justified demands on scarce resource.'"[41] In other words, all the government need do is to take into account the existence of Aboriginal rights in allocating the scarce resource. The requirement that Aboriginal rights have first priority has all but vanished. Justice McLachlin again dissented from this dilution of the justification requirement and pointedly argued that it "ultimately may speak more to the politically expedient than to legal entitlement." In an indication of her appreciation of the increased deference of the section 1 test, she predicted that courts would not "be overly strict in their review"[42] of whether the government had made a reasonable resolution of the conflicting interests in Aboriginal rights cases. She feared this approach would enable the government to take away Aboriginal rights and effectively give them to the majority. The Court's more deferential approach to justification was also applied to Aboriginal title to land in *Delgamuukw*. Although consultation was required, Aboriginal title could generally be expropriated with only the payment of compensation. This decision made Aboriginal land no more secure than other property rights that were not protected in the constitution.[43]

The Court's original insistence that the government must minimally impair Aboriginal rights[44] in its pursuit of a limited range of objectives that regulate, but do not negate, the right has all but vanished. The Court has become more deferential to legislative allocation of scarce resources and more sensitive towards the economic interests of the non-Aboriginal majority as represented by legislation authorizing the development and expropriation of Aboriginal land. Given the considerable latitude that the Court has given governments to limit Aboriginal and treaty rights in favour of a broad range of interests, including the economic and other interests of the non-Aboriginal majority, it can only be concluded that the public and media hysteria about the Supreme Court's so-called embrace of Aboriginal rights is based on deliberate distortions or wilful ignorance of what the cases actually say.

Conclusion

At one level, the story told in this chapter is familiar. It is well known that, after an initial bout of enthusiasm, the Supreme Court has become more deferential in determining whether the government has justified restrictions on *Charter* rights. The Court's increased level of deference started in social policy cases in which it recognized, first, that maximizing rights would have adverse effects on the disadvantaged and, second, that it was not in a good position to second-guess how governments distributed scarce resources among competing groups. What is less well known is that the distinction between judicial deference in social policy cases and insistence on the most proportionate limitation on rights in criminal cases was never stable and that it has been significantly undermined, if not abandoned. The Court has expanded its deferential approach to criminal cases, which constitute the bulk of all cases under the *Charter*. The Court may not even require governments to justify limits placed on the accused's rights under section 1 in those cases in which it defines the accused's rights in a relational manner that respects, but is limited by, competing rights. In any event, the Court now frequently defers to the ability of the state to limit the accused's rights and recognizes that maximizing the accused's rights will have adverse effects on others, including crime victims and groups, such as women and children, who disproportionately suffer some crimes. Section 1 is not a toothless tiger — courts will invalidate measures if the state has not explained the need for the most drastic approach — but its teeth are much less sharp than they used to be.

The evolution of the section 1 test has implications for the judicial activism debate. The most obvious is that the Court will often uphold legislation if the government does a half-way decent job of mounting a section 1 defence. Less obvious is the fact that the Court's deferential turn has been influenced by critics of judicial activism. The Court's decisions to take care that the *Charter* not become an instrument that results in striking down laws designed to assist the disadvantaged is a direct recognition of the arguments (discussed in chapter 5) of left critics of judicial activism that the maximization of rights was not a costless enterprise. The Court's decisions no longer to allow the accused's right to a fair trial to trump other competing rights, including the security, privacy, and equality rights of victims of sexual crimes, is a response to feminist criticisms of the traditional approach to section 1 that saw criminal law as only a matter between the state and the accused. Criticisms of judicial activism from the right also seem to have had some effect on the Court's test for the justification of infringement on Aboriginal and treaty rights. The Court now is prepared to recognize the interests of the non-Aboriginal majority in resource and economic development as a reason to limit Aboriginal title to land, Aboriginal rights to commercial fishing, and rights secured in treaties signed long ago. The Court has diluted the principle that Aboriginal claims have first priority at the real risk of allowing legislatures to limit Aboriginal rights for reasons that simply negate the existence of what critics on the right denounce as special and unwarranted Aboriginal rights. The increased ease with which governments can justify infringements of *Charter* and Aboriginal rights suggests that critics of judicial activism from both the left and the right have had an influence on the Court.

Increased judicial deference to governmental attempts to limit rights has implications for the third of *Charter* cases in which the Court finds there to be an unjustified limitation on a *Charter* right. As we will explore in chapter 10, the limitation of rights cases in this chapter suggests that the legislature may have considerable room to manoeuvre in formulating a reply to *Charter* decisions striking down state action. The government can consciously define an issue as one in which greater judicial deference is warranted. It can stress that the legislation, whether it be criminal or non-criminal law, has an ameliorative purpose that is designed to assist the disadvantaged while, at the same time, it places limits on the rights of others. It can argue that the recognition of Aboriginal rights will adversely affect the economic interests of the non-Aboriginal majority. It can commission work to demonstrate the dangers of maximizing rights in particular contexts, and why options that the Court thought were more respectful of rights will not be as effective in achieving the policy objectives of governments. The Court will not expect certainty from social science evidence and will generally defer to the government so long as it has some evidence to support its position that rights must be limited. All of these factors make it much more likely that the Court will defer to both serious and second tries by the government to limit rights.

Chapter 10
Dialogue between Courts and Legislatures

Every time a government loses a *Charter* case, which happens in the Court approximately one-third of the time, it boosts the popular idea that rights are absolute trumps and that the Court, not the legislature, has the final word. The same pattern can be seen in the United States, where the only response to many controversial decisions under the *Bill of Rights* has been a frustrated attempt to change either the constitution or the Court. These types of responses are even more difficult to achieve in Canada, given the seeming impossibility of amending the constitution and the prime minister's more or less unilateral ability to decide who sits on the Court. The much vaunted section 33 override is hardly better. It has been used a few times to respond to *Charter* decisions, but it is intensely controversial and thought to carry a huge political price. The Court had the last word when it struck down the abortion law or read protection against discrimination on the basis of sexual orientation into Alberta's human rights code. Critics of judicial activism on the left argue that any dialogue between the Court and the legislatures is elitist and undemocratic, while those on the right contend that the dialogue is usually a monologue as the Court orders the government around.[1] This is the crux of the judicial activism problem: nine unelected judges in Ottawa telling elected governments from coast to coast what they must or must not do. The fear is that the Court will have the last word and that legislative supremacy will be replaced with judicial supremacy. In other words, rule by our elected representatives in Parliament will be replaced with rule by unelected judges.

The dangers of judicial supremacy have been grossly exaggerated by the critics of judicial activism. In almost every case in which the Court strikes down state action, its decision need not be, and often has not been, the final word.[2] When the Court does have the last word, the reason is usually more a failure of governmental and public will than a failure of the Court or the *Charter*. The *Charter* rejects the idea found in the American *Bill of Rights* of judicial supremacy over matters that affect rights and freedoms. The Supreme Court has recognized that the structure of the *Charter* means that its decision need not be the final word in democratic debates about how society will treat rights and freedoms. It has acknowledged that its most controversial decisions "can be reacted to by the legislature in the passing of new legislation (or even overarching laws under s. 33 of the *Charter*). This dialogue between and accountability of each of the branches have the effect of enhancing the democratic process, not denying it."[3] The Court has also suggested that if its decisions "were to be taken as establishing the only possible constitutional regime, then we could not speak of a dialogue with the legislature. Such a situation could only undermine rather than enhance democracy."[4] The Court itself accepts that democracy would be undermined in Canada by the type of judicial supremacy found in the United States. Rather, it recognizes that democracy is enhanced when legislatures respond to and even reverse Court decisions under sections 1 and 33 of the *Charter*.

A common mistake made by many who pronounce dialogue to be dead is to focus on the reluctance of legislatures to use the section 33 override in the *Charter*. Section 33 is an important safeguard — the equivalent of shouting to win an argument — but section 1 is the vehicle for the normal conversations and interchanges that regularly occur between courts and legislatures in Canada. In most cases where the Court has struck down laws or illegal state activity, section 1 allows the government to respond by enacting new legislation to advance the government's former objectives and by justifying it to the Court as a reasonable limit on the right that the Court has recognized. One of the reasons why concerns about judicial activism are so off the mark is that the available evidence suggests that the strong legislatures produced by the Canadian parliamentary system have the upper hand in dialogue with the courts, even without pulling out the big gun of section 33.

Dialogues about Police Powers

The Supreme Court's frequent restrictions on police powers raise some tough questions. The justices on the Court are somewhat remote from what happens on the streets and in the squad cars. There is a danger that their idealistic views about what the police should do will be the last word. The Canadian Court has interpreted the right against unreasonable searches and seizures in a generous fashion that has gone further in protecting the accused than the Warren Court did in the United States. Predictably, critics of judicial activism on the left have expressed fear that the Court will impede "the prosecution of business crime," while those on the right are concerned about the "significant effect on law enforcement practices."[5] Parliament's response to almost every search and seizure case, however, demonstrates that it is quite capable of ensuring that the police have ample powers to control crime.

For good reasons, the police take care in dealing with potentially dangerous criminals. As in the movies, they sometimes wear a wire or, better still, have their informers wear one, when talking to the bad guys.

In the 1970s Parliament provided a complex warrant procedure for electronic surveillance, but exempted the police from getting a warrant so long as one party to the conversation, such as the undercover officer or the informer, consented. Even the Warren Court in the United States had agreed to such a procedure on the basis that criminals had to accept the risk that people they spoke with could betray them. Accused were no worse off if a recording, as opposed to the undercover operative's testimony, was used against them. In 1990 the Supreme Court of Canada disagreed and struck down the statutory exemption that allowed people to wear wires without warrants. Justice La Forest, usually a deferential judge when the state had reasons for acting, but one who was passionate about privacy, warned that "a society which exposed us, at the whim of the state, to the risk of having a permanent electronic recording made of our words every time we opened our mouths might be superbly equipped to fight crime, but would be one in which privacy no longer had any meaning." He reasoned that Parliament had struck the appropriate balance between the state's interest in crime control and the individual's interest in privacy when it required the state to obtain a warrant, on the basis that there were reasonable and probable grounds to believe an offence had been or was being committed, the electronic surveillance would reveal evidence of the offence, and less intrusive means of investigation would not work. Parliament had erred in exempting undercover police officers and informers from having to obtain a warrant just because they consented to wearing a wire. There was a danger that the police could engage in electronic surveillance "in their absolute discretion, against whom they wish and for whatever reasons they wish, without any limit as to place or duration. There is a total absence of prior judicial authorization."[6]

Although the Court allowed the recordings taken in reliance on the unconstitutional legislation to be admitted in evidence in the drug trafficking case at hand, the police were not happy about this decision. In a front-page story in the *Globe and Mail*, they complained that the Court's decision meant they had to send "the undercover officer out without a life line ... We've had officers robbed, stabbed, shot at, and it's not getting better."[7] Within two years of this complaint, Parliament responded with new legislation providing for new and simpler warrants to wear wires as well as limited statutory authorization for warrantless uses of wires. The minister of justice observed that the Court's decisions "significantly affect the way police and other agents of the state can do their jobs" and that the legislation would give the police tools "to perform their duties satisfactorily," including "an electronic lifeline to permit police and others in potentially dangerous situations to have their conversations surreptitiously intercepted by backup teams." The opposition members outdid themselves showing that they supported the police and the new legislation.[8] It allowed police officers to obtain, if need be by telephone, warrants that would allow them to intercept private communications, with the consent of one party, for up to sixty days. They first had to provide reasonable grounds for believing that an offence had been committed, and reasonable grounds for believing that information concerning the offence would be obtained. There was no requirement that they use less intrusive means than electronic surveillance. To criticisms from lawyers that the Supreme Court had stressed the dangers of allowing the warrantless use of wires at the discretion of the police, the new legislation also allowed the police to use wires without warrants to respond to a risk of bodily harm or in circumstances where a warrant could not be obtained "with reasonable diligence."[9] Parliament had successfully responded to the Court decision by tailoring wire warrants to its policy objectives and authorizing the use of wires without warrants in some contexts.

The 1993 legislation also contained a new "general warrant" provision that allows judges to authorize the use of any device or investigative technique that, if not authorized, would "constitute an unreasonable search or seizure in respect of a person or a person's property."[10] Although the warrant would only be granted on reasonable grounds and could not be used to invade bodily integrity, it was otherwise as broad as it could possibly be. The legislation responded to cases in which the Court had ruled that the police could not use hidden cameras in washrooms and hotel rooms. Now they could get a warrant to let the cameras roll. The use of videotaping, as well as more intrusive technologies not yet invented, can be authorized by a judge under a general warrant. Parliament was saying to the Court: "Anything that you think violates a reasonable expectation of privacy under section 8 of the *Charter*, we can authorize." Parliament, with the assistance of the experts in the Department of Justice, was becoming clever, perhaps too clever, in devising replies to the Court's *Charter* decisions.

Another example of a prompt legislative reply to a *Charter* search-and-seizure ruling is the response to the Court's controversial decision in *Feeney*.[11] The case involved a warrantless entry into Feeney's trailer, where evidence, including a shirt stained with the blood of the eighty-six-year-old murder victim, was seized. The Court held that the common law power to enter a private dwelling to make an arrest could no longer be justified under the *Charter* and that, except in cases of hot pursuit, a warrant was required. In a strongly worded dissent, Justice L'Heureux-Dubé complained that the police were wrongfully being portrayed "as lawless vigilantes, flagrantly and deliberately violating the Charter at every turn," whereas they were just doing their job.[12] She focused on the entry of the police into Feeney's trailer, not on the breaking down of the door of some innocent person. The Supreme Court's decision was front-page news and was heavily criticized as a sign of judicial activism in protecting the accused's rights under the *Charter*, whereas Feeney's subsequent murder conviction on the basis of the remaining evidence was barely news. Jeffrey Simpson wrote in the *Globe and Mail* that *Feeney* was another example of how the Court's rulings "are now more important in determining a range of criminal law matters than anything Parliament decides."[13]

Contrary to these fears, the Court did not have the last word in *Feeney*. It suspended its decision for seven months to give Parliament an opportunity to enact a new warrant provision. Parliament quickly enacted new legislation that allowed arrest warrants to authorize entry into homes and a separate *Feeney* warrant authorizing entries into houses to make arrests. Some people might criticize these new warrant provisions as negative replies or distortions of Parliament's preferred policy because they essentially followed the Court's ruling that warrants were required.[14] At the same time, however, Parliament also authorized warrantless entries of private dwellings to make arrests in cases where "exigent circumstances" would make it impracticable to obtain a warrant. Parliament defined exigent circumstances to include "reasonable grounds to suspect that entry into the dwelling house is necessary to prevent imminent bodily harm or death to any person" and "reasonable grounds to believe" that warrantless entry "is necessary to prevent the imminent loss or imminent destruction of evidence."[15] This broad definition went beyond *Feeney*, which had approved warrantless entries into homes only in cases of hot pursuit. The new law also expanded the debate by allowing judges, on similar grounds, to exempt the police from making their traditional announcement of police presence when entering a home. As in many other search and seizure cases, Parliament, not the Court, had the last word and established the ultimate rules for police conduct. Dialogue between the Court and Parliament has given the police a wide range of powers to conduct searches with and without warrants. Instead of police officers exercising their own discretion to use wires or cameras or to break down doors, Parliament has required them in most, but not all, cases to obtain a warrant. The result has been clearer rules and greater accountability for both citizens and the police.

Dialogues about the Criminal Trial Process

The Court has been criticized so often for its concerns about the rights of the accused that Chief Justice McLachlin has declared, as one of six myths surrounding the *Charter*, the idea that criminals routinely walk

away from a "criminal justice system in crisis"[16] In fact, prison populations and sentences have increased throughout most of the *Charter* era,
even as reported crime has declined.[17] The Court has not unlocked the
prison gates.

Many people in jail have not been convicted of a crime. Half of
those in provincial jails in Ontario are awaiting trial, and one in five people acquitted at trial have been imprisoned before trial.[18] In a series of
1992 cases, the Supreme Court upheld from *Charter* challenge most of
the provisions that allow people to be locked up before trial. Denial of
bail in order to prevent the substantial likelihood that the accused would,
if released, commit a criminal offence was upheld on the basis that "the
bail system ... does not function properly if individuals commit crimes
while on bail." A reverse onus that required those charged with drug trafficking to show why they should be released was also upheld. The only
provision that the Court struck down was one that allowed bail to be
refused in "the public interest." This vague phrase would, in the Court's
view, allow a person to be locked away before trial on a judicial whim.[19]
A number of commentators concluded that the Court would have the
final word on this one extraordinary ground for denying bail.[20]

Five years later, however, Parliament resurrected denial of bail on
public interest grounds. The new provision does not use the phrase
"public interest," but instead allows bail to be denied for "any other just
cause," including, especially in serious cases, "where detention is necessary in order to maintain confidence in the administration of justice."[21]
In other words, Parliament used fancier language to allow bail to be
denied in the public interest even when there was no reason to believe
that, if released, the accused would flee or commit a crime. People could
be imprisoned before trial simply because the public would feel good
about it and would be shocked if they were released. Parliament again
cleverly tracked the vague due process language of the *Charter* to
authorize the crime control response of pre-trial detention. The
accused's *Charter* right to be denied bail only for a "just cause" was
turned on its head by the drafting experts at the Department of Justice
to authorize the crime control response of pre-trial detention on vague,
albeit "just," grounds not related to legitimate concerns that the accused
might, if released, flee or commit a crime. The Supreme Court will soon
have to evaluate the constitutionality of this legislative reply to its 1992
decision, but most signs point towards judicial deference towards legislative second tries, however unjust and unnecessary.

One Supreme Court case that is associated with opening the prison
gates is *Askov*. Elijah Askov was charged with extortion and other crimes
for demanding a 50 per cent commission on the booking of exotic
dancers. At the time he was making a club owner an offer the man could

not refuse, Askov was brandishing a sawed-off shotgun and a knife. He was arrested, denied bail, and jailed for six months before trial. It took two more years after his preliminary hearing for his trial to start in the busy Peel courts in one of Toronto's rapidly growing suburbs. At that time, Askov argued that his *Charter* right to a trial in a reasonable time had been violated. The Supreme Court agreed and issued a stay of proceedings. Askov walked. The Court stressed that the government had an obligation to put enough resources into the criminal justice system to ensure that not only the accused but victims and society too had the benefit of speedy trials. It also articulated the general proposition that anything beyond six to eight months would constitute unreasonable delay. Immediately, all hell broke loose. To screaming headlines that left the impression of a general amnesty for criminals, the Ontario government — the very government that the Court had criticized for not putting enough resources into the system — announced that thousands of charges that had been "Askoved," or permanently stopped, because of the Court's ruling. The count eventually topped off at over 50,000 charges stayed or withdrawn. Surely this was a dangerous form of judicial activism that imposed unrealistic rules on prosecutors and allowed an alarmingly large number of potentially dangerous criminals to go free?

The answer is, however, not so simple. The media did not report that most accused faced multiple charges, so the real figure of those let go because of *Askov* was closer to 25,000 than 50,000. Moreover, the media did not report that 90 per cent of criminal charges in Ontario at the time were not withdrawn.[22] Still, most people believed that *Askov* had created an amnesty for criminals and they blamed the Court, especially after the justice who had written the decision indicated that "the rigidity of the interpretation by some people came as a shock ... We were not aware of the extent of the impact."[23] In any event, the Court took its first opportunity a year later to reverse a typical *Askov* stay for a thirteen-month delay in a drunk driving case and to indicate that its guidelines were not absolute rules. Although the *Askov* saga underlines the fallibility of judicial decision making, the governments were also at fault for making Peel the slowest court district north of the Rio Grande. In the early 1980s Parliament had considered legislating similar speedy trial standards to many American jurisdictions, but the bill was not a priority and it died on the order paper. The same was true of law reform recommendations that Parliament require prosecutors to disclose their case to the accused before trial. Disclosure and speedy trials are connected. Early disclosure to the defence means charge screening and early plea bargaining, which frees up valuable court space for trials. The backlog that caused Askov to wait two years for a trial was in part caused by a lack of efficient charge screening, disclosure of the Crown's case to the accused, and plea bargaining in what defence lawyers called "no deal Peel." Shortages of judges and prosecutors may also have been a factor. On both speedy trials and disclosure to the defence, the Supreme Court made broad and quasi-legislative judicial decisions in part because of governmental neglect of the criminal trial process.[24] Some critics of judicial activism have defended legislative inertia as a legitimate response by Parliament,[25] but it is difficult to justify this position in the criminal context in which government neglect often means the imprisonment of people and delays for both the victims and the public under archaic laws and practices.[26]

Parliament could have responded to *Askov* by enacting ordinary legislation of the type left to die in the mid-1980s and by enacting disclosure requirements that would have facilitated early charge screening and plea bargaining. Even if the speedy trial standards set by Parliament were held to violate the right to a trial in a reasonable time as interpreted by *Askov*, the Court likely would have held that they were reasonable limits under section 1 of the *Charter*, given Parliament's superior ability to decide how limited resources should be allocated. As matters stood, Parliament did not act even in the midst of the often exaggerated *Askov* crisis,[27] and it has not yet legislated to provide guidance on speedy trials or on most disclosure issues. One of the unfortunate consequences of the *Charter* is that Parliament has abdicated its proactive law reform role and increasingly relies on the Court to articulate and enforce minimum standards of fairness for the accused. This situation, however, is more a failure of parliamentary government than of the Court or the *Charter*.

Dialogues about Criminal Laws

Some conservative judges have criticized the Court for going beyond a concern about fair process in the criminal law and reforming the substantive criminal law. Justice Bastarache, for example, has commented that the Lamer Court "went very far in looking at the substantive law and determining whether Parliament had the right to impose, for instance, the very conditions under which a crime would be created. This means you are way beyond a due process kind of approach."[28] The Court has indeed rewritten important aspects of the law of murder. At the same time, it has not had the final word on even these matters.

René Vaillancourt was a cautious but unlucky robber who, without the Court's intervention, would have been convicted of murder. He robbed a Montreal pool hall with an accomplice, who had a gun. Vaillancourt, who carried a knife but not a gun, was worried about the gun and had his accomplice remove some bullets — unfortunately, not all the bullets. The accomplice got into a struggle with a patron, the gun discharged, and the patron was fatally shot. The accomplice got away, and Vaillancourt was left to face a murder charge. He was charged under a law that provided that a person committing a serious crime was guilty of murder if death resulted from the crime or the use or even possession of a firearm during the crime, even if the accused did not intend for the victim to die. This broadly worded Canadian version of felony murder could result in a murder conviction for an accident with a gun during a robbery. The law had long been criticized by law reform bodies, but Parliament was not likely to reform it. What politician wanted to look soft on gun-wielding robbers or their accomplices?

The Supreme Court intervened on the basis that the stigma of a murder conviction and its mandatory penalty of life imprisonment should require, as a matter of fundamental justice, that the accused knew that the victim was likely to die. Justice Lamer conceded that the objective of deterring the use of firearms and violence was important, but held that a murder conviction for accidental and unintentional killings was not necessary. Parliament could punish the carrying of weapons during offences, and people like Vaillancourt could receive stiff sentences for robbery and manslaughter.[29] Justices McIntyre and L'Heureux-Dubé wrote vigorous dissents, stressing that victims had died, Parliament should be able to decide what constituted murder, the Americans allowed felony murder, and that Justice Lamer's concern "that these offenders not endure the mark of Cain is ... an egregious example of misplaced compassion."[30] In what has been characterized as a "negative reply,"[31] Parliament accepted these decisions by repealing the felony murder offence. The Justice Department may well have been happy to have the Court perform the dirty and dangerous work of law reform, which, if undertaken in Parliament, would have put their minister at political risk. The Court seemed to have the last word.

Parliament still had a wide-open field to regulate and punish the use of the firearms through any means short of a murder conviction. In 1995 it took up the Court's invitation to punish severely the use of weapons during offences and enacted ten mandatory minimum penalties of four years' imprisonment for a variety of serious offences involving the use of firearms. Someone like Vaillancourt would now face a minimum of four years in the penitentiary. The Court has recently upheld these mandatory minimum penalties as not constituting cruel and unusual punishment. The accused that the Court allowed Parliament to send to the penitentiary for four years was not even an experienced armed robber like Vaillancourt, but thirty-five-year-old Marty Lorraine Morrisey. Mr. Morrisey lived with his mother, had no criminal record, and, while distraught and drunk after the breakup of his relationship, unintentionally but negligently shot and killed his best friend.[32] A balanced account of the felony murder saga would also include the Court's 1990 decision to allow Parliament to classify intentional killings committed during serious offences as felony first-degree murder, subject to life imprisonment and ineligibility for parole for twenty-five years.[33] In response to high-profile murders of a child in a biker war and of a female lawyer by her ex-spouse, Parliament has expanded the list of serious offences to include criminal organization and stalking offences. In response to the spectre of mass murderer Clifford Olson's failed attempt to be declared eligible for parole by a jury after serving fifteen years of his first-degree murder sentence, Parliament also restricted access to such faint-hope hearings both for mass murderers and others convicted of first-degree murder.[34] The Court has significantly changed the Canadian law of murder, but even in this context, it has not had the final word.

Conversations about Tobacco Advertising

Parliament may have been able to respond to the Court's murder decisions and use the criminal law to deter the use of guns, but what about another lethal substance, cigarettes? As we saw in chapter 9, a 5 to 4 majority of the Supreme Court struck down a 1988 law prohibiting the advertising of tobacco products. Although the government's defence of the law left much to be desired, critics can make strong arguments that this case represented a dangerous form of judicial activism. Thankfully, the Court did not have the last word.

Within two years of the judgment, Parliament responded with new legislation. It followed the Court's suggestions about less restrictive alternatives to a total ban on tobacco advertising by prohibiting only lifestyle, as opposed to brand preference, advertising and by providing that mandatory health warnings be attributed to Health Canada.[35] The new legislation also contained restrictions on tobacco company sponsorship of sporting and cultural events. These restrictions proved controversial and were eventually subject to a five-year exemption.[36] The new legislation was carefully designed to survive the *Charter* challenge that would undoubtedly be launched by the litigation savy tobacco companies. Parliament clearly articulated the purposes of its new legislation as responding to the "substantial and pressing concern" of smoking as a national public health problem and to concerns about protecting young people from tobacco.[37]

The federal government has been criticized for not being "aggressive in pursuing its legislative initiative" by not questioning "the wisdom of the Court's characterization of tobacco advertising as protected speech" and for accepting "the judiciary's speculative comment" about less-restrictive alternatives to address "a complex social problem that baffles policy experts and can hardly be said to fall within the Court's competence." The result has been described as "less effective legislation that casts doubt on the purported benefits of constitutional dialogue."[38] This criticism raises the issue of the "policy distortion" that "occurs when legislators tailor statutes to 'judicially articulated norms' of constitutional meaning, even when those norms conflict with the legislature's own understanding of constitutional norms."[39] The legislation may be less effective than the old legislation because of attempts to comply with the Court's perhaps mistaken impression about less-restrictive but equally effective alternatives. But we should not throw out the idea of dialogue between the Court and Parliament just because Parliament's response to a particular case was lukewarm. We should also not place all the blame on the Court and the *Charter* and, by doing so, let our elected representatives off easily for their response to the Court's decision.

Parliament could have enacted a more robust reply to the Court's decision. The most drastic option was to re-enact the total ban while declaring, under section 33, that the legislation should operate notwithstanding the right to freedom of expression. There were calls in Parliament to do just that, and the health minister even recommended that option to Cabinet.[40] Perhaps fearful of a negative public reaction to the idea that rights would be overridden, the government decided not to use the override. It is difficult to see why the override was not used if the Court's decision was so bad and if the invalidated legislation was as effective in reducing the harms of smoking as its proponents believed. Surely it would not have been difficult to explain the need for the override to a public that was ready to believe the worst about the tobacco companies and was concerned about rising health care costs. As the minister of health explained, smoking is responsible for one in five deaths in Canada and costs the health care system billions of dollars each year. Over 90 per cent of Canadians supported efforts by government to discourage smoking among young people, and 73 per cent supported efforts to discourage smoking among those who already smoke.[41] Given this level of approval, it is difficult to think that the people would not have accepted the use of the override.

A somewhat less drastic and sneakier option would have been for the government to enact an "in-your-face" reversal of *RJR -Macdonald* without the override. For example, the government could have followed the Court's ruling by placing attributions on the health warnings, but re-enacted a total, or close to total, ban on advertising. Parliament already had experience with such in-your-face reversals or partial reversals of the Court's decision, for in 1995 it had reversed most of the Court's controversial *Charter* decision to recognize a defence of extreme intoxication to charges of sexual assault and assault. An in-your-face reply to *RJR* would have been more defensible if the government was prepared to reveal the studies that were not given to the Court in *RJR* to show that absolute advertising bans were more effective than bans on lifestyle advertising. If the studies did not exist, the government could have commissioned them. Some professor somewhere should have been able to demonstrate that some people identified particular brands of cigarettes with a glamorous lifestyle. The section 1 jurisprudence discussed in chapter 9 suggests that the Court would have deferred to the government if it had had a reasonable basis for acting on such social science evidence. The government's preparation of a full section 1 file could be criticized as a form of policy distortion in itself, but surely requiring research into the effectiveness of alternative policy instruments is not inherently bad or debilitating to democracy.

Why was there no override in response to *RJR-Macdonald*? One hypothesis is that public opinion lags behind the structure of the *Charter* in terms of thinking of rights as absolute and in considering even a temporary and democratic override of rights to be unacceptable. But this view does not give the people much credit. The government could have explained why the override was necessary. It is not acceptable for those who oppose judicial activism in the name of democracy to say that the people are not smart enough to be convinced of the error of the Court's decision and the necessity of the override. Even if the government was not prepared to run the risk of the override, why was there no in-your-face reply? Health officials who had carriage of the legislation had less experience with *Charter* dialogue than the Justice officials who had already crafted one in-your-face reply and were at that time working on another, both in response to controversial Court decisions on the rights of those accused of sexual assault.[42] Most *Charter* litigation affects criminal law, and the Department of Justice has become more expert, clever, and bold over time in responding to *Charter* decisions. My favourite hypothesis is slightly more cynical: think about the strength of the interests that were adversely affected by the legislation. The tobacco companies are rich multinationals that were able to secure significant postponements of the government's ban on sponsorship in part because of the millions they pump into cultural and sporting events. In contrast, the men accused of sexual assault who were adversely affected by in-your-face legislative replies to the Court's sexual assault decisions had little money to spend and less political power.[43] In my view, the government bears a good share of the blame for not using the override or enacting an in-your-face reply to the Court's decision in *RJR*.

It is unfair to place all the blame for the tobacco advertising saga at the feet of the Court. Although the Court may not be in the best position to assess the effectiveness of alternatives to a less than absolute ban on tobacco advertising, the government did not give it much assistance. By assigning the burden of justifying the legislation to the government, section 1 of the *Charter* contemplates that the government will provide the Court with the relevant expert evidence. The Court arrived at its perhaps erroneous conclusion that the government's objectives could be satisfied by a ban on lifestyle advertising only after it concluded that the government had failed to disclose policy studies studying the effectiveness of less-than-absolute bans. The failure either to undertake or to disclose such studies forced the Court to rely on its intuitions about the matter. The Court may be wrong, but the government is equally to blame for not educating the Court in the section 1 inquiry. Once the decision was made, Parliament could have re-enacted a total, or close to total, ban on advertising either with the override or with an in-your-face reply without the override. The latter course would have allowed the government to make a better defence of why a ban on all advertising was necessary, and why the distinction between brand preference and lifestyle advertising can be illusory in an age in which brands are consciously shaped to reflect lifestyles. There is plenty of room under the *Charter* for dialogue, but both Parliament and the Court must make effective contributions to the debate. The blame for policy distortion will, in most cases, fall on both institutions.

Dialogues about Prisoner Voting Rights

Should Richard Sauvé be able to vote in federal elections? As a Canadian citizen, he has a clear right under the *Charter* to vote. As a graduate of Queen's University, he is better educated and informed than the average voter. He also has more time than most of us to study the issues in a campaign. Mr. Sauvé is serving a sentence of life imprisonment for his involvement in a first-degree murder in 1978 when he was a member of the Satan's Choice Biker Club. He will soon return to the Supreme Court for the second time to challenge federal legislation that denies him the vote. The reason why Sauvé must return to the Court a second time is because the Supreme Court does not have the last word when it makes decisions under the *Charter*.

Sauvé first went to the Supreme Court in 1993. In a very brief judgment, the Court indicated that Parliament's denial of the vote to all prisoners "is drawn too broadly and fails to meet the proportionality test, particularly the minimal impairment component of the test."[44] The Court did not go as far as two courts of appeal, which had struck the law down on the grounds that the punitive and symbolic purposes of denying prisoners the vote were not important enough to limit the *Charter* right and that the denial of the vote was not rationally connected to the government's abstract objectives. One court of appeal had dismissed the "widely held stereotype of the prisoner as a no-good almost sub-human form of life to which all rights should be indiscriminately denied."[45] The Supreme Court's decision that the law was overbroad left Parliament more room to respond.

By the time the Supreme Court delivered its decision in *Sauvé I*, Parliament had already enacted new legislation to restrict the ability of prisoners to vote. Although Mr. Sauvé won in court, he lost in Parliament. This outcome is hardly surprising once one accepts that the independent courts are supposed to protect unpopular individuals and minorities, while elected legislatures have no such obligations. The new legislation enacted by Parliament denies all prisoners serving two years or more the right to vote. Parliament decided to cut off the franchise at those prisoners serving federal time in the penitentiary. It rejected less-drastic alternatives, such as a recommendation of a recent royal commission that only prisoners serving ten years or more be denied the vote. A motion to give all prisoners the right to vote was defeated on a voice vote and after a short and unedifying debate in Parliament.[46] Even though the Kingston member of parliament who moved the motion effectively argued that many other countries and some provinces allowed prisoners to vote, his colleagues replied that voting was just one of many privileges that should be lost in prison. One member predictably invoked the spectre of Clifford Olson being able to vote and concluded, "I just cannot get excited about such people losing their rights to vote for the period they are incarcerated."[47] The majority in Parliament had little incentive to protect the right of an unpopular group with no political clout, even though it followed lower court decisions that, under the *Charter*, judges and the mentally disordered should be allowed to vote.[48] Minorities are not always at a disadvantage in the legislative process, but the truly unpopular and powerless ones are. The issue of prisoner voting rights is one in which elected parliamentarians have an incentive to disregard the rights of perhaps the most unpopular and vilified citizens in Canada and to score cheap political points by appearing to be tough not only on crime but on criminals. What will the Supreme Court do in *Sauvé II*?

The Court may be tempted to be deferential towards Parliament's second try in taking the vote away from prisoners and reluctant to second-guess the two-year cut off, especially because the Court's interpretation of the right to vote is not subject to the override. The majority in the Court of Appeal that upheld the new restrictions stressed that the "case is another episode in the continuing dialogue between courts and legislatures" and that, "while the notion of ensuring a 'decent' or 'moral' electorate may have little place in today's society," Parliament's choices of penal and electoral policy "are by definition political and therefore warrant deference ... kindness towards the criminal can be an act of cruelty towards the victims, and the larger community."[49] Despite this deferential abdication of the judicial role in the face of a parliamentary reply to a previous court decision, there are arguments that the Court should strike down the law, even though it is Parliament's second try. The objectives that Parliament asserts — ensuring a law-abiding electorate and bolstering the criminal sanction — are very vague and amount to little more than objections to the idea that prisoners should have the vote.[50] It is not clear that denying prisoners the vote will help stop crime or ensure that those who cast a vote are decent and moral citizens. There are less restrictive alternatives, and any good that the law does is speculative in the extreme compared with the corrosive harm of denying any of our citizens the vote. Disenfranchisement has a long and ugly history in Canada. Aboriginal people, for example, did not have the vote until 1960, and Aboriginal people today fill too many spaces in federal penitentiaries. Aboriginal inmates whose parents and grandparents were denied the vote until 1960 are now denied the vote. The idea of dialogue would be dangerous if the Court automatically deferred to any legislative reply to its previous decisions. A decision upholding the new voting restrictions would confirm the reality of dialogue, but would also suggest that one of the most unpopular groups in our society — prisoners serving federal time — could have its democratic rights totally negated by legislation.

Shouting Matches and Calmer Conversations over Quebec's Language Laws

All the dialogue that has so far been discussed in this chapter was done without legislatures using their ultimate weapon: their ability to enact legislation notwithstanding most of the rights in the *Charter*. The use of the override is perhaps indelibly associated with Quebec's reaction to the enactment of the *Charter* and its use of the override to defend its language laws. Quebec was the only province not to agree to the enactment of the *Charter* and, as a political protest, invoked an omnibus override shortly after the *Charter* was proclaimed in force. Despite the fact that the Quebec Court of Appeal held that the Quebec legislature did not give citizens adequate notice of the particular rights and laws that were subject to the override, the Supreme Court took a deferential approach to reviewing the use of the override and upheld the omnibus override except as it was applied retroactively.[51]

Quebec's most controversial use of the override came after a corporation, Brown's Shoes, challenged provisions in Bill 101 that required commercial signs to be only in French. The Quebec courts held that the law was an unjustified restriction of freedom of expression under both the Quebec and the Canadian charters. The Supreme Court agreed. Although preserving the French language and the "visage linquistique" of Quebec was an important enough goal to justify limiting a *Charter* right and could support a requirement that French have a "marked predominance" in public signs, the total prohibition of languages other than French could not be justified.[52] The lead litigant believed that even a requirement that his advertising be 80 per cent in French was acceptable because it reflected the social reality of Montreal and reconciled collective rights with individual rights.[53] Many in Quebec, however, were in no mood to compromise. Demonstrations involving up to 15,000 people soon occurred in the streets of Montreal, the site of the language wars. The theme was "ne touchez pas Loi 101." Some stores with bilingual signs had their windows broken. Three days after the decision, a bill invoking the notwithstanding clause was introduced in the Quebec legislature and, within a week, it had been debated and enacted. The new law overrode the Court's decision, but only with respect to outdoor signs.[54] As had been the case before the Court's decision, outdoor signs would be only in French; other languages, however, could be used in indoor advertising. Premier Robert Bourassa believed that his "outdoor/indoor" approach was a compromise that recognized the rights of the anglophone minority. Underlining the reality of this compromise was the fact that the separatist Parti Québécois opposed the bill as not going far enough to protect the French language.

Quebec's response was a compromise, but a different one from the solution that had been imagined and suggested by the Court. The Supreme Court had accepted that allowing limited use of languages other than French was a less drastic alternative, but had not specifically considered the new "indoor/outdoor" compromise of the Bourassa government. Indeed, the Court expressed some frustration that Quebec had not even attempted "to justify the requirement of the exclusive use of French" before the Court. [55] As with the *RJR-Tobacco* case, it is possible that a better defence of the law would have convinced the Court to accept, if not the total ban on languages other than French, then at least Bourassa's indoor/outdoor compromise as a reasonable limitation on commercial expression. It is an interesting historical might-have-been to speculate on what would have happened had the override not been used and the Quebec government had defended its outdoor/indoor compromise under section 1 as a reasonable limit on freedom of expression. A Court assisted by better section 1 evidence might have accepted the new law without the override. Not using the override, however, would have meant that the new language law would be tied up in *Charter* litigation or a reference by the Quebec government to the courts. The political pressures on Premier Bourassa to protect and express the collective rights of the francophone majority probably explain the decision to use the override. Quebec's use of the override was candid in its proclamation that collective interests or rights were more important than the interests of language minorities in commercial expression, and in its rejection of the Court's determination that a total prohibition on the use of language other than French in commercial signs had not been justified.

The use of the override was candid, but it was also very controversial. The anglophone minority felt that its rights had been taken away, and three anglophones resigned in protest from Bourassa's Cabinet. The reaction outside Quebec was even more negative and helped to bring about the collapse of the Meech Lake accord. If respect for Quebec's distinct society meant disrespect for *Charter* rights, many outside Quebec were opposed to the accord. The problem may be that the public tends to think of rights in absolutist terms that mimic the judicial supremacy of the American *Bill of Rights*. The majority of the public, both inside and outside Quebec, think that the courts rather than the legislatures "should have the final say"[56] when they declare a law unconstitutional. The public may not appreciate the complex structure of the *Charter*, which, by giving governments a right of reply to court decisions under both sections 1 and 33, suggests that courts should not always have the final say. Unfortunately, politicians outside Quebec did little to help the public understand the *Charter*'s complex and democratic structure. Prime Minister Brian Mulroney played into a simplistic understanding of absolute rights and judicial supremacy when he described the override as the "fatal flaw" of the *Charter* that "holds rights hostage." In a statement that imitated American rhetoric about rights, but revealed a profound ignorance of the innovative Canadian compromise between legislative and judicial supremacy, Mulroney concluded that any constitution "that does not protect the inalienable and inpresciptible individual rights of individual Canadians is not worth the paper it is written on."[57] If their prime minister so poorly understood the structure of the *Charter*, it was not surprising that Canadians also misunderstood the legitimacy of the override.

Public attraction to simplistic notions of absolute rights and judicial supremacy suggests that governments wishing to use the override must be prepared to convince a sceptical public of the legitimacy of their actions. Nevertheless, it is premature to pronounce section 33 dead on arrival. Its use is certainly not politically fatal. The Bourassa government in Quebec was re-elected shortly after using the override in the Bill 101 case, as was the Devine government in Saskatchewan shortly after it used the override in back-to-work legislation.[58] As we will see, the Klein government in Alberta was burned by its attempt to use the override against the mentally challenged people the government had involuntarily sterilized in past decades, but it was re-elected after it had used the override to outlaw gay marriage. Section 33 is not politically fatal. All three provincial governments that have used it have been re-elected shortly thereafter. Running against the Court in Ottawa has been an effective political tactic since Premier Aberhart's opposition to the Court's dismantling of Social Credit in Alberta in the 1930s and Premier Duplessis's opposition to the Court throughout the 1950s in Quebec. The Court is an easy target, especially for provincial politicians. It is vulnerable because it is unelected, does not talk back, and can be portrayed as part of a distant and haughty Ottawa establishment. Under the *Charter*, however, the elected governments cannot only rail against the Court but can actually do something about it by using the override.

Although the override allows the legislature to win an argument with the Court over a particular point by shouting, it requires the conversation to continue five years later, when, as required under section 33, the override expires. The legislature can renew the override, as Quebec has done in some other under-publicized cases.[59] In the Bill 101 case, however, Quebec used the opportunity for sober second thoughts provided by the expiry of the 1988 override. In 1993 it allowed the override to expire and enacted new legislation that closely followed the Supreme Court's original decision by allowing the use of languages other than French in commercial signs, provided that the French language was markedly predominant.[60] Quebec's decision was undoubtedly influenced by criticism of its use of the override, including a decision of the Human Rights Committee of the United Nations that it was "not necessary, in order to protect the vulnerable position in Canada of the francophone group[,] to prohibit commercial advertising in English."[61] In our increasingly globalized and rights-conscious world, the use of the override will often have international repercussions, including further appeals under international rights-protection instruments. The United Kingdom's *Human Rights Act, 1998* allows Parliament to enact legislation in contravention to the *European Convention*, but, like section 33 of the *Charter*, requires Parliament to revisit derogations from that document every five years. The international reaction from the rest of Europe and elsewhere, as well as the domestic reaction, will help determine whether Parliament renews its formal derogations. Section 33 of the *Charter* similarly allows legislatures to shout at courts and override their interpretation of rights, but the five-year sunset provides a salutary time for reflection on the domestic and international reaction to the override.

The denouement of Quebec's shouting match with the Court over Bill 101 illustrates the usefulness of the sober second thoughts encouraged by the five-year sunset on the override. The override preserves the Court decision as a valid point of principle that the legislature cannot temporarily live with. When the override expires after five years, the Court's decision can come back to life. In any event, it will influence debate. The override provides a complex and wise structure for dialogue between courts and legislatures which, unfortunately, is not well enough understood by politicians or the public. At the same time, it is unfair to blame either the Court or the *Charter* for the failure of governments to use and justify to the public the use of the override.

The Failure to Respond to *Morgentaler*

A spectacular example of the Court having the last word is its decision in *Morgentaler* to strike down the abortion law, a decision that has left Canada as one of the few countries that has no regulation or restrictions on even late-term abortions. The explanation for the Court having the last word on abortion lies more with a rare failure of the parliamentary process than with the Court or the *Charter* or even a reluctance to use the override.

The majority of the Supreme Court took pains in *Morgentaler* to avoid the *Roe* v. *Wade* approach that would dictate to elected governments the exact nature of constitutional laws governing abortion. The Conservative government, however, was not eager to legislate with respect to the no-win abortion issue and failed to take leadership on the issue. After five meetings with his caucus, Prime Minister Mulroney announced in May 1988 that a free vote would be held on abortion. The result was a procedural disaster, with five different pro-life and pro-choice amendments being defeated without the prime minister or the leader of the Opposition even bothering to be present. This legislative free for all was a good example of the Americanization of our political process. Without leadership, the rights of the underrepresented were at risk. All the female members of parliament voted against a pro-life amendment that would allow abortions only when continuing the pregnancy would endanger the life of the mother. This motion, however, was the most popular of the five and was defeated only narrowly, 118 to 105, in the male-dominated Parliament.

After the free vote debacle, it was clear that the government would have to do something, even if the issue was a political loser. It debated both a gestational approach, as suggested by Justice Wilson in her judgment, and one that placed restrictions on abortion at all times, as allowed by Justice Beetz's judgment. It eventually settled on Bill C-43, which made abortion at all times an offence punishable by up to two years in prison unless it was performed by a doctor who was "of the opinion that, if the abortion was not induced, the health or life of the female person would be likely to be threatened." The bill passed the House of

Commons in 1990 by a narrow majority of 140 to 131, but only after party discipline was imposed on the Cabinet (though not the back bench). The issue then moved to the Senate, where, for the first time ever, there was a tied vote, in part because of common opposition by pro-life and pro-choice senators to the bill. This result was the first defeat of a government bill in thirty years in the unelected Senate.[62] The government somewhat gratefully allowed the bill to die and did not attempt, as it had done to secure passage of the goods and services tax (GST), to appoint more senators or to strong-arm (or wheel in) the holdouts.

What is to be made of the failure of Parliament to respond to *Morgentaler*? Some have worried that it is an ominous sign of the "politics of rights" that allows "individuals and interest groups ... to recast their policy goals in the rhetoric of rights and then take them to the courts to be 'enforced'" and "a judicialization of abortion" that represents "the triumph of individualism and liberalism" over values such as compassion and responsibility "promoted by other organizing ideas like socialism and toryism."[63] There are some problems with this dire diagnosis. The Supreme Court did not dictate any particular policy on abortion, and it was prepared to balance the rights of women with the state's legitimate interest in protecting the fetus. If "court-room rights talk"[64] was undermining the willingness to make compromises, the talk was not coming from the Court. Popular images of rights may be more absolutist and less compromising than the actual structure of the *Charter* or the decisions of the Court. The make-no-compromises politics of rights thrived in a situation in which elected politicians and appointed senators were allowed to vote without the imposition of party discipline. These conditions make it unfair to blame Parliament's failure to enact abortion legislation on either the Court or the *Charter*.

The failure to enact legislation after *Morgentaler* suggests that a well-functioning parliamentary system may be as important as sections 1 and 33 of the *Charter* to ensuring that the Court does not have the final word on matters of social policy. An elected Senate that regularly vetoed legislation supported by Cabinet or generated counter legislation would make it more difficult for Parliament to respond to *Charter* decisions. Similarly, a relaxation of party discipline could make it more difficult to respond to Court decisions, as backbenchers might hold out if the government reply was thought to be too strong or not strong enough. The present system of Cabinet domination and tight party discipline, however, allows for effective legislative replies. In cases where our elected governments are not prepared to overcome the burden of legislative inertia by a Cabinet decision to enact legislation and apply party discipline, it does not seem unreasonable for the Court's decision to stick. This is especially true if the judges have set the status quo to assist a group whose rights are at stake and if the group may have difficulty having its voice heard in the political process. The fact that Parliament may not be prepared to make the effort of overcoming the burden of legislative inertia in some cases hardly supports the conclusion that the *Charter* is "deeply and fundamentally undemocratic" or that the dialogue is "usually a monologue."[65] When the elected government is firmly committed to responding to the Court's *Charter* decision, it can do so. And, when the elected government does not wish to push the issue, we would be better questioning ourselves why we elected it rather than blaming the Court or the *Charter*.

The Failure to Respond to *Vriend*

Another case that is cited by the critics of judicial activism as evidence of judicial monologues and judicial supremacy is the failure of Alberta to respond to the Supreme Court's decision in *Vriend*. In this case the Court read into Alberta's human rights code protection against discrimination on the basis of sexual orientation, an area that the legislature had deliberately left out. As with *Morgentaler*, however, the failure of the legislature to respond must be assessed in its proper political context.

The story starts in March 1998 when the Alberta government proposed using the override to prevent *Charter* challenges to a law limiting compensation to about 700 people who had been involuntarily sterilized between 1928 and 1972 as part of a eugenics program aimed at those classified as "mentally defective."[66] Premier Klein defended the legislation — which capped awards at $150,000 — as a compromise that avoided litigation and limited the government's exposure to lawsuits claiming over $700 million. Some victims of involuntary sterilization opposed the legislation, arguing, "we have just as much right as he does on this planet. How dare he take my rights away." The proposed use of the notwithstanding clause and understandable sympathy for the victims made the issue front-page news.[67] The very next day the government acknowledged the criticism it had received by scrapping the bill. Klein conceded that his "political sense ... didn't click into gear"; it had become "abundantly clear to individuals in this country that the Charter of Rights and Freedoms is paramount" and that the notwithstanding clause "is something that you use only very, very rarely."[68] On the day that the Supreme Court handed down *Vriend*, and less than two weeks after the retreat on the eugenics override, Klein gave a "public undertaking that if the notwithstanding clause is ever to be even considered again, there would have to be full and open and intensive public consultation."[69] Alberta's inability to use the override in response to *Vriend* was largely a self-inflicted wound.

In any event, it is far from clear that Alberta wanted to use the override. Klein stated in the legislature that "*Vriend* was probably the right decision" and that he abhorred "the thought of discrimination of any kind." Two-thirds of Albertans in a poll conducted for the government supported the decision not to use the notwithstanding clause, and three-quarters believed that people should be able to lodge complaints with the human rights commission about discrimination on the basis of sexual orientation.[70] The use of the override to reverse *Vriend* would have been almost as unpopular with Albertans as its proposed use against those the government had involuntarily sterilized. The same poll also suggested that most Albertans were not opposed to extending benefits to same-sex couples, but that a majority were opposed to gay marriage. As we will see, the government has acted and used the override to outlaw gay marriage. Those who criticize *Vriend* as judicial activism should accept that the elected government could have restored the status quo with the use of the override. *Vriend* enhanced democracy by requiring Alberta to confront the way it treated a disadvantaged minority. It in no way dictated that equal personhood must be extended to the minority, so long as the government was willing to reassert and defend a position that was a product of discrimination and neglect.

A Variety of Responses to *M. v. H.*

Some commentators try to dismiss the struggle for gay rights as a post-modern and postmaterialist campaign for "status and recognition" that is not connected to the elimination of "tangible material disadvantage."[71] The struggle for gay rights is a plea for recognition and belonging, but it is also a fight to keep one's job and to have a roof over one's head. Certainly, Delwin Vriend was making a point when he took Alberta to court, but he was also fighting for his job after he had been fired when his employer learned he was gay. *M. v. H.* was also a case with real life implications. It arose from the breakup of a ten-year relationship. H. was financially dominant, owning the house and contributing the most to the family business. M. devoted more of her time to domestic tasks. As a common law spouse playing the role of the traditional wife, M. would normally have been entitled to apply for support from the financially dominant spouse on the dissolution of the relationship. M., however, was out of luck. It was not because she did not need support — she was unemployed at the time — or that she had not earned it. It was simply because her spouse also happened to be a woman.

The Court decided in *M. v. H.* that the exclusion of same-sex common law partnerships from support provisions in Ontario's *Family Law Act* constituted unjustified discrimination against gays and lesbians. As in *Vriend*, the Court indicated that the inclusion of gays and lesbians would better advance the objectives of the legislature, in this case responding to economic needs arising from the breakup of conjugal relationships. The Court seemed anxious to avoid the charges of judicial activism that accompanied the *Vriend* case[72] and repeatedly stressed that its decision did not involve marriage. It also departed from the *Vriend* remedy of reading in same-sex couples to the legislative definition of common law couples. Instead, the Court simply declared the legislation invalid subject to a six-month delay. This remedy essentially held the ability of heterosexual common law spouses to seek support from their former partners hostage to the legislature's decision whether it was prepared to enact legislation to include same-sex couples — and in a hurry.

Critics of judicial activism describe *M.* v. *H.* as a "blockbuster case" that, because it affects so many spousal benefits laws, "renders denials of judicial activism problematic" and as a "remedial decree" case that "specified a new policy practice to fill the gap" left by the legislature.[73] These claims, however, are themselves rendered problematic by the sheer variety of responses that governments have taken to the Court's decision. On the one hand, a social democratic government in British Columbia quickly moved to equalize the benefits of all same-sex couples with both common law and married couples. It also supported a gay couple who went to court to be allowed to marry and called on the federal government to "send a very positive signal to society that ... discrimination is no longer acceptable."[74] In the neighbouring province of Alberta, a neo-conservative government has yet to equalize benefits for same-sex couples; in addition, it used the notwithstanding clause to outlaw gay marriages for at least five years. These are the extremes, but they demonstrate both democracy and federalism at work. Other governments took positions in the middle and have not yet exhausted the range of reply options. If this is judicial activism, it is judicial activism with a very wide range of legislative endings.

Ontario's response to *M.* v. *H.* was one of prompt but grudging compliance, combined with symbolic opposition to the idea that gays and lesbians can really be spouses. Ontario's neo-conservative government enacted comprehensive legislation that amended more than sixty-five pieces of legislation before the expiry of the Court's six-month delay of the declaration of invalidity. To its credit, the Ontario government did not play the minimalist game of amending only the legislation that had been the subject of litigation. The attorney general explained that "legislation is clearly not part of our agenda" and was introduced only because of the Court's decision. On the surface, this response seemed to imply that the Court had dictated to a reluctant government that common law partnerships included same-sex partnerships. A previous social democrat government had tried to achieve the same result in 1994, but had failed after allowing a free vote on the issue. A closer look, however, suggests that the Ontario government was able to stamp some of its social conservatism on the new legislation. The same press release in which the attorney general complained about having the legislation forced on the agenda by the Court also explained that the bill "responds to the Supreme Court decision while preserving the traditional value of the family in Ontario. Rights and obligations that apply only to married couples are not being extended to same sex partners. The Bill does not alter the traditional meaning of common law spouse in Ontario law."[75] The bill achieved these conservative policy goals by adding a new term — "same-sex partner" — that would receive the same benefits as heterosexual couples, who were still the only ones described in the legislation as "spouses." To be sure, this amendment was largely a matter of semantics and symbols, but one with the policy consequence of affirming traditional family values and being hurtful to those in the gay community who wanted to be recognized as spouses in a family. The Ontario government was able to comply with the Court's decision while, at the same time, indicating its conservative belief that only a man and a woman could be genuine spouses. The successful litigant in the case applied for a rehearing before the Supreme Court on the basis that "the Ontario Legislature has failed gays and lesbians again" by creating "a segregated 'partnership' category." Citing the attorney general's argument about preserving traditional family values, she argued that "the sole purpose of the separate definition is to discriminate" and to indicate that, "under all of the amended laws, gays and lesbians, are not spouses, not family."[76] The Supreme Court denied the request for a rehearing without giving reasons, and other courts have deferred to the legislature's choice of words in creating a separate but equal category of "same-sex partners."[77] The Ontario government was able to put its policy stamp on the legislation it enacted to comply with M. v. H.

The federal government's response to M. v. H. was more enthusiastic. It amended sixty-eight statutes by defining common law partnerships of at least a year between "two persons" as conjugal relationships, thus avoiding criticisms that the separate but equal approach used by Ontario was discriminatory. The legislation was, however, amended in committee to incorporate a motion made by the Reform Party, and passed by a vote of 216 to 55 in Parliament, that nothing in the Act affects the meaning of marriage as "the union of one man and one woman to the exclusion of others."[78] Although the Court repeatedly stressed in M. v. H. that its decision has nothing to do with marriage, Parliament's reply to the decision suggests an opposition to gay marriage. It was opposed by Equality for Gays and Lesbians Everywhere (EGALE) on the basis that it suggested that gay relationships were inherently inferior to heterosexual relationships. Both the Court and Parliament, which has jurisdiction over marriage, will eventually have to deal with the gay marriage issue. Parliament's initial response has unimaginatively defined the issue in the stark and divisive terms of gay marriage or no gay marriage. There are other alternatives, including a wide range of domestic partnership laws, that would allow individuals living together, whether conjugally or not, more choice in structuring the legal significance of their relationship. A conservative government in Nova Scotia has, for example, provided for registered domestic partnerships that will receive the same benefits as married couples.[79]

The least enthusiastic response to *M. v. H.* was Alberta's sullen silence on the issue of equalized benefits and its temper tantrum that shouted down anyone from even litigating the gay marriage issue. Alberta has not yet enacted legislation to comply with *M. v. H.*, despite the public survey which suggests that most Albertans have no problem with the equalization of benefits for gay couples and despite having a perfect opportunity to do so when it enacted legislation in response to court decisions that it had discriminated against opposite-sex common law spouses by not providing them with the same benefits as married partners. The elected representatives of Alberta did, however, find the time to take the strongest possible stance against gay marriage. On 15 March 1999, by a vote of 32 to 15,[80] they passed a private members' bill that defined marriage as a union of a man and a woman and that employed the notwithstanding provisions of both the *Charter* and the *Alberta Bills of Rights*. The preamble accompanying the legislation provided that the public was deeply interested in preserving the "purity" of marriage and that "marriage between a man and a woman has from time immemorial been firmly grounded in our legal tradition, one that is itself a reflection of long standing philosophical and religious traditions." The bill, and particularly the use of the notwithstanding clause, was debated over a number of days. Its sponsor argued that the western premiers had insisted on the inclusion of the notwithstanding clause in the *Charter* to ensure that legislatures "can assert their will in matters of important public policy."[81] The opposition Liberals argued that it was possible to preserve the traditional view of marriage with "*Charter* proof" legislation that did not drag "out the howitzer, section 33 of the Charter." They claimed that, because the people of Alberta were opposed to the override being used against the anglophone minority in Quebec, they should be equally opposed to its use against gays and lesbians, especially before the courts had even had an opportunity to rule on the gay marriage issue. The decision to enact the law with the override, as well as the subsequent and resounding re-election of the Klein government, suggests that reports of the death of section 33 have been exaggerated.

Alberta's use of the override to outlaw gay marriage means that, for five years at least, courts in Alberta cannot even participate in a dialogue about gay marriage, let alone have the final word. The bill's sponsor candidly explained that "if we do not use the notwithstanding clause, we have left the door open to challenges." Another supporter explained that the pre-emptive use of the override was a means to send "a clear message to the court system ... that any move to change the definition of marriage would be a mistaken interpretation of the intent of the Legislature and the Charter."[82] This passage reflects the conservative judicial philosophy of the Reform Party that courts should be held accountable by the legislature whenever they stray from the intent of the legislature. The use of the override was also an exception to the government's commitment in the wake of *Vriend* to consult the public in a referendum before using the override.[83] Perhaps the government felt it could escape responsibility by the use of American-style private members' bills. The override will unfortunately silence meaningful dialogue on gay marriage by denying an unpopular minority access to the courts on an issue that would be quickly voted, if not shouted, down if raised in the legislature. For all intents and purposes, Alberta has stopped democratic dialogue on whether laws that restrict marriage to heterosexuals constitute unjustified discrimination against gays and lesbians. The only saving grace is that, by using the override, Alberta will be forced to revisit the issue when the override expires in 2004. By that time the issue will have been considered by the courts and perhaps the legislatures in other provinces. By 2004 public opinion on gay marriage in Alberta may have caught up to public acceptance of *Vriend* and the equalization of benefits contemplated in *M. v. H.*

Not Even the Final Word Is Final: Remedial Dialogue

One would expect the courts to lay down the law when ordering remedies for proven and unjustified *Charter* violations. Even at the remedial stage, however, the Court has bent over backward to let the legislature have its say. The most visible instrument of remedial dialogue is the Court's invention and widespread use of the delayed declaration of invalidity. This remedy means that even when the Court decides to strike down a law as unconstitutional, it can suspend the possibly disruptive remedy, often for a year, to give the legislature an opportunity to pre-empt that remedy with new legislation. During that time, the unconstitutional legislation remains in force. This Canadian remedial innovation, one that is now entrenched in the new South African Constitution, recognizes the reality of dialogue and the ability of the legislature to respond with new legislation to most *Charter* decisions. It was first used in the 1985 *Manitoba Language Reference* to avoid the "legal vacuum" and "chaos and anarchy" that would have resulted had all of Manitoba's unilingual laws been struck down. From this extraordinary beginning, the use of delayed or suspended declarations of invalidity has grown by leaps and bounds so that they now verge on the routine. The Court's concern about giving governments an opportunity to respond to its rulings has been so strong that it has eclipsed more traditional concerns about giving a successful litigant an immediate remedy. The Court effectively says to the successful litigant: "Congratulations, you have won the case. Even though it has taken many years and your savings, you will not receive an immediate remedy because we are going to give the government a year to decide what to do."[84]

A remedy that is widely misunderstood as a sort of permanent judicial injunction over the legislature occurs when the Court decides to cure a constitutional defect in legislation not by striking it down, but by reading in words that make the legislation constitutional. The Court uses this remedy only when it concludes that both the *Charter* and the intent of the legislature will be better served by judicial amendment, rather than striking down, the legislation. It was first used by lower courts in the *Schachter* litigation after they found that a biological parent was treated unequally by having less parental leave than a parent who adopted a child.[85] Instead of striking down the fifteen weeks of parental leave available to those who adopt children, a remedy that would have achieved equality with a vengeance and harmed adoptive parents who were not represented in the litigation, the lower courts read in the ability of biological parents to obtain such parental leave. Many critics complained that this decision was a bold judicial act of legislation. The court's reading in remedy was not, however, the final word. Parliament was concerned about the budgetary implications of the court's remedy and it amended the legislation to provide that all parents — biological or adoptive — got only ten weeks of parental leave. Adoptive parents were not happy with this reduction, but it was a legitimate option open to the legislature. Parliament was in a better position than the court to know how much parental leave it could afford and parents did not have a *Charter* right to fifteen, as opposed to ten, weeks of leave.

On appeal, the Supreme Court affirmed that the courts could cure constitutional defects by reading in terms to legislation, but suggested that caution was in order before courts used the remedy. The Court concluded that the lower courts had distorted Parliament's intent and blown its budget by extending benefits intended for a small group (adoptive parents) to a much larger group (biological parents). The Supreme Court's remedy was to strike down the benefits received by adoptive parents, albeit subject to a one-year delay. Adoptive (but not biological) parents would still receive parental leave during this time. Parliament could decide which of many options to pursue. It could give all parents fifteen weeks of parental leave, it could give them less than fifteen weeks (such as the ten weeks available under the legislation enacted in response to the lower courts' decision extending fifteen weeks of benefits), or it could abolish parental leave altogether. The case that recognized reading in as a remedy was actually characterized by judicial deference to Parliament's intent and capacities.

The Court's most controversial use of the reading in remedy was *Vriend*, when it read protection against discrimination on the basis of sexual orientation into Alberta's human rights code. The purposes of both the legislation and the *Charter* supported adding sexual orientation rather than striking down the entire human rights code because of its unconstitutional failure to include sexual orientation. The Alberta government complained about judicial legislation and expressed a preference for Justice Major's dissent on the issue of remedy. Justice Major's solution of striking down the entire human rights code because of its failure to include sexual orientation would have effectively held the code hostage to whether the legislature was prepared to include sexual orientation in the law. In any event, the Court's reading-in remedy was not necessarily the final word because Alberta could "modify the amended legislation by passing exceptions and defences which they feel can be justified under s. 1 of the Charter" or it could "turn to s. 33 of the Charter, the override provision, which ... is the ultimate 'parliamentary safeguard.'" This option effectively responded to Justice Major's argument that "it should lie with the elected Legislature to determine this issue. They are answerable to the electorate ... and it is for them to choose the remedy whether it is changing the legislation or using the notwithstanding clause."[86] The difference was that the majority, in a sensible and principled fashion, assigned the burden of legislative inertia so that those who wished to deny protection against discrimination on the basis of sexual orientation had to enact legislation, while Justice Major would have allowed the entire human rights code to be unnecessarily struck down if the legislature had decided simply to do nothing. If anything, Justice Major's approach was the more drastic remedy. In any event, either remedy left room for a response from the legislature.

Is the Court more respectful to the legislature when it fixes unconstitutional aspects of laws by the interpretative devices of reading in or reading down or when it strikes down the entire law? This is a difficult question. In the early years of the *Charter*, the Court tended to strike down constitutionally overbroad legislation, reasoning that the legislature should have an opportunity to redraft the law from scratch. More recently, the Court has found ways to save possibly unconstitutionally laws by interpretative devices. This approach was most dramatically done in the *Sharpe* case: the Court devised and read in to the broad offence of possession of child pornography certain limited exceptions for some privately created and held materials depicting lawful sexual activity. This decision saved the legislation under the *Charter* and meant that the Court did not, as the lower courts in British Columbia had done, strike down the offence because it was unconstitutional in some of its applications. The Court's efforts to save the legislation from invalidation were praised both by the police and by many in government for leaving a useful offence on the books. At the same time, the Court's decision in *Sharpe* did involve a certain amount of judicial amendment of the legislation, albeit amendment that preserved as much of Parliament's intent as was constitutionally permissible. Faced with overbroad legislation, courts can be criticized as activist for both striking down the law or for saving it by interpreting it in a manner not intended by the legislature. In either case, however, the legislature can still enact new legislation in response to the Court's remedy.

Courts in the United Kingdom are now faced with a similar dilemma under the *Human Rights Act, 1998*. They are invited both to interpret legislation as consistent with rights "where possible" and to declare legislation to be incompatible with rights when not possible. A case can be made that the most candid and democratic form of dialogue is achieved when courts do not try to save legislation in ways that Parliament never intended. Striking down a law leaves it up to Parliament to decide how to respond. Still, a declaration of invalidity in Canada, or a declaration of incompatibility in the United Kingdom, may be a needless intrusion when it is clear that the legislature would have preferred that the Court make minor alterations to the legislation to render it compatible with rights that were perhaps not fully considered when the legislation was enacted. In any event, legislatures under the *Charter* possess an excellent mechanism to reply to either a declaration of invalidity or a reading-down or a reading-in remedy: they can respond with new legislation that can be defended as a reasonable limit on the right that the Court has articulated in its first ruling.

With respect to remedies affecting legislation, the Supreme Court has taken positive steps to facilitate a constructive dialogue between the Court and the legislature. The Court has frequently delayed its blunt remedy of striking unconstitutional laws down in order to give the legislature an opportunity to fill any legislative vacuum before it occurs and to select from a wide array of constitutional alternatives. Even when the Court reads in or reads down legislation to cure a constitutional defect, it is careful to do so only when the intent of both the *Charter* and the legislation supports such a remedy. In any event, the Court's reading-in or reading-down remedy need not be the final word, as the legislature can amend the legislation to alter the interpretation that the Court has given it. Even when we most expect the Court to lay down the law as it provides remedies for unjustified *Charter* violations, its judgments are not necessarily the final word.

Conclusion

Even in the one-third of cases in which the Supreme Court invalidates state action under the *Charter*, its judgments need not be the final word. In the vast majority of cases, the legislature can pursue its policy objectives and attempt to justify a legislative response under section 1 as a reasonable limitation on the right. In cases such as *RJR- MacDonald* the resulting legislation may be somewhat less effective in advancing policy objectives than the legislation the Court has struck down, but that policy distortion is related to the unwillingness of Parliament to enact an in-your-face reply that effectively reverses the Court's decision or to use the override, as Quebec did to reinstate its language legislation. In most cases, however, legislatures have been able to advance their objectives with prompt and effective replies to *Charter* decisions without the use of the override. Cases such as *Morgentaler* and *Vriend*, which did not result in a legislative reply, are exceptions that can be explained by a failure of governmental and public will to exercise the strong legislative powers provided by our parliamentary system of government and sections 1 and 33 of the *Charter*. The reluctance to use the override (which Alberta eventually got over in its pre-emptive assault on gay marriage) may be related to governments and citizens being influenced by an American-style vision of judges as supreme in enforcing absolute rights. A reluctance to use the override (which has not proven politically fatal the three major times it has been used by provincial governments) could constrain our ability to reply to judicial decisions, but it cannot be blamed on either the Court or the *Charter*, both of which embrace a more sophisticated understanding of rights and of institutional and democratic dialogue. In any event, dialogue between courts and legislatures has survived and thrived without the use of the override.

Part 3
Beyond Judicial Activism

Chapter 11
The Myths of Judicial Activism

The extent of judicial activism in Canada under the *Charter* has been examined in the last four chapters. My overall conclusion is that critics of judicial activism on both the left and the right have overestimated the extent to which judges have been able to read their own preferences into law, to avoid the constraints of deciding issues as a court as opposed to a legislature, to maximize rights without regard to competing social values, and to have the last word. The accusation of judicial activism is not only inaccurate but unhelpful. The label "judicial activism" obscures more than it illuminates and allows commentators to criticize the Court and the *Charter* without really explaining their reasons for doing so. It hints at, if not judicial impropriety, at least judicial overreaching, while hiding controversial assumptions about judging, rights, and democracy. We need to move beyond loaded labels and American-style debates about judicial activism to more complex discussions about the role of judges, courts, and legislatures in a democracy. Those who criticize or defend judicial activism must try to escape the tyranny of labels and explain more clearly the reasons for their conclusions.

In this chapter I will identify some implicit assumptions made by those who accuse the Court of engaging in judicial activism. It is much easier to see judicial activism as a pressing problem if you believe that judges should decide only what is necessary to resolve disputes between private parties; that judges can legitimately discover only clear answers in the framers' text or intent; that real rights are rarely, if ever, threatened in a liberal democracy; that judges enforce their inflated views of rights as absolute trumps and final words; and that democracy depends on legislative supremacy. Conversely, judicial activism is much less of a problem if you believe that the Supreme Court should decide legal issues of national importance; that all judging involves bounded creativity; that the state does violate real rights; that rights recognized by the Court need not be absolute; and that the Court's decisions are not inherently undemocratic or the last word in a democracy. Revealing the implicit assumptions will not result in agreement; it will, however, result in a better debate.

The Myth That Judges Can Avoid Deciding *Charter* Issues

A common criticism in debates about judicial activism is that courts engage in it when they decide constitutional issues that are not absolutely necessary to settle a live dispute. In the United States there is a long tradition of courts avoiding constitutional decisions and deciding them narrowly on the facts of the particular case.[1] The idea that courts should, whenever possible, avoid or limit constitutional judgment has influenced conservative critics of judicial activism: they argue that the Supreme Court has abandoned its traditional adjudicative function of settling disputes and become an "oracle" that tries "to solve social problems by issuing broad declarations of constitutional policy" and that it regularly displays "judicial hubris" by unnecessarily making constitutional pronouncements.[2] These critics should confront whether they really want judges to duck constitutional issues and explain why the very act of avoidance is itself not an implicit rejection of the merits of the claim being avoided.

The myth that judges can avoid constitutional issues is perhaps best illustrated by the unhappy stories of two unlikely people whose lives intersected because the Court ducked the issue of fetal rights. One was Joe Borowski, a pro-life crusader from the Prairies, and the other was Chantal Daigle, a young woman from Quebec who found that her ex-boyfriend, Jean-Guy Tremblay, had obtained a court order preventing her from obtaining an abortion. Mr. Borowski, who had been a social democrat Cabinet minister in Manitoba for a short time before resigning so he could speak out against abortion, passionately believed that the fetus was protected by the *Charter* and was offended at the idea that Canadian law allowed abortions, even if they were approved by a hospital committee under the *Criminal Code* as necessary to protect a woman's life or health. He wanted to challenge the constitutionality of any legal abortions, but encountered more than his share of roadblocks in persuading the courts to hear his case. He had no legal right to challenge the abortion law because it did not directly affect his own rights. He would not be charged under the law or have an abortion under it. Instead, Borowski relied on a 1974 case that allowed a citizen to raise a serious constitutional issue that could not be decided in litigation by those directly affected. In that case, the Supreme Court had allowed an opponent of bilingualism to argue that the federal government did not have constitutional powers to implement that controversial program. The Court had emphasized the public interest in ensuring that governments acted constitutionally and that Canadian courts, unlike American courts, were not constitutionally restricted to deciding only live cases and controversies.[3] These cases also demonstrate that public interest standing is open to all, not only the left-leaning groups associated with the so-called Court Party.

The Supreme Court granted Borowski public interest standing on the basis that he was raising serious constitutional issues that could not reasonably be raised in litigation by those directly affected by the law. Chief Justice Laskin dissented, arguing that "mere distaste has never been a ground upon which to seek assistance of the court."[4] His uncharacteristic opinion ignored the fact that Borowski's claim was couched not in terms of taste, but in an allegation that the constitution had been violated. If the Court had told Borowski to go away, it would have implicitly been rejecting his argument that legal abortions violated the *Charter*. It is much better to answer such legal questions directly in a manner that can be judged for all, and not through the indirect means of denying standing or deciding that it is too early or too late for the Court to make a decision.

Chief Justice Laskin was on more solid ground when he argued that it was possible for a person more directly affected — for example, a man who fertilized a fetus — to bring a claim that an abortion would violate the rights of a fetus. The problem with this approach, one that the Court would eventually learn, was that such a concrete dispute would be extremely difficult to litigate. Those who are directly affected by a law may not be able to go to the expense, time, or trauma of litigating the issue. Better decisions may emerge when highly motivated and competent public interest litigants are allowed to raise issues that directly affect others. The *Borowski* case took eight years to return to the Court, but this leisurely pace ensured that the affected parties had the time to give the Court their best evidence and arguments.

Borowski's case on the merits finally came back to the Supreme Court in 1989. The Court declined to decide the case on the basis that it had become moot after the Court had, in 1988, struck down the abortion law in *Morgentaler*. Even though the new status quo violated the rights that Borowski claimed for the fetus even more than the old law and there had been full adversarial argument on the issues, the Court feared that a decision might "pre-empt a possible decision of Parliament by dictating the form of legislation it should enact. To do so would be a marked departure from the traditional role of the court."[5] It is difficult to see how deciding the issues raised by Borowski — issues that the Court admitted could have been remitted to them by the government on a reference — would have dictated legislation to Parliament or departed from the Court's role. The issue was whether the fetus had rights under the *Charter*. The Court's eventual decision that the fetus did not have such rights would not have dictated legislation to Parliament because, as recognized in *Morgentaler*, Parliament could still act to protect a fetus that did not have constitutional rights. Even a decision recognizing fetal rights would have left Parliament an important role in striking the balance between fetal rights and the rights of women denied access to abortions. A decision on the merits in *Borowski* would have contributed to the dialogue among the Court, the legislature, and society on abortion, but it would hardly have been the final word.

A ruling on the merits in *Borowski* might have clarified some of the legal questions about abortion that were being debated in Parliament. It would also have given Borowski a meaningful day in Court after he had spent over a decade litigating the issue. In any event, the Court's decision to declare the appeal moot only delayed the inevitable for a short time. Later that same year the Court was summoned back from its summer recess to sit in an emergency session to decide whether Jean-Guy Tremblay had the legal right to prohibit Chantal Daigle from obtaining an abortion in the twenty-second week of her pregnancy. After argument was commenced, the Court was informed that Ms. Daigle had obtained an abortion in the United States. This development meant that the case was moot. Following *Borowski*, the Court should have declined to answer a constitutional question that was no longer necessary to decide a live dispute. The Court now recognized, however, that the controversial issue of fetal rights could not be avoided. It issued its decision that the rights of the fetus and the father were not protected under the Quebec *Charter*, "in order to try to ensure that another woman is not put through an ordeal such as that experienced by Ms. Daigle."[6] This decision has been criticized as favouritism to the pro-choice position,[7] but it extended to the pro-life forces represented by intervenors in the appeal the courtesy of deciding their claims on the merits.

These cases are a good illustration of what Chief Justice McLachlin has called the "myth that courts can decline to decide Charter issues"[8] that are presented to them. The Court simply must decide constitutional issues, however difficult or divisive they may be. Ducking the issue will only delay the inevitable and often constitute an implicit and unjustified dismissal of the merits of the claim. It is also significant that the techniques of judicial avoidance and minimalism were designed in the American context in an effort to minimize the effects of judges having the final word when they define constitutional rights. A decision on the merits in *Borowski*, unlike the American decision in *Roe v. Wade*, would still have left Parliament plenty of room to devise its own abortion policy. Avoiding constitutional issues under the *Charter* is not necessary to create space for democratic decision making. Elected legislatures retain robust powers under sections 1 and 33 of the *Charter* to respond to even bold and broad constitutional judgments that the Court could have avoided.

The Myth That Judges Exercise Open-Ended Discretion when Making Law

Critics of judicial activism on both the left and the right have reached the conclusion that judges have a strong discretion when interpreting the vague phrases of the *Charter* and that they can read their unrepresentative views into the *Charter*. The left concludes that adjudication is inherently indeterminate and political, while the right holds up the often disappointed hope that judges could decide cases in a formalist manner based on the plain words and intent of the *Charter*. The left predicts that judges will use their discretion under the *Charter* to favour the advantaged, while the right predicts that judges will favour the disadvantaged.

Anyone who regularly reads the decisions of the Supreme Court can see the effects of different approaches and personalities on the Court. Justice Michel Bastarache has indicated that, on criminal matters, he is more conservative than the majority of the Court, particularly former chief justice Antonio Lamer.[9] Not many would disagree. My concern in this chapter, however, is only with the strong claim that judges are free to make the law in their own image. This argument may seem like a straw man, because few people would claim that there are absolutely no constraints on judges deciding cases. The problem is that those who criticize judicial activism have often made something very close to such extreme claims. They are forced to argue that judges enjoy a strong discretion under the *Charter*, in order to make their case that judicial law-making allows an almost monarchial elite to impose its personal views on the populace. And it is ironic that these critics diverge so widely on the predictions of what the personal preferences of the judges will be. The left is convinced that judges will favour corporations and the wealthy because the judges are, after all, wealthy lawyers. The right is convinced that judges will favour the minorities preferred by the intellectual elite, groups that have access to them through the law schools, judicial education, and the law clerks.

A number of critics predicted that, once the Court abandoned the proposition that the principles of fundamental justice protected under section 7 of the *Charter* were restricted to matters of procedural fairness, the only alternative was something akin to the substantive due process that constitutionalized *laissez-faire* economics in *Lochner* and abortion policy in *Roe* v. *Wade*. But this concern has proven not to be the case. The Court's decision in *Morgentaler* can be distinguished from *Roe* v.

Wade in the sense that it left the legislature more room to respond and did not attempt to detail a trimester-by-trimester abortion policy. Reply legislation was introduced and almost enacted that would, contrary to *Roe* v. *Wade*, have regulated abortion at all stages of pregnancy. Although the Court has held that the fetus is not protected under the *Charter*, it has also indicated that Parliament could act to protect the fetus. Canadian judges have not written their own views about abortion — whether they be pro-life or pro-choice — into the *Charter*.

What about the Court's later decision to hold that the principles of fundamental justice require Canadian governments to seek assurances that the death penalty will not be applied before it sends fugitives back to face trials in foreign lands?[10] The Court made this decision even though, a decade earlier, it had allowed mass murderer Charles Ng and escaped murderer Robert Kindler to be sent to the United States to face the death penalty. In addition, attempts to amend extradition legislation to ensure that the minister of justice would always seek assurances that the death penalty would not be applied had been defeated in Parliament. The Court refused to decide the case narrowly on the basis that the fugitives, Glen Burns and Atif Rafay, were Canadian citzens and only eighteen years of age when they were accused of clubbing Rafay's mother, father, and sister to death with a baseball bat. The Court's courageous and bold change of heart on extradition to face the death penalty has been criticized in both national newspapers as an affront to democracy and the rule of law. Ted Morton has argued that the decision underlines that the Court stands "in judgment of the policy wisdom of Parliament's decisions — not based on what the *Charter* means, but on the personal beliefs of a majority of these nine unelected judges."[11] The problem with this argument is that the judges on the Court did not assert their personal beliefs in a roll-call voice vote. Rather, they agreed to a lengthy judgment that attempted to justify their decision in relation to the text of the *Charter* and its prior decisions. The Court also drew a distinction between justice issues that were within its expertise — matters such as the risk of wrongful convictions and the execution of the innocent — as opposed to more general issues about the morality and wisdom of the death penalty. The Court's reasons may not convince everyone; reasonable people may disagree and a majority of Canadians may favour the death penalty. But, as the Court noted, if public opinion was decisive there would be no need for the *Charter* or the independent judiciary to provide protections for "the worst and weakest among us." The Court reminded us of our higher aspirations to justice — not their personal beliefs — when, because of our understandable revulsion at crime, we were most likely to forget them.

Does this role justify giving the Court the final word? Probably not. If, despite a growing international consensus against the death penalty and our increasing awareness of people who are wrongfully convicted of murder, Canadians decide in an election or a referendum that they really want the death penalty, the Court's courageous judgment should not be an insurmountable barrier. The Court would not have to be changed, and the constitution would not have to be amended. There would, however, have to be legislation that invoked the override. This process would make us think twice, and might *de facto* require a strong majority and strong legislative will for the death penalty. But this procedure is more democratic than the state of affairs before the case in which the minister of justice, behind closed doors and without having to give reasons, would decide which fugitives would live and which might die and Parliament could debate the capital punishment without necessarily paying attention to the real risk of the execution of the wrongfully convicted. The override also has the advantages of requiring sober second thoughts and deep debate about the death penalty. It can be used to reinstate the death penalty or our ability to extradite people to face the death penalty, if that is really what Canadians want. If, after five years of a death penalty protected by the override, we release another Donald Marshall, David Milgaard, Guy Paul Morin, Thomas Sophonow, or Gregory Parsons, all wrongfully convicted of murder, or if we execute such a person, Canadians would have a perfect opportunity to reconsider the wisdom of the Court's decision, let the override expire, and repeal the death penalty.

Although judges do make a difference in cases like *Burns and Rafay*, the text of the *Charter* still matters. The courts have been reluctant to find economic rights in the *Charter*, given the absence of property rights or explicit guarantees of adequate social services as found in some other constitutions and proposed in the ill-fated Charlottetown accord.[12] Despite impassioned arguments from law professors that health care, housing, and social assistance are within the purposes of the *Charter* in ensuring security of the person and the equal benefit of the law, the courts have generally rejected such claims.[13] In a case refusing to constitutionalize the right to strike as part of the freedom of association to form a union, the Court has indicated that, with the possible exception of specifically entrenched mobility rights, the *Charter* "does not concern itself with economic rights."[14] Chief Justice Dickson and Justices Lamer and Wilson — all judges not noted for their restraint — concluded that the exclusion of property rights from section 7 of the *Charter* "leads to a general inference that economic rights as generally encompassed in the term 'property' are not within the parameters of the s. 7 guarantee." They left the door open a crack by indicating that they did not declare "that no right with an economic component can fall within 'security of the person.'"[15] Justice Lamer, however, subsequently tried to close the door by arguing that section 7 of the *Charter* should not apply to issues of "pure public policy" and did not include "economic liberty," such as freedom of contract and the right to work as a prostitute.[16] The courts have not read libertarian or communitarian economic views into section 7 of the *Charter*. They have been constrained by the omission of economic or property rights from the *Charter* and have not used it to stand in the way of privatization and the shrinkage of the Canadian welfare state throughout the 1990s. Conversely, the Court would not block attempts to revive the welfare state.[17] It still matters very much which type of governments we elect. As in the abortion cases, the economic rights cases[18] suggest that the claims that courts have an open-ended discretion to read their own preferences for the world into the *Charter* are a myth.

The Myth That No Real Rights Are at Stake in *Charter* Litigation

Some critics of judicial activism are sceptical about whether *Charter* litigation involves real rights. Those on the right question rights inflation and group rights, while those on the left express concern about individualistic and negative rights that protect people from the state. Andrew Petter and others worry about the effect of due process rights, which, by protecting the accused from the state, may make it more difficult for the state to protect the victims of crime, who, like the accused, often come from disadvantaged groups — most notably women and children.[19] These concerns speak to the need to balance due process with victims' rights, but they cannot justify scepticism about due process rights. The state is still putting people in jail, and it had better do so fairly. There is also little evidence that abandonment of due process will actually protect the victims of crime.

The right expresses a different type of scepticism about rights. Ted Morton and Rainer Knopff state that "the courtroom politics promoted by the Court Party" are "authoritarian": they undermine the pluralistic politics of liberal democracies and the need for a sovereign people to accept the ability of a temporary majority "to set and conclude the rest." Christopher Manfredi similarly argues that it is wrong to see the legislative process as a "zero sum game" in which some majorities and some minorities are permanent.[20] Behind this defence of pluralistic politics lurks deep scepticism about whether *Charter* litigation involves violation of real rights and concerns that the Court is blurring "the distinction between genuine mistreatment of discrete and insular minorities and the ordinary vicissitudes of democratic politics."[21] Critics on the right suggest that many who are going to Court should accept the win-some / lose-some attitude that is necessary for a healthy democracy.

The defence of *Charter* litigation as a short circuit of pluralistic politics might work if the courts had blown *Charter* rights up so they could be claimed whenever any temporary minority was denied some benefit. This, however, has not been the case. The *Charter* has not been interpreted to protect people against every restraint on their freedom and every inequality in their treatment. Section 7 has generally been restricted to issues that involve the justice system, and equality rights have been narrowed to protect only those who are vulnerable to discrimination and affronts to their human dignity. Once the Court placed these important restrictions on the potentially broadest rights in the *Charter*, scepticism about rights seems unwarranted.

The facts of the cases are probably the most eloquent evidence that *Charter* litigation involves real rights. It would be difficult to tell Burns and Rafay that their rights were not at stake when the minister of justice decided to extradite them without assurances that they would not be housed on death row awaiting lethal injection. Delwin Vriend's rights were at stake when he could not even complain about discrimination after he was fired from his teaching job once his employer learned he was gay. Similarly, M's rights were at stake when she could not apply for support simply because her economically dominant ex-spouse was also a woman. The treatment complained about in these cases is not part of the "ordinary vicissitudes of democratic politics" but the denial of equal citizenship. The complaints of *Charter* applicants in these cases do not seem like moral over-sensitivity, but, rather, claims to treatment as an individual with dignity. It is one thing to criticize the Court for the way it balances rights with other rights and social interests, but it simply will not do to pretend that no rights are at stake in *Charter* litigation.

The Myth That Judges Enforce Absolute Rights under the *Charter*

Many concerns about judicial activism are based on an image of a court that is enforcing rights as absolute trumps over social interests and competing rights. The American experience provides plenty of examples of rights being enforced in this manner, especially in the context of the First Amendment's absolute command that no law shall be made abridging freedom of expression, religion, and association. The Canadian Court, however, has rejected the idea of rights as absolute trumps. In its recent decision upholding the offence of possession of child pornography, Chief Justice McLachlin rejected the idea that any right, even one related to one's privately held written material, would be beyond limitation under section 1 of the *Charter*.[22] Whereas the Canadian Supreme Court has affirmed Jim Keegstra's conviction for hate propaganda, based on his teaching of hateful conspiracy theories about Jews to his students, the United States Supreme Court has struck down a law prohibiting cross burnings and swastika displays as impermissible regulation of the content of speech. Similarly, the Canadian Court upheld restrictions on degrading and dehumanizing pornography that were struck down in the United States as attempts to regulate the content of speech.[23] My purpose is not to join the debate about the merits of these decisions, but simply to indicate the increased margin of deference that Canadian legislatures have over American legislatures when placing content-based restrictions on speech. The idea that courts will enforce absolute rights in Canada is simply a myth.

Some people may reasonably argue that the Court has erred in deciding that all expressive activity short of violence is expression protected under the *Charter*. By allowing limits to be placed on rights, however, section 1 of the *Charter* allows legislatures to limit the damage caused by any judicial overreaching in defining rights. Many people believe that both American and Canadian courts have made serious mistakes in equating freedom of expression with the spending of large amounts of money to influence elections. In the United States the Supreme Court has severely restricted the ability of legislatures to impose limits on campaign financing, despite serious fears that this practice has produced inequities and inequalities in their high-spending electoral system.[24] Canadian courts under the *Charter* had made the same equation, and the National Citizens Coalition has won several cases in Alberta striking down various restrictions on third party spending in an election.[25] The results of these cases were significant because they led to wide-open third party spending in the 1988 and 1993 federal elections. These cases are some of the strongest examples of the dangers of judicial activism under the *Charter*.

Nevertheless, Parliament has not been powerless in crafting a response. After the first National Citizens Coalition case and the free-spending free trade election of 1988, the government appointed a royal commission to examine electoral financing. Several years and millions of dollars later, the commission made strong recommendations about the need for restrictions on campaign spending and the dangers of the approach taken by the American and Canadian courts.[26] A royal commission can be a potent instrument in the government's attempt to influence the Court, because it can produce the social science evidence that the courts will often defer to under section 1 of the *Charter*. In 1997 the Supreme Court indicated that it was entirely permissible under section 1 of the *Charter* for the government to limit the speech and spending of some individuals and groups in order to ensure fairness and to enhance the voice of those who could not spend millions in an attempt to influence an election. The Court quoted the commission report with approval and took notice of the inequities produced by unrestricted spending in the 1988 election.[27] During the 2000 federal election the Court overturned an injunction secured by the National Citizens Coalition against the enforcement of new restrictions on third party spending. The Court did not decide the merits of the challenge, but its actions reaffirmed the legitimacy of the government's objectives in regulating third party spending during elections.[28] When the government gathers the evidence and mounts a strong case, it can often justify reasonable limits on rights.

The ability of governments to justify limitations on rights under section 1 of the *Charter* and the willingness of the Court to listen to the government's case for justification can mitigate any overbroad judicial definitions of rights. Those who criticize the courts for engaging in judicial activism must account for the opportunity that section 1 of the *Charter* provides for government to justify limitations on rights. However tempting it may be, the American image of rights being enforced as absolute and final limits on governments is not an accurate description of the *Charter*. The courts may make mistakes under section 1 of the *Charter* if they are not presented with enough information about the need for limits on rights, but these mistakes can generally be corrected with better legislation and better evidence.

The Myth of Judicial Supremacy under the *Charter*

The critics of judicial activism will not be persuaded by the ability of governments to respond to judicial decisions with legislation that can be defended under section 1 of the *Charter*. After all, courts still decide whether new limits placed on the right are reasonable. These critics dismiss the concept of dialogue between the Court and the legislature. Those on the right argue that mandatory court decisions are "a monologue, with judges doing most of the talking and legislatures most of the listening,"[29] while those on the left complain that any dialogue between courts and legislatures leave citizens as "eavesdroppers at the doors of power." [30] The dialogue metaphor is not perfect, and I will suggest in chapters 13 and 14 that it is open to confusion and abuse. But the baby should not be thrown out with the bath water. Criticisms of dialogue turn into error when commentators assume that the *Charter* is based on judicial supremacy.

Dialogue would be difficult and often illusory if the only effective way to respond to constitutional decisions was to change the constitution or the Court. As we saw in chapter 3, both drastic measures were eventually used to respond to the decisions of the Judicial Committee of the Privy Council that the federal government could not implement a New Deal, including unemployment insurance, to deal with the Great Depression. It may often be difficult for a government whose legislation is invalidated under the division of powers to formulate new legislation to pursue the same policy objectives. As in the United States, it may be necessary to change the constitution or the Court. Dialogue, however, is much easier under the *Charter*. Governments can talk back to the Court under section 1 as they explain their reasons for limiting a right and the alternatives they considered and rejected. If this exchange does not work, governments can shout at the Court by using the section 33 override. Shouting, however, comes with a political price, in terms of heightened public attention and a requirement that the legislature revisit the matter after a five-year cooling-off period when the override expires.

As we discussed in chapter 10, there are plenty examples of legislative responses to court decisions. Parliament responded to the Court's invalidation of a total ban on tobacco advertising with legislation prohibiting lifestyle advertising. This response has been criticized as distorting Parliament's policy to get tough on a serious health risk. All the blame, however, cannot be dumped on the Court or the *Charter*. The government could have done a better job in justifying the necessity of the total ban in the first place by demonstrating, if it could, that it was more effective than the less restrictive lifestyle advertising ban. Even without the override, Parliament could have enacted an "in-your-face" reply that effectively reinstated most of the old law. Parliament has not been shy in reversing *Charter* decisions recognizing a defence of extreme intoxication and access to complainants' private records with in-your-face replies. One reason that the government may not have enacted an in-your-face reply that essentially reversed the Court's decision may be that the tobacco companies who pump millions into the economy through corporate sponsorships have more political power than those accused of sexual assault. This political fact of life, however, cannot be blamed on the false idea that the *Charter* promotes judicial supremacy. Finally, if the government had really wanted to prohibit all tobacco advertising, it need only have pulled the trigger on the section 33 override. If governments in Saskatchewan, Quebec, and Alberta can be re-elected after using the override against unions, non-French speakers, and gays and lesbians, respectively, it is a safe bet that the people of Canada would have accepted the use of the override against the tobacco companies that are contributing to the death of so many of us. Critics of judicial activism who profess to be concerned about democracy should accept with good grace decisions by their elected governments not to use the override.

The Myth of Majoritarian Democracy and Undemocratic Judicial Review

The final myth that should be discarded in our debates about the proper role of the Court is the idea that judicial review is undemocratic and that Canadian democracy has traditionally been based on the wishes of the majority unfettered by judicial intervention. Many critics of judicial activism on all sides of the political spectrum argue with passion that judicial review is inherently undemocratic. Their views cannot be lightly discarded because there is something odd about a Court of nine appointed judges striking down legislation enacted by elected governments. It will not do to say simply that elected governments agreed to entrench the *Charter*. The governments that agreed to the *Charter* may not have foreseen the evolution of judicial review in Canada. In any event, they are our old governments, not our current ones. A slightly different take is to argue that some rights are indispensable to a functioning democracy. Long before the *Charter* the Supreme Court struck down restrictions on a free press on the basis that they were inconsistent with a functioning Parliament, which requires wide and free debate on matters of public controversy. The idea that judicial review can be justified as enforcing the ground rules of democracy will be explored in chapter 12, but at this juncture it must be conceded that it is difficult to justify many *Charter* decisions, especially the majority made with respect to criminal justice, as absolutely or uncontroversially necessary to maintain democracy.

A sense of history is important to understand why judicial review that restrains majorities is not inherently undemocratic. The treaties between the First Nations and the Crown indicate that Aboriginal rights are not some recent invention, but were recognized from the time Europeans came to Canada. Confederation was a creative compromise that tempered majority rule based on the one-person / one-vote principle of representation by population with federalism and minority rights — both of which were subsequently enforced by courts. Canadian history cannot be rewritten so that Lord Durham's dream of a legislative union where the majority could swamp the minority was actually realized.[31] Like Confederation, the creation of the *Charter* was a creative compromise between the rights of individuals and minorities on the one hand and concerns about communal self-government on the other. Pierre Trudeau's insistence on rights for individuals and minorities, which could be enforced by the Supreme Court, was tempered by the insistence of Allan Blakeney and others that rights be subject to both explicit limitation and override by all the elected governments of Canada.

The Supreme Court understands that Canada was never a purely majoritarian democracy. At significant junctures, it has recognized the complexity of Canada. In the implied bill of rights cases from Alberta in the 1930s and Quebec in the 1950s, it reminded us that democracy requires respect for fundamental freedoms. In *Oakes*,[32] Chief Justice Dickson reminded us that a free and democratic society depends on respect for individual and group dignity and diversity, as well as on democratic institutions that "enhance the participation of individuals and groups in society." More recently in the *Quebec Secession Reference*,[33] the Court reminded us that the core values of Canada include not only democracy but federalism, minority rights, and the rule of law. The starkly majoritarian vision of democracy that critics of judicial activism on both the left and the right have embraced is an incomplete vision that does not do justice to the complex and plural commitments of Canada. It has never existed. If the country is to survive, its democracy will never be purely majoritarian. The idea of a purely majoritarian democracy is an unrealistic and ultimately destructive myth. At the very least, it is an inaccurate starting point to measure the effects of the *Charter* on Canada.

As we will elaborate in chapter 14, a better starting point is to see the *Charter* as a continuation of a common law tradition that enhances democracy by requiring legislatures to consider rights, but does not impose the Court's judgments about rights as the absolute final word. In many cases, *Charter* litigation restrains the activities of police officers. Democracy and the rule of law alike are enhanced when Parliament responds to these decisions with new legislation that authorizes and regulates the police conduct in question. Because of Supreme Court decisions, we do not leave the seizure of bodily samples for DNA testing or the entry into homes to make arrests to the discretion of police officers. We now have statutory authorization for when and how the police should invade the bodily integrity and break down the doors of even the "worse and weakest" among us. The Court has not had the last word on police powers, but its decisions have enhanced democracy by generating legislative replies that should have promoted public debate about police powers and accountability for the exercise of police powers.

Even on issues of contentious social policy, the Court's interventions under the *Charter* can be defended as enhancing and forcing democracy. In the Court's decision in *Vriend*, for example, it found that the exclusion of protection from discrimination on the basis of sexual orientation in Alberta's human rights code was an unjustified form of discrimination. As suggested above, this decision can be defended as a just recognition of Delwin Vriend's very real rights to complain that he was fired for discriminatory reasons. Irrespective of the justice of

Vriend's claim, however, the Court's decision can also be defended as promoting democracy in Alberta. Christopher Manfredi has suggested that "*Vriend* represented the boldest step in a sequence of institutional interactions that promotes the transition from legislative to judicial supremacy in Canada." For him, the Court's reference to the ability of Alberta to respond by invoking section 33 was "disingenuous," given "the political delegitimization of the notwithstanding clause."[34] Alberta's subsequent use of the override on gay marriage, however, suggests that Professor Manfredi is wrong to suggest that section 33 is permanently out of bounds. The reason why Alberta did not use the override to over-rule *Vriend* was not that section 33 was illegitimate, but because the people and the premier thought the decision was right. A committed democrat should not complain if the elected government of the people is not prepared to use the override.[35]

Ted Morton and Rainer Knopff take a different tack and argue that *Vriend* took away the government's "preferred choice," which "was not to act at all ... Prior to the ruling, the Klein government could safely ignore this issue, upsetting only a small coalition of activists, few of whom were Tory supporters in any case."[36] Refusing to address an issue may technically be a form of policy making, but it is not a particularly admirable or courageous one, especially if the reason for doing so is that a vulnerable minority can be dismissed as "a small coalition of activists" that the government can ignore. A refusal to address an issue is often the result of legislative inertia and, as such, does not carry the same democratic weight as a recently debated and affirmed policy.[37] The Court's decision in *Vriend* enhanced democracy by addressing this defect of majoritarian politics, while giving the legislature an opportunity to reassert the status quo as the will of the majority if it was willing to do so in a clear and transparent manner. The government was not willing to defend a position that was a product of discrimination and neglect, and not supported by its own electorate.

Vriend enhanced democracy by requiring Alberta to confront how it treated a disadvantaged minority, while in no way dictating that equal personhood must be extended to the gay and lesbian minority. Alberta's acceptance of *Vriend* should help promote faith in democracy by suggesting that, given the opportunity to use the notwithstanding clause in order to discriminate against gays and lesbians, both the government and the people of Alberta chose the high road, albeit with a little help from the Court. If they had chosen discrimination, at least the override would have preserved the Court's point of principle and required the legislature to revisit the matter in five years' time. Unfortunately, Alberta later chose to short-circuit meaningful democratic debate on gay marriage by using the override to prohibit courts from even considering whether present restrictions on marriage are an unjustified form of discrimination against gays and lesbians. It would have been more democratic to have allowed the minority and the courts to speak their lines in the dialogue and then have decided whether to use the override.

Conclusion

Despite its common usage and attraction as a shorthand for more complex ideas, the term "judicial activism" is ultimately not a helpful way to structure debate about judicial review, at least under the *Charter* or other modern bills of rights. The label "judicial activism" obscures more than it illuminates because it allows commentators to criticize the Court without explaining why they believe a particular decision is wrong. Moreover, it allows critics to claim the high moral ground and hint at judicial impropriety, without explaining their often controversial views about judging, rights, and democracy.

All critics of judicial activism should explain why, if judges are free to impose their world views under the *Charter*, they still bother to explain their conclusions not on the basis of personal preferences, but in terms of their interpretation of the text, precedents, and traditions that affect the question before them. It is perhaps inevitable that complex jurisprudential issues cannot always be fully explained, but it would improve the debate if critics of judicial activism made clear what they expect of judges. If this explanation occurs, many people may dismiss both the framers'-intent approach favoured by some conservative critics of judicial activism and the deep indeterminacy approach favoured by some on the left as extreme views about what judges actually do.

Another major limitation of the label "judicial activism" is that it often hides the user's views about rights. Rights are one of the most theoretically and politically charged issues of our age, and reasonable people will disagree about them. At the same time, those criticizing the Court for engaging in judicial activism and those defending the Court from such charges should come clean about their view on rights. Critics on the right have been admirably candid about their views that *Charter* litigation does not generally involve real rights, but rather disputes about thwarted policy preferences that should, in most cases, be resolved in the legislature. Critics on the left have also been candid about their concern that the *Charter* only protects the negative liberty of individuals from the state and does not guarantee their positive liberty. My fear is that those in the media and in politics who raise concerns about judicial activism are often considerably less candid about their scepticism that *Charter* litigation involves real or important rights. Do critics of judicial activism on the right really believe that gay people do not have rights to complain about discrimination or to receive equal benefits? Do critics of judicial activism on the left really believe that accused persons do not have rights to evidence that may be helpful to their defence or protections from the police? The public has a right to know, and people may be dismissive of politicians and pundits who are too dismissive of their rights.

Finally, the critics of judicial activism should make clear their views about democracy. In order to understand why judicial review is not undemocratic, it is helpful to understand something about Canadian history and our evolving common law tradition. Democracy in Canada has never been about unfettered majority rule. From Confederation on, our courts were assigned the important task of enforcing the division of powers and minority rights and of ensuring that governments respect the rule of law by making clear statements if they wished to depart from the fairness values found in the common law. Critics of judicial activism should not be allowed to use the vulnerability of the Court in a populist age to rewrite Canadian history and to recast Canadian democracy in a purely majoritarian light that fails to explain other fundamental aspects of our society, including federalism, minority rights, and the common law.

My intention in identifying some false and unhelpful myths relied upon by those who criticize the Court for engaging in judicial activism has not been to end the necessary and healthy debate about judicial review under the *Charter*. Rather, my goal has been to lay the groundwork for a clearer and more transparent debate about the role of the Court, one that directly engages the complex and important issues of judging, rights, and democracy that are at stake, without obscuring them under the slippery and loaded label of judicial activism.

Chapter 12
The Myths of Right Answers

If the endless debate about whether the Court has engaged in judicial activism is not the answer, where do we go from here? The conventional answer is towards a theory that attempts to define a role for judges that will produce right answers and decisions that are consistent with democracy. One problem, and it is an embarrassing one, is that there are too many right-answer theories. Take the four judgments that were written in *Morgentaler* when the Court struck the abortion law down. In his dissent, Justice McIntyre looked to the text and the intent of the framers for right answers and found that the framers had intended that the *Charter* and the judges remain neutral on the divisive and delicate abortion issue. At the other end of the spectrum, Justice Wilson looked to moral principles for the right answer and found that a woman's right to an early abortion was required in order to respect her liberty and freedom of conscience. In between were the judgments of Chief Justice Dickson and Justice Beetz. They looked for right answers in the balance of substantive values that had already been struck by Parliament and the need that women seeking an abortion be subject to a fair process. All four judgments in *Morgentaler* are arguably "compatible with the Charter of Rights and Freedoms because the Charter is worded generally and subject to varying interpretations."[1] But a conclusion that the judges can be all over the map and that they can all point to a respectable theory to justify their position will hardly satisfy those who are concerned about judicial activism. Nor should it.

Another problem is the very idea that judges can impose one right answer, any right answer, on the people. The three main theories of judicial review — judges finding right answers in the text and intent of the framers, or the ground rules of democracy, or moral principles — were all produced by Americans for Americans. They attempt to justify decisions such as the ruling in *Brown* v. *Board of Education* that racial segregation was unconstitutional while avoiding the excesses of constitutionalizing economic policies, as in *Lochner*, and, for some, abortion policy, as in *Roe* v. *Wade*. All assume that so long as judges reach the right answers, democracy will be preserved, even though the legislature and the people may not agree and have no alternative but to accept the Court's decision. This does not satisfy those concerned that judicial activism will usurp democracy. Nor should it.

A modern bill of rights such as the *Charter*, which allows legislatures to limit or derogate from rights with ordinary legislation and without having to change the Court or the constitution, responds to the failure of conventional theories of judicial review to produce reliably right answers. The awesome and frequently final power of the United States Supreme Court has produced a contest to invent a theory that gives judges right answers that are, by themselves, consistent with democracy. Judicial supremacy makes it necessary to produce a theory that reconciles each and every exercise of judicial power under the American *Bill of Rights* as in itself consistent with democracy. Under the *Charter* and other modern bills of rights, the search for a theory that reconciles every judicial decision with democracy is less desperate because, should judges step over what society believes to be the proper line, all that is necessary to restore the balance is ordinary legislation limiting or overriding the Court's constitutional decision. This flexibility also responds to the democratic deficit in conventional theories of judicial review. When the Court has the last word, it is because the legislature and the people have let it have the last word. Democracy is maintained and even enhanced by the ability of legislatures to limit or even override rights as declared by the courts.

The Intent and Text of the Framers as the Right Answer

The leading exponent of looking to the intent and text of the framers of the constitution as the only legitimate source of right answers to constitutional questions is Robert Bork, the conservative judge who was nominated by President Reagan to serve on the United States Supreme Court, but, amid much controversy, was not confirmed by the Senate. One reason why he was not confirmed was that he had a clear theory of judicial review which suggested that many constitutional decisions made by the Court were illegitimate, simply because they could not be supported by the intent and text of the framers of the constitution. Judges should strike down what the framers clearly prohibited, but in every other case allow democratically elected legislatures and executives to do whatever the constitution does not clearly prohibit. Bork argues that his approach "means that the ratifiers of the Constitution and today's legislators make the political decisions, and the courts do their best to implement them." Looking beyond the text of the constitution means that unelected judges will illegitimately read their political preferences into the constitution. "When the Constitution has not spoken, the Court will be able to find no scale, other than its own value preferences, upon which to weigh the competing claims." The text either speaks clearly to judges or leaves them a wide-open discretion that is not guided by law, but the personal values and politics of the judge. "Where the law stops, the legislator may move on to create more; but where the law stops, the judge must stop."[2] Bork starts from the premise that judicial intervention is inherently anti-democratic and should be limited to those cases in which the democratically enacted constitution clearly mandates it. His approach to democracy is majoritarian, because the worse feature of judicial activism is that it implements "an elite's minority sentiment,"[3] whether the elite is the robber barons who benefited from the *Lochner* era of judicially enforced laissez-faire or the unpopular religious and racial minorities who benefited from the decisions of the Warren Court.

Bork's theory is concerned with the structure of the American *Bill of Rights* and is designed to legitimate "judicial supremacy, the power of the courts to invalidate statutes and executive actions in the name of the Constitution." He assumes that the only alternatives are judicial supremacy and legislative supremacy, and this inflexibility raises the stakes of the quest for limits on judicial review. Judges should lean in the direction of under-enforcement of constitutional norms because this practice preserves "representative democracy," as opposed to over-enforcement, which can produce "an authoritarian judicial oligarchy."[4] Bork's stark choice between judicial supremacy and legislative supremacy reflects the structure of the American *Bill of Rights* and much American constitutional thought. It makes little sense in the context of the *Charter*, however, which is carefully structured to avoid the excesses of both judicial and legislative supremacy. The *Charter* allows the legislatures of today room to respond to decisions that interpret its provisions in a manner that the framers of yesterday may not have expected or foreseen.

In Canada there have been few advocates of looking to the intent of the framers as the source of "right answers," owing, perhaps, to our awareness of the confused and contradictory intent of the many people who contributed to the drafting of the *Charter* just two decades ago. Justice William McIntyre, the judge with the lowest level of acceptance of *Charter* claims on the Dickson Court, came the closest to advocating a framers'-intent approach. In a decision holding that the freedom to associate in a union does not include the right to strike, he warned that "the Charter should not be regarded as an empty vessel to be filled with whatever meaning we might wish from time to time."[5] He also dissented in *Morgentaler* on the basis that the *Charter* was silent on the issue of abortion and that the framers intended it to be neutral on the subject. It was not a coincidence that Justice McIntyre in both decisions rejected attempts to change the status quo. Framers' intent requires that "only the principles contained in the Charter as it was understood at the time of adoption be used to strike down legislation."[6] If requiring a committee to approve a woman's abortion or taking away the right to strike by legislation was permissible in 1982, there would be a very strong presumption that such governmental powers would continue under the *Charter*. The framers'-intent approach ensures that judges will rarely get ahead of the legislature in recognizing rights and, by doing so, undercuts the Court's anti-majoritarian role. By limiting judicial intervention to cases where the text and the intent of the framers are clear, it errs on the side of judicial under-enforcement of constitutional norms.

Despite its claims, the framers' intent approach is no more determinate than other theories of judicial review. Justice McIntyre was praised for following the intent of the framers in the cases mentioned above, but he was criticized for departing from the framers' intent when he held that citizenship was a prohibited ground of discrimination even though it had not been explicitly listed as such by the framers of the *Charter*. In fact, there was textual support for this decision, as section 15 of the *Charter* does not provide that the nine explicitly listed grounds of discrimination are the only possible grounds of discrimination. Reasonable people who are committed to interpreting the vague text of a bill of rights can disagree about its meaning. Judge Bork, for example, found that the First Amendment protected only political speech, so that "constitutionally, art and pornography are on a par with industry and smoke pollution,"[7] while Justice Hugo Black insisted that the reference in the First Amendment to Congress making no law abridging freedom of speech was much broader, because it meant just what it said. The fact that the answers in the text are not as clear as they often seem to Bork and his followers belies their claims to have solved the problem of judicial activism.

The framers' intent approach sits uneasily with both sections 1 and 33 of the *Charter*. Those who helped to draft the *Charter* acknowledged that section 1 left "much margin for judicial creativity in adjudicating permissible limitations on rights," while leaving the legislature an opportunity to defend restrictions on *Charter* rights.[8] Moreover, section 1 does not ask judges to apply limits on *Charter* rights as they were understood in 1982, but rather to determine whether the government in a particular case in the here and now has justified restrictions on *Charter* rights. This is an inherently dynamic and contextual process that does not lend itself to the static methodology of discovering what the framers intended in 1982. The existence of section 33 also suggests that the framers expected that judges might do something unexpected.[9] Prime Minister Pierre Trudeau told the House of Commons that he believed the *Charter* was neutral on abortion, but he added that, should the Court decide oth-

THE MYTHS OF RIGHT ANSWERS | 229

erwise, Parliament could still say: "Notwithstanding this decision, notwithstanding the charter of rights as interpreted by this judge, the House legislates in such and such a manner on the abortion issue."[10] Trudeau, a former law professor, knew very well that the courts might not follow the expectations of the drafters of the *Charter*. As a democrat, however, he believed that future legislatures could assert their own policies — to regulate abortion "in such and such a manner" — should they be prepared to take responsibility for their actions in reversing the Court's decisions. The ability of sections 1 and 33 of the *Charter* to accommodate the current democratic wishes of society makes the issue of the framers' historical intent much less relevant.

Enforcing the Rules of Democracy as the Right Answer

One theory that seems to answer the dilemma of judicial activism is the idea that the Court should enforce only the ground rules of democracy. What could be more democratic than democracy? This approach is associated with the work of John Hart Ely, a former dean at Stanford Law School, who argued that *Brown* v. *Board of Education* and many of the other decisions of the Warren Court were justified on the basis that the Court was simply ensuring the integrity of the political process. Many of the Court's judgments were "fueled not by a desire on the part of the Court to vindicate particular substantive values it had determined were important or fundamental, but rather by a desire to ensure that the political process ... was open to those of all viewpoints on something approaching an equal basis."[11] Substantive values should be left to the legislature, and the Court should perform tasks — the protection of fair process and unpopular minorities — within the particular expertise and ability of the independent judiciary.

The idea that courts should enforce the ground rules of democracy is attractive for two reasons: it bases the role of the Court on the need to ensure that minorities are not ganged up upon and it appeals to the institutional strengths of the judiciary as an independent body concerned primarily with process. At the same time, it has problems — one of which is indeterminacy. Given the importance of voting to democracy, one would have expected Ely to be an unabashed supporter of Warren Court decisions that the one-person / one-vote principle required congressional districts to be of equal population. He was, in fact, surprisingly equivocal on this issue. It was not irrational — "indeed it may ultimately serve the cause of real equality" — to compensate for the advantages that urban residents have, in terms of access to their governments and the media, by allowing those in rural and or less-populous ridings a greater weight for their votes. Ely concluded, however, that the one-person/one-vote decisions were justified simply because they were easier than "an 'in-between' standard" to administer.[12] Canadian courts have, in fact, adopted such "an 'in-between' standard" of relative equality of voting power and have upheld attempts to ensure the effectiveness of rural and northern representation.[13] The Canadian decisions are as consistent with democracy as the American decisions are. Even with respect to issues at the core of democracy, the idea that courts should enforce the ground rules of democracy does not provide clear and reliably right answers.

Another problem is a lack of clarity in identifying the groups that need judicial protection because of a malfunctioning of democracy. Ely argued provocatively that if women "don't protect themselves from sex discrimination in the future, it won't be because they can't." He also stated that the abortion rights decision of *Roe* v. *Wade* was not necessary because women make up a majority and should be able to have their views adequately represented in the elected legislature. These views are controversial, given the traditional under-representation of women in positions of power and the stereotypes they face relating to biology and socially constructed gender. Although he recognized that gays and lesbians can suffer discrimination, Ely confessed that it would be "cheating" under his theory to strike down a law criminalizing their sexual practices because it would require judges to enforce fundamental values such as privacy. Many people would simply not agree with conclusions that women, gays, or the poor are not victims of a malfunctioning democracy and in need of judicial protection.[14] These disagreements would not mollify critics of judicial activism, who are concerned that judges can do whatever they like under the *Charter*.

A democracy re-enforcing approach to judicial review risks the under-enforcement of some important constitutional values. The Warren Court's activism in the criminal justice system may have been justified, but it is a stretch to explain it as preserving the ground rules of democracy. Legal rights and remedies, which lie at the heart of the *Charter*, speak to independent substantive values of privacy, restraint in the use of state coercion, and fair treatment[15] that are increasingly controversial, given the rise of democratic concerns about the protection and rights of crime victims. A democracy re-enforcing approach would also under-enforce other important constitutional values. Ely would protect only political speech in the name of democracy, and he rejects *Roe* v. *Wade* as an illegitimate attempt by the unelected judiciary to protect fundamental values.[16] On these issues, the liberal Ely agrees with the conservative Bork. Perhaps because he dedicated his book to Chief Justice Earl Warren, many fail to recognize the Ely would significantly limit judicial intervention in the name of democracy.

When the Court must intervene to protect democracy, Ely follows the structure of the American *Bill of Rights* and argues that it should go all the way and have the final word. He dismisses analogies between constitutional law and the common law and supports judicial supremacy. Judicial restraint in not interpreting the constitution to include substantive values is necessary because the Court's constitutional decisions can only "be undone ... by the cumbersome process of constitutional amendment." The weight of judicial supremacy under the American *Bill of Rights* helps explains why Ely errs on the side of judicial under-enforcement of constitutional norms. If the decisions of the Court can only be changed by constitutional amendment, it does seem dangerous to ask the Court to enforce its view of fundamental values.

Ely is also no fan of dialogue between courts and legislatures. Allowing the legislature to respond to judicial decisions that are by definition required to ensure a fair democracy and protect society's outcasts would only throw the "case back to a rigged jury."[17] This approach sits uneasily with sections 1 and 33 of the *Charter*, which allows Court decisions on the *Charter* to be thrown back to the "rigged jury" of the legislature, which retains the power to limit and even override the rights of minorities. Under the *Charter* the Court may be able to enforce fundamental values as well as the rights of minorities because its decisions can be altered by ordinary legislation as opposed to constitutional amendment.

Osgoode Hall law professor Patrick Monahan has brought the insights of Ely's theory to bear on the *Charter*. The *Charter* follows Ely's theory more closely than does the American *Bill of Rights* because it does not protect "particular substantive values" such as the right of property or the freedom of contract. Monahan argues that "judicial review should be conducted in the name of democracy, rather than as a means of guaranteeing or requiring 'right answers' from the political process" or enforcing fundamental values. Problems of indeterminacy, however, remain. Telling a judge to protect "the right of equal access to and participation in the political process" and to "maximize openness and the possibility of revision in social life"[18] does not ensure the right answer in deciding whether Parliament can prohibit the possession of child pornography or restrict access to the complainant's private records in sexual assault cases. Critics of judicial activism may still fear that judges can do whatever they want and call it democracy. There is, however, much to be said for Professor Monahan's recognition that sections 1 and 33 of the *Charter* reject judicial supremacy and can re-enforce democracy by allowing the legislature to affirm the values of the community. This approach points in the direction of seeing judicial review as part of an ongoing dialogue between the Court and the legislatures.[19] The idea of dialogue, however, sits uneasily with Ely's view that society's outcasts need permanent and final protection from the legislature by the independent judiciary.

Process-based theories constitute an improvement over framers'-intent theories because they build on the judiciary's unique ability to protect fair process and vulnerable minorities. They can justify strong judicial intervention to protect minorities who are systemically disadvantaged in the legislative process. At the same time, however, process-based theories are not nearly determinate enough to satisfy those who are concerned about judicial activism. There is little agreement about what rights are protected under the rubric of process or what minorities require judicial protection from the majority. Attempts to separate issues of process from substance are not entirely persuasive. Process-based judicial review is either so robust that it blurs into full-blown substantive review or so thin that it risks under-enforcement of many constitutional norms.

Moral Principles as the Right Answer

The foremost theorist of full-blown substantive review that looks to moral principles for right answers is Ronald Dworkin, who teaches jurisprudence at Oxford and at New York University. His theory of judicial review is often associated with judicial activism. Judges in hard constitutional cases should not exercise a discretion informed by their own politics or sense of good policy, but should attempt to interpret correctly the moral principles in the constitution. Rights-based principles trump collective policy goals.[20] Dworkin's favourite principle is the right of individuals to equal concern and respect, which he argues can justify many of the decisions of the Warren Court. Dworkin has restrained some of his earlier enthusiasm for activism in the name of moral philosophy by stressing that the judge has an obligation to respect the integrity of the law and to make sense of the text of the constitution, prior precedents, and traditions.[21] At the same time, he stills believes that much of what would be seen as judicial activism can be justified on the basis that the best judge — someone Dworkin aptly names Hercules — can reach the right answers on the basis of the moral principles that best explain the constitution.

Dworkin's theory runs into problems of indeterminacy. Reasonable people acting in good faith will disagree about what is required to give individuals equal concern and respect. Dworkin concludes that this principle produces a right to abortion and a right to sell violent pornography and allows governments to practise affirmative action. Others, however, reach the opposite conclusions on the basis of the same abstract principles. Even Dworkin concedes that a moral reading of the constitution has "inspired all the greatest constitutional decisions of the Supreme Court, and also some of the worst."[22] This admission is not likely to persuade critics of judicial activism who are concerned about giving unelected judges the power to enforce their views about moral philosophy on the populace.

Dworkin admits that his moral theory of judicial review has not attracted widespread support among American judges. Given judicial supremacy, it remains scary. Hercules applying the American *Bill of Rights* could easily take too much away from the democratic realm. Nevertheless, Dworkin remains undeterred by the argument that "it would be most irksome to be ruled by a bevy of Platonic Guardians, even if I knew how to choose them, which I assuredly do not. If they were in charge, I should miss the stimulus of living in a society where I have, at least theoretically, some part in the direction of affairs."[23] He contents himself with arguments that the moral victories of judicial activism will outweigh its moral losses, and with the prospect that the public can debate and disagree with the Supreme Court while still accepting its constitutional judgments as the final word. Truly awful decisions will not be obeyed by the people, he says, and the president will eventually appoint better judges.[24] As we discussed in chapter 6, this defence of judicial activism is unconvincing because it is far from clear that the benefits of those cases in which judges reach the right answers outweigh the costs of cases such as *Dred Scott*, constitutionalizing slavery, and *Lochner*, constitutionalizing *laissez-faire* economics, in which activist courts have reached the wrong answers. Dworkin also ignores the loss to democracy when citizens are simply forced to watch and obey a Supreme Court, even if that Court could somehow be relied upon to reach reliably right answers.[25]

Like the other theories we have examined in this chapter, Dworkin's theory of judicial review is designed to fit the American *Bill of Rights*. Dworkin is admirably candid about this fact, but it limits the usefulness of his theory to the *Charter* or other modern bills of rights such as the United Kingdom's *Human Rights Act, 1998*, which allow ordinary legislation limiting or derogating from rights as interpreted by the Court. The idea that rights are principled trumps over collective goals sits uneasily with both sections 1 and 33 of the *Charter*. Although Dworkin supported the incorporation of the *European Convention* into English law, there are hints that he is uneasy with the idea that rights in that document can be subject to limits that are found to be necessary in a democratic society or, worse, by explicit derogation by a legislature prepared to accept political responsibility for such an action.[26] Dworkin's sense of what judges should do — elaborate principles found in the abstract guarantees of the American *Bill of Rights* — does not accord well with judges deciding whether legislated limits on rights are reasonable, necessary, and proportionate ways to advance society's collective goals. This process of determining whether limits on rights have been justified is a central concern for judges under section 1 of the *Charter* and under similar provisions in other modern bills of rights. At the same time, however, appointing Dworkin's Hercules to the Court may not be as scary in Canada, New Zealand, or the United Kingdom as in the United States, precisely because judges under a modern bill of rights cannot enforce their view of abstract moral principles as the final word, but must also listen to government's justifications for limiting such rights. If Hercules runs amuck, the legislature can enact ordinary legislation that overrides or derogates from his interpretation of rights.

Some Canadians have tried to adapt Dworkin's approach to judicial review to the structure of the Canadian Constitution. Building on some early *Charter* cases which suggested that "cost, custom and convenience" or the will of the majority could not justify the limitation of rights under section 1 of the *Charter*, my colleague Lorraine Weinrib argues that courts should accept limitations on *Charter* rights only if they are consistent with the values of the *Charter*.[27] Although legislative attempts to advance *Charter* values can constitute a substantial and pressing objective to limit *Charter* rights, I am somewhat uneasy with a "supremacy of rights model" that suggests that rights can only be subject to "principled" limits relating to "the interests for which the rights stand."[28] Section 1 seems designed to allow governments to limit *Charter* rights for a broad range of objectives, many of which do not relate to the rights and freedoms themselves. In *Oakes*, Chief Justice Dickson argued that the final standard for the justification of limits on rights and freedoms was the requirement that Canada be free and democratic. Neverthless, he also concluded that the right to be presumed innocent could be limited to facilitate the conviction of drug traffickers, a "collective goal of fundamental importance," but not one easily related to the rights in the *Charter*, including the presumption of innocence that Parliament had chosen in its war against drugs to violate.[29] Allowing governments to limit rights only in the name of *Charter* values will either drastically restrict the range of legitimate governmental objectives or force the government to squeeze all its objectives under the rubric of *Charter* values. The Supreme Court has recognized that, in cases of conflicting rights, each right should be defined in relation to the other.[30] Although this relational approach limits rights in the name of *Charter* values, it runs the risk of allowing the legislature to minimize the rights of the least popular, such as those accused of crime, while inflating the rights of the more popular, such as crime victims. At the same time, there is much to be said for Professor Weinrib's structural reading of the *Charter*, which insists that denials of rights and legislative reversals of *Charter* decisions should be accomplished only with the special safeguards and sober second thoughts of the section 33 override.[31]

My colleague David Beatty has articulated a very different theory of judicial review, one that is also influenced by the Dworkian quest for right answers to be enforced by the judiciary. Rights are abstract principles, and judges err in Professor Beatty's view when they stop "reading the Charter deductively with a view to promoting the values of pluralism, equality, human dignity etc. on which it was based" and impose definitional limits on rights.[32] The problem, however, is that this expansive approach to rights will produce a *Lochner*-like activism that requires the entire statute book to be justified under section 1 as reasonable limits on seemingly unlimited rights. Beatty counters by arguing that courts should then, for reasons of democracy, defer to the government's choice of objectives for limiting *Charter* rights. Unlike Weinrib, he would not require these objectives to be limited to the values of the *Charter*. Judicial deference to the legislature, however, stops abruptly at this stage. Thereafter the courts should insist that legislatures limit rights only when "there is no other, less drastic policy available that would interfere less with people's rights and freedoms."[33] Beatty contends that this solves the problem of judicial activism because the Court simply tells elected governments "to pursue their political manifestos in ways and by means that impaired the constitutional entitlements of those they affected as little as possible ... Governments can do almost anything they want except act in a heavy-hand and/or discriminatory way."[34] One problem is that some legislative means may be difficult to separate from legislative ends. A mechanical search for less restrictive alternatives may distort the ability of legislatures to advance their chosen policy effectively. For example, should mandatory retirement be struck down simply because some jurisdictions can live without it? At some point there has to be a judicial stopping point, and that point is likely to be informed by the judiciary's own sense of its competence in relation to the legislature. At the same time there is much to be said for Professor Beatty's observation that legislatures can frequently respond to *Charter* decisions by pursuing their democratic platforms in a better-tailored and less heavy-handed manner.

The Potential of Harnessing Hercules by Democratic Dialogue

The theories that judges should enforce the intent of the framers, the ground rules of democracy, or moral principles are all based on the assumption of judicial supremacy in enforcing the constitution, however thick or thin it may be. All three theories were formulated to provide the judges on the United States Supreme Court with right answers that are consistent with democracy. They all assume that those judges should have the final word when enforcing the right answer and the right rights. Unfortunately, there is no agreement about any one of the theories or how they should be applied. It is simply a myth to think that any theory that depends on judges getting the right answers will respond to those who are concerned about judicial activism. An even deeper problem for all democrats is the idea that judges should impose final right answers on the people and their governments. Even if we could rely on judges to reach reliably right answers — which all evidence suggest we cannot — something would be lost from the perspective of democracy by having the unelected judiciary from on high impose right answers as the final answers. What is to be done?

In chapters 13 and 14, I will suggest that the answer is to understand judicial review under the *Charter* as a contribution to an ongoing dialogue between the independent judiciary, the elected legislatures, and the people. The work of the Canadians examined in this chapter points in the right direction. The values of the community can be expressed through ordinary legislation limiting rights under section 1 of the *Charter* or even legislation under section 33 of the *Charter* overriding rights as interpreted by the Court. Judicial invalidation of legislation under section 1 will often mean that the legislature could pursue the very same objective in a less heavy-handed way. Section 1 is thus the main engine of dialogue, not section 33. If the legislature, however, wishes to deny a right completely or reverse a decision of the Court interpreting a *Charter* right, it should have to take responsibility for doing so under section 33, while the Court's point of principle is preserved even if it does not prevail. The Court's judgment can be reconsidered — perhaps accepted, perhaps rejected — when the override expires after five years. The dialogic structure of the *Charter* and similar bills of rights does not mean that the judiciary should abandon the search for the right, or at least the best answers suggested by the *Charter*. It does, however, mean that the judicial answer will not necessarily be the final answer.

Once it becomes clear that the Court need not have the last word, the focus should be less on restraining judges, to make sure they leave space for democracy, and more on judges playing the role that best suits the independent judiciary as an institution and best enhances, and even provokes, democracy. It becomes possible to support the more robust theories of judicial review discussed in this chapter, not because of confidence that judges using them will always reach right answers that are consistent with democracy, but because they encourage judges to inject considerations of moral principles and less restrictive alternatives into democratic debates about the difficult issues that end up in *Charter* litigation. Minimal approaches to judicial review should be avoided precisely because they will stifle dialogue among the court, legislatures, and society about constitutional values such as fair process, fundamental values, and minority rights that are otherwise vulnerable to neglect in the legislative and administrative processes. A minimal approach to judicial review produces a faint-hearted dialogue that threatens to become a complacent monologue. In contrast, when the judiciary vigorously enforces constitutional norms and even when it over-enforces them, dialogue increases and intensifies. The legislature in a Cabinet-dominated parliamentary system of government is in a good position to respond to judicial decisions by reasserting its majoritarian and regulatory objectives and using its powers under sections 1 and 33 of the *Charter* to justify limitations and overrides of the rights proclaimed by the Court. The dialogic structure of the *Charter* suggests that it is better for judges to err on the side of over-enforcing rather than under-enforcing rights because the legislature is much more likely to counter the former than to make up for the latter. Under a modern bill of rights with a parliamentary system, judges can embrace robust theories of judicial review that, if taken in the context of the judicial supremacy of the American *Bill of Rights*, would produce a high risk of excessive judicial activism. The only dangers with robust judicial review under the *Charter* are if the legislative system becomes beset with paralysis, or if the public takes an absolute view of rights that prevents government from making use of its powers to limit or override rights and, ultimately, to justify these actions to the people. These dangers, however, would be more failures of democracy than of the Court, and especially of the *Charter*.

Conclusion

The plurality of respectable theories about how judges should get right answers in difficult constitutional cases lends support to critics of judicial activism on both the left and the right, all of whom argue that judges are free to impose their will and preferences on society. It is a myth to think that there can be agreement on which theory is best supported by the constitution. It is also a myth to think that judges will reliably reach right answers that are themselves consistent with democracy. Reasonable judges will disagree about the meaning of the text, the requirements of democracy, or the appropriate moral principles, and reasonable people will disagree about whether the judges' decisions are consistent with democracy.

The myth that any theory of judicial review will generate reliably right answers that are themselves consistent with democracy points towards the wisdom of not giving judges the final word. The desperate American search for a right-answer theory that reconciles judicial review with democracy is considerably less desperate in Canada, precisely because of the ability of legislatures under sections 1 and 33 to limit and even override the rights that the Court finds in the *Charter*. This advantage does not mean that the conventional theories of judicial review are not valuable or that there is no basis for concluding that some are better than others. In my view, the framers'-intent approach is the least helpful theory because it risks freezing rights as they were understood at the time of the *Charter's* enactment. The approach of enforcing the ground rules of democracy is more helpful because it identifies a unique role for the Court in protecting minorities that are vulnerable in a democracy. At the same time, it risks under-enforcement of constitutional norms such as freedom of expression, privacy, and due process that may protect fundamental values that are not easily related to the functioning of a democracy. Judicial concern with both the ground rules of democracy and moral principles will allow judges to articulate the fullest range of fundamental values that might otherwise be neglected by the legislature or the bureaucrats. Dworkin's approach errs on the side of judicial over-enforcement rather than under-enforcement of the *Charter*. Taken in its indigenous American context, it runs a real risk of allowing the Court to usurp democracy in the name of rights. The Canadian (and the New Zealand and the British) Parliament should, however, be able to harness strong judges like Dworkin's Hercules because they can enact ordinary legislation to limit or override the rights that the Court has generously, perhaps too generously, interpreted. Strong legislatures under a modern bill of rights can counter the activism of a strong Court.

Chapter 13
Democratic Dialogue in Theory

How can a judgment of the Supreme Court, the highest Court in the land, be likened to part of a dialogue? The final judgments of the final Court are not an invitation to further conversation; they are meant to be obeyed. Tell judges to stuff themselves and their judgments and you may end up in jail. Is the idea of judicial review as dialogue not a fantasy of law professors, who are about the only ones in our society who get to talk back after the Court makes its final decisions?

The key to understanding a court judgment, whether under the common law or under a modern bill of rights, as a form of dialogue is to understand and examine the entire legal process. The judgment of the court is final and to be obeyed, as it determines the rights and obligations of the parties to the dispute and serves as a precedent for similar cases. At the same time, the legislature could always respond to judge-made common law by enacting legislation that displaced the Court's decision. In three readings, a legislature could wipe out centuries of common law by enacting a workers' compensation scheme or a criminal code. This process was democracy and it was dialogue. Under the *Charter* and other modern bills of rights, legislatures can still respond to court decisions by limiting or overriding the rights the Court has proclaimed. In chapter 14, I will examine how democratic dialogues among the court, the legislature, and society have worked in practice under both the common law and the *Charter*. In this chapter I will consider the charge that seeing judicial review as part of a dialogue with legislatures and society does not capture the authoritative, principled, and final nature of judicial judgment.[1] I will also consider the charge that seeing judicial review as part of a dialogue reduces the Court's judgments to conversational ploys that will diminish respect for the judiciary and produce moral relativism and judicial deference. Some understandings of dialogue between the Court and the legislature do fall into these traps. Others, however, make room for a strong judicial voice that defends principles such as minority rights, fair process, and fundamental values. They demand that the decisions of the Court be respected and obeyed, while still not giving five justices on the Court the final word in our democracy.

Dialogue between Courts and Legislatures

The dialogue metaphor helps explain much of the judicial process. Much of what judges do is listen and talk, in that order. One of the great virtues of adjudication is that it allows parties to tell judges their stories.[2] Good oral argument before the Court is an exercise in dialogue, often Socratic dialogue, with the litigants being pushed by the probing questions of the judges. Judges on the Supreme Court engage in dialogue among themselves, in the form of concurrences and dissents as well as collegial interchange.[3] They are immersed in a world that gives them plenty of feedback: "[T]he law, as Bentham long ago remarked, is made, not by judge alone, but by judge and company ... the colloquy goes well beyond the profession and reaches deeply into the places where public opinion is formed."[4]

The feedback that the Court receives about its decisions is important and may have some influence on the Court, but it is not the democratic dialogue that is promoted under the common law and the *Charter*. The truly democratic dialogue that occurs under a modern bill of rights is not the professional debate of professors and pundits about whether the Court was right or wrong in reaching its decisions.[5] Rather, it is the democratic debate of citizens whether the power of their elected governments to place limits on the Court's decisions or even to override them by ordinary legislation should be exercised. This democratic debate should be a serious one in which citizens reflect on the responsibility that comes from the fact that their elected governments can do something very meaningful — perhaps very wrong and perhaps very right — in response to the Court's constitutional decisions. Sometimes citizens and their governments may come to the conclusion that the Court's decision should stand. In other cases, however, they will modify the Court's decisions. In rare cases, they will even reverse the Court's decision, with, it is hoped, the special safeguards and sober second thoughts of the section 33 override. In every case, however, democracy will be enhanced both by the Court's contribution in making the citizenry aware of the effects of state actions on even its most unpopular citizens and by the fact that the Court need not have the final word.

In their emphasis on democracy and their failure to insist on final right answers, dialogic theories of judicial review may seem to smack of moral relativism. For many people, the danger of a *Dred Scott* constitutionalizing slavery or a *Lochner* constitutionalizing *laissez-faire* economics may be worth securing the victory of a *Brown* v. *Board of Education* holding that racial segregation is unconstitutional. Dialogic theories, however, would allow judges to decide *Brown* while recognizing that society may do much to resist its just conclusion that racial segregation is evil. We now know that *Brown* was not much of an immediate victory and that it was disobeyed by governments and citizens in the American South. An explicit and temporary southern override of *Brown* may not have been much worse than its *sub rosa*, lengthy and violent resistance. It would have been more candid. Dialogic theories of judicial review can enhance democracy by requiring legislatures and the public to confront their prejudices and fears. Sometimes they will give in to these ugly forces, but not generally. When they do give in, nothing, not even judicial supremacy, will save the society from itself. Theories that allow for dialogue among the Court, the legislature, and the people demonstrate a faith and optimism about democracy that is absent from the conventional theories of judicial review examined in chapter 12. They also place less reliance on judges reaching reliably right answers that are always consistent with democracy. Having discussed the differences between dialogic and conventional theories of judicial review, I must now bring some clarity to the meaning of dialogue by outlining three very different understandings of dialogue, all of which find support in the decisions of the Court.

Dialogue Based on Courts and Legislatures Interpreting the Constitution for Themselves

The oldest dialogic theory is that of coordinate construction, espoused by Thomas Jefferson and James Madison, two of the founders of the American Constitution. Having rebelled against the monarchy, both were unwilling to give the unelected federal judiciary the final say in interpreting the constitution. Jefferson believed that if judges "could decide what laws are constitutional ... for the Legislature and Executive also, would make the judiciary a despotic branch."[6] Madison similarly expressed concerns that if the constitutional interpretations of courts were final, "this makes the Judiciary Dept. paramount in fact to the Legislature, which was never intended and can never be proper."[7] Coordinate construction gives the legislature the power not only to reply to Court decisions but to ignore them and to interpret the constitution for itself. President Andrew Jackson relied on this theory when he vetoed a national bank that he thought was unconstitutional, even though the Court had ruled otherwise. For Jackson, "the opinion of the judges has no more authority over Congress than the opinion of Congress over the judges, and on that point the President is independent of both. Each public official who takes an oath to support the Constitution swears that he will support it as he understands it, not as it is understood by others."[8] This sense that what the courts have found legal may nevertheless be constitutionally improper is not dangerous. Indeed, it is congruent with the understanding of constitutional conventions in the British Constitution: the queen does not use her legal powers, but follows the unwritten constitution by acting only on the advice of her elected governments.[9]

The theory of coordinate construction, however, gets more dangerous and can be downright ugly when governments use it to defy judicial decisions enforcing constitutional rights. President Jackson, who made his fame as an Indian fighter, employed the same theory of coordinate construction to ignore a landmark Court ruling that Georgia had no power over Cherokee land, reportedly by stating that the chief justice "has made his decision and now let him enforce it."[10] Many citizens in the South used this theory to refuse to obey *Brown* v. *Board of Education*, on the basis that desegregation infringed their states' rights as interpreted by state legislatures. When taken to this extreme, the theory of coordinate construction suggests that a judicial decision is just one particular interpretation of the constitution, and not entitled to any more respect than a rival interpretation made by the executive or the legislative.[11] In other words, what the Court has concluded to be illegal and unconstitutional may be considered by the legislature and the executive to be perfectly legal and constitutional.

Despite these fairly radical implications, the doctrine of coordinate construction is making a comeback.[12] Georgetown law professor Mark Tushnet has recently proposed that legislatures practise "populist constitutional law" that would allow them to "ignore what the courts say about the Constitution, as long as they are pursuing reasonable interpretations" of the abstract principles of the *Bill of Rights*.[13] The legislature's interpretations of what constitutes a fair trial or equality would have as much claim to respect as the Court's. Surprisingly, Tushnet does not seem to fear the implications that this process may have for accused persons or minorities.[14] McGill political scientist Christopher Manfredi has similarly argued that "genuine dialogue only exists when legislatures are recognized as legitimate interpreters of the constitution and have an effective means to assert that interpretation."[15] He argues that constitutionalism will become meaningless if courts, just as much as the executive and the legislature, are given unlimited powers to impose their interpretations of the constitution on other branches of governments. This concern would have been shared by both Jefferson and Madison. Manfredi also assumes that legislatures are competent and interested in engaging in constitutional interpretation and that they will not interpret the rights of unpopular individuals and minorities against the state in a self-interested manner.

Despite its lineage, the doctrine of coordinate construction challenges conventional understandings of the rule of law that suggest that the legislature should respect the Court's interpretation of the constitution. The idea that the legislature has as much, if not more, right than the court to say what fundamental freedoms or voting, legal, equality, or minority rights mean in a particular context, and to act on this interpretation, risks making the legislature a judge in its own majoritarian causes. As an elected institution, Parliament has an interest in minimizing the rights of its most unpopular citizens. Elected politicians cannot be expected to respect the rights of an infamous criminal or a vilified minority. Some may take such courageous stands, but most will not. Unlike judges, they must stand for re-election, face party discipline, and answer the calls of their constituents. Finally, coordinate construction sacrifices the distinctive role of independent courts and elected legislatures by suggesting that they both should devote their different talents to the same exercise: constitutional interpretation. The Court and Parliament will get bogged down in arguments about which institution has interpreted the *Charter* correctly.

Despite these powerful objections, the Supreme Court has lent some support to the strong theory of coordinate construction by stating that the "courts do not hold a monopoly on the protection and promotion of rights and freedoms."[16] As we will discuss in chapter 14, this statement was made in a case in which the Court upheld an "in-your-face" parliamentary reply that reversed a previous *Charter* decision based on the rights of those accused of sexual assault. The Court deferred to Parliament's interpretation of the rights of women and children who have been victimized or are vulnerable to being victimized by sexual violence, even though the politicians, quite understandably, minimized the rights of those very unpopular men who are accused, sometimes falsely, of sexual assault. The Court has also implicitly supported coordinate construction by refusing to review the reasons used by legislatures when they invoke the override, including the legislature's implicit or explicit interpretation of the relevant right that might support its use of the override.[17] In chapter 14 I will suggest that Parliament, if it wants to assert a right to act on its own interpretation of the *Charter*, contrary to the way the Court has interpreted it, should invoke the section 33 override. This procedure will ensure continued dialogue about whether society should accept the Court's or Parliament's interpretation of the *Charter*. Judicial decisions will be trivialized if the legislature rejects the Court's interpretation of the *Charter* in favour of its own, without the special safeguards and sober second thoughts of the override.

Dialogue Based on Legislatures Holding the Court Accountable

Another approach to dialogue is that courts are influenced and held accountable by the political feedback they receive from legislatures and society. The premise is that the unelected courts should not stray too far from the democratic mainstream. The origins of this approach are found in an influential 1957 article by Yale political scientist Robert Dahl, who concluded that, as an empirical matter, the "policy views dominant on the Court are never for long out of line with the policy views dominant among the lawmaking majorities of the United States." Dahl also argued as a normative matter that, "if the Court did in fact uphold minorities against national majorities, as both its supporters and critics often seem to believe, it would be an extremely anomalous institution from a democratic point of view." Although he carefully avoided mentioning the Court's biggest challenge to majority preferences ever, its 1954 decision in *Brown* v. *Board of Education*, Dahl even suggested that if the Court supported "minority preferences against majorities," it would "deny that popular sovereignty and political equality, at least in the traditional sense, exist in the United States."[18] At the very moment Dahl wrote these words, the South was resisting *Brown* on the basis that unelected federal judges were interfering with their popular sovereignty and that the majority overwhelmingly supported the racial segregation that, for many of them, constituted the Southern way of life. Dahl's majoritarian view of both democracy and judicial review suggests that *Brown* was illegitimate. It would deprive the Court of its anti-majoritarian role and could allow unpopular minorities to be permanently ganged up upon. It also begs the question of why bother assigning the task of judicial review to the independent judiciary when elected politicians could more safely be relied upon to reflect the wishes of the majority. Despite these disquieting implications, Dahl's approach to dialogue seems to be making something of a comeback.

Many who see dialogue as a form of majorities holding the Court accountable focus on the important task of a positive description of the place of the Court in society. One political scientist has argued that the recognition of rights depends not so much on constitutions or judges but on the support that rights claimants receive from governments and non-governmental groups in society. The necessity for a "support structure" for rights, in his view, helps resolve the tension between democracy and rights.[19] Ted Morton and Rainer Knopff agree about the importance of a support structure for rights litigation in the form of government support for "the Court Party," but not with the idea that this support resolves the tension between democracy and judicially enforced rights. They conclude that the "Charter Revolution" is "deeply and fundamentally undemocratic" because it is "anti-majoritarian."[20] If the *Charter* cannot be abolished, they imply, courts should not stray far from the democratic mainstream and they should listen when governments withdraw their support from those claiming *Charter* rights. Taken to the extreme, the idea that the Court is accountable to government and society suggests that the Court should make "politically sensitive" decisions designed to respond to political messages from other branches of government and to maintain the Court's public support and prestige.[21] Courts and legislatures should speak in similar voices that reflect and defer to majority sentiment. The goal of the dialogue is to reach agreement, with the Court following the election returns, or at least never being too far ahead of the legislature or society.

The Supreme Court has lent some support to this theory by suggesting that it is accountable to the legislature because "its decisions can be reacted to by the legislature in the passing of new legislation."[22] It also appeared to retreat when some of its decisions on Aboriginal rights, especially in the *Marshall* fishing rights case, appeared to be too far ahead of society, and when some of its decisions on the rights of the accused were reversed by the legislature. Whatever its merits as a matter of empirical description, the idea that the independent courts should be accountable to the legislature and to the majority should not serve as a normative guide for the participants in the dialogue. Taken to the extreme, the notion of the Court's accountability to the legislature is in tension to judicial independence and the Court's anti-majoritarian role.[23] Like theories based on coordinate construction, theories of dialogue based on the Court's accountability to the legislature sacrifice the distinctive role of courts and legislatures by suggesting that they both should devote their different talents to the same exercise: the discovery and reflection of majority sentiment.

There are dangers in stressing the Court's accountability to legislatures and society or the importance of agreement in the dialogue. Although the Court should be open to education by the legislature about its objectives and why it has rejected seemingly less intrusive alternatives, it should be true to its anti-majoritarian nature and role, its precedents, and its own way of reasoning, even if such a stand produces judgments that provoke widespread or focused opposition in civil society or the use of the override. The safety valve of the override should allow "courts to be courts and legislatures to be legislatures,"[24] without politically astute switches in time by the Court to save the Court. Judges who have their decisions reversed by the override should not see it as a shameful indication that they were out of touch. If they believe that their decisions were supported by the law, they should wear the override as a badge of pride that they have done their job and done it well. Strong and principled judicial interventions in the dialogue will assure that something of value that would not ordinarily be heard in democratic conversations will be added, even if the Court's contribution ultimately does not prevail. In chapter 14 I will suggest that if the legislature wants to hold the Court accountable by reversing a *Charter* decision that the majority finds to be simply unacceptable, it should use the override.[25] This is the proper way under the *Charter* for the Court to be held accountable to the legislature and society for its decisions. The override will assure that the government is also held accountable by the people for its decision and that the matter will be reviewed again in light of the Court's judgment after the override expires in five years' time.

Dialogue Based on Courts and Legislatures Playing Distinct but Complementary Roles

The two theories we have seen above, of legislatures interpreting the constitution for themselves and of legislatures holding the Court accountable, suggest that dialogue may indeed mean that Supreme Court decisions are not to be taken all that seriously and that the legislature can bully the Court into agreement. There is, however, another understanding of dialogue that sees judicial decisions as a more serious and principled matter, without giving the Court the final word. This approach is reflected in the work of Yale law professor Alexander Bickel, a paradoxical but brilliant figure who defended *Brown* v. *Board of Education* in the face of attempts by the South to claim that it was unconstitutional and unacceptable to the majority, but who criticized other decisions of the Warren Court for unprincipled and unnecessary activism. Bickel, who died in 1974 at the age of fifty, set the stage for those such as Ronald Dworkin and John Hart Ely who, as discussed in chapter 12, later attempted to justify principled, anti-majoritarian, and activist judicial review. Unlike those theorists, however, Bickel believed that even the Court's final judgments on matters of constitutional principle were not, and probably should not be, the final word. In 1970 he wrote that "virtually all important decisions of the Supreme Court are the beginnings of conversations between the Court and the people and their representatives. They are never, at the start, conversations between equals. The Court has the edge ... [but] the effectiveness of the judgment universalized depends on consent and administration."[26] The Court "interacts with other institutions, with whom it is engaged in an endlessly renewed educational conversation ... And it is a conversation, not a monologue."[27] Bickel believed in dialogue between the Court, the legislature, and the people.

The structure of the American Constitution, which has no limitation or override clauses and, since the Court successfully asserted its exclusive right to interpret the Constitution in *Marbury* v. *Madison*, has been based on judicial supremacy in defining the constitution, led Bickel to conclude that dialogues between the Court and the other branches of government were most easily undertaken when the Court found ways not to decide constitutional issues.[28] One of these passive virtues was a presumption by the Court that it would interpret statutes in a manner that complied with constitutional rights unless the legislature has made its intent to violate rights crystal clear. The use of this type of common law presumption allowed the Court to engage "in a Socratic colloquy with the other institutions of government and with society as a whole concerning the necessity for this or that measure, for this or that compromise. All the while, the issue of principle remains in abeyance and ripens."[29] For Bickel, the freest and least dangerous form of dialogue under the American Constitution occurred when the Court based its decision on non-constitutional and common law grounds. Bickel's insights about the dialogue promoted by "quasi-constitutional law,"[30] however, apply to judicial review under the *Charter* and other modern bills of rights because the structure of the *Charter* is "Bickellian" and rooted in the common law in the way it encourages courts to protect rights while inviting the legislature to place and justify clear limits and overrides on those rights.[31]

When the time was ripe and judgment could not be avoided, Bickel argued, the Court should decide constitutional issues, and it should decide them on the basis of principle properly crafted and defended. "The search must be for a function ... which differs from the legislative and executive functions; which is peculiarly suited to the capabilities of the courts; which will not likely be performed elsewhere if the courts do not assume it."[32] In other words, the Court should play a distinct and complementary role to that of the legislature and not try to duplicate legislative efforts to reflect the will of the majority. The Court's use of principle also meant that Bickel did not believe that the dialogue between courts and legislatures was a conversation between equals in which the Court and the legislature had an equal right to act on its own interpretation of the Constitution. The Court played the role of Socrates, while the legislature and society played the role of the sometimes stubborn and strong-willed students. This analogy is not as paternalistic as it sounds, because Socrates' students could always have refused to listen to their frail teacher, or simply overpowered him, if they had been prepared to ignore his words of wisdom.

Unlike proponents of coordinate construction or of dialogue based on the Court's accountability to society, Bickel was sensitive to the fact that the Court spoke through final judgments that should be obeyed, while recognizing that they may not be the final word. He feared that that "political opposition could defeat the Court's decision" in *Brown* v. *Board of Education*. This resistance, whether couched in the constitutional language of states' right or the racist cries of a threatened white majority, did not justify the Court retreating from its point of principle. The Court's subsequent decision to allow desegregation "in all deliberate speed" was based on dialogue that preserved the Court's point of principle in the face of massive resistance. "The Court placed itself in position to engage in a continual colloquy with the political institutions, leaving it to them to tell the Court what expedients of accommodation and compromise they deemed necessary. The Court would reply in the negative — and did eventually once so reply — only when a suggested expedient amounted to the abandonment of principle."[33] The case where the Court would not abandon principle, despite enormous public and governmental resistance, was when all nine members signed a judgment to require the desegregation of Central High in Little Rock, even if that meant disorder and violence.[34] Bickel's eloquent account of dialogue made room for a strong judicial voice of principle, one that would resist opposition from the majority and rival constitutional interpretations from the other branches of government. It also demonstrates that dialogue between courts and legislatures need not be based on moral relativism or judicial deference.

Other commentators have followed in Bickel's footsteps in examining the role that the courts should play in their dialogue with the legislature when they interpret statutes or constitutions. Pride of place should go to a Canadian, Paul Weiler, who played an important role in devising section 33 of the *Charter*. Weiler's early work was sceptical about giving the Court the final word in interpreting the constitutional division of powers or even in enforcing the *Canadian Bill of Rights*. Instead, he praised the Court for intervening in a number of cases in the 1950s to "require a very clear statement from the legislature" of its wish to encroach on a variety of common law principles. The best "technique of judicial restraint of the majority" was not American-style judicial supremacy, but the old common law technique of requiring "a clear and unambiguous legislative statement, sometimes in fact a restatement, of its wish to offend against a fundamental principle of fairness within the society. It is easy to envisage cases where this technique is not effective, but experience suggests that it usually is. When it does succeed, a democracy is richer, not poorer, for it."[35] The common law method of protecting rights, as well as the ability of legislatures to limit or override the Court's decisions under the *Charter*, was based on dialogue between Parliament and the Court.

Seeing the Court's intervention as part of a dialogue does not necessarily mean that the Court should be timid, deferential, or concerned about its popularity. "A major virtue" of the fact that the Court does not necessarily have the last word for Weiler is that it can boldly proclaim and enforce rights with "a sense of security from the presence of a legislative safety net beneath them." The strong governments produced by the Canadian parliamentary system allow effective replies to court decisions. The Canadian system also makes strong judicial review more necessary and less dangerous than in the American system of divided government. Weiler contemplated that courts would focus on issues of legal principle and fairness to unpopular individuals and minorities that the legislatures, and especially administrators, were inclined to neglect, but that legislatures would respond in those cases in which they were prepared to take "the flak" and the democratic responsibility for explicitly stating they could not live with the principles the Court had declared.[36]

Americans who have built on Bickel's understanding of dialogue have had trouble because the structure of the American *Bill of Rights* promotes judicial supremacy, not dialogue, between courts and legislatures. Like Bickel, they have had to recommend that the Court avoid or minimize constitutional judgment in order to allow the legislature an opportunity to respond to its decisions.[37] They have urged courts to invent ways to allow legislatures to take second looks at laws that may violate the constitution, while conceding that the "Canadian innovation,"[38] which allows legislatures to respond to *Charter* decisions with ordinary legislation that limits or overrides the Court's constitutional decisions, is a more natural way to conduct a dialogue between courts and legislatures. Another alternative is to allow the judiciary to be supreme, but to see as dialogue those extraordinary moments where Americans have been able to change the constitution or the Court in response to overwhelmingly unpopular judicial decisions. As we saw in chapter 2, however, these extraordinary "constitutional moments"[39] in American history have been difficult and dangerous to achieve. Constitutional amendments in the wake of a bloody Civil War were necessary to reverse the Court's constitutionalization of slavery in *Dred Scott* and the president had to threaten to pack the Court before it backed down from *Lochner* and upheld New Deal regulation of the economy during the midst of the Depression.

The Canadian *Charter*, however, promotes a much less difficult and dangerous dialogue than the American *Bill of Rights* because the *Charter* allows rights as interpreted by the Court to be openly limited or overridden by ordinary legislation. The Supreme Court of Canada has contemplated a dialogue in which courts and legislatures play distinct and complementary roles that enhance democracy, follow the tradition of the common law,[40] and respect the structure of the *Charter* as formulated by Weiler and others. Under the *Charter*, "the work of the legislature is reviewed by the courts and the work of the courts in its decisions can be reacted to by the legislature in the passing of new legislation (or even overarching laws under s. 33 of the Charter. This dialogue between

... each of the branches ha[s] the effect of enhancing the democratic process, not denying it."[41] The Court promotes democracy not because every one of its decisions is consistent with or required by democracy, but because it requires the elected government to take responsibility for and justify to the people its decisions to limit or override rights that are liable to be neglected in the legislative and administrative process. The Court forces Parliament to consider the rights of minorities and the unpopular, while not dictating the final word about matters involving these rights. Democracy is enhanced by combining judicial activism under the common law and the *Charter* with legislative activism, as legislatures enact ordinary legislation that places reasonable and justified limits on rights or even clearly override rights as proclaimed by the Court.

Conclusion

To critics who argue that the dialogue model does not adequately capture the nature of a judicial process that renders final judgment on the basis of principle, my response is to give courts and legislatures distinctive but complementary roles. As I will argue more fully in chapter 14, this response also explains ordinary dialogue under both the common law and section 1 of the *Charter*. Courts remind legislatures of values that might otherwise be neglected, and legislatures respond by expanding or refining the terms of the debate and by making clear why rights have to be limited in particular contexts. This response explains less well the extraordinary dialogues that occur when legislatures and courts engage in shouting matches and showdowns over whether a particular decision made by the Court was right or acceptable. In these cases, the legislature may be claiming to correct a Court that has wrongly interpreted the constitution or has rendered a decision that is unacceptable to society. The extraordinary nature of these claims and the conflict they produce between the Court and the legislature suggest that they should be made only with the special safeguards of the section 33 override.

The exact nature of the dialogue between courts and legislatures will be revealed in those cases — judicial second looks at legislative second looks — in which the Court examines legislation that was enacted in response to its previous decisions. From the perspective of dialogue as accountability, they involve a showdown between the Court and the legislature, with the latter having the most majoritarian muscle. From the perspective of coordinate construction, they pit the Court's interpretation of the constitution against the legislature's rival interpretation. From the perspective of courts and legislatures playing distinct roles, they provide an opportunity for the Court to be educated about the practical effects of its prior rulings, while also allowing the legislature an opportunity to demonstrate what it has learned from the Court's previous ruling and to refine debate about legislative objectives and alternatives. In chapter 14 I will examine a number of these difficult cases. In my view, courts should uphold reply legislation only when the legislature has refined the law so that it is justified under section 1 of the *Charter*. They should not defer to the legislature's interpretation of the constitution or its assertion of majority sentiment. If, however, the legislature wants to make these extraordinary claims, it can do so with the special safeguards and sober second thoughts of the override.

It is a fair point that theories of dialogue do not tell judges how difficult cases must be decided. No less than the theories examined in chapter 12, they do not ensure that judges will get reliably right answers. What theories of dialogue between courts and legislatures do achieve, however, is a process in which all of us in a democracy can struggle together for the right answers, without relying on the monologues and concentrated power produced by either judicial or legislative supremacy. The Court can bring to the attention of legislatures and society important values, such as fairness and minority rights, that politicians and bureaucrats would often prefer to ignore, but it need not have the last word should the legislature take responsibility for limiting or overriding the Court's decisions.

Democratic Dialogue in Practice

Both those who criticize the Court for judicial activism and those who offer conventional defences of judicial review agree that the *Charter* was a revolution in the relationship between the Supreme Court and the legislatures. These commentators focus on the fact that the *Charter* allows the Court to strike down legislation that violates rights as found by the Court in the broad guarantees of the *Charter*. The critics of judicial activism fear the revolutionary new powers of judges under the *Charter*, while defenders of judicial review express hopes that the judges will use their new powers in a manner consistent with their favoured theory of judicial review. If you accept the widely held premise that the *Charter* was a revolution that gave the judges the last word, there are real reasons to fear judicial activism. There is no agreement about how judges should interpret a constitutional bill of rights or how we can ensure that their decisions are consistent with democracy. If the *Charter* were a northern version of the American *Bill of Rights*, Canadians, like Americans, would be caught between the dangers of an underactive judiciary that leaves room for legislatures, but frequently fails to protect fundamental values and the rights of minorities, or an overactive judiciary that dictates some important and contentious policy issues to the legislature — unless the Court or the constitution could be changed.[1]

Those who see the *Charter* as either a welcome revolution or a terrible one are not paying enough attention to the ability of legislatures, by limiting or overriding rights under sections 1 and 33 of the *Charter*, to sustain the type of dialogue that has always occurred between courts and legislatures under the common law. They also ignore what the *Charter* did not change — a parliamentary system of government that has the potential to produce legislative activism[2] to counter judicial activism. Ignoring either the structure of the *Charter* or the continued relevance of parliamentary government means that those who criticize the Court for judicial activism and those who offer conventional defences of judicial review run the serious risk of wrongly conflating the *Charter* with the particular problems of judicial supremacy under the 1791 American *Bill of Rights*. Canadians, and perhaps others who live under a modern bill of rights, are quickly driving down a dead end towards American-styles debates about whether the Court is too activist or too restrained, all the time ignoring the fact that their elected governments can always place limits or even override rights as interpreted by the Court. The ability to limit and override rights makes the vast majority of *Charter* decisions closer to common law decisions, which could always be amended or abolished by ordinary legislation, than to American *Bill of Rights* decisions or even to division of powers decisions, which can often only be circumvented by the difficult process of changing the Court or the constitution. Understanding the common law nature of the *Charter* should ease concerns about judicial activism, but it may raise alarms for those who are relying on the Court, as opposed to the legislature, as the ultimate protector of rights. The *Charter* is not the revolution that many have hoped for and many have feared. It is, rather, a continuation and enrichment of our common law and democratic traditions.[3]

The Common Law Approach to Protecting Rights

Much of criminal, administrative, and Aboriginal rights law — all areas that now dominate the so-called Charter Revolution — was made by courts reading concerns about fairness into the common law long before the *Charter*. The common law allowed the Court to call the attention of society and the legislature to fairness values that were liable to be neglected by politicians and bureaucrats, without giving the judges the awesome responsibility of necessarily having the final word. If the Court applied the common law presumption in a way that society found to be unacceptable or mistaken, the answer was simply to enact ordinary legislation that clearly displaced the Court's common law presumption. In 1938 an astute Canadian legal scholar, John Willis, recognized that courts used presumptions of statutory interpretation to enforce "a sort of common law 'Bill of Rights' or 'ideal constitution.'"[4] Today, judges still use these presumptions, albeit updated to account for the post-Second World War concern about human rights. They also recognize that while the presumptions may protect important rights, they must yield to a clear expression of the legislative will. "If the legislation is clear, of course, the intent of the legislation must be respected. But what these presumptions ensure is that a law that appears to transgress our basic political understandings should be clearly expressed so as to invite the debate which is the lifeblood of Parliamentary democracy."[5] The common law presumptions require legislatures to be candid about their treatment of fundamental values. This approach should produce conditions conducive to accountability and democracy.

The best of what the independent courts did before the *Charter* was to engage legislatures in a dialogue by articulating, in the harsh reality of individual cases brought by aggrieved and often unpopular litigants, the requirements of important values that might otherwise have been ignored or finessed in the legislative and administrative processes. At the same time, the Court did not insist that it would have the final word. It often invited, and sometimes dared, the legislature to depart from its principled starting point. It was always open to Parliament to prescribe by law its intent to depart from the values of the common law constitution in particular contexts. Common law judicial review reenforced democracy by requiring debate, reflection, and clear statements by legislatures about how they would treat the fundamental values identified by the court.

The answer to the judicial activism of the common law presumptions was legislative activism in which our elected governments clearly took responsibility for rejecting the fairness concerns articulated by the Court. It simply was not necessary to attack or change the Court or to try to amend the constitution. Ordinary legislation would do the job.

COMMON LAW DIALOGUES ABOUT ABORIGINAL RIGHTS

The common law approach to protecting rights was democratic, but it should not be romanticized. Sometimes democracy can be ugly. Our shameful treatment of Aboriginal rights in the past may explain why Aboriginal and treaty rights are now not only constitutionally protected under the *Constitution Act, 1982* but also not subject to either the section 33 override or the section 1 reasonable limits provision. Before 1982 Parliament used its powers of legislative supremacy to override treaty rights and extinguish Aboriginal title, even though this unjust result did not accord with the honour of the Crown or the solemn promises made in the treaties.[6] Before 1982, judges had limited tools to stop this assault, but they did have some tools. Some judges quickly accepted the unjust proposition that Aboriginal rights had been extinguished simply because Europeans had exercised sovereignty. Others, however, demanded more. Justice Emmett Hall, today best known as the founder of medicare, ruled in the 1973 Nishga land claim case that a decision of the legislature to extinguish Aboriginal rights must be "clear and plain." It was not sufficient to find that the majority had exercised power inconsistent with Aboriginal title; the right had to be clearly extinguished by democratically debated and enacted legislation.[7] This common law protection of Aboriginal rights left the rights vulnerable, but at least it ensured that the legislature would have to prescribe its intention to extinguish rights in a statute and be held accountable for that act of injustice by the people and by future generations. Chief Justice Brian Dickson, who, like Justice Hall, came from the Prairies and was adept at using the common law to protect rights, took the same clear-statement approach that required the legislature explicitly to state its intent to infringe Aboriginal rights. He reasoned that, "given the serious and far-reaching consequences of a finding that a treaty right has been extinguished, it seems appropriate to demand strict proof of the fact of extinguishment in each case where the issue arises ... extinguishment cannot be lightly implied."[8] He also applied the clear-statement rule to determining whether Aboriginal and treaty rights had been extinguished before they were recognized and affirmed in the 1982 constitution, and he created a common law presumption that "treaties and statutes relating to Indians should be liberally construed and doubtful expressions resolved in favour of the Indians."[9] The common law approach to protecting Aboriginal rights does not guarantee the protection of rights as absolutes and it leaves rights vulnerable at the hands of the majority, but it does require legal authority, democratic debate, and accountability for the exercise of the power to be unjust.

COMMON LAW DIALOGUES ABOUT ADMINISTRATIVE JUSTICE

Judges have long used the common law to protect people from arbitrary and unfair exercises of administrative power. The most famous case remains *Roncarelli* v. *Duplessis*,[10] in which the Supreme Court held that the premier of Quebec, Maurice Duplessis, had acted without legal authority when he revoked Frank Roncarelli's liquor licence "forever" because the restaurant owner had posted bail for some of his fellow Jehovah's Witnesses. Even though the legislation granted a "discretion" to grant or revoke the liquor licence and one judge was prepared to read this power literally, Justice Ivan Rand, the Court's most civil libertarian judge, concluded: "[T]here is no such thing as absolute and untrammeled 'discretion' ... no legislative Act can, without express language, be taken to contemplate an unlimited arbitrary power exercisable for any purpose, however capricious or irrelevant." In this case, there was no legal authorization for Duplessis to "arbitrarily and illegally ... divest a citizen of an incident of his civil status." Under the common law, the exercise of all power must be justified. The Court did not provide absolute protection to Roncarelli's freedom of conscience, but it recognized that his rights were at stake. The only response open to the government would be to enact legislation that explicitly allowed the premier to revoke the licences of Jehovah's Witnesses or of Frank Roncarelli. If the legislature ever adopted such a law, it is difficult to believe that, at that point, even judges who were prepared to assert the absolute final word over the legislature would be able to do so in a society that would obviously value brute power over law, equality, and the need for reasons to justify the exercise of power.[11]

Without any guidance from the legislature, the Court recognized common law rights of individuals to hearings or at least some form of participation before their interests were adversely affected by administrative decisions.[12] As one judge suggested as early as 1863, "the justice of the common law will supply the omission of the legislature."[13] The Court left open the possibility that the legislature could enact statutes that explicitly precluded its common law presumptions of fairness, but legislatures generally had little appetite for clearly expressing their desire to act in an unfair or arbitrary manner. Legislatures did, however, routinely enact legislation that was designed to shelter the decisions of administrative agencies from judicial review. The legislatures often had good reason to fear judicial interference with the legitimate regulatory activities of the state. The courts, however, were not overly impressed by such "do not enter" signs and generally asserted their power to review decisions. At first they insisted that administrators reach "right answers," but this demand was effectively criticized as unwarranted judicial activism by many on the left who were suspicious of courts as inexpert meddlers in good administration. Later on the courts, again under the leadership of Justice Dickson, insisted only that administrators justify their decisions as not patently unreasonable.[14] This attitude showed increased respect for the reasons that administrators gave for their use of power while not allowing them to exercise power unfairly and without reasons and justifications. It contemplated a process, not altogether different from section 1 of the *Charter*, in which the Court reminded the government of limits on its power, and the government reminded the Court about why power was exercised. Much of the common law of administrative law can be seen as "embodying a culture of justification" that allows the state to act "on the condition that the procedures which are utilized are fair and facilitate participation and justification."[15]

Common law concerns about fairness continue to evolve. The Court has recently insisted on reasons from those officials who decide whether people should be saved from deportation on compassionate grounds. As in *Roncarelli* v. *Duplessis*, the Court stressed that discretion must be exercised in an unbiased fashion and must respect the values of the rule of law and the *Charter*.[16] To assess whether state power has been justified, the Court indicated that those affected by such decisions are entitled, under the common law, to reasons for the state's decisions. The immigration officer who had decided that Mrs. Baker should not be saved from deportation to Jamaica was found to have a reasonable apprehension of bias because his notes focused on the fact that the applicant was a single mother on welfare who had eight children and had been diagnosed with a mental illness. As my colleague David Dyzenhaus has suggested, *Baker* unifies the common law approach of administrative law around the idea, inherent in *Roncarelli*, that "legal authority differs from sheer power because it is by definition exercised in accordance with the fundamental principles of the rule of law. But the agency's sense of what is considered appropriate under the rule of law will be deferred to, as long as the agency supports its decisions with adequate reasons."[17] Again, this approach followed section 1 of the *Charter* in requiring the state to write down and justify its reasons for exercising power.

COMMON LAW DIALOGUES ABOUT CRIMINAL FAULT

For many people who travel it's a recurring nightmare: someone slips drugs into their suitcase without their knowledge and they are discovered at customs; or someone sells them oregano, but it is found to be stronger and illegal stuff. Not likely to happen, but it could. The criminal law simply says that it is illegal to possess certain drugs. Parliament, in its hurry to win the war on drugs, did not bother to say whether the accused must know that he or she has drugs. A court that was unconcerned with fairness and unwilling to read into the law things not found in its literal text would quickly convict the unknowing and unwitting drug smuggler, even though that person's only real crime may be gullibility. Fortunately, the courts have taken a more robust approach at common law that is concerned with the injustice of convicting someone who is not at fault.

In 1957 the Beaver brothers sold an undercover officer what they thought was powered milk, but was, in fact, heroin. Upright citizens may not have much sympathy for the Beavers, who were, after all, trying to rip someone off during a drug deal, but they would have more sympathy if they themselves were caught unaware at the border with drugs in their possession. The Supreme Court read the offence of possession of narcotics subject to the common law presumption that, unless Parliament clearly states otherwise, the prosecutor should have to establish that the accused was subjectively at fault. This presumption arose because of the Court's concern about punishing the morally innocent even in exceptional and strange cases such as the Beaver brothers'. It also arose in response to continued legislative neglect: Parliament never seemed to turn its mind to the issue of requiring fault for most criminal offences. Parliament's failure was not surprising given that legislated fault requirements would make it more difficult for its prosecutors to secure convictions. In its judgment overturning the Beavers' conviction, the Court, in a decision by former defence lawyer Chief Justice Cartwright, relied on an old common law presumption that Acts of Parliament should not, by a "literal construction," be interpreted to allow an innocent person to be punished. Parliament could jail people who did not know they had drugs, but the Court "would refuse to impute such an intention to Parliament unless words of the statute were clear and admitted of no other interpretation. To borrow the words of Lord Kenyon [in a 1798 common law case] ... 'I would adopt any construction of the statute that the words will bear, in order to avoid such monstrous consequences.'"[18] The Court strongly made the point about the injustice of convicting someone in the absence of fault and stopped the legislature from sneaking in doctrines that could punish the innocent. It dared Parliament to declare its willingness to be so unjust.

But what about the reality that judges could make mistakes when creating and applying the common law presumptions of fault? In a subsequent case, Chief Justice Cartwright would have applied the same presumption of subjective fault to protect a corporation that was found to have twenty-six undersized lobsters in a catch of 50,000 or 60,000 pounds. He was arguably wrong in that case to apply the presumption of subjective fault when Parliament was trying to conserve a natural resource and not put someone in jail. His colleagues thought so, and he wrote in lone dissent.[19] Even if he could have persuaded four of his colleagues to join him, Parliament could have responded with clear legislation to displace the common law presumption of subjective fault. As under section 1 of the *Charter*, Parliament would have had to explain in law why the accused's rights must be limited in the particular context of possession of undersized lobsters. Even a wrongly applied common law presumption may re-enforce democracy by requiring the legislature to justify its actions clearly. If we have faith in the democratic process and the clarity of the judicial error, we should not be overly concerned about requiring the legislature to correct judicial mistakes.

The result espoused by the majority in the lobster case was not without its own problems because it allowed a conviction even if the corporation was not at fault and had done everything that was reasonably possible to ensure that it did not catch undersized lobsters. Fortunately, the Court crafted a more principled common law presumption eight years later. In the landmark *Sault Ste. Marie* case, Justice Dickson articulated strong common law presumptions of subjective fault (in criminal cases such as *Beaver*) and fault based on negligence (in regulatory offence cases such as the lobster case). The Court explained the reasons for requiring a "vicious will" to be convicted of a true crime and also the danger of convicting "the morally innocent,"[20] who could have done nothing more to prevent undersized lobsters from being caught. These rationales represented concerns about fairness to the accused that were likely to be neglected when the legislature affirmed its concerns about harms by enacting offences. At the same time, if they clearly expressed their intention to do so, legislatures could still enact no-fault regulatory offences and criminal offences that did not require subjective fault. By requiring such clear statements, the common law presumptions facilitated democratic accountability and debate for legislative departures from the principles of fault. *Sault Ste. Marie* is an excellent example of how the Court can initiate and structure a dialogue with the legislature and how the judiciary can add its distinctive voice and concerns to the dialogue without necessarily having the final word.

To be sure, the common law presumptions in *Sault Ste. Marie* were a strong form of judicial law making that made it more difficult to prosecute over 40,000 regulatory offences enacted by municipalities and both levels of governments. More even than *Charter* cases like *M.v. H.* requiring equal benefits for same-sex spouses, it was "a single blockbuster case" that could be said to render "denials of judicial activism problematic."[21] The Court might well have been reluctant to proclaim its strong presumptions of fault as the absolute final word. The beauty of the presumption, however, is that, if the legislature found it unworkable, all it had to do was to engage in the democratic process of clearly stating a departure in ordinary legislation. Presumptions do not have to be based on a claim that judges cannot make mistakes or that they will always be able to perceive compelling cases for contextual exceptions to general principles. The more presumptive the ruling, the stronger the judicial voice can be because judges need not fear imposing the last word.[22] Common law dialogues between courts and legislatures are ideal vehicles by which to implement the insight that "no good society can be unprincipled; and no viable society can be principle-ridden."[23] Common law presumptions are an invitation to the legislature to respond to the judicial decision and to explain to both the public and the Court why limits on the values articulated by the Court are necessary in particular contexts. The fact that legislatures may not respond does not mean that the dialogue has been an unsuccessful monologue. The legislature may have thought through the implications of a possible reply and have discovered other less intrusive alternatives to advance its policies. Sometimes even having to formulate in clear language the transgression of fundamental values will persuade the legislature of the error of its ways.

SUMMARY

The common law approach to rights protection with respect to Aboriginal rights, administrative law, and the criminal law is one in which the judge calls the attention of society and the legislature to important values and limits on powers, but does not enforce them as absolute rights or limits. What makes the common law democratic[24] is that the judge does not assert the final word if the legislature is prepared to take democratic responsibility for displacing the Court's decision. What makes the common law dialogic is that the legislature can reverse or revise the Court's decision and that the judges' acceptance or rejection of assertions of state authority depend not so much on abstract values and principles that can be determined by the judges in solitary splendour, but on the particular reasons that are given by the state for limiting those values. As we will see, the *Charter* builds on the democracy-enhancing clear-statement requirements of the common law as well as its demands for a process of dialogue in which the use of state power is justified and brought within a range of reasonableness.

From the Common Law to the *Charter*

Despite triumphs such as Justice Hall's decision in *Calder*, Justice Rand's decision in *Roncarelli*, and many of Justice Dickson's decisions concerning Aboriginal rights, administrative law, and criminal law, the Court has not always applied common law presumptions of fairness and respect for rights in a robust fashion. This is unfortunate because such presumptions can promote greater transparency and attention to principle in the legislative process, while recognizing that the Court is not infallible and that principles are not absolutes. The value of common law presumptions can be seen in a number of cases in the early 1980s in which Justice Dickson dissented from the decision of the Court to read a variety of police powers into the statutes that failed explicitly to authorize such police powers. Dickson's point was not that the police had gone over some absolute limit on their powers, but that there should be explicit legal authorization and democratic discussion of their powers. As we will see in the next section, his vision of partnership and dialogue between courts and legislatures over the ambit of police powers came to fruition under the *Charter*.

Justice Dickson dissented from an oft-criticized 1979 decision of the Supreme Court to convict a cyclist of obstruction of justice for refusing to identify himself to a police officer after he ran a red light. He interpreted the offence of obstruction of justice in light of the common law presumption that an accused should not be required to assist the police unless there was a clear legal duty to do so. There was nothing in the statute that said a person had to answer when a police officer asked for identification. Judicial creation of exceptions to this basic rule of liberty were "unsound in principle and unworkable in practice ... the criminal law is no place within which to introduce implied duties, unknown to statute and common law, breach of which subjects a person to arrest and imprisonment."[25] This presumption did not mean that the legislature could not require such cooperation, and Justice Dickson cited numerous examples where legislatures had done so. Nevertheless, he believed that it was for the Court to articulate the general principle of liberty and for the legislature to articulate and justify the need for a clear exception to the principle. The result of this institutional division of labour would be greater accountability and transparency for the accused, the police, and society. If Parliament wanted people to be guilty of a crime for not identifying themselves when asked by the police, it had better say so directly and take democratic responsibility for its actions.

Justice Dickson also dissented when the Court, in the early 1980s, found implicit in a warrant for electronic surveillance the power to break into the target's home to install the recording device. He invoked the common law presumption "in favour of vested rights ... as well as the presumption that express language must be found to demonstrate that a legislative body intended to authorize an act otherwise unlawful at common law." He also stressed "the traditional legal protection accorded private property and the long-standing refusal of the judiciary to impair that protection where Parliament has not itself done so expressly."[26] Dickson's dissents were an invitation to Parliament to conduct a democratic debate about police powers. If Parliament believed that police break and enters were justified, it should initiate a public debate and explicitly authorize them. The government might have been unwilling to have such a democratic debate soon after the public had learned that the Royal Canadian Mounted Police had burned down a barn and committed other illegalities. But this discomfort was the point of requiring clear statements in legislation to authorize police break and enters. The approach taken by the majority of the Court unfortunately allowed Parliament implicitly to authorize police law breaking and avoid a democratic debate about a contentious police power.

Chief Justice Dickson's use of common law presumptions to promote both democracy and the rule of the law culminated in his dissenting statement in *Dedman* [27] that "it is the function of the legislature, not the courts, to authorize the arbitrary police action that would otherwise be unlawful as a violation of rights traditionally protected at common law." In that case, he dissented from the majority's judgment that the common law duties of police officers authorized random stops and spot checks of drivers to detect and deter drunk driving. The random stops were a popular and effective means to deter drunk driving, especially during the holiday season, and there was little doubt that the legislature would be prepared to authorize them. In fact, by the time the Supreme

Court decided the case, Ontario had already amended its *Highway Traffic Act* [28] to authorize the popular anti-drunk driving-initiative. Nevertheless, Chief Justice Dickson continued to argue that it was an important principle — ultimately one that spoke to the procedures of democracy more than the substantive content of the law — that the police power be clearly authorized in legislation, and not read in by the judiciary.

The dissents in these cases did not mean that Chief Justice Dickson believed that the police powers he refused to imply into silent legislation could not be justified. Three years after *Dedman*, he joined the Court's judgment in holding that the Ontario law authorizing the random stops was a justified and reasonable limitation, under section 1, on the *Charter* right not to be arbitrarily detained by a police officer. [29] Many of the values found in the common law presumptions in the criminal law were now proclaimed as constitutional rights, but not absolute rights of the type found in the American *Bill of Rights*. The legislature could justify reasonable limits on the right without having to assert that the right against arbitrary detention was not violated by random traffic stops or attempting to curb a Court that might invalidate a popular initiative against drunk driving. As required under section 1, the legislature was obliged to prescribe by law and to justify the limits it placed on the right. The structure of the *Charter* continued the common law dialogue between courts and legislatures. It meant that a conclusion that a right was violated was only the start of a conversation about whether legislative limitations on the rights were necessary.

Those who look only at the bottom line will see very little difference between the results reached in the above two cases. There was a world of difference because democracy and the rule of law had both been enhanced when the legislature spoke its lines in the dialogue. The legislature had authorized state power by democratically enacting laws and justifying limits on the rights of the individuals under the common law and the *Charter*. The dialogue that Chief Justice Dickson had tried to promote with his earlier common law dissents — a dialogue in which courts and legislatures played distinct and complementary roles — had been achieved under the *Charter*.

Dialogue between Courts and Legislatures under the *Charter*

Judicial review under a modern bill of rights can be seen as a continuation and enrichment of common law dialogues between the Court and the legislature. The legislature can respond to *Charter* decisions, as it could to common law decisions, with ordinary legislation that justifies the limit placed on the right or derogates from the right. The ability of legislatures to reply to Court decisions explains what David Dyzenhaus has called the "democratic" character of the *Charter* and similar modern bills of rights, as opposed to the "liberal" character of the American *Bill of Rights*, which is based on judicial supremacy and finality in defining and enforcing the enumerated rights. This insight also opens the possibility that *Charter* review can be seen as public law "writ large,"[30] and not as a revolution that gives unelected judges new and dangerous powers. The *Charter* can be understood as a continuation and enrichment of the best of our common law and public law traditions.

As suggested in the last chapter, there are different types of dialogues that may occur between the Court and the legislatures. Will the two institutions attempt to learn from each other in a respectful conversation in which each brings different concerns and information to the table? Will they shout at each other about which one has interpreted the *Charter* correctly? Will there be showdowns about who is the bigger kid on the block? The structure of the *Charter* provides some helpful ground rules and processes to govern respectful conversations, shouting matches, and showdowns between the Court and the legislature.

The limitation clause in the *Charter* and most other modern bills of rights facilitates a respectful and constructive conversation that allows each institution to learn from the other. By providing for the judicial protection of rights, section 1 of the *Charter* allows the Court to focus the attention of legislatures, executives, and society on fundamental values and minority rights that might otherwise be neglected or ignored. By allowing a wide range of reasonable limits on rights to be prescribed and justified, it also allows the government to educate both the Court and society about its objectives and the alternatives rejected in pursuing these objectives. Section 1 is a vehicle for an enriching conversation in which both the Court and Parliament expand the horizon of each other while being true to their own distinctive capacities as elected and non-elected institutions. It is based on the idea that the independent Court and the elected Parliament can play distinct and complementary roles, as opposed to being engaged in the same process of interpreting the law or responding to the wishes of the people. It provides the structure for the constructive dialogue that often occurs between people who, despite their very different experiences and values, respect each other and converse not by arguing over specific points, but by introducing the other to new perspectives and new ways of looking at the problem. The conversation is refined and sharpened, without getting bogged down over sticking points and direct confrontations.

Human experience tells us, however, that people do occasionally get hung up on particularly contentious points. Voices can be raised. At this point, section 33 provides a carefully structured outlet for the extraordinary dialogue that occurs when the Court and the legislature cannot get over a fundamental disagreement on a particular point and a showdown looms. It allows a legislature to reverse a Court decision with an "in-your-face" reply that suggest that the Court wrongly interpreted the constitution or that its decision was simply unacceptable to the majority. The ability to derogate from rights under the *Charter* and other modern bills of rights also allows the legislature to cut off debate with the courts by a pre-emptive use of the override. This use is unfortunate because it amounts to the legislature saying, "I do not even want to hear what you have to say," something that, if not fatal, is especially corrosive to healthy and respectful relationships.[31] Although section 33 resembles the way that legislatures could abolish the common law, it constitutes an improvement by requiring the public to be more clearly warned about what is being done in its name and by preserving the Court's point of principle, to be reconsidered in calmer times when the override expires after five years. The override can result in legislative tyranny, but it is a tyranny that is explicit for all the world to see and that must be revisited when the override expires. Even when it is not frequently used, the override remains a powerful metaphor and reminder of the common law nature of the *Charter* and its innovative balance of judicial and legislative activism.

Charter Dialogues about Search and Seizure Powers

The Supreme Court's generous interpretation of the right against unreasonable searches and seizures has generated concerns by critics of judicial activism on both the left and the right. The end result of these cases has, however, been the antithesis of the judicial monologue that the critics of judicial activism fear. Parliament has responded to almost every major Court decision striking down search powers in a way that not only made such searches possible but enhanced democracy, the rule of law, and accountability for the exercise of police powers,[32] all without coming close to having to shout at the Court and use the override. These cases demonstrate that ordinary and respectful dialogue between the Court and Parliament under the *Charter* is similar to the type of dialogue that Justice Dickson tried to promote under the common law.

Critics of judicial activism on the left expressed fears that the Court's decision striking down the power of state investigators to search without a warrant would result in a *Lochner*-like paralysis of the regulatory state. But Parliament responded to the Court's first search-and-seizure case with new legislation that allowed combines investigators to obtain a warrant on the basis of reasonable grounds that a crime had been committed and that the search would find evidence.[33] This process has been described as a negative form of dialogue because the law struck down by the Court was repealed and replaced by Parliament, but it seems to be a case "in which elected officials reflect on the implications of judicial decisions and revise statutes to advance legislative objectives in a manner that complies with the Charter." Parliament did, however, accept the Court's judgment that warrants were required for searches.[34] Those who subscribe to a theory of coordinate construction might see this process as a negative reply or a form of policy distortion because Parliament did not act on its own interpretation of the right against unreasonable search and seizure. The problem, however, is that Parliament would have a conflict of interest in acting on its own interpretation of a right that restricts the activities only of its own investigators.

Critics of judicial activism on the right expressed fears that the Court's decisions requiring warrants for searches would handcuff the police. The Court struck down writs of assistance, which authorized police officers and customs officials to conduct searches and seizures without prior judicial authorization.[35] The use of such writs by English officials had been one of the causes of the American Revolution. Two hundred years later, Canadians started to become disenchanted with them and governments stopped issuing such general warrants to search. By the time the Court finally held that the writs of assistance violated the right against unreasonable search and seizure, Parliament had already replaced them with telewarrants, which allowed police to obtain warrants quickly, before evidence such as drugs was destroyed.[36] The Court itself would not have had the information or the resources to create the telewarrant procedure, but Parliament could. This entire process provides a good example of constructive and respectful dialogue: Parliament introduced a new warrant procedure that could serve the same objectives as writs of assistance, while complying with the constitutional norms of prior judicial authorization of searches and seizures wherever feasible. For those still worried that drugs might be flushed down the toilet while the police dial up a telewarrant, the law now authorizes warrantless searches, if reasonable grounds for obtaining a warrant exist, but "by reason of exigent circumstances it would be impracticable to obtain one."[37]

There are many more examples of respectful dialogue between the Court and Parliament over search-and-seizure powers. In 1994 the Court excluded illegally seized evidence of a DNA match in a sexual assault case. The public was understandably outraged when the accused's lawyer explained that "the freeing of a man who was proven 'beyond a scintilla of doubt' to have raped a 69 year old woman at a senior citizen's home is a good thing."[38] Unfortunately, this case was necessary to prompt Parliament into creating legislation to allow the police to obtain warrants to seize bodily material for DNA testing. The legislation was fast-tracked and, with cooperation from all parties, went through the House of Commons in one day.[39] The Canadian parliamentary system is particularly amenable to rapid responses to Court decisions, but this may not be so in countries with more divided forms governments. If, as occurred with respect to the failed reply to *Morgentaler*, party discipline is relaxed and the Senate exercises a more powerful role, there is a greater chance that the Court will have the last word. Dialogic theories of judicial review depend on the structure not only of the bill of rights but also of government.

Parliament's delay in providing for DNA warrants had some unfortunate consequences. In 1997 the Court decided another case involving the seizure of bodily material for DNA testing before Parliament had provided for warrants. The case was an awful one. A seventeen year old, Billy Stillman, was accused of raping and murdering fourteen-year-old Pamela Bischoff. The police arrested Stillman and seized a number of DNA samples, without his consent and without a warrant. In order to match teeth marks found on the victim, the police also forced Stillman to submit to a two-hour procedure to obtain dental impressions. I represented the Canadian Civil Liberties Association in its intervention in this appeal, and the forced dental impressions was, by far, the worst police conduct in the case. A majority of the Court excluded the teeth impressions, as well as hair and saliva samples obtained without a warrant, characterizing them as illegal and particularly intrusive invasions of the sanctity of the body. The very same year, however, Parliament responded by enacting a provision that allowed a justice to issue a warrant authorizing police officers to take body impressions, including dental impressions.[40] Unfortunately, there was little public debate about these new provisions. All citizens must continue to be vigilant about the way the legislature treats rights, and we should not accept as necessary or wise any measure that could survive *Charter* review.

It is easy to be cynical about the frequent legislative replies to the Court's search-and-seizure decisions. Critics of due process will point out that Parliament followed the Court's directions by providing for warrants. For them, due process is still due process, even when enacted by Parliament and not the Court. Supporters of due process will point out that Parliament tailored the warrants to its own interests and authorized some warrantless searches. For them, the Court's due process decisions produced only more efficient and legitimate crime control. These are valid points, but it would take a strong faith in legislatures to suggest that Parliament should have ignored or defied Court decisions that were designed to protect those inherently unpopular people who are suspected by the police of crimes. The interests of such groups are likely to be ignored in the legislative process, and the courts have special concerns and expertise in promoting fairness in the criminal justice system. Similarly, it would take a strong faith in courts to suggest that their rulings should be final in defining police powers and procedures. Parliament had a role to play in indicating to the Court the objectives secured by police powers and the contexts in which the Court's principles were not practicable. Parliament must update the law to accommodate new technologies such as telewarrants and DNA. Legislation can, to the benefit of both the police and the public, promote greater clarity and certainty about the limits of police powers. The legislation enacted in reply to the Court's decisions may not be perfect, but at least there was an opportunity for democratic debate about police powers. These cases, and Parliament's frequent replies, enhanced democracy and the rule of law in a way that Chief Justice Dickson tried to do in his pre-*Charter* dissents against implied police powers.

Charter Dialogues about Sexual Assault Law

The most tense dialogues between the Court and Parliament under the *Charter* have occurred over sexual assault laws. Sexual assault is one of the most difficult issues in our society. The Court and Parliament can learn from each other, and each has an important role to play. Parliament can act on information about who suffers sexual violence and why most victims decide not to report it to the authorities. Parliament can change the offence — replacing rape in 1983 with sexual assault — and other rules and procedures governing trials. The independent judiciary can ensure fairness to the accused — by definition, people who are unpopular if not demonized — and it can require the state to justify any limitations it places on the accused's rights and to be clear if it must override the accused's rights. If the judges do not protect the accused, it is not likely the politicians will, especially when faced by a powerful lobby of women's groups and the public's understandable revulsion at violent and sexual crime.

CONSTRUCTIVE DIALOGUES ON STATUTORY RAPE, VAGRANCY, AND THE RAPE SHIELD

There have been a number of constructive interactions between the Court and Parliament over sexual offences, where each institution has played a distinct and complementary role and respected the prerogatives of the other institution. One example was the Court's 1990 decision to strike down the offence of statutory rape, which provided that a man could be punished by up to life imprisonment for having consensual sexual intercourse with a girl under fourteen years of age regardless of his belief that she was older. This offence was a legislative exception to the common law principle that a person who honestly believed in a state of affairs that would make his conduct innocent should not be convicted of a criminal offence. Justice Wilson explained for the Court that the offence could punish those who were mentally innocent of the crime because they honestly believed that the girl was older. In such circumstances, the law could not be justified as a reasonable limit that would help deter sex with underage girls. Justice McLachlin dissented on the basis that, although the law could punish the mentally innocent, it was justified because of its role in deterring men from having sex with girls who might be "jail bait."[41] The Court made a point about the possible injustice of the law: a concern that was very unlikely to be heard in Parliament. A politician who even approached the subject would risk being accused of approving of sex with children — a political kiss of death. Taken on its own terms, however, the Court's decision might be criticized as excessive judicial activism that went beyond the American courts and disrupted Parliament's policy in protecting young girls from the very real dangers of premature sex.

Fortunately, by the time of the Court's ruling, Parliament had already enacted a new offence that provided better protection for children and was fairer to the accused. The new offence protected both boys and girls under fourteen years of age from any form of sexual interference, touching, or invitation to touching. Issues of whether intercourse occurred would no longer be relevant, as they had been under the archaic statutory rape offence. Parliament also allowed screens and videotaped evidence to be used to make it easier for child victims to testify. The new offences did not follow the common law subjective fault principles espoused by the Court, but allowed the accused a defence only if he or she had taken all reasonable steps to ascertain the child's age. This provision afforded more protection than the old law to accused, who might think the child was older than fourteen years of age, but not as much as the common law presumption that honest but unreasonable mistakes should exonerate the accused. The result was successful and respectful dialogue on a delicate subject that allowed the Court and Parliament to meet halfway. The Court brought to Parliament's attention a potential injustice that would not likely concern the elected politicians, while Parliament, after conducting research on the matter, did not accept the Court's decision as the final word and engaged in comprehensive law reform that provided better and modern protection for the sexual integrity of children.

Another example of a constructive dialogue between the Court and Parliament occurred with respect to an offence that allowed all convicted sexual offenders to be convicted of vagrancy if found loitering in or near a school ground, playground, public park, or bathing area. The offence applied without specific notice to all sexual offenders, not just pedophiles, and for the duration of their lives. The overkill of this vagrancy offence was not likely to be corrected in the legislative process because convicted sexual offenders are not a popular constituency. The offence had rarely been used and was, at one point, rendered useless when Parliament forgot to update the reference numbers in the offence to the predicate sexual offences. This legislative error was fixed and the offence was used to convict Robert Heywood, a retired Victoria schoolteacher with convictions for sexual assault against two young girls, of vagrancy for hanging around a playground and taking pictures of the crotches of young girls. Heywood appealed to the Supreme Court, which, in a 5 to 4 decision, held that the offence violated the principles of fundamental justice under the *Charter*. Many no doubt would agree with Justice Gonthier, who argued in dissent that the offence should have been upheld and applied vigorously to those who, like Heywood, loitered in a children's playground with a malevolent intent. Nevertheless the majority held that the offence should be struck down because it applied without notice to too many people for too long a period and prohibited too much conduct, including being in parks without a bad intent and where no children could reasonably be expected to be present. In a world without dialogue between the Court and Parliament, this decision would have been disturbing and even dangerous.

Fortunately, by the time the Supreme Court rendered its decision, Parliament had already enacted a new offence.[42] Judges could ban, if need be for life, those convicted of sexual crimes against children both from loitering in public areas where children would reasonably be expected and from having a position of trust and authority over children. Parliament expanded the terms of the debate by providing also that a peace bond could be obtained on the basis of reasonable fears that any person would commit a sexual offence against a child. The new offence was used by the majority of the Supreme Court as evidence that Parliament could accomplish its legitimate aims in protecting children from being victims of sexual offences in a more tailored manner than the old overbroad law.[43] Despite the Court's approval for the new law, which was already in force, the case was presented in the media as a sign of "how far our courts, and particularly the Supreme Court, has gone from reflecting the need for public safety."[44] The courts never doubted the need for public safety, but their decisions rejected Parliament's sledgehammer approach. The new offence created by Parliament more carefully targeted those most likely to commit sexual crimes against children. As in the statutory rape case, a controversial Court decision prompted Parliament to consider fairness issues that it otherwise would not have considered and to engage in comprehensive law reform that, in the end, provided children with stronger protections against sexual predators. These cases are good examples of the constructive dialogue that can occur between the Court and Parliament when they each stick to what they do best. The Court reminded Parliament of the unjust effects of its laws in exceptional cases, and Parliament used its power to enact new offences and new procedures to remind the Court of the need to provide children with the greatest protection possible from sexual exploitation. The Court's concern with ensuring fairness to the accused and avoiding the conviction of the morally innocent was not one that normally would have been considered by Parliament. Unlike the Court, Parliament was able to engage in comprehensive law reform after having commissioned extensive research on the subject. A strong Court and a strong Parliament each played distinct and complementary roles and together made the law better.

The final sexual assault case that fits this pattern is the Court's decision to strike down categorical "rape shield" restrictions on the admissibility of the complainant's prior sexual conduct in a criminal trial, and Parliament's response both with less categorical restrictions on such evidence and a more comprehensive reform of sexual assault law. In *Seaboyer*,[45] the accused argued that his right to a fair trial was violated because he could not use evidence of the complainant's prior sexual conduct in his defence. Putting the victim on trial for her sexual history had long been an effective and, for the victim, very hurtful and humiliating defence strategy in sexual cases. Parliament had responded in 1983 with legislation that prevented most prior sexual history evidence from being used at the trial. In a 7 to 2 decision the Court decided that Parliament had struck "the wrong balance between the rights of complainants and the accused" by categorically excluding evidence that could be essential to the accused's defence, including the controversial defence that he made an honest but perhaps unreasonable mistake that the victim consented to the sexual activity. Justice McLachlin argued that no less than the "precept that the innocent must not be convicted" was at stake. "One has only to think of the public revulsion at the improper conviction of Donald Marshall in this country or the Birmingham Six in the United Kingdom to appreciate how deeply held is this tenet of justice." Even if the victim's rights to security of the person were at stake, the accused's right must prevail and the Court could not accept a risk that the innocent would be convicted. In her dissent, Justice L'Heureux-Dubé refused to focus on "the narrow interests of the accused" and stressed the risk that women would be sexually assaulted. She concluded that any evidence excluded by the rape shield law was not relevant unless the accused "has the right to a biased verdict."[46]

Although the Court struck down the categorical exclusion of evidence of the complainant's prior sexual conduct, it was careful not to create a vacuum that would return the law to the bad old days of women being discredited simply because of prior sexual activity. It established new common law guidelines that would not admit evidence of the complainant's prior sexual conduct with the accused or others to support an inference that the woman consented or was less worthy of belief as a witness. The new common law guidelines were presented as "a middle way that offers the maximum protection to the complainant compatible with the maintenance of the accused's fundamental right to a fair trial."[47] The Court subsequently explained that if its own common law guidelines had been the only permissible response, it would not have been meaningful to speak of a dialogue between the Court and Parliament.[48]

Despite the attempt to prevent the worst abuses of the past, the Court's decision was denounced in the press as "a devastating blow" and a "slap in the face" to victims of sexual assault. The chair of the Parliamentary Committee on the Status of Women repeated that committee's call that the section 33 override be used to re-enact the rape shield law in order to protect women from "brutal interrogation about their sexual history and reputation."[49] Some have argued that the override could and should have been immediately invoked "without significant political backlash, given the overwhelming extent of the public outcry against the *Seaboyer* decision."[50] The override would have been the appropriate vehicle had Parliament simply re-enacted the very law that the Court had struck down. Parliament would have been telling the Court that its interpretation of the *Charter* was wrong or that its decision was simply unacceptable. Parliament would have won its shouting match with the Court, but, after a five-year cooling-off period, it would have had to revisit the matter by deciding whether the expired override should be renewed.

Instead of telling the Court that it was wrong and its decision was unacceptable, the government slowed down and consulted with women's groups. It decided that the more constructive and more permanent response to *Seaboyer* was to engage in comprehensive reform of sexual assault law. This reform included a new "rape shield" that established a more flexible test to establish whether the complainant's prior sexual conduct should be admitted. The test would ask judges to consider not only the accused's rights but society's interests in encouraging the reporting of sexual assault and possible prejudice to the complainant's privacy, dignity, and right to the equal and non-discriminary protection of the law. Parliament also restricted one of the grounds for admitting evidence of the complainant's prior sexual conduct by requiring that an accused who mistakenly believed that the complainant was consenting had taken reasonable steps to ascertain that she had consented — something that was now explicitly defined as voluntary agreement to the particular sexual activity. The reply to *Seaboyer* was constructive, respectful, and effective precisely because Parliament used its institutional advantage over the Court by comprehensively reforming the law of sexual assault. It did not provoke a showdown or shouting match with the Court by telling the judges that their decision about the old rape-shield law was wrong or unacceptable. Parliament could have taken this route, but it would have had to use the override and revisit the matter after a five-year cooling-off period. Parliament arguably accomplished more by not shouting.

The Supreme Court subsequently upheld the new rape shield law, concluding that it was "in essence a codification by Parliament of the Court's guidelines in *Seaboyer*." Unfortunately, this statement suggests something closer to monologue, whereas a fair amount of dialogue between the Court and Parliament actually occurred. Parliament introduced some significant changes to the Court's guidelines in *Seaboyer*, including protecting the complainant from having to testify at the hearing to determine if her prior sexual conduct was admissible along with legislative directions to judges to consider her privacy and equality rights and the social interest in encouraging the reporting of sexual assault. These changes were subsequently upheld by the Court on the basis that the accused's right should be defined in relation to the competing equality and privacy rights of the complainant, and that it "would belie the mutual respect that underpins the relationship" between the Court and Parliament to "insist on slavish conformity" with the Court's prior pronouncements.[51] More important, but unmentioned by the Court, was the point that Parliament had broadened the debate by engaging in comprehensive reform of the sexual assault offence in a way that should make evidence of the complainant's prior sexual conduct less relevant in sexual assault trials. The Court did not have the final word on the rape shield and, without using the override, Parliament responded to the Court's controversial decision with legislation that comprehensively reformed the law of sexual assault.

"IN-YOUR-FACE" DIALOGUES AND SHOUTING MATCHES ON INTOXICATION AND ACCESS TO RECORDS

The next two cases are less about respectful conversations that expand the debate between the Court and Parliament, and more about shouting matches over whether the Court was right or wrong. They involve what has become known in Ottawa as "in-your-face" replies to the Court. The in-your-face reply is a form of dialogue that minimizes policy distortions caused when the legislature responds to a Court's decision because the legislature essentially rejects or reverses the Court's decisions on the basis that the Court has wrongly interpreted the *Charter* or that its decision is simply unacceptable. The United States Supreme Court has not put up with this sort of reply and has quickly struck down legislative attempts to reverse *Miranda* and other unpopular constitutional decisions. The Canadian Supreme Court has been much more willing to accept such legislative lip. My concern about in-your-face replies is not that they are unacceptable under the *Charter*, but that they should have been enacted with the override, which provides a special structure to govern shouting matches and showdowns between the Court and Parliament. Section 33 requires Parliament to alert the people about what is being done and to revisit the matter after a five-year cooling-off period. It ensures more, not less, dialogue.

The first sexual assault case that earned an in-your-face reply from Parliament involved a seventy-two-year-old alcoholic, Henri Daviault, who sexually assaulted his wife's friend, a sixty-five-year-old woman confined to a wheel chair. It was estimated that Daviault had, after consuming about eight beers and a bottle of brandy, a blood alcohol level five times the legal limit and one that would produce a coma or death for a non-alcoholic. It did not have that effect on Daviault, who attempted to rape the victim. Under the existing law, *Daviault* was an easy case because drunkenness was not a defence to sexual assault or assault. Nevertheless, a majority of the Supreme Court concluded that convicting Daviault of sexual assault would violate the *Charter* if he was so extremely intoxicated that he acted involuntarily and without any intent at the time the crime was committed. The dissenters favoured the traditional common law: even if the accused was so drunk that he acted without fault at the time of the sexual assault, the fault in becoming so drunk was good enough to convict him of sexual assault.

Even though the Court did not acquit Daviault, but sent the case back for a new trial in which he would have to prove with expert evidence that he was so extremely intoxicated that he did not know what he was doing, the public was outraged at the Court's decision. The Court was denounced for declaring open season on women and for excusing the drunken commission of violent crimes. "For weeks the ruling was fodder for radio hotline shows and newspaper letter-to-the-editor writers. Opposition to *Daviault* united both feminists and law-and-order-advocates."[52]

The Court in its judgment anticipated public concerns and invited Parliament to respond by enacting a new offence that would ensure that the Daviaults of this world would never be acquitted. The new offence that the Court proposed would convict the extremely intoxicated not of sexual assault or assault — on the Court's reasoning they were not at fault for such crimes — but of a new crime based on causing harm while severely intoxicated. Such a legislative response, like the comprehensive changes to sexual assault law in response to *Seaboyer*, would have traded on Parliament's institutional advantage by doing something that the Court could not — namely, creating a new crime. It also would have broadened the debate away from whether the majority in *Daviault* was right and towards the public interest in protection from the extremely intoxicated. Such a legislative response would have avoided a direct confrontation with the Court's ruling and allowed the legislature to add something to the debate that the Court never could have done. It would have produced a dialogue in which both the Court and Parliament acted in a way that the other institution could not have.

A private member introduced a new offence that would have made it an offence punishable by up to fourteen years' imprisonment to commit sexual assaults while extremely intoxicated. This was no slap on the wrist and would have increased the maximum exposure of the severely intoxicated to imprisonment. Nevertheless, the minister of justice, reflecting the public clamour against the unpopular decision and concerns expressed by women's groups about a new intoxication-based offence, denounced the bill as raising the spectre of a "drunkenness discount." Instead of creating a new intoxication-based offence that would have recognized both the harm caused by the accused and his diminished level of fault, Parliament effectively reversed *Daviault* with legislation that followed the logic of the three dissenting judges: it deemed that the fault of becoming extremely intoxicated could be substituted for the fault of assault or sexual assault. This legislation constituted much more of an in-your-face reply to the Court's decision than the response to *Seaboyer* or the introduction of a new offence.

The new law was quickly passed with approval by all parties. Politicians on the left stressed that the bill was a progressive response to violence against women and children, while those on the right argued that it responded to the wishes of the majority of Canadians who were "upset and disgusted" at Supreme Court decisions that lacked "common sense" and were "better-suited for the faculty club."[53] Unfortunately, there was no serious discussion in Parliament of whether the reversal of the Court's *Charter* decision required the use of section 33. The use of the override would have required Parliament to revisit the matter when it expired after five years and when the panic over *Daviault* acquittals would likely have subsided as courts made clear how limited and rare the defence would be. Parliament would have had an opportunity to rethink the need for the override. In any event, the override was not used and the Supreme Court will eventually have to decide whether the new provision can survive *Charter* challenge.

By following the logic of the dissenting judges, Parliament has placed the Court in a difficult position by suggesting that the majority in *Daviault* was wrong to interpret the *Charter* as it did. Parliament's right to tell the Court that it was wrong in this way can only be supported on the basis that Parliament is entitled to act on its own interpretation of the constitution, even when it is at odds with that of the Court, or to override *Charter* decision that it determines are unacceptable to the majority of Canadians. There are elements in the preamble to the legislation which reflect both strong theories of dialogue. The preamble asserts the relevance of the equality rights of women, parts of the *Charter* that were not considered by the Court in its original judgment. The preamble also suggests that the Court may have been wrong when it suggested that extreme intoxication could produce involuntary behaviour. A Court that accepted coordinate construction would ask itself whether it was prepared to defer to Parliament's interpretation of the relevant *Charter* rights. The preamble also appeals to majority sentiment by asserting that Parliament "shares with Canadians the moral view that people who, while in a state of self-induced intoxication, violate the physical integrity of others are blameworthy." A Court that accepted a theory of dialogue in which it was accountable to the majoritarian branches of government would consider whether public outrage at its decision affected its continued commitment to such an unpopular precedent. It is also possible for the Court to see the legislation as an attempt by Parliament to refine debate under section 1 of the *Charter* by abolishing only the *Daviault* defence for crimes of violence and not property offences. Such a section 1 approach could fit into a model of constructive dialogue in which Parliament was more intent on telling the Court its objectives and alternatives than whether it agreed with the Court's original decision. The Court's ultimate response to the inevitable *Charter* challenge it will hear to this provision may do much to clarify what sort of dialogue from Parliament the Court is willing to accept without the use of the override.

Professors Manfredi and Kelly characterize Parliament's in-your-face reply to *Daviault* as "an excellent example of genuine dialogue,"[54] presumably because Parliament did not accept the Court's interpretation of the *Charter*. For them, the way to avoid judicial supremacy is not to give the Court a monopoly on how the *Charter* should be interpreted. Under their doctrine of coordinate construction, Parliament apparently can reject and reverse the Court's *Charter* decisions without using the override. But such reliance on coordinate construction is dangerous because it diminishes respect for the Court as an institution, trivializes the Court's precedents, and allows the rights of the most unpopular people to be defined by elected politicians — all without the special safeguards and sober second thoughts of the override. Parliament will have an incentive to minimize the rights of the most unpopular — the Daviaults of the world — and maximize the rights of the more popular — women, children, and others who could be victimized by drunken violence. In-your-face replies without the override are not necessary to avoid judicial supremacy. Parliament could have enacted a new intoxication-based offence that would have ensured that people like Daviault did not go free. Any violation of the accused's rights could be justified under section 1 of the *Charter*. If Parliament thought this resolution would distort its policy by producing a drunkenness discount, it could have enacted its in-your-face reply with the override. This reaction would ensure continued dialogue and reconsideration of *Daviault* when the override expired after five years. If *Daviault* was still considered a public menace at that time, the override could easily be renewed. The override simply commits the government to more democracy and debate.

The last example of dialogue is particularly interesting because it involves an unpopular *Charter* decision, an in-your-face parliamentary reply that reversed that decision, and a subsequent Court decision to uphold the parliamentary reply. The unpopular decision was the Court's decision in the *O'Connor* case.[55] The case involved an all-too-familiar story of a person in a position of trust and authority, in this case a bishop, accused of raping four Aboriginal women in a residential school in the 1960s. The bishop, O'Connor, wanted access to the confidential counselling records of the complainants while the complainants saw these requests as a further violation. The Court divided 5 to 4 on the proper way to handle the frequent requests made by defence counsel for the records of complainants, especially in historic sexual assault cases. The majority stressed the danger of placing the accused in a Catch 22 of having to establish the relevance of documents he had never seen and the possibility of wrongful convictions by denying the accused access to important evidence. The prosecution must therefore turn over to the defence all records in its possession. For other records that might be in the offices of doctors, therapists, and rape crisis counsellors, the trial judge should look at any possibly relevant record and hand them over to the accused after balancing the accused's right to make a defence with the complainant's privacy rights. The minority took a very different approach. It was sceptical that the records would contain relevant information and worried about the effects on the complainants of not only disclosure to the defence but even production to the trial judge. The issue for the minority was not just the complainant's privacy rights but the social interest in encouraging people to report sexual violence and the equality rights of women, children, and the disabled who were vulnerable to sexual violence. All these concerns had to be balanced before the judge even decided whether to look at the records.

The division on the Court ran deep and was affirmed when the same majority stayed proceedings in a case in which a rape crisis centre had followed its policy of destroying all notes of interviews with its clients. It again stressed the difficulty of establishing the relevance of a document that had been shredded, while the same minority stressed that the accused had not demonstrated the relevance of the documents and could still receive a fair but perhaps not a perfect trial.[56] The split on the Court was reflected in public debate, with feminists stressing the revictimization caused by any production or disclosure of private records, and defence lawyers stressing the relevance of confidential records, especially with respect to the dangers of therapy in producing false memories of sexual abuse.

Parliament responded to these cases with an in-your-face reply that has been described by many commentators as "a direct, almost point-by-point repudiation of the majority judgment ... vindicating the approach taken by the minority."[57] A representative of LEAF similarly explained that the new legislation told a five-judge majority of the Court that they were "wrong in constitutional law."[58] The legislation followed the dissent in *O'Connor* by subjecting all records, whether in the possession of the Crown or a third party, to a two-stage process that balances the accused's rights against the complainant's privacy and equality rights and the social interest in encouraging the reporting of sexual assaults. It also followed the dissent by outlining ten allegations that, alone or together, were not sufficient to establish that a record was relevant. This long list included allegations that the record related to the subject matter of the case or to the complainant's credibility and that it might disclose a prior inconsistent statement. On its face, the legislation seemed to place the accused in an impossible Catch 22. He had to prove the relevance of private records he had never seen, and Parliament told him that almost any reason he could give for wanting access to the record was by itself not good enough. As in the *Daviault* reply, the reply to *O'Connor* indicated that Parliament was prepared, quickly, to reverse a Supreme Court decision favourable to the rights of the accused with legislation patterned on dissenting judgments that gave greater weight to the rights of women and victims of sexual assault.

If the *Charter* had produced judicial supremacy in Canada, the Court should have struck down Parliament's reversal of *O'Connor*. The United States Supreme Court had little trouble striking down Congress's attempt to overrule *Miranda*, on the basis that the legislature may not "supersede our decisions interpreting and applying the Constitution."[59] The story was different in Canada. Although recognizing "significant differences" between the *O'Connor* regime and the new legislation, the Supreme Court upheld Parliament's reply.[60] Noting that it would adopt "a posture of respect" towards Parliament and presume that its legislation was constitutional, the Court gave Parliament more respect than the majority in *O'Connor* received from the elected branch of government. Parliament was free not to follow *O'Connor* and "to insist on slavish conformity would belie the mutual respect that underpins the relationship between the courts and legislature that is essential to our constitutional democracy." The Court characterized *O'Connor* as a common law decision, rather than one based on the *Charter*, and argued that, "if the common law were to be taken as establishing the only possible constitutional regime[,] then we could not speak of a dialogue with the legislature." In this way, the Court equated the scheme created in *O'Connor* with the common law rules created in *Seaboyer* and *Daviault*. This approach suggests that the Court recognizes the similarities between its relation with legislatures under the common law and under the *Charter* and will be cautious about offering its rules as the only or final solutions to difficult problems.

The Court did hint that parts of the new legislation might be overbroad. It may have authorized trial judges in individual cases to read down, or create exemptions from, certain parts of the legislation, including the long list of insufficient allegations and restrictions on the initial production to trial judges, when it suggested that "where there is a danger that the accused's right to make full answer and defence will be violated, the trial judge should err on the side of production to the Court."[61] By delegating the task of reading down the legislation or crafting exemptions from it to trial judges, the Court may have prevented the more visible and democratic debate that would have occurred had the Court struck down the overreaching parts of the law and given Parliament an explicit opportunity to reconsider the law. The ten insufficient allegations and the restrictions on production to trial judges were, in my view, a serious violation of the accused's rights, but they were also intended by Parliament. Parliament should have an opportunity to reconsider its commitment to these provisions after being told clearly by the Court the effect they could have on the accused, however unpopular he might be. Parliament could then go back to the drawing board or it could use the override to reinstate legislation that could result in the conviction of the innocent. The attempts made by the Court in this and other recent cases to save possibly unconstitutional laws by reading down the terms used by Parliament manage to avoid direct conflict with Parliament, but they also distort Parliament's intent to enact possibly unconstitutional legislation. By having the Court fix the law by itself, they may inhibit further democratic dialogue about the Court's decision and Parliament's apparent desire to violate the accused's rights.[62]

The Court gave several reasons for the deference it showed Parliament in upholding the in-your-face reply. One was that Parliament was acting to protect women and children who had been harmed by stereotypes and mistreatment as victims of sexual assault. The Court suggested that, "if constitutional democracy is meant to ensure that due regard is given to the voices of those vulnerable to being overlooked by the majority, then this court has an obligation to consider respectfully Parliament's attempt to respond to such voices." The history of discrimination against complainants in sexual assault cases is undeniable, and Parliament has a legitimate role in responding and in attempting to end it. Women and children remain underrepresented in Parliament. Nevertheless, the Court's deference to Parliament's attempt to respond to such voices raised the question of who would look out for those men accused of sexual assault — a group that had less political clout than the organized women's groups who have so effectively campaigned for this and other legislation. The Court also stressed that Parliament had more information than it had in *O'Connor* and had received "many submissions ... that private records were routinely being produced to the court at the first stage, leading to the recurring violation of the privacy interests of complainants." The number and nature of these submissions underlined the political strength of those opposed to *O'Connor*. But political opposition to a controversial decision does not make legislation reversing that decision constitutional.[63]

In upholding the reply, the Court also indicated that it does "not hold a monopoly on the protection and promotion of rights and freedoms; Parliament also plays a role in this regard and is often able to act as a significant ally for vulnerable groups."[64] This statement lends some support for the doctrine of coordinate construction discussed in chapter 13, especially because the Court saw the case as one of interpreting the extent of conflicting rights in a relational manner rather than requiring the state to justify its restrictions on the accused's rights under section 1 of the *Charter*. The reading out of section 1 is unfortunate, because Parliament's special expertise and distinctive contribution to dialogues about sexual assault is likely to be on section 1 matters such as defining its regulatory objectives and assessing the effectiveness of alternative policy instruments to achieve those objectives. Parliament does not have comparable expertise in interpreting rights. Moreover, as an elected institution, Parliament will have an interest to maximize the rights of more popular groups, such as the women's groups, and to minimize the rights of less popular groups, such as those who stand accused of sexual assault. A theory that gives legislatures the equal right to interpret the content of the *Charter* will often make Parliament a judge in its own majoritarian cause. It could be argued that the alternative is to make the judiciary a judge in its own cause, but because the judiciary is independent it should have no incentives other than to achieve justice as best it can.

The Court also suggested that it would approach legislative replies to its *Charter* decisions with a considerable amount of deference and it expressed concern that not upholding Parliament's reply might not enhance democracy. This response ignores the possibility, one previously recognized by the Court when it read in protection for gays and lesbians into Alberta's human rights code, that one way in which the legislature could respond to an unpopular *Charter* ruling was by using the section 33 override. The use of the override in this case would have encouraged a more wide-ranging debate on this complex piece of legislation, and it would have ensured continued discussion of this evolving subject when the override expired after five years. As matters stand, the Court's decision upholding the legislation under the *Charter* may actually inhibit further dialogue on this difficult subject by legitimating the legislation as consistent with the *Charter*, even while parts of the legislation may be unconstitutional and parts of the Court's judgment may encourage trial judges in individual cases to read down some aspects of the legislation in order to protect the accused's rights. Upholding legislation as constitutional sends a message to the legislature and society that all is well, and it may actually discourage continued legislative debate and reform of this controversial and possibly unconstitutional law.

SUMMARY

The effective replies to the Court's controversial decisions about sexual assault reveal much about Parliament's ultimate power in its dialogue with the Court. Legislatures that are firmly committed to policies can gain the upper hand, even without using the override. The Court's *Charter* decisions, like its common law decisions, need not be the final word when the legislature is determined to assert its policy interests. If anything, it was too easy for Parliament to reverse unpopular Court decisions without using the override.

Parliament's replies to the statutory rape, vagrancy, and rape shield cases provide good examples of the constructive and respectful dialogue that can emerge when each institution does what it does best without engaging in shouting matches or showdowns on particular points. In each case, Parliament used its institutional advantage by engaging in law reform that was much more comprehensive than the Court's decision. Like a good conversation between different people, both the Court and Parliament made contributions that the other could not. The replies to *Daviault* and *O'Connor* produced a more confrontational dialogue because Parliament seemed to tell the Court that its decisions were wrong or unacceptable. The result was a less constructive and more confrontational dialogue. Parliament and the Court did not seem to learn from each other, but simply concluded that the other institution was wrong. Parliament engaged in piecemeal reform and demonstrated a degree of disrespect for the Court's *Charter* decision. The normalization of in-your-face replies without the special safeguards of the override would be unfortunate. It would suggest that legislatures can routinely attempt to reverse or minimize court decisions by enacting in-your-face replies. Section 33 provides an admirable structure for shouting matches and showdowns between Parliament and the Court. It requires Parliament to signal to the public that it is reversing the Court's decision, and it requires Parliament to reconsider both the Court's decision and whether the override is necessary after a five-year cooling-off period. The criticisms I have made of Parliament's in-your-face reversals of *Daviault* and *O'Connor* do not mean that the Court should have had the final word, but only that there should be more, not less, dialogue and debate when the legislature reverses the Court's *Charter* decisions.

The Dangers of Underenforcement of Constitutional Norms

Dialogue occurs not only when the Court strikes down legislation but also when it upholds legislation. A decision upholding a law "can generate consent and may impart permanence"[65] by legitimating questionable policies as constitutional. *Plessy* v. *Ferguson* was no less important in sanctioning apartheid than *Brown* v. *Board of Education* in attempting to dismantle it. The most dangerous and debilitating consequence of judicial review for Canadian democracy may be to inhibit criticism and reform of dubious laws that have been held to be consistent with the *Charter*.[66]

The dangers of *Charter* proofing questionable laws and practices is a particular concern in the area of criminal justice, where most *Charter* decisions are made and where the accused affected by the law are often unpopular and without political power. Once the Court has decided that a particular criminal law or practice is *Charter* proof, it is unlikely that legislative reform will occur. This is a stark contrast from the 1970s, when Parliament decided to abolish the death penalty, require warrants for wiretapping, and prevent appeal courts from convicting the accused in the face of a jury acquittal even after the courts had decided that those practices did not violate the *Canadian Bill of Rights*. The minimum standards of the *Charter* have quickly become *de facto* maximum standards, and the question of whether a criminal law is *Charter* proof has replaced the question of whether it is wise and just. Parliament has approved a general warrant that is *Charter* proof, but it also authorizes the use of technologies not yet invented to invade our privacy. Parliament has tracked the language of the *Charter* in authorizing judges to imprison people before trial, not because they may flee or commit offences if released, but on the vague but *Charter*-proof basis of "any other just cause."[67] In criminal justice there is a real danger that Parliament is abdicating the task of proactive law reform to the Court,[68] and that the Court's *Charter* standards have become the maximum, at least when Parliament is not prepared to ignore them. Even when Parliament accepts the Court's decisions, there are limits to the Court's ability to reform the criminal law. Even robust judicial regulation of interrogations, disclosure, or speedy trials is often inferior and inefficient as compared with legislative regulation. When the Court becomes more restrained in its commitment to due process, the dangers of *Charter* proofing become even greater.

In areas in which *Charter* litigants may have political power, the dangers of *Charter* proofing are not as great. The Court's decision in *Edwards Books* to uphold Sunday closing laws was not the final word, as most jurisdictions bowed to economic pressures from retailers and consumers to allow Sunday shopping. The Court held that the obligation of a custodial parent, most often a woman, to pay income tax on child support payments received from an ex -spouse did not violate the equality rights of women.[69] Despite the fact that the Court had *Charter* proofed the status quo, within two years the federal government amended the *Income Tax Act* to make child support payments no longer taxable for the mainly female custodial parents and no longer deductible for the mainly male noncustodial parents. The effects of this amendment are complex, but it does indicate that *Charter*-proofed laws can nevertheless be amended if the groups adversely affected by them have enough political power. It has been suggested that "legislators are not indifferent to the equality and civil liberties concerns that are raised in Charter cases, and do not always wait for a court to 'force' them to amend their laws before they are willing to consider fairer, less restrictive, or more inclusive laws."[70] This conclusion may be overly optimistic in cases in which the *Charter* claim rejected by the Court is raised by groups without some power and influence. A decision holding that a restriction on the rights of the accused or unpopular forms of speech or religion is "*Charter* proof" is much more likely to be the final word on the matter. The greatest danger of the Court having the last word in its dialogue with legislatures and society is not when it strikes down a popular law, but when it decides that a popular but questionable law is *Charter* proof.

The real risk that the Court will have the final word when it upholds laws or practices as consistent with the *Charter* illustrates a larger danger of judicial underenforcement of constitutional norms. When a Court upholds a challenged law or activity as consistent with the *Charter*, it is in a sense agreeing with the legislature. Business as usual can continue. Systematic judicial underenforcement of the *Charter* can turn dialogues between litigants, the court, legislatures, and societies into complacent monologues that fail to generate self-criticism or moral growth. It is the harmful effects of mechanical and unwarranted judicial deference that makes the criticisms of judicial activism so dangerous. If the Court takes criticism that it has been overactive to heart, and as we saw in chapter 5 there are some signs that the Court may have done so, the result may be judicial deference that underenforces constitutional norms. The Court may effectively fall silent and fail to remind legislatures and society about anti-majoritarian and often unpopular principles. Some groups may still be able to achieve reforms that the Court has been unwilling to undertake, but the most unpopular will be left without recourse. The unwarranted fear of judicial supremacy could produce a muted and complacent dialogue that is only one deferential step removed from legislative supremacy.

I do not mean to suggest that the optimal dialogue would be produced by a Court that accepts every *Charter* claim and then allows the legislature to respond under sections 1 and 33. Such an approach would swamp the capacities of even the strong legislatures produced by our parliamentary system to engage in dialogue. A Supreme Court that rejects two-thirds of the *Charter* claims it hears, however, does not appear to be in danger of overenforcing constitutional norms, especially when the many effective legislative replies to the remaining one-third of cases are considered. An appreciation of the dialogue that is promoted by the structure of the *Charter* suggests that, at the margin, the Supreme Court should run the risk of being overly active rather than overly deferential. Overenforcement of the *Charter* will result in a spirited and self-critical dialogue in which Parliament considers and responds to *Charter* decisions, whereas underenforcement will result in complacency in which Parliament is unlikely to reform laws and practices that have been declared "*Charter* proof." For example, many would argue that the Court has overenforced the due process rights of the accused in sexual assault cases. The result, however, has not been the judicial monologue that critics of judicial activism fear, but, rather, a spirited and robust democratic dialogue that has seen frequent legislative replies, including in-your-face replies, to the Court's *Charter* decisions. Conversely, the courts may well have underenforced constitutional norms relating to the security and equality interests of the poor. The result has been closer to a complacent monologue in which economic claims made by the poor and the homeless have often been ignored. To be sure, judicial enforcement of economic rights is a risky proposition and there are genuine fears about the adverse effects of overenforcement on the budgetary priorities of governments. Legislatures, however, have the tools to respond to overenforcement by justifying limits on rights or even overriding such rights. More robust judicial enforcement of the rights of the economically disadvantaged would enrich democratic debate by requiring legislatures to turn their minds to a neglected constituency that does not have political power. The Court would not and probably should not have the final word, but more robust judicial participation in the dialogue would enrich democracy by forcing legislatures to clarify and justify what they would otherwise ignore.

The greatest tragedy of the judicial activism debate is that unwarranted concerns about judicial supremacy may persuade the Court to err on the side of underenforcement of rights. This outcome would ensure that values and groups that are neglected in the legislative process will continue to be neglected. What could have been a self-critical and genuinely democratic dialogue will degenerate into a complacent monologue in which the Court routinely defers to the legislature. This would be a shame, because a more robust approach need not result in the Court having the last word so long as our elected governments are prepared to take responsibility for limiting and overriding the rights that the Court reminds us about.

Conclusion

Courts and legislatures under both the *Charter* and the common law engage in dialogue with the other institution. The Court, prompted by the efforts of aggrieved litigants, starts the conversation by drawing the attention of the legislature and society to fundamental values. The Court is the one that must initiate the conversation, because the principles of fairness, fundamental freedoms, and respect for the rights of minorities are ones that are likely to be ignored or finessed in the legislative and administrative processes. The Court, however, does not conduct a monologue in which its common law or *Charter* rulings are the final word. The common law can be displaced by clear legislation. The underlying assumption is that democracy is enhanced by requiring the legislature to debate and to indicate clearly its desire to depart from the values of the common law constitution.

The structure of the *Charter* and similar modern bills of rights contemplates two different forms of dialogue between courts and legislatures, both of which continue but improve common law dialogues. The commonest form of dialogue is conducted under section 1 of the *Charter*, which requires legislatures to prescribe by law the limits they place on *Charter* rights and to justify to the court that such limits are reasonable and necessary to advance their objectives. This dialogue encourages courts and legislatures to be themselves: the courts bring to the table the importance of fundamental values and procedures that may be inconvenient for the legislature to consider, and legislatures bring a knowledge of the regulatory objectives and obstacles that the court may otherwise have difficulty appreciating. The justification of reasonable limits on rights is the engine for dialogue in which each institution listens and learns from the other, while also being true to its own concerns and institutional identity. It is premised on the courts and the legislatures playing distinctive and complementary roles. Like a conversation between people with different interests and perspectives who respect each other, this system allows the dialogue between courts and legislatures to be expanded and refined without being bogged down in disagreements over particular points.

The ability to enact legislation that expressly overrides or derogates from rights under section 33 of the *Charter* provides a carefully structured outlet when the Court and a legislature cannot agree on a particular point and a shouting match or showdown looms. It allows the legislature to reverse a Court decision and even to tell the Court that it was wrong in the way it interpreted the *Charter* or that its decision was fundamentally unacceptable to the majority of Canadians. Although section 33 resembles the way that legislatures could assert their will to abolish the common law, it constitutes an improvement both by requiring that the public be more clearly warned about what is being done in its name and by preserving the Court's point of principle to be reconsidered in calmer times when the override expires. Quebec's decision not to renew the override used to prohibit the use of languages other than French on commercial signs is a good example of how a Court decision subject to an override does not go away and, indeed, may influence democratic debate in calmer times. Express derogations from rights will trigger debate and scrutiny both at home and abroad: one of the reasons why Quebec did not renew its override was an adverse decision from the United Nation's Human Rights Committee. Section 33 can enhance democracy by focusing public attention and debate on controversial questions of rights.

One exception is when the legislature uses the override to pre-empt the courts from even deciding whether legislation or a policy violates the *Charter*. In Alberta the override was recently used in a pre-emptive fashion to preclude courts from even considering whether the prevention of gay marriage was discriminatory. It would have been more democratic for Alberta to have allowed this issue to be litigated, and to decide then whether to reverse a judicial decision recognizing gay marriage with the override or to respond with some compromise measure that could perhaps be justified as a reasonable limit on the equality rights of the gay and lesbian minority. This reaction would still have been democratic — perhaps too democratic for the minority — but at least it would not have shouted down the dialogue before it even started.

A key issue in the future will be whether dialogues will be conducted by justifying limits on rights under section 1 or whether they will be conducted under section 33 by formally overriding and derogating from rights as they have been interpreted by the Court. Legislatures have an incentive not to pay the political price for using the override when, in fact, they should. If courts accept reversals of their decisions without the override, the legislatures may be encouraged to act routinely on their own interpretation of the constitution or their sense that the majority finds the Court's interpretation unacceptable. This behaviour could erode respect for the Court and its anti-majoritarian role. The Court may have to force the issue by invalidating in-your-face legislative reversals of its prior *Charter* decisions that do not invoke the override. This response will not end the dialogue. It may produce a shouting match between the court and the legislature, in which the legislature responds with the override. The legislature can use the override to win the argument, but section 33 ensures that, after a cooling-off period, the Court and the legislature must keep talking about their disagreement. The legislature must decide whether to renew the override, or the decision subject to the override will rise from the ashes of the prior argument. Used in this way, the override encourages more, not less, democratic dialogue.

Another alternative will be that the Court will uphold legislation that may violate the *Charter*, but alter it through a creative use of its power to interpret or read down the legislation. A court concerned about being criticized for being activist may well embrace this more minimal approach. Indeed, there are some signs that the Canadian Court is moving in this direction, as the English courts may well do under the *Human Rights Act, 1998*. The dialogue produced by preserving, but reinterpreting, possibly unconstitutional legislation seems less transparent and less democratic than if the Court took the bull by the horns and declared the offending parts of the legislation to be unconstitutional. Such judicial decisions make headlines. The issues are debated in Parliament, and, under a modern bill of rights, the legislators retain many response options, including the power to limit and override the rights boldly and broadly declared by the Court. They force Parliament to address the issue of how rights will be treated, without imposing the final word. More minimal decisions that read down legislation to make it constitutional can also be subject to legislative responses under section 1 of the *Charter*, but they tend to make headlines only in the law reports and to be debated only among lawyers.

The greatest danger to democratic dialogue is not when the Court strikes down legislation, but when it upholds legislation that may clearly and unreasonably violate the *Charter* or the common law constitution. In these cases the Court does not play its role of alerting the legislature and the public to values that they are liable to neglect or ignore. The very fact that legislation that may infringe the *Charter* or the common law has been upheld by the Court will discourage legislative reconsideration of the matter, unless the groups whose interests are infringed have significant political power. The greatest danger of the current debate about judicial activism is that it may produce excessive deference in an institution — the independent judiciary — that has the power to turn contented and majoritarian monologues, where the powerful dominate, into more self-critical and tolerant dialogues, where the weak are at least heard.

The *Charter* is not a revolutionary departure from a common law approach that requires legislatures to make clear statements when they wish to limit or deny rights and freedoms. The Court's interventions in the name of the common law constitution and the *Charter* enhance democracy by requiring the legislature to be candid with the public when it wishes to limit or deny rights that are liable to be neglected and finessed in the legislative and administrative processes. The clear statement rules of the common law and the *Charter* promote the rule of law and accountability for the use of state power. The *Charter* goes beyond the common law by requiring that limits on rights be justified as reasonable and proportionate limits under section 1 and that overrides or derogations from rights be subject to the extraordinary signals and sober second thoughts of section 33. These key features of the *Charter* improve, sharpen, and prolong the dialogue that has traditionally occurred at common law between the Court and the legislatures.

Chapter 15
Judicial Activism and Democratic Dialogue

If the *Charter* is not very different from the common law and if Canadian legislatures can generally have the last word under the *Charter* in a democratic dialogue with the Court, why has there been so much fuss about judicial activism? Why have Canadians on both ends of the political spectrum been so concerned that the Court will create rights and thwart the democratic wishes of governments and the people?

One reason is the large shadow cast by the American experience of judicial review and the endless American debate about judicial activism, as discussed in chapter 2. Most writing about judicial activism is based on the American *Bill of Rights*. This focus is understandable — the Americans have the most experience with a bill of rights enforced by a Supreme Court. It is, however, unfortunate because the American experience with judicial review is unique and even idiosyncratic, given the absence of any explicit clause in the 1791 *Bill of Rights* that allows government either to limit or to override rights as they have been interpreted by the Supreme Court. Most post-Second World War bills of rights, including the 1950 *European Convention on Human Rights* and the 1966 *International Covenant on Civil and Political Rights*, contemplate that some rights can be limited by ordinary legislation for important objectives and that there can be derogations from certain rights in some situations. The 1982 *Canadian Charter of Rights and Freedoms* extended these features of modern bills of rights by providing, in section 1, a general clause that allows legislatures to justify reasonable limits on all rights and, in section 33, that legislatures could enact legislation notwithstanding certain *Charter* rights for a renewable five-year period. These key provisions anticipated concerns about judicial activism by allowing legislatures to respond to bills of rights' decisions with ordinary legislation without, as so often must occur in the United States, having to change the constitution or the Court.

The *Charter*'s response to concerns about judicial activism has, as discussed in chapter 4, influenced the development of subsequent bills of rights in New Zealand, Israel, South Africa, and the United Kingdom. One of the main arguments of this book has been that there is a fundamental difference between the Canadian *Charter* and other similar modern bills of rights and the American *Bill of Rights*. The ability of Canadian legislatures to justify limits on *Charter* rights and even override those rights for a period of time, combined with the strength of governments produced by the parliamentary system of government, ensures that the Court need not have the last word on policy matters affected by the *Charter*. As under the common law, legislatures can limit or override the Court's decisions with ordinary legislation. It is not necessary, as it often has been in the United States and as it was in response to the judicial invalidation of the Canadian version of the New Deal, to change either the constitution or the Court.

By avoiding judicial supremacy, the *Charter* is more democratic and more continuous with the common law than the American *Bill of Rights*. That *Bill of Rights*, most famously in its First Amendment ("Congress shall make no law ...") , proclaims liberal rights as interpreted by the Court as absolute and subject neither to justifiable limitation nor explicit derogation.[1] It is rooted in a horse-drawn age that predates the modern state and it often allows the Court to impose its constitutional decisions in a more or less absolute fashion on the elected representatives. The American tradition of judicial supremacy shows no sign of abating in the new century: in the disputed presidential election of 2000 the bitterly divided United States Supreme Court effectively decided the result, as the liberal minority accused the conservative majority of judicial activism.[2] All through the election, judicial appointments were a key issue, and one of President George W. Bush's most potent levers on power will be the people he nominates to sit on the Court. The result is a much less democratic state of affairs than prevails in countries, like Canada, that can limit or even derogate from the decisions of their highest Court by ordinary legislation and that can counter judicial activism by legislative activism.

Some commentators have optimistically predicted that the ability of the Canadian *Charter* to combine "the best of both worlds"- judicial activism and legislative activism — will make the power of judges under the *Charter* "less fearsome, less threatening, to the politicians and others now so exercised and angered by what they perceive to be excesses of 'judicial imperialism.'"[3] Unfortunately, this happy outcome has not occurred. As discussed in chapter 5, the American debate about judicial activism has been imported into Canada, and with it plenty of fear and anger has been directed at the Supreme Court. Canadian judges have, at times, been unfairly criticized for engaging in judicial activism by reading their personal preferences into the *Charter*; for deciding constitutional issues that could have been avoided; for enforcing rights without regard to the public interest; and for imposing their judgments as the final word on controversial matters of public policy. The Canadian debate has even echoed the politics of the American debate with, first, the left raising concerns that the Court would use the *Charter* to restrain legitimate government regulation and redistribution and, second, the right contending that the Court is forcing an unwilling society to accept the rights of unpopular minorities and those accused of crimes. Many have lost sight of the genius of the *Charter* and its distinctiveness from the American *Bill of Rights*. This conflict may result in the same type of endless and frustrating debates over whether the Supreme Court is too activist or too restrained, while ignoring the fact that elected governments in Canada can take responsibility for limiting and overriding rights as interpreted by the Court. To the extent that the Canadian debate about judicial activism has been conceived in Americanized terms that ignore structural differences between the two bills of rights and suggest that judges can impose the last word on controversial issues of social policy, it is an unhelpful dead end. This is a tragedy not only for Canadians but for other countries that have adopted modern bills of rights similar to the *Charter*.

The Canadian debate about judicial activism reflects original hostility to the enactment of the *Charter* by some conservative tories and some democratic socialists. Those who opposed the enactment of the *Charter* have, not surprisingly, been inclined to complain of judicial activism under it. There are some signs of a similar debate already emerging in the United Kingdom, as critics of incorporating the *European Convention* into British law are already warning that unelected judges will usurp democracy under the *Human Rights Act, 1998.*[4] These critics have mainly been progressives on the left, but the Canadian experience suggests that conservatives on the right cannot be far behind. Critics on both the left and the right may well, as in Canada, drag their opposition to bills of rights, their suspicions that judges will read their personal preferences into the law, and their faith in majoritarian democracy into a heated debate about the evils of judicial activism.

The Canadian debate about judicial activism has had effects beyond the borders of Canada. Concerns about the growth of judicial activism under the *Charter* influenced decisions in both New Zealand and the United Kingdom during the 1990s not to give courts the power to strike down legislation inconsistent with their recent bills of rights; similar concerns influenced decisions in Australia not to enact even a statutory bill of rights.[5] In 1996 the former British prime minister John Major lumped the Canadian *Charter* with the American *Bill of Rights* when he argued that they both erode "the supremacy of elected representatives ... It is not as though the processes of judicial interpretation are infallible. In the United States at different times, the Bill of Rights was held both to support and to outlaw slavery. More recently, Canada's 1982 Charter of Rights has been held to be inconsistent with earlier laws on Sunday Trading, drug trafficking and abortion. It is no slur on our judicial system to say that such great issues should be decided by elected representatives, not judges and courts."[6] There were also hints in Prime Minister Tony Blair's government's white paper leading to the enactment of the *Human Rights Act, 1998*[7] that the Canadian experience could impair the ability of elected legislatures to exercise their "democratic mandate" to determine vital matters of public policy. A Canadian-style bill of rights might, it was feared, produce a state of affairs closer to the other America, in which the courts have the last word on many matters of social policy. Some people in the common law world have seen the experience under the Canadian *Charter* as too American and too radical a departure from legislative supremacy.

One of my main arguments in this book, however, has been that it is a serious mistake to lump the Canadian *Charter* with the American *Bill of Rights*. The *Charter* has not taken away from the ability of strongly committed elected governments to determine matters of public policy, albeit in a manner that recognizes limits on and derogations from rights. The *Charter* has created a fertile and democratic middle ground between the extremes of legislative and judicial supremacy. Those who look to the Canadian experience under the *Charter* as an example of American-style judicial activism are ignoring how the structure of the *Charter* promotes and enriches the democratic dialogues that have always occurred between the courts and the legislatures under the common law. They ignore the many options that the strong governments produced by the Canadian parliamentary system retain in crafting responses to the Court's decisions.

Those unfamiliar with the Canadian experience usually associate the possibility of legislative replies to *Charter* decisions of the court with the section 33 override.[8] Express derogations from rights are controversial matters in a democratic society that respect rights. The section 33 override has never been used by the federal Parliament in Canada and has been used by only a few provinces with respect to legislation restricting the ability of public employees to strike, same sex couples to marry, and advertisers to use languages other than French on outdoor signs. The most famous use of the override was in Quebec in 1988, when the provincial legislature employed it a few days after the Supreme Court had found that Quebec's prohibition on the use of languages other than French on commercial signs was an unreasonable limitation on freedom of expression. The use of the override can be seen as the legislature engaging in a shouting match in order to win an argument with the Court. After the five-year cooling-off period, Quebec decided not to renew its use of the override, which had proved to be controversial both at home and abroad, including an adverse decision from the United Nation's Human Rights Committee. The override remains an important and valuable safeguard against the excesses of judicial activism, but the Canadian experience suggests that governments may often be reluctant to invite the controversy and the public and international scrutiny that accompanies its use. The override invites and even commands continued debate and dialogue even while it allows legislatures temporally at least to win their argument with the Court. This experience provides a warning for those in the United Kingdom, New Zealand and elsewhere[9] who would rely on the use of express legislative derogations or overrides of rights to limit judicial power.

The override is an important symbol of the ability of elected legislatures to have the final say, but the real engine of dialogue[10] in Canada between the courts and the legislatures is the ability of legislatures to enact laws and justify them as reasonable limits on rights as interpreted by the Court. Section 1 allows governments to justify limits on every *Charter* right, and it does not attempt to limit the reasons for legislative limitations on rights. It enhances democracy by requiring that limits on rights be democratically enacted and debated in legislation, and not be created by police officers or bureaucrats in the exercise of their discretion. Section 1 has been copied in recent bills of rights in New Zealand, Israel, and South Africa. Precursors to section 1 that allow limits that are necessary in a democratic society to be imposed by law can also be found in some, but not all, of the articles of the *European Convention.* Section 1 of the *Charter* lends itself to a particular institutional division of labour and type of dialogue between courts and legislatures. The court reminds the legislature about rights that are liable to be neglected in the legislative and administrative processes. The legislature reminds the court about the reasons why limits on rights are required in particular contexts and the alternatives that the government has considered and rejected. The government's justification for limiting rights can subsequently be reviewed by the court. The dialogue that emerges under section 1 of the *Charter* is not a shouting match over a particular point, but an expanding and constructive conversation that avoids the extremes of either legislative or judicial supremacy.

As discussed in chapter 14, dialogues between Canadian legislatures and the Court under sections 1 and 33 of the *Charter* have their origins in dialogues between courts and legislatures over the common law. Much criminal law and administrative law has been made by common law presumptions that the legislature intends to respect a "common law bill of rights,"[11] one that includes presumptions of fault and respect for the presumption of innocence in the criminal law, and fairness and access to courts in administrative law. The common law allowed the courts to remind politicians and bureaucrats about important values of fairness that they were liable to neglect. At the same time, the Court under the common law did not assume the awesome responsibility of having the last word. The legislature could always take responsibility for enacting legislation that clearly displaced the common law. Democracy was enhanced by requiring limits or derogations from common law rights to be prescribed in democratically debated and enacted laws.

The *Charter* and other modern bills of rights improve on the common law by providing a democratically enacted text to outline the values that the Court should enforce. The rights enforced are no longer found only in the minds and precedents of unelected judges, but must be located in the text of a democratically enacted law. The values in the *Charter* and other modern bills of rights are important components of a free and democratic society that cannot be reduced to majority rule and that respect the rule of law and the rights of minorities.[12] For that reason, they rightly enjoy the burden of legislative inertia after they have been proclaimed by the Court. At the same time, however, there are reasonable disagreements about these matters, and elected governments may want to take responsibility for revising and even reversing judicial decisions that stand in the way of their democratically endorsed and debated programs. For that reason, neither the common law nor the *Charter* or other modern bills of rights assign the Court the final word. In almost all cases, the legislature can respond to the Court's ruling by articulating clear departures from and limitations on the starting point set by the Court's rulings. Democracy is enhanced, however, by requiring legislatures to clearly articulate, justify, and be held accountable for their decisions to limit or depart from the constitutional or common law principles articulated by the Court.

The common law process of requiring the legislature to make clear statements when it wishes to limit or deny rights identified by the Court promotes candour and democratic accountability about how we as a society treat people affected by the law. Clear-statement rules promote democratic debate in courts, legislatures, and the media about some of society's most difficult decisions. They force society to bring its dirty little secrets out into the open and they ensure that the police and other officials are required to abide by the rule of law. The ability of the legislature to clearly limit or deny rights under the common law and the *Charter* presents a risk that our rights will be seriously curtailed and perhaps legislated out of existence. At the same time, this risk is always present in a democracy. What judicial review under either the common law or modern bills of rights such as the *Charter* can achieve is to create a society in which citizens are better aware of the implications of what bureaucrats and the legislature is doing in their name.

When the courts' judgments prevail, respect for rights is produced not by judicial supremacy, but by the decision of the elected government of the day not to risk the "political troubles" that would accompany the clear legislative statements (and consequent debate at home and abroad) necessary to depart from the court's decisions.[13] Dialogue between courts and legislatures under the common law and modern bills of rights such as the *Charter* is indeed based on "active citizenship," because the elected legislature can take responsibility for reversing or revising the Court's decision. It is not the false dialogue of a "star-struck people" speculating about what "a few black-robed celebrities" on the Supreme Court "will do next on abortion or some similar issue," but one in which the citizens decide whether their elected government will enact ordinary legislation to place limits on or even override rights as interpreted by the Court.[14]

A constructive and democratic dialogue between courts and legislatures under a modern bill of rights such as the *Charter* can improve the performance of both institutions. The independent judiciary can be robust and fearless in its protection of rights and freedoms, knowing that it need not have the last word. The legislature will be encouraged to consider whether it can pursue its objectives in a manner more respectful of rights and to establish rules in legislation to authorize and justify the conduct of the police and other state officials. The elected government can be explicit and candid about why it is necessary to limit or depart from the Court's rulings with ordinary legislation. It need not manipulate the appointment power or the Court's jurisdiction, or attempt the often futile quest to amend the Constitution in order to respond to a controversial Court decision. The democratic dialogue between courts and legislatures under a modern bill of rights such as the *Charter* can avoid the monologues and unchecked power that may be produced by either unfettered legislative supremacy or unfettered judicial supremacy. It is especially necessary to diffuse power in countries where the parliamentary system of government , combined with tight party discipline, gives governments more or less absolute power between elections. Strong courts are needed to balance the power of strong legislatures.

The greatest danger in the dialogue between courts and legislatures is not excessive judicial activism, because legislatures can and will correct judicial overreaching on behalf of minorities and the unpopular. The result will be a self-critical and democratic dialogue, even if judicial decisions do not prevail. If, however, the Court is too weak in protecting the rights of minorities and the unpopular, it is less likely that elected governments will do more. The result can be a complacent and majoritarian monologue that is less truly democratic. Excessive judicial deference will allow legislatures and officials to act without being questioned by the Court about the effects of their actions on the most unpopular among us. The sense that courts will not challenge questionable laws may inhibit their reform, especially if those adversely affected by the law have little political power. The greatest danger of the judicial activism debate is that it may produce excessive judicial deference. If this happens — and there are signs that it may be happening in Canada, and that misperceptions about the Canadian experience have dampened enthusiasm for judicial review in other places — then the democratic and dialogic potential of the *Charter* will be squandered by the unnecessary importation of an American-style judicial activism debate based on the false dichotomy of judicial supremacy or legislative supremacy. This failure would be a tragedy not only for Canada but for other countries as well. It might mean that we will all continue to spin our wheels in the two-century American debate about judicial activism, one that ignores the potential under modern bills of rights with parliamentary forms of government to have the benefits and the responsibility of both judicial activism and legislative activism.

The answer to unacceptable judicial activism under a modern bill of rights is legislative activism and the assertion of democratic responsibility for limiting or overriding the Court's decisions. Citizens can enjoy the benefits of judicial activism without the costs of judicial supremacy. They can have the cake of justice, but they can eat it if they do not like how it turns out. Some day, however, we will all have to stand on the scales of justice. Modern bills of rights and their robust judicial enforcement allow governments to be put on trial for the way they treat the weakest and worst among us. But the Court is also on trial because governments can, under the *Charter*, limit and even reverse its decisions. In the end, all of us are on trial for how we exercise our powers of self-government. That is the burden and the privilege of democracy.

Notes

Preface

1 Throughout this book, the short form "Court," with a capital "C," is reserved for the Supreme Court of Canada.

2 On the basis of my one year as a clerk and my subsequent academic career, Professors Morton and Knopff characterize me as a member of "the jurocracy." F.L. Morton and Rainer Knopff, *The Charter Revolution and the Court Party* (Peterborough: Broadview Press, 2000) at 112. If only they had known about my work for what they call the Court Party! When cases I have been involved in are discussed in the chapters that follow, I will indicate my involvement. For the record, I have represented Aboriginal Legal Services of Toronto in *Williams* and *Mankwe* (screening jurors for racial prejudice), *Corbiere* (*Charter* right of non-resident Indian band members to vote in band elections), *Gladue* and *Wells* (sentencing Aboriginal offenders), *Golden* (constitutionality of strip searches), and *Sauve II* (prisoner voting rights under the *Charter*). I have also represented the Canadian Civil Liberties Association in *Hill* (libel and free expression), *Stillman* (exclusion of evidence under s. 24(2) of the *Charter*), and *Latimer* (constitutionality of mandatory life imprisonment). I have represented the Ontario Criminal Lawyers Association in *Dunedin Construction* (costs as a *Charter* remedy) and the Ontario Metis Association in *Perry* and *Lovelace* (rights of the Métis and non-status Indians).

3 See my *Due Process and Victims' Rights: The New Law and Politics of Criminal Justice* (Toronto: University of Toronto Press, 1999); *Constitutional Remedies in Canada* (Aurora: Canada Law Book, as updated); "The Effects of the Canadian Charter of Rights on Criminal Justice" (1999) 33 *Israel Law Review* 607; "The Attorney General and the Charter Revisited" (2000) 50 *University of Toronto Law Journal* 1; and "Chief Justice Lamer and Some Myths about Judicial Activism" (2000) 5 *Canadian Criminal Law Review* 21. On my understanding of the legal process, see "What's New and Old about the Legal Process" (1997) 47 *University of Toronto Law Journal* 363.

PART ONE

Chapter 1: The Supreme Court on Trial

1 Canada, House of Commons, *Debates,* 1 March 2001 at 1400.

2 Richard Gywn, "If there is anarchy today, the Supreme Court has to take responsibility for that," *St. John's Telegram*, 12 October 1999, 6.

3 "Ex-premiers call for the use of charter's 'safety valve,'" *National Post*, 1 March 1999, A1. The first quotation is from Lougheed and the second is from Blakeney.

4 He added, "I'm not saying that's the case now, but I personally would favour reconsidering a certain number of decisions of the court." Cristin Schmitz, "Supreme Court goes 'too far': Judge," *National Post*, 13 January 2001, A1, A7; Cristin Schmitz, "Settle native issues with talks: Judge," *National Post*, 15 January 2001, A4. Subsequent complaints by Aboriginal groups and defence lawyers that they could not receive a fair hearing from Justice Bastarache were dismissed by the Canadian Judicial Council. Kirk Makin, "Accusations against judge rejected," *Globe and Mail*, 17 March 2001, A7.

5 Kirk Makin, "Lamer worries about public backlash," *Globe and Mail*, 6 February 1999, A1; Luiza Chwialkowska, "Rein in lobby groups, senior judges suggest," *National Post*, 6 April 2000, A1.

6 Janice Tibbetts, "Lamer attacks Alliance 'yelping,'" *National Post*, 14 April 2001, A1.

7 Kirk Makin "Canadians believe Supreme Court rulings are influenced by politics: poll" *Globe and Mail* July 3, 2001 A1.

8 Alexander Bickel, *The Least Dangerous Branch: The Supreme Court at the Bar of Politics*, 2d ed. (New Haven: Yale University Press, 1986) at 1.

9 Chief Justice Antonio Lamer as quoted in F.L. Morton and Rainer Knopff, *The Charter Revolution and the Court Party* (Peterborough: Broadview Press, 2000) at 13.

10 Preston Manning, "Strong Roots, Bright Future," Reply to the Speech from the Throne, October 1999 at 12.

11 Alan Cairns, *Reconfigurations* (Toronto: McClelland & Stewart, 1995), chapter 4.

12 Morton and Knopff, *The Charter Revolution and the Court Party*.

13 F.L. Morton, Peter Russell, and Troy Riddell, "The Canadian Charter of Rights and Freedoms: A Descriptive Analysis of the First Decade" (1995) 5 *National Journal of Constitutional Law* 1 at 5; James Kelly, "The Charter of Rights and Freedoms and the Rebalancing of Liberal Constitutionalism in Canada" (1999) 37 *Osgoode Hall Law Journal* 625 at 636.

14 Interestingly, those who raise concerns about excessive civil litigation in Canada, like those who raise concerns about *Charter* activism, often ignore important structural differences between American and Canadian law. In Canada, as almost everywhere else in the world, the losing party in civil litigation must pay a significant amount of the costs incurred by the winner. The American rule of no cost shifting, combined with the heavy use of contingency fees, can make even unsuccessful litigation almost costless. See Kent Roach and Michael Trebilcock, "Private Enforcement of Competition Laws" (1996) 34 *Osgoode Hall Law Journal* 461.

15 There is disagreement on the exact number of cases that results in legislative replies. Some argue that legislatures have crafted replies in about two-thirds of cases. See Peter Hogg and Allison Bushell, "The Charter

Dialogue between Courts and Legislatures (or Perhaps the Charter of Rights Isn't a Bad Thing after All" (1997) 35 *Osgoode Hall Law Journal* 75. Others argue that there have been meaningful legislative replies in only about a third of the cases. See Christopher Manfredi and James Kelly, "Six Degrees of Dialogue: A Response to Hogg and Bushell" (1999) 37 *Osgoode Hall Law Journal* 513. My approach will not be a quantitative one that attempts to provide a scientific measure of activism, but a qualitative one that focuses on the Court's major decisions in a wide variety of constitutional contexts. Quantitative analysis can be useful, but the issues of whether courts are usurping democracy and deciding cases legitimately are far too value laden to be resolved by a battle over numbers. Peter Hogg and Allison Thornton, "Reply to 'Six Degrees of Dialogue'" (1999) 37 *Osgoode Hall Law Journal* 529.

16 Chief Justice McLachlin has identified some of the myths of judicial activism under the *Charter*. They are the myth 1) that the *Charter* for the first time bestowed individual rights on Canadians; 2) that it created absolute rights that the legislature cannot abridge; 3) that it replaced parliamentary supremacy with judicial supremacy; 4) that judges can decline to decide *Charter* issues; 5) that criminals "walk" under the *Charter*; and 6) that the courts and legislatures are adversaries. Beverley McLachlin, "Charter Myths" (1999) 33 *University of British Columbia Law Review* 23.

17 *R. v. Mills* (1999), 139 CCC (3d) 321 at paras. 57-58; *Vriend v. Alberta*, [1998] 1 SCR 493 at para. 139.

Chapter 2: The Endless American Debate

1 Federalist 78 and Federalist 81 in Alexander Hamilton, James Madison, and John Jay, *The Federalist Papers* (New York: Mentor, 1961) at 465, 485.

2 5 U.S. (1 Cranch) 137 (1803).

3 Herbert McClosky, *The American Supreme Court* (Chicago: University of Chicago Press, 1960) at 43; Samuel Morison et al., *The Growth of the American Republic*, 7th ed. (New York: Oxford University Press, 1980) at 346.

4 Sheldon Goldman, *Constitutional Law and Supreme Court Decision-Making* (New York: Harper and Row, 1982) at 33.

5 Alexis de Tocqueville, *Democracy in America* (Garden City: Doubleday, 1969) at 151.

6 *Dred Scott v. Sanford*, 19 Howard 393 (1857).

7 Louis Fisher, *Constitutional Dialogues: Interpretation as Political Process* (Princeton: Princeton University Press, 1988) at 278; Morison et al., *The Growth of the American Republic* at 595.

8 For Lincoln, the case was binding "so far as it decided in favor of Dred Scott's master and against Dred Scott and his family," but was not "a rule of political action for the people and all the departments of the government ... By resisting it as a political rule, I disturb no right of property, create no disorder, excite no mobs." Lincoln as quoted in George Swan,

"Roe from Lincoln's Dred Scott Viewpoint" (1984) 15 *Lincoln Law Review* 23 at 38, 41-42.

9 163 U.S. 537 (1896). See also *Bradwell* v. *Illinois*, 16 Wallace 130 (1873); *The Civil Rights Cases*, 109 U.S. 3 (1883).

10 Gary McDowell, *Curbing the Courts* (Baton Rouge: Louisana State University Press, 1988) at 3.

11 198 U.S. 45 (1905).

12 *In re Debs*, 158 U.S. 564 (1895); *Truax* v. *Corrigan*, 257 U.S. 312 (1921).

13 *United States* v. *E.C.Knight*, 156 U.S. 1 (1895); *Pollock* v. *Farmers' Loan and Trust Co.*, 158 U.S. 601 (1895).

14 *Hammer* v. *Dagenhart*, 247 U.S. 251 (1918); *Bailey* v. *Drexel Furniture*, 259 U.S. 20 (1922). The Court itself eventually corrected this mistake and upheld such federal legislation. *United States* v. *Darby*, 312 U.S. 100 (1941). See also Fisher, *Constitutional Dialogues* at 204-5.

15 Bruce Ackerman, *We the People*, vol. 2 (Cambridge: Harvard University Press, 1998) at 2: 327.

16 *United States* v. *Butler*, 297 U.S. 1 (1936).

17 Louis Goldberg and Eleanore Levinson, *Lawless Judges* (New York: Rand School Press, 1935) at 231-32, 240-41.

18 Robert Jackson, *The Struggle for Judicial Supremacy* (New York: Knopf, 1941) at 320-21.

19 Ibid. at 343-44.

20 Merlo Pusey, *The Supreme Court Crisis* (New York: Macmillan, 1937) at 105.

21 Fisher, *Constitutional Dialogues* at 215.

22 *West Coast Hotel* v. *Parrish*, 300 U.S. 379 (1937).

23 *United States* v. *Carolene Products*, 304 U.S. 144 at 152 (1938).

24 *Korematsu* v. *United* States, 323 U.S. 214 (1944); *Dennis* v. *United States*, 341 U.S. 494 (1951).

25 *Minersville* v. *Gobitis*, 310 U.S. 586 (1940); *West Virginia State Board of Education* v. *Barnette*, 319 U.S. 624 at 638 (1943).

26 347 U.S. 483 (1954).

27 Clifford Lytle, *The Warren Court and Its Critics* (Tucson: University of Arizona Press, 1968) at 12-21; McDowell, *Curbing the Courts* at 152.

28 Gerald Rosenberg, *The Hollow Hope: Can Courts Bring about Social Change?* (Chicago: University of Chicago Press, 1991) at 52.

29 Herbert Wechsler, "Towards Neutral Principles of Constitutional Law" (1959) 73 *Harvard Law Review* 1.

30 *Brown* v. *Board of Education II*, 349 U.S. 294 (1955).

31 *Cooper* v. *Aaron*, 358 U.S. 1, 18 (1958).

32 *Swann* v. *Charlotte-Mecklenburg Board of Education*, 402 U.S. 1 at 16 (1971).

33 Nathan Glazer, "Towards an Imperial Judiciary" (1975) 41 *The Public Interest* 104; Lino Graglia, *Disaster by Degree* (Ithica: Cornell University Press, 1976). On the change in attitude among progressives, compare Owen Fiss, *The Civil Rights Injunction* (Bloomington: Indiana University Press, 1978), praising the structural injunction in which judges manage

state institutions, with Felix Frankfurter and Nathan Greene, *The Labor Injunction* (New York: Macmillan, 1930), criticizing the use of injunctions against unions. The limited Canadian experience with injunctions in enforcing constitutional rights will be examined in chapter 8 at p. 152 ff.

34 Lytle, *The Warren Courts and Its Critics* at 29-37.

35 Ibid. at 48. The Court's decisions in *Engel* v. *Vitale*, 370 U.S. 421 (1962), and *Abington School District* v. *Schempp*, 374 U.S. 203 (1963), drew a dissent from Justice Stewart that the Court was defying both tradition and the text of the constitution.

36 Fisher, *Constitutional Dialogues* at 204; McDowell, *Curbing the Court* at 156.

37 Liva Baker, *Miranda* (New York: Antheum, 1983) at 245.

38 *Dickerson* v. *United States*, 2000 WL 807223 per Rehnquist CJ. Justice Scalia, in dissent, argued that because the *Miranda* rule was not required by the constitution, the Court was asserting "an immense and frightening antidemocratic power" to make legislative rules to prevent constitutional violations.

39 William Rehnquist, "Who Writes the Decisions of the Supreme Court," *U.S. News and World Report*, 13 December 1957, 75. Even Rehnquist, however, admitted that "the specter of the law clerk as a Legal Rasputin, exerting an important influence on the cases actually decided by the Court, may be discarded at once ... It is unreasonable to suppose that a lawyer in middle age or older, of sufficient eminence in some walk of life to be appointed as one of nine judges of the world's most powerful court, would consciously abandon his own view as to what is right and what is wrong in the law because a stipling clerk just graduated from law school tells him."

40 Bob Woodward and Scott Armstrong, *The Brethren* (New York: Simon and Schuster, 1979) at 76.

41 *Griswold* v. *State of Connecticut*, 381 U.S. 479 (1965).

42 Alexander Bickel, *The Supreme Court and the Idea of Progress* (New Haven: Yale University Press, 1978).

43 410 U.S. 113 (1973).

44 John Hart Ely, "The Wages of Crying Wolf: A Comment on *Roe v. Wade*" (1973) 82 *Yale Law Journal* 920; Alexander Bickel, *The Morality of Consent* (New Haven: Yale University Press, 1975) at 27-28.

45 *Harris* v. *McRae*, 448 U.S. 297 (1980).

46 Robert Bork, *The Tempting of America* (New York: Free Press, 1990) at 116.

47 *Planned Parenthood* v.*Casey*, 505 U.S. 833 at 998-99 (1992).

48 *Texas* v. *Johnson*, 491 U.S. 397 (1989); *United States* v. *Eichman*, 486 U.S. 310 (1990).

49 *Employment Division* v. *Smith*, 494 U.S. 872 (1990) (holding that the use of peyote is not protected as a religious practice); *City of Boerne* v. *Flores*, 117 S. Ct. 2157 (1997) (striking down the *Religious Freedom Restoration Act* of 1993 as beyond Congress's powers).

50 *United States* v. *Virginia*, 116 S. Ct. 2264 at 2292 (1996).

51 Robert Bork, *Slouching toward Gomorrah: Modern Liberalism and the American Decline* (New York: Basic Books, 1996) at 108. For an argument that the Court was influenced by Ivy League law professors "who live professionally in a world of words" and "tend overwhelming to be people of the left with adversarial attitudes to the beliefs and traditions of most of their fellow citizens ... The nightmare of the typical American intellectual, therefore, is that public policymaking should fall into the hands of the American people," see Lino Graglia, "*Romer v. Evans*: The People Foiled again by the Constitution" (1997) 68 *University of Colorado Law Review* 409 at 412. For similar arguments in the Canadian context, see F.L. Morton and Rainer Knopff, *The Charter Revolution and the Court Party* (Peterborough: Broadview Press, 2000).

52 *Romer v. Evans*, 116 S. Ct., 1620 at 1628, 1637 (1996).

53 *Bakke v. California*, 438 U.S. 265 (1978); *Shaw v. Hunt*, 517 U.S. 899 (1996); David Chang, "Discriminatory Impact, Affirmative Action and Innocent Victims: Judicial Conservatism or Conservative Justices?" (1991) 91 *Columbia Law Review* 790 at 831.

54 *United States v. Lopez*, 514 U.S. 549 (1995); *Printz v. United States*, 117 S. Ct. 2365 (1997); Alexander Rose, "Democrats fighting court's curtailment of federal influence" *National Post*, 3 October 2000 at A14.

55 531 U.S. (2000).

56 Bruce Ackerman, *We the People: Foundations* (Cambridge: Harvard University Press, 1997) at 12.

57 McDowell, *Curbing the Courts* at 165.

58 Jesse Choper, *Judicial Review and the National Political Process* (Chicago: University of Chicago Press, 1980) at 55.

59 Robert Dahl, "Decision-Making in a Democracy: The Supreme Court as a National Policy-Maker" (1957) 6 *Journal of Public Law* 279.

60 *Ex parte McCardle*, 73 U.S. 318 (1868).

61 Michael Perry, *The Constitution, the Courts and Human Rights* (New Haven: Yale University Press, 1982) at 138. Perry sees the Canadian approach as "an effort to have the best of two worlds: an opportunity for a deliberative judicial consideration of a difficult and perhaps divisive constitutional issue and an opportunity for electorally accountable officials to respond, in the course of ordinary politics." Michael Perry, "The Constitution, the Courts and the Question of Minimalism" (1993) 88 *Northwestern Univiversity Law Review* 84 at 158-59; Michael Perry, *The Constitution and the Courts* (New York: Oxford University Press, 1994) at 200.

62 In 1948 the Court invalidated a law that gave the police discretion to prohibit sound trucks, while, the next year, it upheld a better-tailored and content neutral restriction of loud and raucous noises. *Saia v. New York*, 334 U.S. 558 (1948); *Kovacs v. Cooper*, 336 U.S. 77 (1949).

Chapter 3: Judicial Activism before the *Charter*

1 See, for example, F.L. Morton and Rainer Knopff, *The Charter Revolution and the Court Party* (Peterborough: Broadview Press, 2000) at 22.

2 Kenneth McNaught, "Political Trials and the Canadian Political Tradition," in Martin L. Friedland, ed., *Courts and Trials* (Toronto: University of Toronto Press, 1975) at 137. See, generally, Kent Roach, "The Role of Litigation and the Charter in Interest Advocacy," in Leslie Seidle, ed., *Equity and Community* (Montreal: Institute for Research on Public Policy, 1993) at 160-65; Ian Brodie, "Lobbying the Supreme Court," in Hugh Mellon and Martin Westmacott, eds., *Political Dispute and Judicial Review* (Toronto: Nelson, 2000) at 195-96.

3 See, generally, Kent Roach, *Constitutional Remedies in Canada* (Aurora: Canada Law Book, 1994), chapter 1; Douglas Schmeiser, *Civil Liberties in Canada* (Oxford: Oxford University Press, 1964), chapter 4.

4 James Snell and Frederick Vaughan, *The Supreme Court of Canada* (Toronto: The Osgoode Society, 1985) at 142.

5 As quoted in David Ricardo Williams, *Duff: A Life in the Law* (Toronto: The Osgoode Society, 1984) at 146.

6 *Edwards* v. *A.G. Canada*, [1930] AC 123 (PC).

7 *Cunningham* v. *Tomey Homma*, [1903] AC 151 (PC); *Co-operative Committee on Japanese Canadians* v. *A.G. Canada*, [1947] AC 87 (PC). See Bruce Ryder, "Racism and the Constitution" (1991) 29 *Osgoode Hall Law Journal* 619.

8 Douglas Schmeiser, *Civil Liberties in Canada* (Oxford: Oxford University Press, 1964) at 260.

9 *Quong Wing* v. *The King* (1914), 18 DLR 121 (SCC); *Christie* v. *York*, [1939] 4 DLR 723. See James W.St.G. Walker, *"Race," Rights and the Law in the Supreme Court of Canada: Historical Case Studies* (Waterloo: Wilfred Laurier Press, 1997) at 100, 158.

10 *Re Drummond Wren*, [1945] 778 at 783 (HC).

11 Walker, *"Race," Rights and the Law in the Supreme Court of Canada* at 231.

12 Thomas Berger, *Fragile Freedoms* (Toronto: Clarke Irwin, 1981) at 232-36.

13 *Calder* v. *British Columbia*, [1973] SCR 313.

14 As quoted in P.B. Waite, ed., *The Confederation Debates* (Toronto: McClelland & Stewart, 1963) at 44.

15 *Severn* v. *The Queen*, [1878] SCR 70; Ian Bushnell, *The Captive Court* (Montreal: McGill-Queen's University Press, 1992) at 92; Snell and Vaughan, *The Supreme Court of Canada* at 31-32, 113.

16 Lord Haldane, "Lord Watson" (1899) 11 *Juridical Review* 278 at 281; Premier Howard Ferguson on Lord Haldane, as quoted in Alan Cairns, "The Judicial Committee and Its Critics" (1971) 4 *Canadian Journal of Political Science* 301 at 317 Lord Haldane, as quoted in Williams, *Duff* at 102; A Parliamentarian, as quoted in Cairns, "The Judicial Committee and Its Critics" at 304 -5.

17 As in the United States, the courts held that federal powers to regulate commerce did not extend to the regulation of local production. *A.G. B.C.* v. *A.G. Canada (The Natural Products Marketing Act)*, [1937] AC 377 aff. [1936] SCR 398.

18 The courts held that the legislation, which infringed provincial jurisdiction over property and civil rights, could not be justified as an emer-

gency measure because it was designed to be permanent. A.G. *Canada* v. *A.G. Ontario (The Employment and Social Insurance Act)*, [1937] AC 355 aff. [1936] SCR 427.

19 *A.G. Canada* v. *A.G. Ontario (Labour Conventions)*, [1937] AC 326 on appeal from [1936] SCR 461.

20 *A.G. B.C.* v. *A.G. Canada (Natural Products Marketing Act)*, [1937] AC 377. The Court had, in fact, earlier struck down a provincial marketing scheme as infringing federal powers over interprovincial and international trade and commerce.

21 F.R. Scott, "The Privy Council and Mr. Bennett's 'New Deal' Legislation" (1937) 3 *Canadian Journal of Economics and Political Science* at 240

22 F.R. Scott, "Some Privy Council" (1950) 28 *Canadian Bar Review* 780.

23 F.R. Scott, "The Consequences of the Privy Council's Decisions" (1937) 15 *Canadian Bar Review* 485 at 491, 494.

24 W.P.M. Kennedy, "The British North America Act: Past and Future" (1937) 15 *Canadian Bar Review* 393 at 399.

25 Senate of Canada, *Report Relating to the Enactment of the British North America Act, 1867, and Lack of Consonance between Its Terms and Judicial Construction of Them and Cognate Matters* (Ottawa: Queen's Printer, 1939) at 12-13.

26 Cairns, "The Judicial Committee and Its Critics" at 301.

27 R.C.B. Risk, "The Many Minds of W.P.M. Kennedy" (1998) 48 *University of Toronto Law Journal* 353 at 384.

28 Canada, House of Commons, *Debates*, 14 April 1939 at 2812-13.

29 Peter Russell, *The Judiciary in Canada* (Toronto: McGraw-Hill Ryerson, 1987) at 339.

30 The attorney general resigned in part on the basis that "his professional oath as a barrister made it necessary for him to uphold the law and prevented him from giving advice contrary to what was to him the plain letter of the law." J.R. Mallory, *Social Credit and the Federal Power in Canada* (Toronto: University of Toronto Press, 1956) at 75, 185.

31 John Irving, *The Social Credit Movement in Alberta* (Toronto: University of Toronto Press, 1959) at 165.

32 *Reference re Alberta Statutes*, [1938] SCR100.

33 Thomas Berger, *Fragile Freedoms* (Toronto: Clarke, Irwin, 1981), chapters 5 and 6; William Kaplan, *State and Salvation: The Jehovah's Witnesses and Their Fight for Civil Rights* (Toronto: University of Toronto Press, 1989), chapter 8.

34 Conrad Black, *Duplessis* (Toronto: McClelland & Stewart, 1977) at 386.

35 *Boucher* v. *The Queen*, [1951] SCR 265 at 291-92.

36 *Switzman* v. *Elbing*, [1957] SCR 285 at 290.

37 As quoted in Pierre Trudeau, *Federalism and the French Canadians* (Toronto: Macmillan, 1968) at 112.

38 Edward McWhinney, *Judicial Review*, 4th ed. (Toronto: University of Toronto Press, 1968) at 244, 260. See also F.R. Scott, "Areas of Conflict in the Field of Public Law and Policy" (1956) 3 *McGill Law Journal* 29 at 48-49.

39 *Henry Birks* v. *Montreal,* [1955] SCR 799.
40 As quoted in Fred Kaufman, "Case Comment" (1953) 1 *McGill Law Journal* 223 at 223-24.
41 *Saumur* v. *The City of Quebec*, [1953] SCR 299 at 333, 318. Justice Kerwin upheld provincial jurisdiction over freedom of speech and religion and dismissed an argument based on an implied bill of rights on the basis that "we have not a Bill of Rights such as is contained in the United States Constitution and decisions on that part of the latter are of no assistance." Ibid. at 324.
42 SQ 1953-4, c.15, ss. 2a, 2b, 2c.
43 Black, *Duplessis* at 389.
44 Petition for interlocutory relief, as quoted in *Saumur and Jehovah's Witnesses* v. *A.G. of Quebec* (1962), 37 DLR (2d) 703 at 718 (Que. CA).
45 *Saumur* v. *A.G. of Quebec*, [1964] SCR 252.
46 SQ, c. 96, s. 175. A somewhat similar municipal bylaw in Quebec was recently struck down again when the Jehovah's Witnesses challenged it, this time under the *Charter*. Municipalities, unlike provincial governments, do not have the option of using the notwithstanding clause to override *Charter* rights.
47 Morton and Knopff argue that "deciding under the Charter whether government as such may (or must) do something, goes far beyond deciding which government may do it" under the division of the powers. Morton and Knopff, *The Charter Revolution and the Court Party* at 53. My conclusion that the division of powers presents a greater risk of judicial activism than the *Charter* is consistent with the work of Weiler, who argued that the Court should not enforce the division of powers but a bill of rights subject to a notwithstanding clause. See Paul Weiler, *In the Last Resort* (Toronto: Carswell, 1974); Paul Weiler, "Of Judges and Rights, or Should Canada Have a Constitutional Bill of Rights" (1980) 60 *Dalhousie Review* 205. The intrusiveness of judicial rulings on the division of powers can, however, be mitigated by various instruments of cooperative federalism such as the federal government's ability to spend in areas of provincial jurisdiction or to declare provincial undertakings to be of national importance. See Patrick Monahan, *The Politics of the Constitution* (Toronto: Carswell, 1987).

Chapter 4: The *Charter's* Influential Response to Judicial Activism

1 See Peter Russell, "A Democratic Approach to Civil Liberties" (1969) 19 *University of Toronto Law Journal* 109; Donald Smiley, "The Case against the Canadian Charter of Human Rights" (1969) 2 *Canadian Journal of Political Science* 277; Robert Samek, "Untrenching Fundamental Rights" (1982) 27 *McGill Law Journal* 755. At the Joint Committee on the Constitution, which held hearings in 1980 and 1981 and is generally credited with increasing support for the *Charter*, twenty-one groups and forty-one individuals opposed the idea of entrenchment, compared with fifty-four groups and fifty-three individuals who supported it. See

Proceedings of the Joint Committee on the Constitution, 1980-1981, issue 57: 92. The significant number of opponents of entrenchment suggests that the *Charter* had not yet become a civic religion.

2 Janet Hiebert, "Why Must a Bill of Rights Be a Contest of Political and Judicial Wills? The Canadian Alternative" (1999) 10 *Public Law* 22 at 23.

3 "Small package, small target," *Maclean's*, 13 October 1980 at 31; Robert McKercher, *The United States Bill of Rights and the Canadian Charter* (Toronto: Ontario Economic Council, 1983) at 19; Manitoba, *Legislative Debates*, 3 March 1981 at 1247.

4 Joint Committee on the Constitution 30: 8, 37.

5 Ibid. at 38-39.

6 Paul Weiler, "Of Judges and Rights, or Should Canada Have a Constitutional Bill of Rights" (1980) *Dalhousie Review* 205 at 232-34.

7 Ibid. at 206, 214, 233. When Minister of Justice Jean Chrétien introduced the notwithstanding clause in the House of Commons, he used almost identical language: "The purpose of an override clause is to provide the flexibility that is required to ensure that legislatures rather than judges have the final say on important matters of public policy." Canada, House of Commons, *Debates,* 20 November 1981 at 13043.

8 Paul Weiler, *In the Last Resort* (Toronto: Carswell, 1974) at 212.

9 Saskatchewan, *Legislative Debates*, 26 November 1981 at 1.

10 Ibid., 2 December 1981 at 134.

11 Ibid., 9 December 1981 at 400, 402.

12 *Ford* v. *Quebec* (1988), 54 DLR (4th) 577 (SCC).

13 Robert Sharpe and Katherine Swinton, *The Charter of Rights and Freedoms* (Toronto: Irwin Law, 1998) at 57.

14 For example, Article 10(2) of the *European Convention* provides that freedom of expression may be subject to limitations "as are prescribed by law and are necessary in a democratic society, in the interests of national security, territorial integrity or public safety, for the prevention of disorder or crime, for the protection of health or morals, for the protection of the reputation or rights of others, for preventing the disclosure of information received in confidence or for maintaining the authority and impartiality of the judiciary." Article 19(2) of the *International Convention* similarly provides that restrictions can be placed on freedom of expression if they are "provided by law and are necessary for respect of the rights or reputations of others; for the protection of national security or of public order or of public health or morals." Some rights, such as fair trial rights in Article 6 or equality rights in Article 14 in the *European Convention*, are not subject to any limitations.

15 Section 5 of the New Zealand *Bill of Rights* provides "the rights and freedoms contained in this Bill of Rights may be subject only to such reasonable limits prescribed by law as can be demonstrably justified in a free and democratic society."

16 Article 8 of the *Basic Law on Human Dignity and Liberty* provides: "There shall be no violation of rights under this Basic Law except by a Law fit-

ting the values of the State of Israel, designed for a proper purpose, and to an extent no greater than required."

17 Section 36 of the South African *Bill of Rights* provides: "The rights in the Bill of Rights may be limited only in terms of law of general application to the extent that the limitation is reasonable and justifiable in an open and democratic society based on human dignity, equality and freedom, taking into account all of the relevant factors, including the nature of the right; the importance of the purpose of the limitation; the nature and extent of the limitation; the relation between the limitation and its purpose; less restrictive means to achieve the purpose."

18 *FirstCertification Judgment* [1996] 4 SA 744 at paras. 77 and 78; *Soobramoney* v. *Minister of Health*, [1998] 1 SA 765 at para. 29 (CC). If adequate reasons are not given, the Court may require, for example, adequate medical treatment.

19 *Grootboom*, October 2000 at para. 44.

20 Section 8 of the *Basic Law*, Freedom of Occupation, allows for statutes to be enacted with an express statement that they shall be valid notwithstanding the *Basic Law*, but that the validity of such a statute shall expire in four years. This particular override has subsequently been extended by legislation indefinitely. Tsvi Kahana, "The Partnership Model" (SJD thesis, University of Toronto, 2000) at 19-20.

21 *Human Rights Act*, 1998 c. 42, ss. 16,3.

22 Ibid., s. 4; *Moonen* v. *Film and Literature Board of Review* (1999), 5 HRNZ 224 at para. 20.

23 *Rights Brought Home*, CM 3872 at 2.13.

24 Michael Taggart, "Tugging on Superman's Cape: Lessons from Experience with the New Zealand Bill of Rights" [1998] *Public Law* 266.

25 Contrary to James Allen, who lumps the *Charter* with the American *Bill of Rights* as "Superman" bills of rights. James Allen, "Turning Clark Kent into Superman" (2000) 9 *Otago Law Review* 613 at 623.

26 Justice Iacobucci has warned that "if statutory meanings must be made congruent with the Charter even in the absence of ambiguity, then it never would be possible to apply, rather than simply consult, the values of the Charter. Furthermore, it would never be possible for the government to justify infringements as reasonable limits under s.1 of the Charter, since the interpretative process would preclude one from finding infringements in the first place." *Symes* v. *Canada* (1993), 110 DLR (4th) 470 at 549 (SCC). See also *Canada (A.G.)* v. *Mossop* (1993), 100 DLR (4th) 658 at 673 (SCC). For another recognition by Justice Iacobucci that where "Parliament has not turned it mind to the issue at hand, striking down the legislation may encourage much need changes" and dialogue between the Court and Parliament, see *Little Sisters* v. *Canada (A.G.)* (2001) 38 CR (5th) 209 at para. 268 (in dissent) (SCC).

27 For an early indication that English courts may engage in creative forms of interpretation, see *R.* v. *D.P.P. ex p. Kebeline*, [1999] 4 All ER 803 at 837 (HL), suggesting that a persuasive burden requiring the accused to prove

something on a balance of probabilities could be interpreted as only an evidential burden to raise a reasonable doubt. For a contrasting recognition of Parliament's intent to impose a burden on the accused under the New Zealand *Bill of Rights*, see *R.* v. *Phillips*, [1991] 3 NZLR 175 (CA). With respect to legislation enacted before the minister, under section 19 of the *Human Rights Act, 1998*, addressed the issue of compatibility with *Convention* rights, courts might distort what might have been, had the minister turned his or her mind to it, an intent to limit or derogate from the right. With respect to new legislation, the courts may take a ministerial declaration of compatibility as *carte blanche* for strong interpretation, again in possible defiance of the purpose and intent of the legislation, and in particular an intent to justify limits on *Convention* rights.

28 *Bonham's Case* (1610), Co. Rep. 113b per Lord Coke. Some common law judges have come close to reviving Lord Coke's robust approach to judicial review. For example, Sir Robin Cooke has suggested that "some common law rights presumably lie so deep that even Parliament could not override them." *Taylor* v. *New Zealand Poultry Board*, [1984] 1 NZLR 394 at 398, and the Hon. Sir John Laws has also suggested that courts might at common law be able to strike down laws because they are inconsistent with "a fundamental right" or "democracy itself." The Hon. Sir John Laws, "Law and Democracy" [1995] *Public Law* 72 at 87.

29 Ronald Dworkin, *Taking Rights Seriously* (Cambridge: Harvard University Press, 1977); Ronald Dworkin, *A Matter of Principle* (Cambridge: Harvard University Press, 1985).

30 Lord Irvine, "Judges and Decision Makers: The Theory and Practice of Wednesbury Review" [1996] *Public Law* 59 at 76-78; Michael Zander, *A Bill of Rights?* 4th ed (London: Sweet and Maxwell, 1997) at 109, 120.

31 Jeffrey Jowell, "Beyond the Rule of Law: Towards Constitutional Judicial Review" (2000) *Public Law* 671 at 675.

32 *West Virginia State Board* v. *Barnette* 319 US 625 at 638 (1942).

33 Contrary to Jeremy Waldron's arguments that dialogue between the people and the United States Supreme Court under the American *Bill of Rights* is false and undemocratic. See Jeremy Waldron, *Law and Disagreement* (Oxford: Clarendon Press, 1999) at 291.

34 The Hon. Sir John Laws, "The Limitation of Human Rights" [1998] *Public Law* 254 at 261-62, quoting from *R.* v. *Ministry of Defence ex parte Smith*, [1996] 1 All ER 257. See also Hon. Sir John Laws, "Is the High Court the Guardian of Fundamental Constitutional Rights?" [1993] *Public Law* 59 at 74-78, where he champions the idea that judges should employ strong common law presumptions that legislatures will respect rights unless they make clear statements to the contrary and that administrators should give reasons and justifications for their decisions.

35 Lord Irvine, "The Development of Human Rights in Britain under an Incorporated Convention on Human Rights" [1998] *Public Law* 221 at 225-26.

36 *Reference re s.94(2) of the B.C. Motor Vehicle Act* (1985), 23 CCC (3d) 289 at 298 (SCC).

Chapter 5: An American Debate Comes to Canada

1 Andrew Petter, "The Politics of the Charter" (1986) 8 *Supreme Court Law Review* 473 at 476.
2 Patrick Monahan and Andrew Petter, "Developments in Constitutional Law: 85-86 Term" (1987) 9 *Supreme Court Law Review* 69 at 71, 178, 180.
3 Petter, "The Politics of the Charter" at 496, 500, 482.
4 Andrew Petter, "Immaculate Deception: The Charter's Hidden Agenda" (1987) 45 *The Advocate* 857. The next year Petter, writing with Allan Hutchinson, did advert to "traces of a more positive and communitarian strand of politics" in the *Charter*, but stressed that they "find voice only in the qualifications of and limitations on Charter guarantees ... they may occasionally serve as brakes on the full expression of Charter rights, but they do not alter the fact that liberal individualism is the engine that drives the Charter carriage." Allan Hutchinson and Andrew Petter, "Private Rights/Public Wrongs: The Liberal Lie of the Charter" (1988) 38 *University of Toronto Law Journal* 278 at 283.
5 Michael Mandel, *The Charter of Rights and the Legalization of Politics in Canada*, rev. ed. (Toronto: Thomson, 1994) at 85, 271, 354, 440, 461.
6 Allan Hutchinson, *Waiting for CORAF: A Critique of Law and Rights* (Toronto: University of Toronto Press, 1995) at 131,15, 58, 170, 181.
7 Andrew Petter and Allan Hutchinson, "Rights in Conflict: The Dilemma of Charter Legitimacy" (1989) 23 *University of British Columbia Law Review* 531 at 540, 544.
8 Joel Bakan, *Just Words: Constitutional Rights and Social Wrongs* (Toronto: University of Toronto Press, 1997).
9 Allan Hutchinson, "The Rule of Law Revisited: Democracy and Courts," in David Dyzenhaus, ed., *Recrafting the Rule of Law* (Oxford: Hart Publishing, 1999) at 197, 218, 220. Hutchinson has not been totally won over to the *Charter* and has urged the British not to entrench a bill of rights on the basis that "the response to a deficit in democratic justice is not less democracy (in the form of an unelected jurocracy), but more democracy (in the form of engaged citizens)." Allan Hutchinson, "Supreme Court Inc.: The Business of Democracy and Rights," in Gavin Anderson, ed., *Rights and Democracy* (London: Blackstone Press, 1999) at 44. As we will see, the rhetoric of the courts as an unelected "jurocracy" has been picked up by critics of judicial activism in the United Kingdom, but is primarily used in Canada today by critics of judicial activism on the right.
10 See my *Due Process and Victims' Rights: The New Law and Politics of the Charter* (Toronto: University of Toronto Press, 1999) at 70-71.
11 F.L. Morton and Rainer Knopff, *The Charter Revolution and the Court Party* (Peterborough: Broadview Press, 2000) at 47, 50.
12 F.L. Morton and Rainer Knopff, "Permanence and Change in a Written Constitution: The 'Living Tree' Doctrine and the Charter of Rights" (1990) 2 *Supreme Court Law Review* 533 at 545.
13 Samuel LaSelva, *The Moral Foundations of Canadian Federalism* (Montreal and Kingston: McGill-Queen's University Press, 1996) at 77. As LaSelva

recognizes, "the Charter can be law to judges even though its provisions cannot be mechanically applied by them: for it restricts and guides judges and sets standards of reasoning for them."

14 Morton and Knopff, *The Charter Revolution and the Court Party* at 58; Rainer Knopff and F.L. Morton *Charter Politics* (Toronto: Nelson, 1992), chapter 7.

15 Knopff and Morton, *Charter Politics* at 198, 225-26. Writing in 1987, Morton similarly concluded that "it is easy to overstate the problem of 'judicial supremacy.'" When, as in most cases, the Court considered challenges to the behaviour of police and bureaucrats, "they are usually enforcing legislative policy, not obstructing it"; moreover, section 33 provided a check on judicial mistakes and judicial supremacy. F.L. Morton, "The Political Impact of the Canadian Charter of Rights and Freedoms" (1987) 20 *Canadian Journal of Political Science* 31 at 52-54.

16 Morton and Knopff, *The Charter Revolution and the Court Party* at 166.

17 Ibid. at 153, 149. The quote from Lord Durham is taken from G.M. Craig, ed., *Lord Durham's Report* (Toronto: McClelland & Stewart, 1963) at 50.

18 F.L. Morton and Rainer Knopff, "Canada's Court Party," in Anthony Peacock, ed., *Rethinking the Constitution* (Toronto: Oxford University Press, 1996) at 72.

19 See chapter 8 at p. 145 ff for a further critique of this aspect of the Court Party thesis.

20 Christopher Manfredi, *Judicial Power and the Charter* (Toronto: McClelland & Stewart, 1993) at 60, 147. The Court's decision on these matters is examined in chapter 7 at p. 127 ff.

21 Ibid. at 207-8.

22 Christopher Manfredi, *Judicial Power and the Charter*, 2d ed. (Toronto: Oxford University Press, 2001) at 188, 134.

23 Ibid. at ix, 22.

24 Christopher Manfredi and James Kelly, "Six Degrees of Dialogue" (1999) 37 *Osgoode Hall Law Journal* 513 at 520-21.

25 Manfredi, *Judicial Power and the Charter*, 2d ed. at 180.

26 Robert Martin, "The Judges and the Charter" (1984) 2 *Socialist Studies* 66 at 71.

27 Robert Hawkins and Robert Martin, "Democracy, Judging and Bertha Wilson" (1995) 41 *McGill Law Journal* 1 at 10-11, 3-4, 27. They argued that a reading that integrated section 15(1) and section 15(2) by Justice Wilson "effectively stripped the word 'equality' of the meaning it was generally understood to have in 1982 and replaced it with the meaning she wanted it to have." Ibid. at 45.

28 Manfredi, *Judicial Power and the Charter*, 2d ed. at 135.

29 Gad Horwitz, *Canadian Labour in Politics* (Toronto: University of Toronto Press, 1968); W.A. Bogart, *Courts and Country* (Toronto: Oxford, 1994).

30 Alan Cairns, *Reconfigurations* (Toronto: McClelland & Stewart, 1995) at 120.

31 Russell taught Morton and Knopff as well as me. No one can accuse him of producing clones! On his diverse contributions, see Joe Fletcher, ed.,

The Democratic Imagination: Essays in Honour of Peter Russell (Toronto: University of Toronto Press, 1999).

32 In 1969 he argued against entrenchment of a *Charter*, based on "the legal profession's limited social vision," which saw the "struggle for civil liberty ... in terms of a sagacious judiciary, periodically prodded by some liberal counsel, restraining the overreaching programmes of the demos." Peter Russell, "A Democratic Approach to Civil Liberties" (1969) 19 *University of Toronto Law Journal* 109 at 128, 131.

33 Peter Russell, "The Effect of a Charter of Rights on the Policy-Making Role of Canadian Courts" (1982) 25 *Canadian Public Administration* 1 at 12, 33.

34 Peter Russell, "The First Three Years in Charterland" (1985) 28 *Canadian Public Administration* 367 at 391, 394.

35 Peter Russell, "Canada's Charter of Rights and Freedoms: A Political Report" [1988] *Public Law* 385 at 390, 387.

36 Peter Russell, "Canadian Constraints on Judicialization from Without" (1994) 15 *International Political Science Review* 165 at 168, 169.

37 Canada, House of Commons, *Debates,* 8 June 1998 at 1205 (Eric Lowther, Calgary Centre, Reform).

38 Ibid. at 1640 (Gerry Ritz, Battlefords Lloydminister, Reform).

39 Ibid. at 1630.

40 House of Commons, *Debates,* 13 October, 1999 at 1600, 1605.

41 Manning criticized Court decisions that required warrants to enter a house (*Feeney*), excluded unconstitutionally obtained evidence (*Therens*), stayed proceedings because of unreasonable delay (*Askov*), expanded the intoxication defence (*Daviault*), struck down offences of vagrancy (*Heywood*) and possession of child pornography (*Sharpe*), and having an abortion without a hospital committee's approval (*Morgentaler*), and granted prisoners the right to vote (*Sauvé*).

42 Preston Manning, "Supreme Court Reform," *Globe and Mail,* 16 June 1998, A21.

43 The New Canada Act (draft), Reform Party of Canada, December 1999 at 13.

44 House of Commons, *Debates,* 1 March 2001 at 1400.

45 Janice Tibbetts, "Lamer attacks Alliance 'Yelping,'" *National Post,* 14 April 2001 at A1; Norma Greenway, "Lamer's rebuke was out of bounds: CA," ibid., 17 April 2001 at A6.

46 Susan Delacourt, "The Media and the Supreme Court of Canada" in Hugh Mellon and Martin Westmacott, eds., *Political Dispute and Judicial Review Assessing the Work of the Supreme Court of Canada* (Toronto: Nelson, 2000) at 35.

47 Patricia Hughes, "Judicial Independence: Contemporary Pressures and Appropriate Responses" (2000) 80 *Canadian Bar Review* 181 at 200ff.

48 Rory Leischman, "Robed Dictators," *The Next City,* October 1998.

49 Celeste McGovern, "Benevolent Monarch," *Western Report,* 21 September 1998, 21-23.

50 Delacourt, "The Media and the Supreme Court of Canada" at 35.

51 Andrew Coyne, "That's what judges are for," *National Post*, 7 April 2000, A18.

52 Susan Ruttan, "Some fads not worth importing from U.S.," *Edmonton Journal*, 19 June 1999, H2.

53 "Judicial Activism is not a figment of the imagination," *Globe and Mail*, 26 October 1999, A20.

54 "Judging the judges," ibid., 8 February 2000, A18.

55 Andrew Coyne, "The Charter under attack," *National Post*, 3 May 1999, as quoted in Delacourt, "The Media and the Supreme Court" at 38.

56 "Supreme Self-Restraint," ibid., 7 April 7 2000, A20.

57 Neil Seeman, "Who runs Canada?" ibid., 24 July 1999.

58 "Letter to the editor," ibid., 28 July 1999, A15.

59 As quoted in "Gavels and microphones don't mix," *Globe and Mail*, 26 August 1998, A14.

60 Kirk Makin, "Lamer worries about public backlash," ibid., 6 February 1999, A1, quoted in Delacourt, "The Media and the Supreme Court" at 38.

61 "Rein in lobby groups, senior judges suggest," *National Post*, 6 April 2000, A1. Chief Justice McLachlin added: "We don't consider ourselves the final word on things ... generally one can say that when we say a certain particular law is inconsistent with the Charter, there is some room to manoeuvre, and often there is a great deal of room."

62 Other judges, including Justices L'Heureux-Dubé and Abella, who had both been targeted in the press for engaging in judicial activism, took the opportunity in public speeches to dissect what was entailed in the loaded charge of judicial activism and to defend the role of courts in a democracy. In a speech in Australia, Justice L'Heureux-Dubé commented that "the mere assertion of activism, without a full discussion of where the court has erred and in the absence of an explicit argument of how, and on which grounds, a different solution is better justified, serves no useful purpose." She also stated that "to suggest that there is a neutral ground somewhere, a judicial terra nullius on which courts can stand when expounding the common law is a pure fallacy." Claire L'Heureux-Dubé, "Judicial Activism and the Rule of Law: Doing Away with Terra Nullius Once and for All," unpublished paper, July 1998 at 8, 19. Justice Abella argued that democracy as opposed to totalitarianism "is not — and never was — just about the wishes of the majority." Rosalie Abella, "The Judicial Role in a Democratic State," unpublished paper, April 2000 at 7. The *Globe and Mail* responded with complaints that Justice Abella "holds legislatures in low repute" and that "we should know who superior judges are before they are confirmed" and they should "leave necessary remedies for the legislature to devine." "Judges and the public interest," *Globe and Mail*, 14 April 2000.

63 *Edwards Books* (1986), 35 DLR (4th) 1 at 49 (SCC).

64 *Irwin Toy* (1989), 58 DLR (4th) 577 at 623 (SCC).

65 *R. v. Marshall* (1999), 138 CCC (3d) 97 at paras. 58-59.

66 Jeffrey Simpson, "The Supreme Court as battering ram," *Globe and Mail*, 7 October 1999, A14.

67 *R. v. Marshall* (1999), 139 CCC (3d) 391 at paras. 20, 42, 44.

68 As quoted in Ken Coates, *The Marshall Decision and Native Rights* (Montreal and Kingston: McGill- Queen's University Press, 2000) at 19.

69 Cristin Schmitz, "Settle native issues with talks: Judge," *National Post*, 15 January 2001, A4; Cristin Schmitz, "SCC wrong forum for native land claims: Bastarache," *Lawyers Weekly*, 19 January 2001, 20.

70 The Court's strict test for establishing an Aboriginal right will be examined in chapter 7 at p. 134 ff, and its generous test for allowing the government to justify limits on *Charter* rights will be examined in chapter 9 at p. 160 ff.

71 Bruce Feldhusen, "Access to the Private Therapeutic Records of Sexual Assault Complainants" (1996) 75 Canadian Bar Review 537 at 562; Manfredi, *Judicial Power and the Charter*, 2d ed. at 182-83.

72 *R. v. Mills* (1999) 139 CCC (3d) 321 at paras 20, 56, 58 (SCC). The Court did hint that trial judges might have to read down some of the more extreme implications of the law that would deny them, and not only defence lawyers, access to the documents that might be relevant to the accused's defence. The accused was subsequently acquitted. See chapter 14 at p. 278 ff for more discussion of this case.

73 *R. v. Morrisey*, [2000] 2 SCR 90.

74 *R. v. Latimer*, 2001 SCC 1 at para. 88. I represented the Canadian Civil Liberties Association, which intervened to argue that the mandatory penalty was cruel and unusual punishment.

75 "Better Judgment," *National Post*, 24 January 2001, A19; "Sharpe Ruling," ibid., 27 January 2001, A17; Luiza Chwialkowska, "Revamped Bench," ibid., 22 January 2001, A8. Patrick Monahan observed that *Charter* applicants were successful in three of the nine *Charter* cases that the Supreme Court heard in 2000 and that in none of these cases was legislation struck down. He concludes: "There was little evidence of the sort of activism that has prompted critics in previous years to complain that the Court was encroaching on the prerogatives of the legislature." Patrick Monahan, "The Supreme Court's 2000 Term," *Supreme Court Law Review*, forthcoming.

76 *R. v. Burns*, [2001] SCC 7 at para. 67.

77 Ted Morton, "What Chrétien once believed," *National Post*, 19 February 2001, A14; Neil Seeman, "Who do you think you are?" *Globe and Mail*, 20 February 2001.

Chapter 6: Four Dimensions of Judicial Activism

1 See, for example, Neil Tate and Torbar Vallinder, *The Global Expansion of Judicial Power* (New York: New York University Press, 1995).

2 Rory Leishman, "Robed Dictators," *The Next City*, October 1998.

3 Bertha Wilson, "Law and Policy in a Court of Last Resort," in Frank McArdle, ed., *The Cambridge Lectures, 1988* (Montreal: Yvon Blais, 1989)

at 220. See also Rosalie Silberman Abella, "The Judicial Role in the Development of the Law: The Impact of the Charter," in Joe Fletcher, ed., *Ideas in Action* (Toronto: University of Toronto Press, 1999) at 271.

4 Paul Sniderman et al., *Rights in Conflict* (New Haven: Yale University Press, 1996) at 164.

5 Richard Posner, *The Federal Courts* (Cambridge: Harvard University Press, 1996) at 314, 318.

6 Robert Bork, *The Tempting of America* (New York: Basic Books, 1990) at 16-17.

7 To their credit, Morton and Knopff recognize that judicial activism has become "a loaded and hotly disputed term." They have offered a more precise and multi-tiered definition of judicial activism as "the disposition to interpret rights broadly and to enforce them vigorously. Activist judges display 'a readiness to veto the politics of other branches of governments on constitutional grounds' usually by striking down statutes or excluding evidence in criminal cases. Self-restraint by contrast 'connotes a judicial presupposition to find room within the constitution for the policies of democratically accountable decision-makers." F.L. Morton and Rainer Knopff, *The Charter Revolution and the Court Party* (Peterborough: Broadview Press, 2000) at 15; Rainer Knopff and F.L. Morton, *Charter Politics* (Toronto: Nelson, 1992) at 19, 98.

8 See E.R. Elhauge, "Does Interest Group Theory Justify More Intrusive Judicial Review" (1991) 101 *Yale Law Journal* 31; Kent Roach, "The Problems of Public Choice" (1993) 31 *Osgoode Hall Law Journal* 721.

9 Ronald Dworkin, *Taking Rights Seriously* (Cambridge: Harvard University Press, 1977) at 142.

10 Ronald Dworkin, *Law's Empire* (Cambridge: Harvard University Press, 1986) at 398, 378.

11 Dworkin, *Taking Rights Seriously* at 143, 148.

12 Dworkin, *Law's Empire* at 375-76.

13 Dworkin is clear that his approach to judicial activism, like his theory of judicial review, is built around the American *Bill of Rights* and that other approaches to rights protection are not only possible but "may well be better from the point of view of ideal theory." Ibid. at 379. Although Dworkin has proposed that the United Kingdom adopt the *European Convention*, he seems to have some misgivings about the ability of Parliament to limit or derogate from rights in that document. See Ronald Dworkin, *A Bill of Rights for Britain* (London: Chatto, 1990).

14 Guido Calabresi, "Foreword: Antidiscrimination and Constitutional Accountability (What the Bork-Brennan Debate Ignores)" (1991) 105 *Harvard Law Review* 80.

15 Lorraine Weinrib, "Canada's Constitution Revolution: From Legislative to Constitutional State" (1999) 33 *Israel Law Review* 13 at 47, 45.

16 Paul Mahoney, "Judicial Activism and Judicial Restraint in the European Court of Human Rights: Two Sides of the Same Coin" (1990) 11 *Human Rights Law Journal* 57 at 86. He cautioned that "the judges' power to

update the Convention through ... interpretation is not boundless. Fear of subjective judicial tyranny or of the supremacy of the judiciary is misplaced since serious constraints exist on their power."

17 Bradley Canon has argued that judicial activism is a matter of degree measured on six different dimensions, including the degree to which judicial decisions negate democratically enacted legislation, depart from earlier Court decisions or the text of the constitution, make decisions about substantive policy as opposed to process, substitute judicial policies for legislative and executive policies, and prevent other branches of government from developing their own policy. Bradley Canon, "Defining the Dimensions of Judicial Activism" (1983) 66 *Judicature* 237; Bradley Canon, "A Framework for the Analysis of Judicial Activism" in Stephen Halpern and Charles Lamb, eds., *Supreme Court Activism and Restraint* (Lexington: D.C.Heath, 1982) at 385. For an early argument by a Canadian commentator that the contrast between judicial activism and restraint, so popular in the United States, "may not be pure dichotomy at all and intellectual differences on the Supreme Court might better be represented as different points on a continuum ... the real question may be questions of degree," see Edward McWhinney, "The Great Debate: Activism and Self-Restraint and Current Dilemmas in Judicial Policy-Making" (1958) 33 *New York University Law Review* 775 at 790.

18 Knopff and Morton, *Charter Politics* at 101.

19 See, for example, John Daley, "Defining Judicial Restraint," in Tom Campbell and Jeffrey Goldsworthy, ed., *Judicial Power, Democracy and Legal Positivism* (Aldershot: Dartmouth, 2000); Christopher Wolfe *The Rise of Modern Judicial Review: From Constitutional Interpretation to Judge-Made Law* (NewYork: Basic Books, 1986).

20 Alexander Bickel defended avoidance of constitutional issues as a means to allow legislatures an opportunity to refine their views on controversial matters that could have been subject to constitutional judgment. See Alexander Bickel, *The Least Dangerous Branch: The Supreme Court at the Bar of Politics*, 2d ed. (New Haven: Yale University Press, 1986), chapter 4. More recently, Cass Sunstein has defended constitutional minimalism, or deciding one case at a time, as minimizing the costs of judicial error and maximizing the space for democracy. See Cass Sunstein, *One Case at a Time: Judicial Minimalism on the Supreme Court* (Cambridge: Harvard University Press, 1999) at 53.

21 Although recognizing that a restrictive approach to procedural issues such as standing "generally favours governments" that are the defendants in litigation, and may not be desirable if court decisions are thought to enhance either liberty or rationality in governance, an Australian commentator has included procedural conservatism within his definition of judicial restraint. Daley, "Defining Judicial Restraint" at 288, 307.

22 Mary Ann Glendon, *Rights Talk* (New York: The Free Press, 1991) at 13, 167.

PART TWO

Chapter 7: The Constrained Creativity of Judicial Law Making

1 Cristin Schmitz, "Supreme Court goes 'too far': Judge," *National Post*, 13 January 2001, A1.
2 *Hunter v. Southam* (1984), 14 CCC (3d) 97 (SCC).
3 F.L. Morton and Rainer Knopff, *The Charter Revolution and the Court Party* (Peterborough: Broadview Press, 2000) at 47.
4 Madame Justice Bertha Wilson, "The Making of a Constitution: Approaches to Judicial Interpretation" [1988] *Public Law* 370 at 380.
5 John Willis, "Statute Interpretation in a Nutshell" (1938) 16 *Canadian Bar Review* 1 at 17.
6 Bertha Wilson, "Law and Policy in a Court of Last Resort," in Frank McArdle, ed., *The Cambridge Lectures, 1989* (Montreal: Yvon Blais, 1990) at 220, quoting one of the earliest popular pieces to criticize the Court for activism - Robert Fulford, "Probing the Supreme Court," *The New Federation*, January/February 1989 at 43.
7 As suggested in Rainer Knopff and F.L. Morton, *Charter Politics* (Toronto: Nelson, 1992) at 117-25.
8 *Heydon's Case* (1584), 76 ER 637 638
9 *Interpretation Act*, RSC 1985, c. I-21, s. 12; *Interpretation Act of 1849* (12 Vict., c. 10, s. 5(28)).
10 *R. v. Big M Drug Mart*, [1985] 1 SCR 295 at 344.
11 *Separate Schools Reference*, [1987] 1 SCR 1148; *Adler v. The Queen*, [1996] 3 SCR 609.
12 *Reference re Electoral Boundaries Commission Act (Saskatchewan)* (1991), 81 DLR (4th) 16 (SCC).
13 *Reference re Public Service Employee Relations Act*, [1987] 1 SCR 313; *A.G. Quebec v. Irwin Toy*, [1989] 1 SCR 927; *Reference re ss. 193 and 195.1 of the Criminal Code*, [1990] 1 SCR 1123.
14 As quoted in *Reference re B.C. Motor Vehicles* (1985), 23 CCC (3d) 289 at 303 (SCC).
15 *R. v. Sault Ste Marie* (1978), 40 CCC (2d) 353 (SCC).
16 Patrick Monahan and Andrew Petter, "Developments in Canadian Constitutional Law: The 1985-86 Term" (1987) 9 *Supreme Court Law Review* 69 at 96.
17 Christopher Manfredi, *Judicial Power and the Charter* (Toronto: McClelland & Stewart, 1993) at 60. See also Robert Hawkins, "Interpretivism and Sections 7 and 15 of the Charter" (1990) 22 *Ottawa Law Review* 276 at 287, 291, arguing that the decision was a form of substantive due process that was "an invasion of the democratic sphere by the judiciary ... which knows no bounds."
18 Her famous statement that "it is probably impossible for a man to respond, even imaginatively," to the dilemma faced by a woman with an unwanted pregnancy did not go much beyond Chief Justice Dickson's recognition of the psychological trauma caused by the delays of the committee system or the fact that the committee made its decisions on a

basis other than the pregnant woman's own "priorities and aspirations." In any event, it addressed only the issue of whether a woman's liberty was violated, not whether the violation was in accordance with the principles of fundamental justice or could be justified under section 1 of the *Charter*.

19 Her statement that the *Charter* erects "around each individual, metaphorically speaking, an invisible fence over which the state will not be allowed to trespass" should also be read in light of her comments about Parliament being able to place limits on the rights of women to obtain abortions.

20 Ted Morton describes Justice Wilson's judgment as "one of the purest examples of noninterpretivist judicial activism under the Charter" and suggests that, "to feminists[,] this was the new gospel, pure and simple. That it had now received judicial consecration was reason to celebrate. To those who did not expouse this new gospel, it was a breathtaking assertion of raw judicial power." F.L. Morton, *Morgentaler v. Borowski* (Toronto: McClelland & Stewart, 1992) at 236-37.

21 Knopff and Morton, *Charter Politics* at 268.

22 *Reference re B.C. Motor Vehicle Reference* (1985), 23 CCC (3d) 289 at 293 (SCC).

23 Even Ted Morton and Rainer Knopff were, in 1992, prepared to admit that "the majority's reasoning favoured neither side in the very heated public controversy about whether there is, or should be, a right to abortion" and that it did not attempt "to construct a new national abortion policy in one bold stroke of the judicial pen." Knopff and Morton, *Charter Politics* at 136, 288.

24 Rainer Knopff, "Courts Don't Make Good Compromises" (1999) 20 (3) *Policy Options* 31 at 33; F.L. Morton, "Dialogue or Monologue" (1999) 20 (3) *Policy Options* 23 at 24; Manfredi, *Judicial Power and the Charter* at 118-19.

25 As quoted in Kent Roach, *Due Process and Victims' Rights: The New Law and Politics of Criminal Justice* (Toronto: University of Toronto Press, 1999) at 47.

26 Kent Roach, "Constitutionalizing Disrepute: Exclusion of Evidence after *Therens*" (1986) 44 *University of Toronto Faculty of Law Review* 209.

27 David Paciocco, "The Judicial Repeal of s. 24(2) and the Development of the Canadian Exclusionary Rule" (1990) 32 *Criminal Law Quarterly* 326 at 364; Richard Mahoney, "Problems with the Current Approach to Section 24(2)" (1999) 42 *Criminal Law Quarterly* 443 at 446-50.

28 *R. v. Collins* (1987), 33 CCC (3d) 1 (SCC).

29 *R. v. Stillman* (1997), 113 CCC (3d) 321 at para. 235 (in dissent). See also Knopff and Morton, *Charter Politics* at 50-57. I represented the Canadian Civil Liberties Association, which argued that the unconstitutionally obtained evidence in *Stillman* should have been excluded because of the seriousness of the police's deliberate violation of the accused's rights.

30 As quoted in Schmitz, "Supreme Court goes 'too far': Judge," A1, A4.

31 *R. v. Mohl* (1989), 37 CCC (3d) 565 (SCC); *R. v. Harper* (1994), 92 CCC

(3d) 423 (SCC). See Kent Roach, "The Evolving Fair Trial Test under Section 24 (2) of the Charter" (1996) 1 *Canadian Criminal Law Review* 117.

32 *R. v. Stillman* (1997), 113 CCC (3d) 321 (SCC); *R. v. Feeney* (1997), 115 CCC (3d) 129 (SCC).

33 David Paciocco, *Getting Away with Murder* (Toronto: Irwin Law, 1999) at 243.

34 Beverley McLachlin, "Charter Myths" (1999) 33 *University of British Columbia Law Review* 23.

35 *Institute of Edible Oil Foods* v. *Ontario* (1987), 47 DLR (4th) 368 aff'd 64 DLR (4th) 380n (Ont. CA); *R. v. Myrrmidon Inc.* (1988), 43 CCC (3d) 137 (Man. CA); *Skalbania (Trustee of)* v. *Wedgewood Village Estates Ltd.* (1989), 60 DLR (4th) 43 (BCCA), leave denied 62 DLR (4th) viii (SCC); *538745 Ontario Inc.* v. *Windsor (City)* (1988), 64 OR (2d) 38 (CA), leave denied [1988] 1 SCR.

36 *R. v. D'Entremont* (1987), 81 NSR (2d) 134 (Co. Ct.); *Piercey* v. *General Bakeries Ltd* (1986), 31 DLR (4th) 373 (Nfld. SC).

37 Gwen Brodsky and Shelagh Day, *Canadian Charter Equality Rights for Women: One Step Forward or Two Steps Back* (Ottawa: Canadian Advisory Council of Women, 1989).

38 *Andrews* v. *Law Society of British Columbia* (1989), 56 DLR (4th) 1 (SCC).

38 *Reference re Validity of Sections 32 and 34 of the Workers Compensation Act* (1989), 56 DLR (4th) 765 (SCC); *R. v. Turpin* (1989), 48 CCC (3d) 8 (SCC); *R. v. S(S)* (1990), 57 CCC (3d) 115 (SCC); *Rudolph Wolff and Co.* v. *Canada*, [1990] 1 SCR 695.

39 In *Andrews*, the Court specifically rejected a broad approach advocated by Peter Hogg that "would treat every distinction drawn by law as discrimination under s. 15(1)." For other criticisms by law professors that *Andrews* was too limited, see Dale Gibson, "Equality for Some" (1991) 40 *University of New Brunswick Law Journal* 2; Anne Bayefsky, "Case Comment" (1990) 1 *Supreme Court Law Review* (2d) 503; Richard Moon, "A Discrete and Insular Right to Equality" (1989) 21 *Ottawa Law Review* 563; Marc Gold, "Case Comment" (1989) 34 *McGill Law Journal* 1063; David Beatty, "The Canadian Conception of Equality" (1996) 46 *University of Toronto Law Journal* 349.

40 Sheilah Martin, "Balancing Individual Rights to Equality and Social Goals" (2001) 80 *Canadian Bar Review* 299.

41 (1999) 170 DLR (4th) 1.

42 Ibid. at para. 97.

43 Ibid. at paras. 108, 106, 95.

44 *Lovelace* v. *Ontario* 2000, SCC 37 at para. 7. Justice Iacobucci elaborated that the non-*Indian Act* communities did not have the same land base or involvement in gambling and that the purpose of the Rama project was "consistent with s. 15(1) of the Charter and the exclusion of the appellants does not undermine this purpose since it is not associated with a misconception as to their actual needs, capacities and circumstances." Ibid. at para. 87. I acted *pro bono* as one of the counsel for the Ontario

Metis Aboriginal Association and the Be-Wab-Bon Metis and Non-Status Indian Association in the Court of Appeal and on the factum for the Supreme Court.

45 *Egan and Nesbit* v. *Canada*, [1995] 2 SCR 513 at para. 5 per La Forest J.

46 Ibid. at paras. 173-74.

47 Morton and Knopff, *The Charter Revolution and the Court Party* at 43.

48 Ibid. at 44.

49 *Richardson* v. *Ramirez*, 418 U.S. 24 (1974).

50 *Badger* v. *A.G. Manitoba* (1986), 55 Man. Rep. (2d) 198 at 209-10 (CA) per Lyon JA. Rainer Knopff and F.L. Morton, *Charter Politics* (Toronto: Nelson, 1992) at 298-99. Christopher Manfredi similarly suggests that "an interpretivist approach to s. 3 of the Charter would accept as 'reasonable' all limits that predated the Charter (ie, that existed prior to 1982)." Christopher Manfredi, *Judicial Power and the Charter*, 2d ed. (Toronto: Oxford University Press, 2001) at 240 n.41.

51 Cristin Schmitz, "Settle native issues with talks: Judge," *National Post*, 15 January 2001, A4.

52 Robert Sheppard and Michael Valpy, *The National Deal* (Toronto: Fleet Books, 1982) at 294; Roy Romanow et al., *Canada Notwithstanding* (Toronto: Carswell, 1984) at 213, 268.

53 Morton and Knopff, *The Charter Revolution and the Court Party* at 43.

54 See, for example, *Calder* v. *B.C.*, [1973] SCR 313 at 404, requiring a clear and plain intent to extinguish Aboriginal title. Other examples of the common law requiring clear statements by the legislature before rights were violated are discussed in chapter 14 at p. 254 ff.

55 *R.* v. *Sparrow*, [1990] 3 CNLR 160 at 170 (SCC).

56 *R.* v. *Van Der Peet*, [1996] 4 CNLR 177 at para. 168 (SCC).

57 Jonathan Rudin, "One Step Forward, Two Steps Back" (1998) 13 *Journal of Law and Social Policy* 67 at 73.

58 John Borrows, *Recovering Canada: The Resurgence of Indigenous Law* (Toronto: University of Toronto Press, forthcoming) (emphasis in the original).

59 *R.* v. *Van Der Peet*, [1996] 4 CNLR 177 (SCC).

60 *R.* v. *Pamajewon* (1996), 109 CCC (3d) 275 (SCC).

61 "The burden of language in the Mi'kmaq case," *Globe and Mail*, 6 October 1999, A10. See also "The Supreme Court all at sea," ibid., 5 October 1999, A12, and "Top-court judge denies activism," ibid., 21 October 1999, A4.

62 *R.* v. *Marshall* (1999), 138 CCC (3d) 97 at para. 5 (SCC).

63 Ibid. at para. 57, 59.

64 Russel Lawrence Barsh and James (Sa'ke'j) Youngblood Henderson, "Marshalling the Rule of Law in Canada: Of Eels and Honour" (1999) 11 *Constitutional Forum* 1 at 10.

65 *R.* v. *Marshall* (1999), 139 CCC (3d) 391 at para. 19. The second judgment was discussed in chapter 5 and will also be discussed in chapter 9.

66 Preston Manning has criticized the trial judge in *Sharpe* for not acknowledging the relevance of the *Charter*'s preamble recognizing the supremacy of God to the question of whether the offence of possession of child

pornography was a justified violation of freedom of expression. In a March 2000 speech to Trinity Western University, Manning commented: "The B.C. judge pronounced the supremacy of God 'dead' and capable of 'resurrection' only by the Supreme Court. I venture to say that if this judge had so cavalierly dismissed a faith-based argument advanced by an aboriginal believer or a committed practitioner of Judaism or Islam - if any judge had taken such a back-handed crack at the most sacred doctrines of those faiths — every editorialist and civil libertarian in the country would have risen up in indignation ... But not so, when the object of contempt is the most sacred doctrine of the Christian faith." Ian Hunter, "Preach on, Preston Manning," *National Post*, 6 April 2000, A19. Manning's criticisms are interesting because they suggest that he believes the reference to God in the preamble is to a Christian God, whereas the Court has noted that there is no reference to "an identifiably Christian conception of God" in the preamble and indicated the need to interpret God in a manner consistent with Canada's multicultural society. See *R. v. Big M Drug Mart* (1985), 18 DLR (4th) 321 (SCC).

67 *Reference re Public Sector Pay Reduction Act (P.E.I.)* (1997), 118 CCC (3d) 193 (SCC). See also Jacob Ziegel "The Supreme Court Radicalizes Judicial Compensation" (1998) 9(2) *Constitutional Forum* 31; W.H. Hurlburt, "Fairy Tales and Living Trees: Observations on Some Recent Constitutional Decisions of the Supreme Court of Canada" (1999) 26 *Manitoba Law Journal* 181; Morton and Knopff, *The Charter Revolution and the Court Party* at 108-10 for the expression of similar concerns.

68 *Reference re Secession of Quebec*, [1998] 2 SCR 217 at para. 51.

69 Donna Greshner, "The Quebec Secession Reference: Goodbye to Part V?" (1998) 10 *Constitutional Forum* 19; W.H. Hurlburt, "Fairy Tails and Living Trees: Observations on Some Recent Constitutional Decisions of the Supreme Court of Canada" (1999) 26 *Manitoba .Law Journal* 181 at 184-86.

70 Sujit Choudhry and Robert Howse, "Constitutional Theory and the *Quebec Secession Reference*" (2000) 13 *Canadian Journal of Law and Jurisprudence* 143.

71 Benjamin Cardoza, *The Nature of the Judicial Process* (New Haven: Yale University Press, 1921) at 141.

Chapter 8: The Limits of Public Law Adjudication

1 See, for example, Rainer Knopff and F.L. Morton, *Charter Politics* (Toronto: Nelson, 1992), chapter 7; F.L. Morton and Rainer Knopff, *The Charter Revolution and the Court Party* (Peterborough: Broadview Press, 2000) at 53-57.

2 The lawyers' fees were $50,000. The government's costs were assessed at $40,000, but were eventually forgiven. *Charter* litigants must establish enough adjudicative facts to decide the case and, under the traditional Anglo-Canadian rule in civil litigation, they may have to pay a good portion of the winner's costs. See, generally, Kent Roach, *Constitutional*

Remedies in Canada (Aurora: Canada Law Book, as updated) at 4.20, 5.490, 11.930ff.

3 *Canadian Council of Churches v. Canada* (1992) 88 DLR (4th) 193 (S.C.C.).

4 Ian Brodie, Friends of the Court, http::\\publish.uwo.ca/irbrodie/fotc/ table 2.7, 2.9 as of March 2001. When Morton and Knopff discuss governmental involvement in *Charter* litigation, they focus on the rare cases when governments have conceded *Charter* issues, and not on their normal opposition to *Charter* claims. See Morton and Knopff, *The Charter Revolution and the Court Party* at 117-23.

5 Compare Morton and Knopff, *The Charter Revolution and the Court Party* at 56 with the report of the appearances by the intervenors in *R. v. Sparrow*, [1990] 1 SCR 1075 at 1082.

6 Kenneth Swan, "Intervention and Amicus Curiae Status in Charter Litigation," in Robert Sharpe, ed., *Charter Litigation* (Butterworths: Toronto, 1987).

7 Alexander Bickel, *The Least Dangerous Branch: The Supreme Court at the Bar of Politics*, 2d ed. (New Haven: Yale University Press, 1986); Cass Sunstein, *One Case at a Time: Judicial Minimalism on the Supreme Court* (Cambridge: Harvard University Press, 1999).

8 *R. v. Smith* (1987), 34 CCC (3d) 97 (SCC).

9 *R. v. Morrisey*, (2000) 148 CCC (3d) 1 (SCC).

10 *R. v. Latimer*, (2001) 150 CCC (3d) 129 (SCC) 1 at para. 88. For further criticism of the constitutional minimalism and one-case-at-a-time approach taken in these last two cases, see my "Searching for Smith: The Constitutionality of Mandatory Sentences" (2001) *Osgoode Hall Law Journal* (forthcoming). The reader should know that I acted for the Canadian Civil Liberties Association, which argued that the mandatory penalty should be struck down in part on the basis of hypothetical examples.

11 *United States of America v. Burns and Rafay* (2001), 151 CCC (3d) 97 (SCC).

12 *R. v. Sparrow*, [1990] 1 SCR 1075 at 1105.

13 Patrick Monahan, "The Supreme Court of Canada in the 21st Century" (2001) 80 *Canadian Bar Review* 374 at 392.

14 Ibid. at 391. The fact that the Court in *Marshall II* took a minimalist fact-specific approach to the right in question did not stop it from going beyond the government's refusal to justify limits on the treaty rights and speculating about possible justifications that the government might have for closed seasons and licensing requirements as restrictions on the treaty right.

15 Morton and Knopff, *The Charter Revolution and the Court Party* at 55; Christopher Manfredi, *Judicial Power and the Charter*, 2d ed. (Toronto: McClelland & Stewart, 1993) at 135.

16 American critics of Sunstein's constitutional minimalism often make this point, but they yearn for some way to minimize judicial supremacy by making the Court's articulation of broad principles provisional. See

Christopher Peters, "Assessing the New Judicial Minimalism" (2000) 100 *Columbia Law Review* 1455, and Neal Devins, "The Democracy Forcing Constitution" (1999) 97 *Michigan Law Review* 1971.

17 Morton and Knopff, *The Charter Revolution and the Court Party* at 15; Manfredi, *Judicial Power under the Charter* at 177ff.

18 *Manitoba Language Reference* (1985), 19 DLR (4th) 1 (SCC), supplementary reasons (1986) 26 DLR (4th) 767; [1990] 3 SCR 1417; [1992] 1 SCR 212. See, generally, Roach, *Constitutional Remedies in Canada* at 2.160-220, 13.420-530.

19 These cases are examined in Christopher Manfredi, "Appropriate and Just in the Circumstances: Public Policy and the Enforcement of Rights under the Canadian Charter of Rights and Freedoms" (1994) 27 *Canadian Journal of Political Science* 435, and in chapter 13 of my *Constitutional Remedies in Canada*. Manfredi expresses concerns about remedial activism that can result in judicial management of schools, but the judicial interventions in these cases left the schools significant scope for management and imposed more intrusive remedies only when they seemed to resist the minority language right. My own view is that courts should not hesitate to order mandatory remedies once a government proves defiant, but that governments and school boards should first be given an opportunity to take good-faith steps to implement the right as articulated by the court.

20 *Mahe v. Alberta* (1990), 68 DLR (4th) 69 at 106; *Reference re Public Schools Act (Man.)* (1993), 100 DLR (4th) 723 at 740; Beverley McLachlin, "The Charter: A New Role for the Judiciary" (1991) 29 *Alberta Law Review* 540 at 558.

21 (1997), 151 DLR (4th) 577 at 631-32 (SCC).

22 *Little Sisters Book and Art Emporium v. Canada (Minister of Justice)* (2001), 38 CR (5th) 209 at para. 158. The Court noted that it did not have the information, given that six years had elapsed since the trial judge decided the case.

23 In his study of remedial decisions of lower courts between 1982 and 1992, Professor Manfredi similarly found that declarations dominated and that, while such remedies "may have a long term policy impact, they do not involve courts in the formulation or management of positive orders affecting public policy." Manfredi, "Appropriate and Just in the Circumstances," at 453. Manfredi's own findings may overestimate remedial decree litigation by classifying as remedial decrees those cases involving delayed declarations of invalidity with the possibility of interim relief during the delay. As suggested below at p. 200 ff, I see the delayed declaration of invalidity not as an injunction on the legislature, but as an opportunity should the legislature so desire to pre-empt the Court's negative remedy with one based on its own formation of policy.

Chapter 9: Judicial Acceptance of Limits on Rights

1 Cristin Schmitz, "Settle native issues with talks: Judge," *National Post*, 15 January 2001, A4.

2 Janet Hiebert, *Limiting Rights: The Dilemma of Judicial Review* (Montreal: McGill-Queen's University Press, 1996), chapter 4; Lorraine Weinrib, "The Supreme Court and Section 1 of the Charter" (1988) 10 *Supreme Court Law Review* 469.

3 *R. v. Big M Drug Mart*, [1985] 1 SCR 295 at 352, 337. Justice Wilson also concluded in her concurring opinion that "legislation cannot be regarded as embodying legitimate limits within the meaning of s. 1 where the legislative purpose is precisely the purpose at which the Charter right is aimed." Ibid. at 362.

4 Leon Trakman et al., "R. v. Oakes 1986-1997: Back to the Drawing Board" (1998) 36 *Osgoode Hall Law Journal* 83 at 95.

5 *R. v. Edwards Books*, [1986] 2 SCR 713 at 779.

6 See, for example, Andrew Petter, "The Politics of the Charter" (1986) 8 *Supreme Court Law Review* 473, discussed above in chapter 5.

7 *R. v. Edwards Books* at 795, 810.

8 Michael Mandel, *The Charter of Rights and the Legalization of Politics in Canada*, rev. ed. (Toronto: Thomson, 1994) at 325-26.

9 *R. v. Edwards Books*, [1986] 2 SCR 713 at 772, 781-82.

10 *Irwin Toy Ltd. v. A.G. Quebec* (1989), 58 DLR (4th) 577 at 626, 630.

11 David Beatty, *Constitutional Law in Theory and Practice* (Toronto: University of Toronto Press, 1995) at 82ff; Hiebert, *Limiting Rights* at 87-88.

12 See Kent Roach, "Justice La Forest: A Bickelian Balancer of State and Individual Interests," in Rebecca Johnson et al., eds., *Gerard La Forest at the Supreme Court of Canada, 1985-1997* (Winnipeg: Canadian Legal History Project, 2000) at 189-91; Robert Sharpe, "The La Forest Years: The Vocation of Judging - A Judge's Perspective," ibid. at 512-15.

13 *McKinney v. University of Guelph* (1990), 76 DLR (4th) 545 at 648, 651, 654. Although she dissented on the basis that governments could hire more young people by not imposing cuts on the university and by offering attractive retirement options without the arbitrary and absolute requirement of retirement at the age of sixty-five, even Justice Wilson recognized in her dissent that when the legislature was balancing the claims of competing groups, "a healthy measure of restraint" was in order. Ibid. at 616.

14 The majority's judgment has subsequently been interpreted by the Court as rejecting a formalistic test that applied uniformly in all the circumstances, in favour of a more flexible approach of the type contemplated in *Edwards Books* and *Irwin Toy*. See, for example, *Ross v. School District no. 15*, [1996] 1 SCR 825 at 871-72.

15 *RJR -MacDonald Inc. v. Canada*, [1995] 3 SCR 199 at para. 138.

16 Ibid. at 343-43.

17 *R. v. Oakes* (1986), 24 CCC (3d) 321 (SCC).

18 *R. v. Downey* (1992), 72 CCC (3d) 1 (SCC); *R. v. Laba* (1994), 94 CCC (3d) 385 (SCC).

19 *R. v. Chaulk* (1990), 62 CCC (3d) 193 at 220-23 (SCC).

20 Kent Roach, *Due Process and Victims' Rights: The New Law and Politics of*

Criminal Justice (Toronto: University of Toronto Press, 1999) at 118-19.

21 *Re re ss.193 and 195.1(1)(c) of Criminal Code* (1990), 56 CCC (3d) 65 at 122, 134 (SCC).

22 *Levogiannis* (1993), 85 CCC (3d) 327 at 333 (SCC).

23 *Dagenais* v. *C.B.C.* (1994), 94 CCC (3d) 289 (SCC).

24 *R.* v. *Mills* (1999), 139 CCC (3d) 321 at para. 56. As discussed in chapter 14, this case goes beyond the idea that Parliament can place reasonable limits on rights and may suggest that it can actually interpret the ambit of rights.

25 *R.J.R.-MacDonald* at 331-32. See also *Thomson Newspapers*, [1998] 1 SCR 877 at 942.

26 *R.A.V.* v. *City of St. Paul*, 112 S. Ct. 2538 (1992).

27 *R.* v. *Keegstra* (1990), 61 CCC (3d) 1 at 118-19 (SCC).

28 *R.* v. *Butler* (1992), 70 CCC (3d) 129 at 164, 166 (SCC).

29 *American Booksellers Association* v. *Hudnut*, 777 F. 2d 323 (7th Cir. 1985) aff'd 106 S. Ct. 1172 (1986).

30 *Stanley* v. *Georgia*, 394 U.S. 557 (1969).

31 *R.* v. *Sharpe*, 2001 SCC 2 at para. 80. Note that the American Court has upheld a similar offence by classifying child pornography as "not speech." *Osborne* v. *Ohio*, 110 S. Ct. 1691 (1990).

32 *R.* v. *Sparrow*, [1990] 3 CNLR 160 at 180-81.

33 *R.* v. *Badger*, [1996] 1 SCR 771 at para. 76.

34 *R.* v. *Marshall* (1999), 139 CCC (3d) 391 at para. 41.

35 Tom Flanagan, *First Nations? Second Thoughts* (Montreal: McGill-Queen's University Press, 2000) at 151-65. For criticisms of this limitation test as itself a form of judicial activism, see Len Rotman, "Marshalling Principles from the Marshall Morass" (1999) 23 *Dalhousie Law Journal* 5 at 43.

36 *R.* v. *Sparrow* at 183, 186.

37 *R.* v. *Gladstone*, [1996] 2 SCR 723 at para. 75.

38 *R.* v. *Van Der Peet*, [1996] 2 SCR 507 at paras. 305-6, 315.

39 *Delgammukw* v. *British Columbia*, [1997] 3 SCR 1010 at para. 165.

40 Kent McNeil, *Defining Aboriginal Title in the 1990's: Has the Supreme Court Finally Got It Right?* (Toronto: Robarts Centre for Canadian Studies, 1998) at 20.

41 *R.* v. *Gladstone* at para. 63.

42 *R.* v. *Van Der Peet* at paras. 308-10.

43 John Borrrows, "Soveregnty's Alchemy: An Analysis of *Delgamuukw*" (1999) 37 *Osgoode Hall Law Journal* 537; Lisa Dufraimont, "From Regulation to Recolonization: Justifiable Infringement of Aboriginal Rights at the Supreme Court of Canada" (2000) 58 *University of Toronto Faculty of Law Review* 1 at 25.

44 See Dwight Newman, "The Limitation of Rights: A Comparative Evolution and Ideology of the Oakes and Sparrow Tests" (1999) 62 *Saskatchewan Law Review* 543 at 559.

Chapter 10: Dialogue between Courts and Legislatures

1 Allan Hutchinson, *Waiting for CORAF* (Toronto: University of Toronto Press, 1995) at 170; F.L. Morton, "Dialogue or Monologue" (1999) 20 (3) *Policy Options* 23 at 26.

2 Peter Hogg and Allison Bushell have argued that two-thirds of *Charter* cases striking legislation down have resulted in a legislative reply, while Christopher Manfredi and James Kelly contend that the figure is closer to one-third because legislative repeal of offending statutes and other forms of compliance do not constitute true dialogue. Compare Peter Hogg and Allison Bushell, "The Charter Dialogue between Courts and Legislatures" (1997) 35 *Osgoode Hall Law Journal* 75, with Christopher Manfredi and James Kelly, "Six Degrees of Dialogue: A Response to Hogg and Bushell" (1999) 37 *Osgoode Hall Law Journal* 513. I will not join the quantitative debate because "the question of what to count is always open to argument." Peter Hogg and Allison Thornton, "Reply to 'Six Degrees of Dialogue'" (1999) 37 *Osgoode Hall Law Journal* 529 at 533. Moreover, it is often connected with the substantive issue of what constitutes good dialogue, an issue that I will discuss in chapter 14.

3 *Vriend* v. *Alberta*, [1998] 1 SCR 493 at para. 139.

4 *R.* v. *Mills* (1999), 139 CCC (3d) 321 at para. 57.

5 Michael Mandel, *The Charter of Rights and Freedoms and the Legalization of Politics in Canada*, rev. ed. (Toronto: Thomson, 1994) at 233; Rainer Knopff and F.L. Morton, *Charter Politics* (Toronto: Nelson, 1992) at 21.

6 *R.* v. *Duarte* (1990), 53 CCC (3d) 1 (SCC).

7 "Ruling removes 'life line' police say," *Globe and Mail*, 26 July 1991, A1.

8 Canada, House of Commons, *Debates*, 25 February 1993, 16491, 16564, 16588.

9 *Criminal Code*, s. 184.

10 *Criminal Code*, s. 487.01.

11 (1997), 115 CCC (3d) 129 (SCC).

12 *R.* v. *Feeney* (1997), 115 CCC (3d) 129 at 204.

13 Jeffrey Simpson, "When things get awkward under the Charter of Rights," *Globe and Mail*, 24 August 1997, A14.

14 Mark Tushnet, "Policy Distortion and Democratic Debilitation" (1995) 94 *Michigan Law Review* 245; Christopher Manfredi, *Judicial Power and the Charter*, 2d ed. (Toronto: Oxford University Press, 2001) at 178.

15 *Criminal Code*, s. 529.1-5.

16 Beverley McLachlin, "Charter Myths" (1999) 33 *University of British Columbia Law Review* 23 at 33.

17 During the heyday of the Court's Charter activism from the early 1980s to the mid-1990s, Canada's prison population increased by 50 per cent. See Kent Roach, *Due Process and Victims' Rights: The New Law and Politics of Criminal Justice* (Toronto: University of Toronto Press, 1999) at 1.

18 Ontario Commission on Systemic Racism, *Report* (Toronto: Queens Printer, 1995) at 113, 123.

19 *R.* v. *Morales* (1992), 77 CCC (3d) 91 at 107.

20 Hogg and Bushell, "The Charter Dialogue between Courts and Legislatures" at 121; Manfredi and Kelly, "Six Degrees of Dialogue" at 527.

21 *Criminal Code*, s. 515(10)(c), as amended by SC 1997, c. 18, s. 59.

22 Carl Baar, "Criminal Court Delay and the Charter" (1993) 72 *Canadian Bar Review* 305.

23 "Hampton calls for review of ruling in Askov case," *Globe and Mail*, 17 July 1991, A5.

24 *R. v. Stinchcombe* (1991), 68 CCC (3d) 1 (SCC).

25 F.L. Morton and Rainer Knopff, *The Charter Revolution and the Court Party* (Peterborough: Broadview Press, 2000) at 162ff.

26 Michael Code, who was not only Askov's counsel but subsequently became one of the high-ranking Ontario officials who dealt with the fall-out, has argued that proactive legislative guidance for all affected parties would have been far preferable to reliance on after-the-fact litigation and the drastic remedy of a stay of proceedings. Michael Code, *Trial within a Reasonable Time* (Toronto: Carswell, 1992).

27 Ontario responded by appointing more prosecutors and judges, building new courtrooms, and placing a new emphasis on prompt and efficient charge screening, pre-trial disclosure, and plea bargaining.

28 As quoted in Cristin Schmitz, "Supreme Court goes 'too far': Judge," *National Post*, 13 January 2001, A4. See also Justice McIntyre's argument in dissent in *R. v. Vaillancourt* (1987), 39 CCC (3d) 118, that "while it may be illogical to characterize an unintentional killing as murder," no principle of fundamental justice was offended and Parliament could do so.

29 *Vailancourt v. The Queen* (1987), 39 CCC (3d) 118; *Martineau v. The Queen* (1990), 58 CCC (3d) 353 (SCC).

30 *Martineau v. The Queen* at 385-86.

31 Manfredi and Kelly, "Six Degrees of Dialogue: A Response to Hogg and Bushell" at 526.

32 *R. v. Morrisey* (2000), 146 CCC (3d) 1 (SCC).

33 *R. v. Luxton* (1990), 58 CCC (3d) 449 (SCC).

34 *Criminal Code*, ss. 231(6)(7) and 745.

35 *The Tobacco Act*, SC 1997, c. 13, s. 22.

36 *An Act to Amend the Tobacco Act*, SC 1998, c. 38.

37 *The Tobacco Act*, SC 1997, c. 13, s. 4.

38 Janet Hiebert, "Wrestling with Rights: Judges, Parliament and the Making of Social Policy," in Paul Howe and Peter Russell, eds., *Judicial Power and Canadian Democracy* (Montreal: McGill-Queen's University Press, 2001) at 181, 183, 200.

39 Manfredi, *Judicial Power and the Charter* at 178.

40 Hiebert, "Wrestling with Rights" at 210 n. 39.

41 House of Commons, *Debates*, 5 December 1996 at 7112.

42 Note, however, that the Health Ministry would have been assisted by its legal service unit of Justice lawyers. See James Kelly, "Bureaucratic Activism and the Charter" (1999) 42 *Canadian Public Administration* 476.

43 The fact that the tobacco companies would bring a *Charter* challenge to new legislation was not a good reason for not enacting an in-your-face

reply. It was inevitable that the accused, financed by legal aid because they faced imprisonment, would challenge the in-your-face replies to the Court's sexual assault decisions. The Court's response to these in-your-face replies is discussed in chapter 14 at p. 273 ff.

44 *Sauvé v. Canada*, [1993] 2 SCR 438.
45 *Belczowski v. Canada*, [1992] 2 FC 440 (CA); *Sauvé v. Canada* (1992), 89 DLR (4th) 644 at 650-51 (Ont. CA).
46 House of Commons, *Debates*, 2 April 1993, 18011-21.
47 Ibid., 18016.
48 *Canadian Disability Rights Council v. Canada*, [1988] 3 FC 622 (TD); *Muldoon v. Canada*, [1988] 3 FC 628 (TD); *An Act to Amend the Canada Elections Act*, SC 1993, c. 19, s. 23.
49 *Sauvé v. Canada* (1999), 180 DLR (4th) 385 at para. 59, 137.
50 Rainer Knopff, F.L Morton, and Christopher Manfredi have all expressed concern that such an approach would amount to judicial denigration of the retributive case for seeing disenfranchisement as part of punishment and "judicial preference" for rehabilitation over retribution. Manfredi, *Judicial Power and the Charter* at 147; Knopff and Morton, *Charter Politics* at 329. Their objections would also have to extend to the few cases discussed in chapter 9 at p. 156 ff, in which the Court found legislative purposes to be unconstitutional because they conflict with the very nature and purpose of the right. Thus, in *Big M Drug Mart,* the Court preferred the principle of religious freedom and equality to the enforcement of a state religion, and in *Vriend*, the Court preferred the principle of non-discrimination to discrimination against gays and lesbians.

I will act as counsel for Aboriginal Legal Services of Toronto, which has been granted intervenor status in *Sauvé II*, and will argue that the denial of the vote constitutes unjustified discrimination against prisoners and Aboriginal prisoners, as well as an unjustified denial of the right to vote. On this case I am not the only one with a conflict, as Professor Manfredi was an expert witness for the federal government in *Sauvé II* and Professor Morton has been an expert witness for governments in other voting rights case and is associated with Albertans for a Civil Society, a group that has also been granted intervenor status in *Sauvé II*, and will argue in favour of prisoner disenfranchisement.

51 *Ford v. Quebec (A.G.)*, [1988] 2 SCR 712.
52 Ibid. at 780.
53 Errol Mendes, "Two Solitudes, Freedom of Expression and Collective Linguistic Rights in Canada: A Case Study of the *Ford* Decision" (1991) 1 *National Journal of Constitutional Law* 283 at 287-90.
54 *An Act to Amend the Charter of the French Language*, SQ 1988, c. 54, s. 10.
55 *Ford v. Quebec* (1988), 54 DLR (4th) 577 at 628. See Mandel, *The Charter of Rights and the Legalization of Politics in Canada* at 162-63.
56 Paul Sniderman et al., *The Clash of Rights* (New Haven: Yale University Press, 1996) at 164.
57 House of Commons, *Debates*, 6 April 1989, 153, as quoted in Manfredi, *Judicial Power and the Charter* at 186.

58 The preamble of the Saskatchewan law invoking the override started the task of educating the public about the legitimacy of the override by providing that "whereas s. 33 of the Charter exists for the purpose of permitting publicly accountable legislatures to finally determine essential economic and social policy." *The SGEU Dispute Settlement Act*, SS 1984-85-86, c. D.1.1.

59 Quebec has used and renewed the override to protect pension plans that treated women and men unequally, to protect denominational schools, and to protect age restrictions on agricultural grants from *Charter* challenges. See Tsvi Kahana, "The Partnership Model of the Canadian Notwithstanding Mechanism: Failure and Hope" (SJD thesis, University of Toronto, 2000), chapter 5.

60 *An Act to Amend the Charter of the French Language*, SQ 1993, c. 40, s. 18. The law also allows regulations to be passed that would require signs to be only in French. This power has been used to require large billboards and advertising in public transit to be in French only. Kahana, "The Partnership Model" at 188.

61 *Ballantyne, Davidson and McIntyre* v. *Canada*, Communications 359 and 385/1989, Human Rights Committee, established under Article 28 of the *International Convenant on Civil and Political Rights*, 31 March 1993.

62 Janine Brodie, Shelley Gavigan, and Jane Jenson, *The Politics of Abortion* (Toronto: Oxford University Press, 1992) at 67, 87-88, 98, 115.

63 F.L. Morton, *Morgentaler v. Borowski* (Toronto: McClelland & Stewart, 1992) at 304; W.A. Bogart, *Courts and Country* (Toronto: Oxford University Press, 1994) at 149.

64 Morton and Knopff, *The Charter Revolution and the Court Party* at 149.

65 Ibid. at 149, 165-6.

66 *Muir* v. *Alberta* (1996), 132 DLR (4th) 695 (Alta. QB).

67 Brian Laghi, "Alberta to limit compensation for eugenics victims," *Globe and Mail*, 11 March 1998. A1.

68 Brian Laghi, "Klein retreats in rights scrap," ibid., 12 March 1998, A1.

69 Alberta, Legislative Assembly, *Debates*, 2 April 1998.

70 Alberta, Department of Justice, *Report of the Ministerial Task Force*, 3 March 1999 at 5.

71 Manfredi, *Judicial Power and the Charter* at 133-34.

72 Brenda Cossman and Bruce Ryder, "*M.* v. *H.*: Time to Clean Up Your Acts" (1999) 10 *Constitutional Forum* 59.

73 Morton and Knopff, *The Charter Revolution and the Court Party* at 20; Manfredi, *Judicial Power and the Charter* at 152.

74 British Columbia, Legislative Assembly, *Debates*, 26 June 2000 at 14349 per then attorney general Ujjal Dosanjh. See, generally, Jason Murphy, "Dialogic Reponses to *M. v. H.*: From Compliance to Defiance" (2001) 59 *University of Toronto Faculty of Law Review* 299, on which this section draws.

75 Press release, Ontario attorney general Jim Flaherty, 25 October 1999.

76 Press release of M., 25 November 1999.

77 *Vincent* v. *Ontario* (1999), 70 CRR 365 (Ont. SCJ).

78 House of Commons, *Debates*, 8 June 1999 at 16069, 15960.
79 Nick Bala, "Alternatives for Extending Spousal Status in Canada" (2000) 17 *Canadian Journal of Family Law* 169; *Law Reform (2000) Act*, SNS 2000, c. 29, s. 52.
80 Neither Premier Klein nor Stockwell Day, before his election as leader of the Canadian Alliance, the neo-conservative Official Opposition in the federal Parliament, voted. Missing votes is another example of an American-style politics with loose party discipline.
81 Alberta, Legislative Assembly, *Debates*, 23 February 2000.
82 Ibid. (Committee of the Whole), 7 March 2000 per Mr. Doerksen and per Mr. Langevin.
83 Stockwell Day deftly turned this issue on its head by arguing that "we don't have the mandate as I see it, from our citizens to change this centuries-old definition, nor do we have the mandate, without a full discussion, to stand up and say that we will set up a directory and every other kind of relationship that you can imagine can then qualify." Ibid.
84 *Corbiere* v. *Canada* (1999), 173 DLR (4th) 1 (SCC) (eighteen-month delayed declaration of invalidity that restrictions on voting in band elections were unconstitutional applied to the successful applicant as well as others similarly situated). In this case I represented an intervenor, Aboriginal Legal Services of Toronto, which unsuccessfully argued that the successful applicant should be exempted from the period of delay.
85 If a similar case arose today, it is unlikely that biological parents could even establish that they were an analogous group protected under section 15 or that the legislation violated their human dignity. See chapter 7 at p. 127 ff on the Court's restrictive approach to equality rights.
86 *Vriend* v. *Alberta* at para. 178, 197.

Chapter 11: The Myths of Judicial Activism

1 Alexander Bickel, *The Least Dangerous Branch: The Supreme Court at the Bar of Politics*, 2d ed. (New Haven: Yale University Press, 1986); Cass Sunstein, *One Case at a Time: Judicial Minimalism on the Supreme Court* (Cambridge: Harvard University Press, 1999).
2 F.L. Morton and Rainer Knopff, *The Charter Revolution and the Court Party* (Peterborough: Broadview Press, 2000) at 53, 58l. F.L. Morton and Rainer Knopff, *Charter Politics* (Toronto: Nelson, 1992), chapter 7; Chistopher Manfredi, *Judicial Power and the Charter*, 2d ed. (Toronto: Oxford University Press, 2001) at 134-35, 179; Christopher Manfredi and James Kelly, "Six Degrees of Dialogue" (1999) 37 *Osgoode Hall Law Journal* 513 at 522-26. Some of the cases that the Court is criticized for deciding because the law had already been changed by Parliament were still very much live disputes, since legislative changes to the law did not apply retroactively to the case. For example, in *R.* v. *Sieben*, [1987] 1 SCR 295, the Court had to determine the admissibility of evidence seized under the writs of assistance; in *R.* v. *Heywood*, [1994] 3 SCR 761, it had to determine whether the accused could be convicted under the old

vagrancy law; and in *Schachter*, [1992] 2 SCR 679, it had to determine eligibility to benefits under the law as it existed at the time the claim was made.

3 *Thorson* v. *A.G. Canada (no. 2)*, [1975] 1 SCR 138.

4 *Canada (Minister of Justice)* v. *Borowski* (1981), 130 DLR (3d) 588 (SCC).

5 *Borowski* v. *Canada* (1989), 57 DLR (4th) 231 at 249 (SCC).

6 *Tremblay* v. *Daigle* (1989), 62 DLR (4th) 634 at 648 (SCC).

7 F.L. Morton, *Morgentaler vs. Borowski* (Toronto: McClelland & Stewart, 1992) at 285.

8 Beverley McLachlin, "Charter Myths" (1999) 33 *University of British Columbia Law Review* 23 at 31.

9 Cristin Schmitz, "Supreme Court goes 'too far': Judge," *National Post*, 13 January 2001, A1.

10 *United States* v. *Burns and Rafay* (2001), 151 CCC 97 (SCC).

11 Ted Morton, "What Chrétien once believed," *National Post*, 19 February 2001, A14.

12 Joel Bakan and David Schneiderman, eds., *Social Justice and the Constitution* (Ottawa: Carleton University Press, 1992).

13 John Whyte, "Fundamental Justice: The Scope and Application of the Charter" (1983) 13 *Manitoba Law Journal* 455; Martha Jackman, "The Protection of Welfare Rights under the Charter" (1988) 20 *Ottawa Law Review* 257.

14 *Reference re Public Service Employee Relations Act (Alta)*, [1987] 1 SCR 313 at 412.

15 *Irwin Toy Ltd.* v. *Quebec (A.G.)*, [1989] 1 SCR 927 at 1003-4.

16 *Reference re ss. 193 and 195.1 of the Criminal Code* (1990), 56 CCC (3d) 65 at 96, 104 (SCC).

17 See, for example, *Masse* v. *Ontario (Ministry of Commercial and Social Services)* (1996), 134 DLR (4th) 20 (Ont. Ct. Gen. Div.), upholding significant cuts in social assistance and the many cases listed in John Laskin et al., *The Canadian Charter of Rights and Freedoms Annotated* (Aurora: Canada Law Book, 2000) at 7.900-1100. The United Nations Committee on Economic, Social and Cultural Rights has made adverse comments about the treatment of social and economic rights under the *Charter*. See William Schabas, "Freedom from Want" (2000) 11 *National Journal of Constitutional Law* 189 at 210; Martha Jackman, "Poor Rights: Using the Charter to Support Social Welfare Claims" (1993) 19 *Queen's Law Journal* 65; Robert Sharpe and Katherine Swinton, *The Charter of Rights and Freedoms* (Toronto: Irwin Law, 1998) at 148-50.

18 The Court's fear about intruding on the economic choices of governments has influenced its interpretation of other rights, notably equality rights. Even in its cases dealing with mobility rights, which specifically provide that every person has the right to the gaining of a livelihood in any province, the Court has taken pains to stress that the right does not guarantee the right to work, or even free trade within Canada, and prohibits discriminatory treatment only on the basis of province of resi-

dence. *Law Society of Upper Canada* v. *Skapinker* (1984), 9 DLR (4th) 161(SCC); *Canadian Egg Marketing Agency* v. *Richardson* (1998), 166 DLR (4th) 1 (SCC).

19 Andrew Petter, "The Politics of the Charter" (1986) 8 *Supreme Court Law Review* 473; Michael Mandel, *The Charter of Rights and the Legalization of Politics in Canada*, rev. ed. (Toronto: Thomson, 1994).

20 Morton and Knopff, *The Charter Revolution and the Court Party* at 149-50; Manfredi, *Judicial Power and the Charter* at 198.

21 Ibid. at 135.

22 *R.* v. *Sharpe*, 2001 SCC 3 at para. 80.

23 Compare *Keegstra* with *R.A.V.* v. *St. Paul*, 112 S. Ct. 2538 (1992). On pornography, compare *Butler* with *American Booksellers* v. *Hudnut*, 777 F. 2d 323 (7th Cir. 1985) affd 106 S. Ct. 1172 (1986). On the willingness of the Canadian court to see the state not as the antagonist of freedom, but as the proponent of equality rights, see Mayo Moran, "Talking about Hate Speech" [1994] *Wisconsin Law Review* 1425.

24 *Buckley* v. *Valeo*, 424 U.S. 1 (1976); *FEC* v. *National Conservative Political Action Commission*, 470 U.S. 480 (1985).

25 *National Citizens Coalition* v. *Canada (A.G.)* (1984), 11 DLR (4th) 481 (Alta. QB); *Somerville* v. *Canada (A.G.)* (1996), 136 DLR (4th) 205 (Alta. CA).

26 The Royal Commission on Electoral Reform, *Reforming Electoral Democracy: Final Report* (Ottawa: Queen's Printer, 1991) at 337ff.

27 *Libman* v. *Quebec (A.G.)* (1997), 151 DLR (4th) 385 at para. 56 (SCC). The Court will still require the legislature to justify restrictions on campaign spending and, in that case, struck down what amounted to a total ban on the ability of people to spend money in the Quebec referendum, except through the official Yes and No campaigns. Manfredi has criticized the case for continuing "the trend toward unregulated election spending" and for engaging in "judicial micro-management of public policy," by holding that a $600 restriction on third party spending in a Quebec referendum campaign was unreasonable, but a proposed $1000 limit in federal elections was not. Manfredi, *Judicial Power and the Charter* at 150-51. The $600 limit under Quebec law was restricted to the costs of holding a meeting and prevented a third party not associated or affiliated with official Yes and No committees from spending any money on ads or handbills.

28 *Harper* v. *Canada* (2000), 193 DLR (4th) 37 (SCC).

29 F.L. Morton, " Dialogue or Monologue?" in Paul Howe and Peter Russell, eds., *Judicial Power and Canadian Democracy* (Montreal and Kingston: McGill-Queen's University Press, 2001) at 117.

30 Allan Hutchinson, *Waiting for CORAF* (Toronto: University of Toronto Press, 1995) at 170.

31 Contrary to Morton and Knopff's arguments that we should reclaim Lord Durham's idea that "parliamentary sovereignty was the key to protecting rights." *The Charter Revolution and the Court Party* at 153.

32 (1986), 26 DLR (4th) 200.

33 [1998] 2 S.C.R. 217.

34 Manfredi, *Judicial Power and the Charter* at 5, 134.
35 Jeff Goldsworthy, "Legislation, Interpretation and Judicial Review" (2001) 51 *University of Toronto Law Journal* 75 at 80-82.
36 Morton and Knopff, *The Charter Revolution and the Court Party* at 165.
37 The decision not to address the issue may carry more democratic weight if it is a recent one, such as the 1994 decision of the Ontario legislature on a free vote not to equalize spousal benefits for same-sex couples. This qualification does not mean, however, that such a legislative decision can be immune from *Charter* review.

Chapter 12: The Myths of Right Answers

1 Ian Greene et al., *Final Appeal Decision-Making in Canadian Courts of Appeal* (Toronto: Lorimer, 1998) at 14.
2 Robert Bork, *The Tempting of America* (New York: Basic Books, 1990) at 177, 257, 151.
3 Ibid. at 17
4 Ibid. at 160.
5 *Reference re Public Service Employee Relations Act*, [1987] 1 SCR 313 at 394.
6 Robert Hawkins, "Interpretivism and Sections 7 and 15 of the Charter" (1990) 22 *Ottawa Law Review* 276 at 310.
7 Robert Bork, "Neutral Principles and Some First Amendment Problems" (1971) 47 *Indiana Law Journal* 1 at 29, 31.
8 Barry Strayer, "Life under the Canadian Charter: Adjusting the Balance between Legislatures and Courts" [1988] *Public Law* 347 at 352-53.
9 Patrick Monahan, *Politics and the Constitution* (Toronto: Carswell, 1987) at 81.
10 Canada, House of Commons, *Debates*, 27 November 1981, as quoted in Monahan, *Politics and the Constitution* at 80.
11 John Hart Ely, *Democracy and Distrust* (Cambridge: Harvard University Press, 1980) at 74.
12 Ibid. at 123-24.
13 *Reference re Electoral Boundaries (Saskatchewan)* (1991), 81 DLR (4th) 16 (SCC).
14 Ely, *Democracy and Distrust* at 169, 256, 162.
15 Monahan recognizes that legal rights do "not have this obvious and direct link to the democratic process" and argues that they are not based on privacy or dignity, but rather fair process and the state's superior power when prosecuting crime. Monahan, *Politics and the Constitution* at 110-11. Even accepting these arguments, however, does not establish that the most frequently litigated *Charter* rights are necessary for a functioning democracy.
16 Ely, *Democracy and Distrust* at 94.
17 Ibid. at 68, 169.
18 Monahan, *Politics and the Constitution* at 99, 109, 124-25.
19 Professor Monahan has accepted this view in later work. See Patrick Monahan, "The Supreme Court in the 21st Century" (2001) 80 *Canadian Bar Review* 374.

20 Ronald Dworkin, *Taking Rights Seriously* (Cambridge: Harvard University Press, 1977) at 82.
21 Ronald Dworkin, *Law's Empire* (Cambridge: Harvard University Press, 1986).
22 Ronald Dworkin, *Freedom's Law* (Cambridge: Harvard University Press, 1996) at 3.
23 A famous statement by Judge Learned Hand, for whom Dworkin clerked. See Dworkin, *Freedom's Law* at 342.
24 Dworkin, *Taking Rights Seriously* at 143; Dworkin, *Law's Empire* at 375-76.
25 Jeremy Waldron, *Law and Disagreement* (Oxford: Oxford University Press, 1999), chapter 10.
26 Ronald Dworkin, *A Bill of Rights for Britain* (London: Chatto, 1990).
27 Lorraine Weinrib, "The Supreme Court and Section One of the Charter" (1988) 10 *Supreme Court Law Review* 469 at 496, 506-8.
28 Lorraine Weinrib, "Limitations on Rights in a Constitutional Democracy" (1996) 6 *Caribbean Law Review* 428 at 445.
29 *R. v. Oakes* (1986), 24 CCC (3d) 321 at 349-50 (SCC).
30 *Dagenais* v. *C.B.C.* (1994), 94 CCC (3d) 289 (SCC); *R. v. Mills* (1999), 139 CCC (3d) 321 (SCC).
31 Lorraine Weinrib, "Canada's Constitutional Revolution: From Legislative to Constitutional State" (1999) 33 *Israel Law Review* 13 at 49.
32 Ibid. at 80. See also David Beatty, *Talking Heads and the Supremes* (Toronto: Carswell, 1990) at 84-88.
33 David Beatty, *Constitutional Law* (Toronto: University of Toronto Press, 1995) at 70.
34 David Beatty, "The Canadian Charter of Rights: Lessons and Laments" (1997) 60 *Modern Law Review* 481. "Except for their proscription against laws that serve no other purpose than denying people the freedom to choose how they will go about their lives, the principles of rationality and proportionality impose almost no constraints on what goals and aspirations communities can pursue." Beatty, *Constitutional Law* at 146.

Chapter 13: Democratic Dialogue in Theory

1 F.L. Morton and Rainer Knopff, *The Charter Revolution and the Court Party* (Peterborough: Broadview Press, 2000) at 162. Professor Morton argues: "If I go to a restaurant, order a sandwich, and a waiter brings me the sandwich I ordered, I would not count this as a 'dialogue'. Yet this is how the concept is used in Hogg and Thornton's 1997 study." F.L. Morton, "Dialogue or Monologue?" in Paul Howe and Peter Russell, eds., *Judicial Power and Canadian Democracy* (Montreal and Kingston: McGill-Queen's University Press, 2001) at 111.
2 Martha Minow, "Foreword: Justice Engendered" (1987) 101 *Harvard Law Review* 10; Lon Fuller, "The Forms and Limits of Adjudication" (1978) 92 *Harvard Law Review* 353.
3 Barry Friedman, "Dialogue and Judicial Review" (1993) 91 *Michigan Law Review* 577.

4 Alexander Bickel, *The Least Dangerous Branch: The Supreme Court at the Bar of Politics*, 2d ed. (New Haven: Yale University Press, 1986) at 240.

5 Jeremy Waldron rejects the idea that dialogue between courts and legislatures can be one based on active citizenship when he argues that "the exercise of power by a few black-robed celebrities can certainly be expected to fascinate an articulate population. But that is hardly the essence of active citizenship." Jeremy Waldron, *Law and Disagreement* (Oxford: Clarendon Press, 1999) at 291. His criticisms, however, are directed at Dworkin, who is concerned only with judicial review under the American *Bill of Rights*, and do not include a modern bill of rights where the processes of democracy would still operate when deciding whether rights, as articulated by the Court, should be subject to limitation or derogation by the legislature.

6 Jefferson to Abigail Adams, as quoted in Mark Tushnet, *Taking the Constitution Away from the Courts* (Princeton: Princeton University Press, 1999) at 15.

7 As quoted in Christopher Wolfe, *The Rise of Modern Judicial Review* (New York: Basic Books, 1986) at 96. As Wolfe notes, Madison's view was that "other branches, in matters before them, are not bound by judicial opinions of constitutionality." Ibid. at 96. See also Robert Burt, *The Constitution in Conflict* (Cambridge: Harvard University Press, 1992), chapter 2, on Madison's views.

8 As quoted in John Agresto, *The Supreme Court and Constitutional Democracy* (Ithica: Cornell University Press, 1984) at 118.

9 *Patriation Reference* (1981), 125 DLR (3d) 1 (SCC). For arguments about the danger of reducing issues of constitutionality, including respect for conventions, to bare issues of legality under the *Charter*, see my "The Attorney General and the Charter Revisited" (2000) 50 *University of Toronto Law Journal* 1.

10 Sheldon Goldman, *Constitutional Law and Supreme Court Decision-Making* (New York: Harper and Row, 1982) at 33.

11 "Under the adjudicative version of the separation of powers, unpersuaded governments would be free to disregard such judicial opinions and continue acting on their own views of constitutional requirements." Rainer Knopff and F.L. Morton, *Charter Politics* (Toronto: Nelson, 1992) at 179.

12 Robert Burt has defended a strongly dialogic theory of the American Constitution that would make the Supreme Court "equal, not hierarchically superior, to other branches." Burt, *The Constitution in Conflict* at 3. See also Agresto, *The Supreme Court and Constitutional Democracy*.

13 Tushnet, *Taking the Constitution Away from the Courts* at 175, 33, 186. Tushnet's preference is for democracy, but he seems to assume that the people will want to think in terms of constitutional law, which is not the most obvious vehicle for populism. See Michael Mandel, "Against Constitutional Law (Populist or Otherwise)" (2000) 34 *University of Richmond Law Review* 443 at 459.

14 In earlier work, he suggested that it might be imprudent to endorse legislative enactment of a criminal law that the courts would surely hold unconstitutional. Mark Tushnet, "Policy Distortion and Democratic Debilitation: Comparative Illumination of the Countermajoritarian Difficulty" (1995) 94 *Michigan Law Review* 245 at 262-63.

15 Christopher Manfredi and James Kelly, "Six Degrees of Dialogue" (1999) 37 *Osgoode Hall Law Journal* 513 at 524. See also Christopher Manfredi, *Judicial Power and the Charter*, 2d ed. (Toronto: Oxford University Press, 2001) at 199.

16 *R. v. Mills* (1999), 139 CCC (3d) 321 at paras. 56-58 (SCC).

17 *Ford* v. *Quebec* (1988), 54 DLR (4th) 577 (SCC). See Brian Slattery, "A Theory of the Charter" (1987) 25 *Osgoode Hall Law Journal* 732 at 740-43, arguing that legislatures employing the override are still bound by the rights and are interpreting the rights that are being overridden.

18 Robert Dahl, "Decision-Making in a Democracy: The Supreme Court as National Policy-Maker" (1957) 6 Journal *of Public Law* 279 at 285, 291, 283.

19 Charles Epp argues that the rights revolution in Canada relies less on either the *Charter* or the policy dispositions of the Court and more on the support structure provided by rights advocacy groups, legal aid, lawyers, and government support. Charles Epp, *The Rights Revolution* (Chicago: University of Chicago Press, 1998) at 197-99; Charles Epp, "Do Bills of Rights Matter? The Canadian Charter of Rights and Freedoms" (1996) 90 *American Political Science Review* 765.

20 Morton and Knopff, *The Charter Revolution and the Court Party* at 25, 149. See chapter 5 above for further discussion of their majoritarian premises.

21 Terri Peretti, *In Defence of a Political Court* (Princeton: Princeton University Press, 1999) at 188.

22 *Vriend* v. *Alberta*, [1998] 1 SCR 493 at para. 139.

23 Antonio Lamer, "The Rule of Law and Judicial Independence" (1996) 45 *University of New Brunswick Law Journal* 3 at 13; Patricia Hughes, "Judicial Independence: Contemporary Pressures and Appropriate Responses" (2001) 80 *Canadian Bar Review* 181.

24 Lorraine Eisenstat Weinrib. "Learning to Live with the Override" (1990) 35 *McGill Law Journal* 541 at 568. For arguments that section 33 allows the courts to be bolder in their interpretation of rights, see Paul Weiler, "Of Judges and Rights, or Should Canada Have a Constitutional Bill of Rights" (1980) *Dalhousie Review* 205; Paul Weiler, "Rights and Judges in a Democracy: A New Canadian Version" (1984) 18 *University of Michigan Journal of Law Reform* 51; Lorraine Eisenstat Weinrib, "Canada's Constitutional Revolution: From Legislative to Constitutional State" (1999) 33 *Israel Law Review* 13 at 49.

25 The analogy under the United Kingdom's *Human Rights Act, 1998* would be to make a legislative declaration of incompatibility or even derogation from the rights of the *Convention*, unless legislation responding to judicial decisions could be defended under one of the reasonable limit provisions that apply to some rights in the *Convention*.

26 Alexander Bickel, *The Supreme Court and the Idea of Progress* (New Haven: Yale University Press, 1970) at 91.

27 Alexander Bickel, *The Morality of Consent* (New Haven: Yale University Press, 1975) at 111.

28 Thus a decision employing the passive virtues to avoid a constitutional issue "radiates little of general consequences," while a full-blown constitutional decision "can be revised or reversed — at least in theory — only by the Court itself." Bickel, *The Least Dangerous Branch* at 202-3. Some doctrines of constitutional law, such as striking down the law on the grounds of vagueness or impermissible delegation, allowed legislatures an opportunity to reply and make clear that rights were being deliberately limited "by the full, pluralist, open political process, not by someone down the line." Bickel, *The Morality of Consent* at 79.

29 Bickel, *The Least Dangerous Branch* at 70-71.

30 William Eskridge and Phillip Frickey, "Quasi-Constitutional Law: Clear Statement Rules as Constitutional Law-Making" (1992) 45 *Vanderbilt Law Review* 593 at 597, 631. See also William Eskridge, *Dynamic Statutory Interpretation* (Cambridge: Harvard University Press, 1994) at 294, 276.

31 Guido Calabresi, "Foreword: Anti-discrimination and Constitutional Accountability — What the Bork-Brennan Debate Avoids" (1991) 105 *Harvard Law Review* 80 at 124-25.

32 Bickel, *The Least Dangerous Branch* at 24.

33 Ibid. at 258, 267, 254.

34 *Cooper* v. *Aaron*, 358 U.S. 1 (1958).

35 See Paul Weiler, *In the Last Resort* (Toronto: Carswell, 1974) at 192, 212. The cases Weiler praised were the criminal law case of *Boucher*, [1951] SCR 265, in which the Court interpreted the offence of seditious libel in light of common law presumptions about freedom of speech, and the administrative law cases of *Smith* v. *Rhuland*, [1953] 2 SCR 95, and *Roncarelli* v. *Duplessis*, [1959] SCR 121, which required clear legislative statements before officials could refuse to certify a union because there were communists on its executive or revoke a liquor licence because its holder had posted bail for Jehovah's Witnesses.

36 Weiler, "Of Judges and Rights" at 232-34; Weiler, "Rights and Judges" at 82-84.

37 Cass Sunstein, *One Case at a Time* (Cambridge: Harvard University Press, 1999).

38 Michael Perry, *The Constitution in the Courts* (New York: Oxford University Press, 1994) at 200; Michael Perry, "The Constitution, the Courts and the Question of Minimalism" (1993) 88 *Northwestern University Law Review* 84 at 158. Guido Calabresi has argued that American courts should try to create some space between the extremes of judicial and legislative supremacy and should re-enforce democracy by requiring legislatures to take a second look at the law. He sees the notwithstanding clause in both the *Charter* and the 1960 Canadian *Bill of Rights* as a common law style "clear statement rule" that required legislatures "to speak to their constituents in open and candid ways" before vio-

lating rights. Guido Calabresi, "Foreword: Anti-discrimination and Constitutional Accountability — What the Bork-Brennan Debate Avoids" (1991) 105 *Harvard Law Review* 80 at 124; Guido Calabresi, *The Common Law in the Age of Statutes* (Cambridge: Harvard University Press, 1981) at 18. Calabresi and Perry have focused on the override, but section 1 of the *Charter*, as recognized by Mary Ann Glendon, can also serve many of the same purposes in forcing the legislature to take responsibility for the limits placed on rights. Mary Ann Glendon, *Rights Talk* (New York: The Free Press, 1991) at 13, 167.

39 Bruce Ackerman, *We the People: Foundations* (Cambridge: Harvard University Press, 1997) at 13. Ackerman recognizes that the Court enforces rights as principled trumps in normal times, but argues that the American people can reverse judicial decisions in quasi-revolutionary "constitutional moments." His approach attempts to reconcile judicially enforced rights with democracy, but like the theories examined in chapter 12, reproduces the difficulties and democratic deficits that come with the judicial supremacy of the American *Bill of Rights*. Without a provision allowing legislatures to justify limits on rights or derogate from them with ordinary legislation, the Court's constitutional decisions are final absent extraordinary changes to the Court or the Constitution.

40 In *Mills* (1999), 139 CCC (3d) 321, the Court recognized an analogy between the common law and the *Charter* and indicated that, "if the common law were to be taken as establishing the only possible constitutional regime, then we could not speak of a dialogue with the legislature."

41 *Vriend* v. *Alberta*, [1998] 1 SCR 493 at para. 139.

Chapter 14: Democratic Dialogue in Practice

1 As Mark Tushnet concluded in his survey of American approaches to judicial review, we would unhappily be "left with a choice of dictatorships: sometimes the majority will be the dictator and sometimes the judges will be. Judicial review is often defended as the only way to escape the potential tyranny of the majority, but it simultaneously creates the potential for the tyranny of the judges." Mark Tushnet, *Red, White and Blue* (Cambridge: Harvard University Press, 1988) at 16.

2 This legislative activism is assisted by "bureaucratic activism," in the form of expert advice from the Department of Justice about how to "*Charter* proof" legislation. James Kelly, "Bureaucratic Activism and the Charter" (1999) 42 *Canadian Public Administration* 476.

3 My focus is on the institutional relations between the Court and the legislatures. It is still possible that the values of the *Charter* — especially outside the context of the legal rights — could be classified as a revolutionary change in the way that Canadians, including judges, think about rights. See, for example, Alan Cairns, *Reconfigurations: Canadian Citizenship and Constitutional Change* (Toronto: McClelland & Stewart, 1995).

4 John Willis, "Statutory Interpretation in a Nutshell" (1938) 16 *Canadian Bar Review* 1 at 17, 23. With the exception of presumptions that the pros-

ecutor must establish fault in the criminal law, Willis was quite critical of "ancient presumptions," such as those against expropriation without compensation, because they restrained the ability of legislatures to enact reform legislation that was desperately needed during the Depression. The presumptions have been modernized to take into account the role of the positive state and the post-Second World War concern about human rights. For an argument that independent courts have always used the common law to restrain and discipline the legislature, see John Whyte, "Legality and Legitimacy: The Problem of Judicial Review of Legislation" (1987) 12 *Queen's Law Journal* 1.

5 *Re Estabrooks Pontiac Buick* (1982), 44 NBR (2d) 201 at 210-11 (CA). The case dealt with presumptions concerning respect for property rights, but La Forest JA warned that courts must afford "the Legislature the widest possible scope in the performance of its tasks of adjusting private rights to meet evolving social realities. The courts should not, for example, place themselves in the position of frustrating regulatory schemes or measures obviously intended to reallocate rights and resources simply because they affect vested rights." Ibid. at 213-14.

6 *Sikyea* v. *The Queen*, [1964] SCR 642; *R.* v. *George*, [1966] SCR 267.

7 *Calder* v. *British Columbia*, [1973] SCR 313 at 404 per Hall J. In contrast, Judson J was prepared to find, in the absence of a clear legislative statement, that Aboriginal title had been extinguished.

8 *Simon* v. *The Queen*, [1985] 2 SCR 387 at 405-6.

9 *R.* v. *Sparrow*, [1990] 1 SCR 1075 at 109; *Nowegijicvk* v. *The Queen*, [1983] 1 SCR 29 at 36.

10 [1959] SCR 121.

11 See, generally, David Dyzenhaus, "Form and Substance in the Rule of Law: A Democratic Justification for Judicial Review," in Christopher Forsythe, ed., *Judicial Review and the Constitution* (Oxford: Hart, 2000).

12 *Nicholson* v. *Haldimand-Norfolk Regional Board of Commissioners*, [1979] 1 SCR 311.

13 *Cooper* v. *Board of Works for Wandsworth District* (1863), 143 ER 414 at 420 (CP).

14 *CUPE* v. *New Brunswick Liquor Corporation*, [1979] 2 SCR 227.

15 Beverley McLachlin, "The Roles of Administrative Tribunals and Courts in Maintaining the Rule of Law" (1999) 12 *Canadian Journal of Adminstrative Law and Practice* 171 at 188; David Dyzenhaus, "The Legitimacy of Legality" (1996) 46 *University of Toronto Law Journal* 129.

16 *Baker* v. *Canada*, [1999] 2 SCR 817.

17 David Dyzenhaus, "The Justice of the Common Law: Judges, Democracy and the Limits of the Rule of Law," unpublished manuscript.

18 *R.* v. *Beaver*, [1957] SCR 531 at 537.

19 [1970] 5 CCC (3d) 193 (SCC).

20 *R.* v. *Sault Ste. Marie*, [1978] 2 SCR 1299 at 1303, 1310.

21 F.L. Morton and Rainer Knopff, *The Charter Revolution and the Court Party* (Peterborough: Broadview Press, 2000) at 20.

22 Even with the checks and balances of sections 1 and 33 of the *Charter*, there is a danger that the Court has diluted some of the common law presumptions of fault as it has created constitutional requirements of fault under section 7. See Alan Brudner, "Guilt under the Charter: The Lure of Parliamentary Supremacy" (1998) 40 *Criminal Law Quarterly* 287; Kent Roach, *Criminal Law*, 2d ed. (Toronto: Irwin Law, 2000) at 129-36. Part of the dilution may be because of the reluctance to uphold section 7 violations under section 1. This reluctance makes it much more difficult for legislatures to respond to rulings about constitutional fault.

23 Alexander Bickel, *The Least Dangerous Branch: The Supreme Court at the Bar of Politics*, 2d ed. (New Haven: Yale University Press, 1986) at 64.

24 The terms have been coined by my colleague David Dyzenhaus. See David Dyzenhaus, "Law as Justification: Etienne Mureinik's Conception of Legal Culture" (1998) 14 *South African Journal of Human Rights* 11 at 32.

25 *Moore* v. *The Queen*, [1979] 1 SCR 195 at 212-13. In an earlier dissent in *R.* v. *Biron*, [1976] 2 SCR 56 at 64, Chief Justice Laskin also interpreted the offence of resisting arrest against the "social and legal, and indeed political, principle upon which our criminal law is based, namely, the right of an individual to be left alone, to be free of private or public restraint, save as the law provides otherwise. Only to the extent to which it so provides can a person be detained or his freedom of movement arrested."

26 *Reference re Wiretaps*, [1984] 2 SCR 697 at 709, 722. He added: "[T]he right to be free from unwanted intrusion is important and fundamental. It leaves no room for casual inference of Parliamentary sanction of illegality ... It is for Parliament, not the judiciary, still less the police themselves, to fill any gap in the Criminal Code." Ibid. at 727. See also *Lyons* v. *The Queen*, [1984] 2 SCR 633.

27 [1985] 2 SCR 2 at 15.

28 RSO 1980, c. 193, s. 189a. This legislation did not apply in the case.

29 *R.* v. *Hufsky* (1988), 40 CCC (3d) 398 (SCC). The Court also held that the denial of the right to counsel when a person was required to provide a roadside breath sample was a reasonable limit.

30 Dyzenhaus, "Law as Justification," at 32. Dyzenhaus refers to *Charter* review as "administrative law writ large." As I suggested earlier in this chapter, a similar approach is also seen in Aboriginal and in criminal law, suggesting that *Charter* review can be seen as public law "writ large."

31 It would be better if the ability to override rights under the *Charter* or to derogate by legislating in explicit contravention of rights in the *Human Rights Act, 1998* could be employed only after the Court has made a ruling that the legislature finds unacceptable. Such a proposal has been made by Christopher Manfredi, *Judicial Power and the Charter*, 2d ed. (Toronto: Oxford University Press, 2001) at 193.

32 Peter Hogg and Allison Bushell, "The Charter Dialogue between Courts and Legislatures" (1997) 35 *Osgoode Hall Law Journal* 75 at 88. See also

my *Due Process and Victims' Rights: The New Law and Politics of Criminal Justice* (Toronto: University of Toronto Press, 1999) at 69-86. This conclusion is subject to the caveat that the warrant process works effectively — something, unfortunately, there is reason to doubt.

33 *Competition Act*, SC 1986, c. 26, s. 124.

34 Christopher Manfredi and James Kelly, "Six Degrees of Dialogue: A Response to Hogg and Bushell" (1999) 37 *Osgoode Hall Law Journal* 513 at 520-26.

35 *R. v. Sieben*, [1987] 1 SCR 295; *R. v. Hamill*, [1987] 1 SCR 301.

36 *Criminal Law Amendment Act*, SC 1985, c. 19, s. 70. See also Canada, House of Commons, *Debates*, 20 December, 1984 at 1390.

37 *Controlled Drugs and Substance Act*, SC 1996, c. 19, s. 11(7), following *R. v. Grant* (1993), 84 CCC (3d) 173 (SCC). Manfredi and Kelly, "Six Degrees of Dialogue" at 527, classify this process as a negative form of dialogue on the formalistic basis that the *Narcotics Control Act* was repealed and replaced by new legislation. Even Hogg and Bushell, "The Charter Dialogue between Courts and Legislatures" at 122, underestimate the amount of dialogue by suggesting that all searches conducted under the new *Controlled Drugs and Substances Act* "are to be conducted pursuant to a warrant."

38 "Critics find top court guilty of neglecting victims," *Winnipeg Free Press*, 14 October 1994.

39 *Criminal Code*, s. 487.04, amended in response to *R. v. Borden* (1994), 92 CCC (3d) 404 (SCC).

40 *Criminal Code*, s. 487.091, as amended by 1997 SC c. 18, s. 45, in response to *R. v. Stillman* (1997), 113 CCC (3d) 321 at 366 (SCC).

41 *R. v. Hess* (1990), 59 CCC (3d) 161 (SCC). In *Michael M*, 450 U.S. 464 (1981), the United States Supreme Court upheld a similar statutory rape offence.

42 The Court still had to decide Heywood's fate and the constitutionality of the old law that applied to his conduct. The new criminal law could not apply retroactively to his conduct.

43 *R. v. Heywood* (1994), 94 CCC (3d) 481 at 523 (SCC).

44 Sean Fine, "Ban on loitering struck down," *Globe and Mail*, 25 November, 1994 at A1, quoting Priscilla de Villiers of the crime victims' advocacy group CAVEAT.

45 (1991) 66 CCC (3d) 321 at 403, 387 (SCC).

46 Ibid. at 370, 372.

47 Ibid. at 409, 381.

48 *R. v. Mills* (1999), 139 CCC (3d) 321 at para. 57 (SCC).

49 As quoted in Kent Roach, *Due Process and Victims' Rights: The New Law and Politics of the Charter* (Toronto: University of Toronto Press, 1999) at 170-71.

50 Lois MacDonald, "Promoting Social Equality through the Legislative Override" (1994) 4 *National Journal of Constitutional Law* 1 at 19.

51 *R. v. Darrach*, 2000 SCC 46 at para. 20, 28, 34, 43.

52 As quoted in Roach, *Due Process and Victims' Rights* at 178.

53 Roach, *Due Process and Victims' Rights* at 180

54 Manfredi and Kelly, "Six Degrees of Dialogue" at 520. It is not clear why Manfredi does not criticize the legislative reply as simply embracing the approach of the minority of the Court, as he criticized the in-your- face legislative reply to *O'Connor* as discussed in the following paragraphs. Manfredi, *Judicial Power and the Charter* at 180.

55 *R. v. O' Connor* (1995), 103 CCC (3d) 1 at 65, 69 (SCC).

56 *R. v. Carosella* (1997), 112 CCC (3d) 289 (SCC).

57 Bruce Feldthusen, "Access to the Private Therapeutic Records of Sexual Assault Complainants" (1996) 75 *Canadian Bar Review* 537 at 562; Janet Hiebert, "Wrestling with Rights: Judges, Parliament and the Making of Social Policy" (1999) 5 *Choices* 1 at 22; Manfredi, *Judicial Power and the Charter* at 180-83.

58 As quoted in Roach, *Due Process and Victims' Rights* at 188.

59 *Dickerson* v. *United States*, 26 June 2000 per Rehnquist CJ. See Jamie Cameron, "Dialogue and Hierarchy in Charter Interpretation : A Comment on *R. v. Mills*" (2001) 38 *Alberta Law Review* 1051 at 1062.

60 (2000), 139 CCC (3d) 321 at 356-57.

61 Ibid. at 38-87.

62 The analogous concern under the United Kingdom's *Human Rights Act, 1998*, would be that dialogue based on powers of interpretation under section 3 of that Act will be less transparent than dialogue based on clear declarations by either the courts or Parliament that legislation is incompatible with the convention. A clear judicial declaration of invalidity under the *Charter* or a declaration of incompatibility under the *Human Rights Act, 1998* puts the ball back into Parliament's court, with the result that Parliament can decide what, if any, corrective steps to take, including whether to override or derogate from the relevant right. If the derogation procedures are used, both the Canadian and British Parliaments will have to revisit the matter every five years until the derogation is allowed to lapse.

63 Jamie Cameron, "Dialogue and Hierarchy in Charter Interpretation: A Comment on *R. v. Mills*"(2001) 38 *Alberta Law Review* 1051 at 1061-62.

64 *R. v. Mills* at 357, 360, 386-87. Professor Manfredi is not impressed with the Court's bow to coordinate construction because Parliament's legislation was based on the judgment of the four judges in the minority in *O'Connor*. He suggests, therefore, that any dialogue that occurred was internal to the Court. Manfredi, *Judicial Power under the Charter* at 180. The Court, however, did not overrule *O'Connor*, and it upheld a very different interpretation of the conflicting rights involved after they were endorsed by Parliament. Manfredi's approach suggests that there is only one genuine example of coordinate construction: when Parliament reverses a unanimous *Charter* decision by the Court.

65 Bickel, *The Least Dangerous Branch* at 129.

66 Bickel drew on the work of Thayer, who argued that one of the greatest dangers of judicial review was that the people and the legislators would turn many "subjects over to the courts; and what is worse ... fall into a

habit of assuming that whatever they could constitutionally do they may do — as if honor and fair dealing and common honesty were not relevant to their inquiries ... [the practice of judicial review] is always attended with a serious evil, namely, that the correction of legislative mistakes comes from the outside, and the people thus lose the political experience, and the moral education and stimulus that comes from fighting the question out in the ordinary way, and correcting their own errors. The tendency of a common and easy resort to this great function, now lamentably too common, is to dwarf the political capacity of the people and to deaden its sense of moral responsibility." Ibid. at 21-22.

67 *Criminal Code*, s. 487.01 (general warrants), s. 515(10)(c) (tertiary grounds for denial of bail).

68 Stanley Cohen, "Law Reform, the Charter and the Future of the Criminal Law," in Jamie Cameron, ed., *The Charter's Impact on the Criminal Justice System* (Toronto: Carswell, 1996).

69 *Thibaudeau* v. *Canada*, [1995] 2 SCR 627.

70 Hogg and Bushell, "The Charter Dialogue between Courts and Legislatures" at 105.

Chapter 15: Judicial Activism and Democratic Dialogue

1 See David Dyzenhaus, "Law as Justification: Etienne Mureinik's Conception of Legal Culture" (1998) 14 *South African Journal of Human Rights* 11 at 31 ff, for a helpful contrast between "liberal" models of judicial review, based on the American *Bill of Rights*, and "democratic" and "common law" models, based on a modern bill of rights such as Canada's and South Africa's.

2 *Bush* v. *Gore*, 531 U.S. (2000). See Alan Dershowitz, *Supreme Injustice* (New York: Oxford University Press, 2001).

3 Michael Perry, *The Constitution in the Courts* (New York: Oxford University Press, 1994) at 200. See also Guido Calabresi, "Foreword: Antidiscrimination and Constitutional Accountability (What the Bork-Brennan Debate Ignores)" (1991) 105 *Harvard Law Review* 80 at 124-25; Mary Ann Glendon, *Rights Talk* (New York: The Free Press, 1991); Paul Weiler, "Rights and Judges in a Democracy: A New Canadian Version" (1984) 18 *University of Michigan Journal of Law Reform* 51.

4 J.A.G.Griffith, "The Brave New World of Sir John Laws" (2000) 63 *Modern Law Review* 159; J.A.G.Griffith, "The Common Law and the Political Constitution" (2001) 117 *Law Quarterly Review* 42 at 60ff; J.A.G. Griffith, "Making Rights Real," in Penny Smith, *Making Rights Real* (Dartmouth: Ashgate, 1999); Conor Gearty, "What Courts Are For" (2001) 23 (2) *London Review of Books* 10.

5 Grant Huscroft and Paul Rishworth, eds., *Rights and Freedoms* (Wellington, New Zealand: Brookers, 1995); George Williams, *Human Rights under the Australian Constitution* (Melbourne: Oxford University Press, 1999), chapter 10

6 As quoted in Robert Blackburn *Towards a Constitutional Bill of Rights for the United Kingdom* (London: Pinter, 1999) at 915. James Allen lumps the

Charter together with the American *Bill of Rights* as a "Superman" bill of rights, compared with watered-down statutory "Clark Kent" bills of rights found in New Zealand and also in Hong Kong and the United Kingdom. James Allan, "Turning Clark Kent into Superman: The New Zealand Bill of Rights Act 1990) (2000) 9 *Otago Law Review* 613 at 623.

7 *Rights Brought Home*, CM 3782 at 2.13.

8 The cursory examination of the Canadian experience in the 1997 white paper *Rights Brought Home* focused only on the ability of Canadian legislatures explicitly to override or derogate from rights. *Rights Brought Home*, CM 3782 at 2.11.

9 As I discussed in chapter 4, bills of rights in New Zealand, Israel, and the United Kingdom allow governments to enact legislation that explicitly derogates from protected rights, so it is impossible for courts to interpret this legislation as consistent with the rights contained in those documents. They also contemplate that statements can be made in Parliament that proposed legislation is inconsistent with the particular bill of rights. These provisions serve some of the same clear statement purposes of the Canadian override. In addition, section 16 of the *Human Rights Act, 1998*, c. 42, follows section 33 of the *Charter* in providing that derogations from the *European Convention* will expire five years after they are made, but can be renewed. Like section 33 of the *Charter*, this provision attempts to ensure a continuing democratic dialogue about the override of rights.

10 The leading explanation of dialogue under the *Charter* is found in Peter Hogg and Allison Bushell, "The Charter Dialogue between Courts and Legislatures (Or Perhaps the Charter Isn't a Bad Thing After All" (1997) 35 *Osgoode Hall Law Journal* 75.

11 John Willis, "Statute Interpretation in a Nutshell" (1938) 16 *Canadian Bar Review* 1 at 17, 23.

12 *Reference re Secession of Quebec*, [1998] 2 SCR 217.

13 Paul Rishworth, "Affirming the Fundamental Values of the Nation: How the Bill of Rights and the Human Rights Act Affect New Zealand Law," in Huscroft and Rishworth, eds., *Rights and Freedoms* at 88.

14 This is Jeremy Waldron's characterization of dialogue between the United States Supreme Court and its citizenry in his *Law and Disagreement* (Oxford: Clarendon Press, 1999) at 291 and his rebuttal to Ronald Dworkin's argument that judicial review in the United States improves debate about public issues. Ronald Dworkin, *Freedom's Law* (Cambridge: Harvard University Press, 1996) at 345. Both Waldron and Dworkin, however, can be criticized for assuming that the judicial supremacy of the 1791 American Bill *of Rights* is the norm and for ignoring the potential of modern bills of rights, such as the Canadian *Charter*, the *New Zealand Bill of Rights*, and the United Kingdom's *Human Rights Act, 1998*, to promote democratic dialogues between courts and legislatures which avoid both legislative and judicial supremacy.

Acknowledgments

I received much help in writing this book, with a number of colleagues and friends talking me through two years of research and writing. John Borrows, Sujit Choudhry, David Dyzenhaus, Bill Kaplan, Jonathan Rudin, Robert Sharpe, John Whyte, and an anonymous reviewer all made excellent suggestions that, in their own distinct ways, helped improve this book. Jason Murphy and Trish McMahon, now both in their third year at the University of Toronto Faculty of Law, provided excellent research assistance. The students who took my seminar in the fall of 2000 on the Role of Courts in a Democracy made helpful contributions to my thinking about these topics. Bill Kaplan and Jeff Miller of Irwin Law encouraged the idea for this book and remained enthusiastic and supportive throughout its writing. Rosemary Shipton provided expert editing that much improved the book. An earlier version of chapters 13 and 14 appeared in the *Canadian Bar Review*, and an earlier version of chapter 11 appeared in the *Supreme Court Law Review*. Ron Daniels, the dean of the University of Toronto's Faculty of Law, provided essential support that allowed the book to be written. The financial assistance of the Wright Legal Foundation is gratefully acknowledged.

As with all things, my family's support was a blessing. My parents, aunts, and in-laws all provided much needed help. My wife, Jan Cox, understood my sometimes obsessive need to write this book and provided perspective whether things were going well or not. I am grateful that my daughters, Erin and Carey, take an interest in their father's work, including several interesting and helpful suggestions for the jacket design.

This book reflects in many ways the influence of a number of extraordinary teachers I have had over the years. I continue to learn from family, friends, colleagues, and students, but owe a special debt to a number of teachers who, in ways they may not realize, have helped to shape what appears on these pages. Kent Hamilton and Kenneth McNaught, both deceased, first taught me the importance of history and its relevance to the law, and Marty Friedland and Dick Risk continue to teach me about the wisdom of history. Peter Russell and the late John Edwards taught me to look at the law through the eyes of a student of politics. Alan Cairns taught me much about the politics of rights and the changes the *Charter* was making to Canada in an extraordinary summer before I started law school. Drew Days, Owen Fiss, and Paul Gewirtz taught me about the grandeur and the tragedy of American law. The Hon. Bertha Wilson taught me lessons I will never forget about the importance of courage, independence, and empathy in judging. I am especially grateful to Guido Calabresi for introducing me to the world of legal process and to Robert Sharpe for teaching me how to represent intervenors before the Court and introducing me to the world of Brian Dickson. It is to all my teachers that I dedicate this book.

Index